美国文学视听说

American Literature:
Viewing, Listening, and Speaking

肖明文 主编

·广州·

版权所有　翻印必究

图书在版编目（CIP）数据

美国文学视听说：英文/肖明文主编． -- 广州：中山大学出版社，2025.5. --
ISBN 978-7-306-08308-1

Ⅰ. H319.9

中国国家版本馆 CIP 数据核字第 2025WOM186 号

MEIGUO WENXUE SHI TING SHUO

出 版 人：	王天琪
策划编辑：	张　蕊
责任编辑：	张　蕊
封面设计：	曾　婷
责任校对：	杨曼琪
责任技编：	靳晓虹
出版发行：	中山大学出版社
电　　话：	编辑部 020-84111997，84113349，84110283，84110779，84110776
	发行部 020-84111998，84111981，84111160
地　　址：	广州市新港西路 135 号
邮　　编：	510275　传　　真：020-84036565
网　　址：	http://www.zsup.com.cn　E-mail：zdcbs@mail.sysu.edu.cn
印 刷 者：	广东虎彩云印刷有限公司
规　　格：	787mm×1092mm　1/16　17.75 印张　368 千字
版次印次：	2025 年 5 月第 1 版　2025 年 5 月第 1 次印刷
定　　价：	65.00 元

如发现本书因印装质量影响阅读，请与出版社发行部联系调换

编 委 会

主　编： 肖明文（中山大学）

副主编： 王丽萍（南昌大学）

编　者： 金　天（中山大学）

　　　　　林　芸（上海外国语大学贤达经济人文学院）

　　　　　李奕奇（广东财经大学）

　　　　　唐　苇（南昌大学）

　　　　　黄　勉（广东技术师范大学）

前　言

在新时代教育改革不断深化的背景下，本教材以全国教育大会精神为指引，全面落实《教育强国建设规划纲要（2024—2035年）》关于创新人才培养的要求，以《外国语言文学类教学质量国家标准》为核心框架，结合《普通高等学校外国语言文学类专业教学指南》的具体规范编写完成。作为教学改革的新成果，本教材致力于构建多维度的学习体系，助力培养具有文化素养与跨文化交流能力的复合型人才。

本教材采用"听说结合、学用贯通"的创新形式，系统梳理了从19世纪早期到当代的美国文学发展历程。全书共设置16个教学单元，每个单元均包含三大核心模块：首先，通过时代背景解析揭示文学创作的社会文化根基；其次，以文学流派为脉络展开作家作品分析；最后，设置实践环节强化知识应用。这种"历史语境—文学脉络—实践提升"的三维结构，既展现文学发展的历史轨迹，又注重培养学生的批判性思维能力。

在教材设计上，我们着力突破传统教学模式。每个单元设置渐进式学习环节：通过热身问题激活思维，借助4~5个精选视听素材（含短视频与长视频）构建知识框架，最终通过主题陈述实现能力转化。短视频侧重提炼核心概念，长视频着力于深度解析，二者配合形成从认知到理解的知识建构过程。口语训练环节注重引导学生将输入信息转化为个性化表达，培养学术思辨能力。

不同于现有的美国文学教材，本教材高度重视学生的听、说能力。学生不再是单一地阅读材料，而是通过更为生动的视听方式来获取有价值的信息和观点。在充分有效的信息输入基础上，结合课堂讲解和课外阅读，进行充满思辨性的信息输出。

本教材主要面向英语专业核心课程教学，同时兼顾非专业学生的通识教育需求。对于文学爱好者与自学者，教材的模块化设计支持个性化学习路径。愿这本教材能成为学习者探索美国文学世界的有效指南。

限于编写时间与编者水平，本教材在当代文学前沿领域的覆盖仍有完善空间，部分教学资源的选编也有待优化，甚至存在一些疏漏和错误。我们诚挚欢迎专家和读者批评指正，共同推动外国文学教材建设的创新与发展。

编者

2025年春于康乐园

Contents

Chapter 1	Romanticism I	1
Chapter 2	Romanticism II	11
Chapter 3	Realism	20
Chapter 4	Naturalism	27
Chapter 5	Modernist Poetry	37
Chapter 6	Modernist Fiction	44
Chapter 7	Literature of the 1930s	56
Chapter 8	Southern Literature	67
Chapter 9	Drama	76
Chapter 10	Post-war Fiction	89
Chapter 11	Postmodernism I	98
Chapter 12	Postmodernism II	104
Chapter 13	Jewish American Literature	113
Chapter 14	African American Literature	122
Chapter 15	Asian American Literature	131
Chapter 16	Native American Literature	137

Key to Exercises and Transcripts ········ 143

Chapter 1	143
Chapter 2	154
Chapter 3	161
Chapter 4	171
Chapter 5	179
Chapter 6	187
Chapter 7	197
Chapter 8	206
Chapter 9	214

Chapter 10 ………………………………………………………… 226
Chapter 11 ………………………………………………………… 233
Chapter 12 ………………………………………………………… 240
Chapter 13 ………………………………………………………… 248
Chapter 14 ………………………………………………………… 254
Chapter 15 ………………………………………………………… 261
Chapter 16 ………………………………………………………… 268

Chapter 1　Romanticism I

Part Ⅰ　Warm-up

Discuss the following questions in pairs or groups.
1. How did Washington Irving contribute to the development of American literature?
2. What was James Fenimore Cooper's contribution to the development of the historical novel genre?
3. What are the key characteristics of American Transcendentalist literature?
4. Who were some prominent American Transcendentalist writers and what were their contributions?

Part Ⅱ　Tracing the Haunting Roots of *The Legend of Sleepy Hollow*

Watch the video. Write *T* for true or *F* for false for each statement.
1. (　) *The Legend of Sleepy Hollow* was written by Will Rogers.
2. (　) *The Legend of Sleepy Hollow* has been quite popular in America, both as a story and a movie.
3. (　) People know that the legend of the headless horseman took off 25 miles north of New York City.
4. (　) Elizabeth Bradley is an expert on the horseman.
5. (　) There are three protagonists in *The Legend of Sleepy Hollow*.
6. (　) Washington Irving moved out of New York City because of a pandemic of yellow fever.
7. (　) People can visit the bedroom where Washington Irving died in 1859.
8. (　) The house, as we see it today, was all built in 1656.
9. (　) The bridge featured in the cemetery is the bridge figured in the legend.
10. (　) North Terrytown renamed itself to Sleepy Hollow because of the great fame of the legend.

Part III James Fenimore Cooper

Watch the video and answer the following questions.

1. What was the term "Manifest Destiny" used to describe?
2. What did the frontiers look like in O'sullivan's remarks?
3. How was the West transformed into a romantic idyll?
4. What secured James Fenimore Cooper a place in the APUS history Hall of Fame?
5. By what was "the era of good feelings" characterized?
6. Why does the author introduce Nathaniel Hawthorne and Herman Melville as well as their works in the ending part?

Watch the video again and fill in the blanks.

Cooper's debut novel *The Spy*, published in 1821, told the story of a heroic 1) _____ fighting alongside George Washington in the Revolutionary War. Being the first American novel to achieve worldwide 2) _____, it catapulted Cooper onto the national scene and 3) _____ him as the first American to write with a style distinctly different from that seen in Europe. The specific genre employed by Cooper was called historical 4) _____ and it dramatized the events surrounding the American Revolution in a pious 5) _____ vein. This mirrored the national psyche at the time, and was therefore very well received by the public. 6) _____, the writing itself was highly praised, with Victor Hugo calling it the greatest writing of the century.

At last, the United States was in 7) _____ of a talented writer who is distinctly American, but Cooper had only just begun to make his 8) _____ on the national identity. In response to the fame he achieved by *The Spy* Cooper began working on *The Pioneers*, a novel 9) _____ a family's journey into the New York State frontier. Utilizing a similar style to his previous work, Cooper's first leatherstocking tale 10) _____ frontiersman as American nobility and thus galvanized the American public. Showcasing the power of the common man in natural environment, Cooper painted Americans as bold, daring and 11) _____ man, and his popularity ensured that they would be seen as such throughout the world. Moving farther and farther from its British roots, the United States had become a society of ardent 12) _____, and James Fenimore Cooper was at the center of it.

In addition, *The Pioneers* 13) _____ the character Natty Bumpo who quickly became an archetypal American hero. He 14) _____ the qualities Cooper so staunchly advocated and other characters modeled off Bumbo continued to

15) _____ American literature. In Melville, Thoreau and Twain, Cooper's writings and characters are clearly emulated, leaving no doubt to his 16) _____ on American literature. Still, Cooper's influence didn't end with his writing. As the American identity became increasingly associated with 17) _____ ideas, such as that of the common man, so too did American politics. In 1828, Cooper's message had become so popular in American society that Andrew Jackson, running on a platform of agrarian individualist democracy, won in a 18) _____. While it was Jackson's beliefs and 19) _____ that endeared him to voters, it was Cooper's romanticism of democratic ideals that made such popularity possible. Without Cooper, the American identity may have been vastly different, 20) _____ social and political structures for generations.

Part IV Ralph Waldo Emerson

Watch the video and answer the following questions.

1. What did Ralph Waldo Emerson change in a series of strikingly original essays written in the mid-19th century?
2. What did Emerson's ejection of cultural traditions bring about?
3. Who strongly influenced Emerson and in what way?
4. What were the two crucial things happened to Emerson on his tour of Europe?
5. What was Emerson's epiphany in the famous Jardin des Plantes?
6. What kind of insight did Emerson draw from the fact he found about Samuel Taylor Coleridge and William Wordsworth?
7. What were the two ideas that Emerson found that would guide his life's work?
8. What was the key element of Emerson's new philosophy?
9. What was an extension of Emerson's ideas about the significance of the individual?
10. Why could not people be themselves?
11. What did Emerson think of history, religion and society?
12. What was sacred at last according to Emerson?
13. What is your nature once you have rid yourself of history tradition and religion?
14. What did nature refer to according to Emerson?
15. Who does a pantheist look like?
16. Which releases the inner vision in the romantic tradition on which Emerson draws?
17. What do the rare transcendent moments reveal?
18. What was another aspect of the epiphany that was to have a profound effect on

American literature?

19. Why was everyday a proper subject for literature according to Emerson?

20. How were American writers like Henry David, Emily Dickinson and Hermann Melville influenced by Emerson?

Part V Henry David Thoreau

Watch the video and answer the following questions.

1. What was Henry David Thoreau known for?
2. How many children did the Thoreau family have?
3. Did Thoreau graduate from Harvard University successfully?
4. Who was Thoreau's guide, father and friend?
5. What did transcendentalism focus on?
6. If one wants to be successful in a transcendental world, what should he/she do?
7. What was abolitionism?

Watch the video again and fill in the blanks.

Thoreau's literature was his main contribution to the 1) _____ movement. With the help of Ralph Waldo Emerson, he wrote *The Dial*. *The Dial* was a magazine led by Emerson that supported the transcendentalist writers as well as their ideas and 2) _____ of many of Thoreau's poems and essays. One of Thoreau's first chapter essays, *Natural History of Massachusetts*, was published in *The Dial* as a book review, and with this he proved his calling as a nature style author. The magazine 3) _____ publication in April, 1844.

In 1845, Thoreau experimented with his view of transcendentalism by living in full 4) _____ and leisure, which inspired the creation of his work *Walden*, consisting of 18 essays which described the things he saw, smelt, touched, heard and tasted on his journey to live self-sufficiently. Thoreau spent two years living at Walden Pond, but his work only 5) _____ for one year. The work was written in first person as he stresses his beliefs on how society should live with simplicity and not 6) _____. The work was eventually published in 1854. After leaving Walden Pond in 1849, Thoreau wrote *A Week on the Concord and Merrimack Rivers* which reflected a boating trip that he and his brother John took in 1839. Many of Thoreau's works consisted of 7) _____ experiences as well as his views on a simple way of life.

Henry David Thoreau was a key player in the fight against 8) _____. After he left Walden Pond, Thoreau's transcendentalist beliefs faded and he turned his focus on being an abolitionist in his later life. John Brown, an abolitionist, 9) _____ Thoreau, and Thoreau thought of him as an idol. Thoreau wrote many papers on the 10) _____ of slavery, including one of his most important works, known as *Slavery in Massachusetts*. These papers were one of his contributions to the abolitionist movement. Also, Thoreau helped many slaves escape through a secret 11) _____ known as the Underground Railroad. One of Thoreau's most important contributions, however, was advocating for 12) _____ resistance and protests in the fight for abolishing slavery. In one of his most famous works, *Civil Disobedience*, Thoreau 13) _____ that it is okay to intentionally break unjust laws in order to better the government. Also known as resistance to the government, *Civil Disobedience* showed the power of the role of the individual to determine what is right versus what is wrong, while 14) _____ what society says is right or wrong. These views paralleled to slavery in that even though society may 15) _____ of slavery, it was not necessarily just. Thus, like with his previous work *Slavery in Massachusetts*, Thoreau used literature to 16) _____ against the government and support the fight against slavery.

Henry David Thoreau's impact on the society was immense because of his talent and achievements. As a result of his literature such as *Walden*, people of the 19th century were 17) _____ to transcendental writing at its best. His focus on simplicity and balance between man and nature showed people another way to live their lives as the country was industrializing. His literature, as a whole, affected the people, because it made them think about and 18) _____ their intentions.

Part VI Projects and Presentations

Choose one of the following projects, or design one of your own closely related to the theme of the unit. Finish the project by giving a presentation in class and leading a discussion afterwards.

1. Four important writers as well as their representative works were introduced in this unit. Work in groups and select one of the works to read together. Share with group members the part that you like the best as well as the reasons.

2. All of the four writers introduced in this unit came from America. Do you know some British or European writers in the period of Romanticism? Give a brief talk on "The British or European Romanticism Writers I Know".

3. Confucian influences are vital and notable in American Transcendentalism. Do

some research and give a presentation in response to the following questions. Why did Transcendentalists turn to Confucianism? What are the Confucian influences in Thoreau's writings? How did Emerson use Confucian quotes in transcendentalism?

Part Ⅶ Vocabulary and Notes

Video 1

take a stab at to try（**doing something**）尝试着做……

villain [ˈvɪlən] *n.* the main bad character in a story, play, etc.（小说、戏剧等中的）主要反面人物，反派主角，坏人

mischievous [ˈmɪstʃɪvəs] *adj.* enjoying playing tricks and annoying people 顽皮的，捣蛋的

anarchic [æˈnɑːkɪk] *adj.* with no controlling rules or principles to give order 无政府的；无法无天的；无秩序的

unspool [ˌʌnˈspuːl] *v.* unwind from or as if from a spool 从线轴上解绕开

oddball [ˈɒdbɔːl] *n.* a person who behaves in a strange or unusual way 行为古怪者；反常者；怪人

phantom [ˈfæntəm] *n.* a ghost 鬼；鬼魂；幽灵

Hessian [ˈhesiən] *n.* a German mercenary serving in the British forces during the American Revolution; broadly a mercenary soldier 黑森；赫森；黑森州；雇佣军；海森

spawn [spɔːn] *v.* to lay eggs 产卵

adaptation [ˌædæpˈteɪʃn] *n.* a film/movie, book or play that is based on a particular piece of work but that has been changed for a new situation 改编本，改写本

contagion [kənˈteɪdʒən] *n.* something bad that spreads quickly by being passed from person to person 传播，蔓延，扩散

eerie [ˈɪəri] *adj.* strange, mysterious and frightening 怪异的；神秘的；恐怖的

penchant [ˈpɒnʃɒn] *n.* a special liking for something 爱好；嗜爱

authenticity [ˌɔːθenˈtɪsəti] *n.* the quality of being genuine or true 真实性；确实性

adjacent [əˈdʒeɪs(ə)nt] *adj.* next to or near something 与……毗连的；邻近的

cemetery [ˈsemətri] *n.* an area of land used for burying dead people, especially one that is not beside a church （尤指不靠近教堂的）墓地，坟地，公墓

haunted [ˈhɔːntɪd] *adj.* believed to be visited by ghosts （被认为）闹鬼的，有鬼魂出没的

nebulous [ˈnebjələs] *adj.* not clear 模糊的；不清楚的

capitalize [ˈkæpɪtəlaɪz] to gain a further advantage for yourself from a situation 充分利用；从……中获得更多的好处

pliable [ˈplaɪəbl] *adj.* easy to bend without breaking 易弯曲的；柔韧的

Video 2

Manifest Destiny [ˈmænɪfest ˈdestəni] *n.* (especially in the 19th-century US) the belief that the US was a chosen land that had been allotted the entire North American continent by God（尤指在19世纪的美国）命定扩张论，该理论认为美国是上帝的选中之地，上帝将整个北美洲赐给了美国

lay claims to 宣称有；表示自己有权利去获得

validity [vəˈlɪdəti] *n.* the state of being legally or officially acceptable（法律上的）有效，合法；（正式的）认可

idyll [ˈɪdɪl] *n.* a happy and peaceful place, event or experience, especially one connected with the countryside（尤指乡下的）愉快恬静的地方（或事情、经历）

fledgling [ˈfledʒlɪŋ] *n.* a person, an organization or a system that is new and without experience 初出茅庐的人；无经验的组织；新体系

debut [ˈdeɪbjuː] *n.* the first public appearance of a performer or sports player（演员、运动员）首次亮相；初次登台（或上场）

acclaim [əˈkleɪm] *v.* to praise or welcome somebody/something publicly 称誉某人/事物（为……）；给予高度评价

catapult [ˈkætəpʌlt] *v.* to throw somebody/something or be thrown suddenly and violently through the air（被）猛掷，猛扔

pious [ˈpaɪəs] *adj.* having or showing a deep respect for God or religion 虔诚的；虔敬的

psyche [ˈsaɪki] *n.* the mind; your deepest feelings and attitudes 灵魂；心灵；精神；心态

chronicle [ˈkrɒnɪkl] *v.* to record events in the order in which they happened 把……载入编年史；按事件发生顺序记载

galvanize [ˈɡælvənaɪz] *v.* to make somebody take action by shocking them or by making them excited 使震惊；使振奋；激励；刺激

showcase [ˈʃəʊkeɪs] *v.* to display or present something to its best advantage 展示（优点）

ardent [ˈɑːd(ə)nt] *adj.* very enthusiastic and showing strong feelings about something/somebody 热烈的，激情的

archetypal [ˌɑːkiˈtaɪpl] *adj.* having all the important qualities that make somebody/something a typical example of a particular kind of person or thing 典型的

staunchly [ˈstɔːntʃli] *adv.* in a staunch manner 坚定地

emulate [ˈemjuleɪt] *v.* to work in the same way as another computer, etc., and perform the same tasks 仿真；模仿

agrarian [əˈɡreəriən] *adj.* connected with farming and the use of land for farming 农业的；土地的；耕地的

landslide [ˈlændslaɪd] *n.* an election in which one person or party gets many more votes than the other people or parties 一方选票占压倒多数的选举；一方占绝对优势的选举

cement [sɪˈment] *v.* to make a relationship, an agreement, etc., stronger 加强，巩固（关系等）

wind down [waɪnd daʊn] reduce gradually in activity as something comes to an end 逐渐减少至终止，逐步结束

upheaval [ʌpˈhiːvl] *n.* a big change that causes a lot of confusion, worries and problems 剧变；激变；动乱；动荡

turmoil [ˈtɜːmɔɪl] *n.* a state of great anxiety and confusion 动乱；骚动；混乱

Video 3

transatlantic [ˌtrænzətˈlæntɪk] *adj.* crossing the Atlantic Ocean 横渡大西洋的；横越大西洋的

courtly [ˈkɔːtli] *adj.* (formal or literary) extremely polite and full of respect, especially in an old-fashioned way （尤指老式）极其恭敬有礼的，温文尔雅的

Muse [mjuːz] *n.* (in ancient Greek and Roman stories) one of the nine goddesses who encouraged poetry, music and other branches of art and literature 缪斯（古希腊和罗马神话中执掌诗歌、音乐和其他文学艺术分支的九位女神之一）

ejection [ɪˈdʒekʃən] *n.* the act of forcing out someone or something 驱逐；逐出；赶出

bedrock [ˈbedrɒk] *n.* a strong base for something, especially the facts or the principles on which it is based 牢固基础；基本事实；基本原则

piety [ˈpaɪəti] *n.* the state of having or showing a deep respect for somebody/something, especially for God or religion; the state of being pious 虔诚

resonate [ˈrezəneɪt] *v.* to remind somebody of something; to be similar to what somebody thinks or believes 使产生联想；引起共鸣；和……的想法（或观念）类似

ordain [ɔːˈdeɪn] *v.* to make somebody a priest, minister or rabbi 授予圣秩（品）；授予圣职

orthodoxy [ˈɔːθədɒksi] *n.* the Orthodox Church, its beliefs and practices 正教会；正教信仰与做法

tuberculosis [tjuːˌbɜːkjuˈləʊsɪs] *n.* a serious infectious disease in which swellings appear on the lungs and other parts of the body 结核病

epiphany [ɪˈpɪfəni] *n.* a moment of sudden insight or understanding 顿悟；突然明白

centipede [ˈsentɪpiːd] *n.* a small creature like an insect, with a long thin body and many legs 蜈蚣

caiman [ˈkeɪmən] *n.* any of several Central and South American crocodilians similar to alligators 凯门鳄

grotesquery [grəʊˈteskərɪ] *n.* ludicrous or incongruous unnaturalness or distortion 怪诞

meek [miːk] *adj.* quiet, gentle, and always ready to do what other people want without expressing your own opinion 温顺的；谦恭的；驯服的

bourgeois [ˈbʊəʒwɑː] *adj.* belonging to the middle class 中产阶级的

turbulence [ˈtɜːbjələns] *n.* a situation in which there is a lot of sudden changes, confusion, disagreements and sometimes violence 骚乱；动乱；动荡；混乱

germ [dʒɜːm] *n.* an early stage of the development of something 起源；发端；萌芽

sepulcher [ˈsepəlkə] *n.* a small room or monument, cut in rock or built of stone, in which a dead person is laid or buried 岩穴墓；石墓

impertinence [ɪmˈpɜːtɪnəns] *n.* behaving in a rather impolite and disrespectful way 不礼貌；傲慢；莽撞

conspiracy [kənˈspɪrəsi] *n.* a secret plan made to do something harmful or illegal 密谋策划；阴谋

self-indulgence [ˌself ɪnˈdʌldʒəns] *n.* excessive or unrestrained gratification of one's own appetites, desires, or whims 自我放任

hedonism [ˈhedənɪzəm] *n.* the belief that pleasure is the most important thing in life 享乐主义

narcissism [ˈnɑːsɪsɪzəm] *n.* (formal, disapproving) the habit of admiring yourself too much, especially your appearance 自我陶醉，自赏，自恋（尤指对自己的容貌）

pantheist [ˈpænθiːɪst] *n.* someone who believes that God and the universe are the same 泛神论者

fickle [ˈfɪkl] *adj.* (of people) often changing their mind in an unreasonable way so that you cannot rely on them 反复无常的

blithe [blaɪð] *adj.* (literary) happy; not anxious 快乐的；无忧无虑的

egotism [ˈɛɡətɪz(ə)m] *n.* the practice of talking and thinking about oneself excessively because of an undue sense of self-importance 自我中心；利己主义；自私自利

sublime [səˈblaɪm] *adj.* of very high quality and causing great admiration 崇高的；

壮丽的；宏伟的；令人赞叹的

  foul [faʊl] *adj.* dirty and smelling bad 肮脏恶臭的；难闻的

  elusive [iˈluːsɪv] *adj.* difficult to find, define, or achieve 难找的；难以解释的；难以达到的

  cosmos [ˈkɒzmɒs] *n.* the universe, especially when it is thought of as an ordered system（尤指被视为有序体系时的）宇宙

  simmer [ˈsɪmə(r)] *v.* to be filled with a strong feeling, especially anger, which you have difficulty controlling 充满（难以控制的感情，尤指愤怒）

  allegory [ˈæləgəri] *n.* a story, play, picture, etc., in which each character or event is a symbol representing an idea or a quality, such as truth, evil, death, etc.; the use of such symbols 寓言；讽喻；寓言体；讽喻法

  defiance [dɪˈfaɪəns] *n.* the act or an instance of defying; disposition to resist 违抗；反抗；拒绝服从

  momentum [məˈmentəm] *n.* the ability to keep increasing or developing 推进力；动力；势头

  profane [prəˈfeɪn] *adj.* (formal) having or showing a lack of respect for God or holy things 亵渎神灵的；亵圣的

Video 4

  transcendental [ˌtrænsenˈdentl] *adj.* going beyond the limits of human knowledge, experience or reason, especially in a religious or spiritual way（尤指宗教或精神方面）超验的，玄奥的

  abolitionist [ˌæbəˈlɪʃənɪst] *n.* a person who is in favour of the abolition of something 主张废除……的人

  poll-tax [ˈpəʊl tæks] *n.* a tax that must be paid at the same rate by every person or every adult in a particular area 人头税

  transcendentalist [ˌtrænsenˈdentəlɪst] *n.* advocate of transcendentalism 先验论者；超验主义者

  reliability [rɪˌlaɪəˈbɪlɪti] *n.* the quality of being dependable or reliable 可靠性

  immanence [ˈɪmənəns] *n.* the state of being within or not going beyond a given domain synonym 内在（性）；固有（性）；包含；含蓄

  avid [ˈævɪd] *adj.* very enthusiastic about something (often a hobby) 热衷的；酷爱的

  self-sufficient [ˌself səˈfɪʃ(ə)nt] *adj.* able to do or produce everything that you need without the help of other people 自给自足的；自立的

  mentor [ˈmentɔː(r)] *v.* to advise or train (someone, especially a younger colleague) 指导；培训

Chapter 2　Romanticism II

Part Ⅰ　Warm-up

Discuss the following questions in pairs or groups.

1. What are the key characteristics of American Romanticism in literature?

2. Who were some notable American Romantic writers and what were their contributions to the movement?

3. How did American Romanticism influence the development of American literature?

4. How did American Romanticism reflect the cultural and social climate of the United States during the 19th century?

Part Ⅱ　Walt Whitman Revolutionized American Poetry

Watch the video. Write T for true or F for false for each statement.

1. (　) Whitman revolutionized American poetry.

2. (　) Walt Whitman was born on May 13th, 1819 in West Hills, New York.

3. (　) Whitman largely received his education at schools.

4. (　) Whitman had strong ideas about men's property rights, about immigration, and about the major issue of the day-slavery.

5. (　) Whitman's free verse is stitching together of encyclopedic lists, completely broke with poetic and literary convention and vastly influenced poets worldwide ever after.

6. (　) From his experience with local people during the war, he produced a small book of poems called *Drum Taps*.

7. (　) Whitman was called the poet of democracy.

8. (　) All of his poems are based on the notion of a universal brotherhood.

9. (　) In his lifetime, *Leaves of Grass* was considered by many people as a good book.

10. (　) Whitman really received the attention that he deserved during his lifetime.

Part III Symbolism in *The Scarlet Letter*

Watch the video and answer the following questions.
1. What is one of the main topics of *The Scarlet Letter*?
2. What are the examples of symbolism in the book mentioned by the speaker?
3. What is the symbolic meaning of the reflection in the armor at governor Bellingham's mansion?
4. Is there any change in the symbol of the scarlet letter?
5. What does the brook or stream represent in Chapter 19 of the novel?

Watch the video again and fill in the blanks.

There are a lot of different things going on in *The Scarlet Letter*. One of the main topics of the book is 1) _____ . We will explore some examples of symbolism in the book.

The scaffold plays a vital role in *The Scarlet Letter*. In the novel, it's both the symbol of sin and shame as well as the site of ultimate 2) _____ . Dimmesdale finally decided to act upon his guilt since he had been driven hither to the 3) _____ by the impulse and remorse which dogged him everywhere. And the scaffold as this 4) _____ comes full circle, a process that begins with shame and ends with 5) _____ for himself, for Dimmesdale, and for their daughter Pearl.

Ah, *The Scarlet Letter*, since it's the 6) _____ of the book, you know it's got to be important and it is, the scarlet letter, is a symbol for a 7) _____ of things like identity, shame, sin, and grace. Hester wears it on her chest throughout the novel, so naturally it's going to have a lot of meanings. At first, the scarlet letter is symbolic of Hester's sin and 8) _____ . She commits adultery and has a child as a result. The letter A is sewn into her clothing, literally marking her as an 9) _____ . She takes ownership of that letter which makes it sort of a cool symbol for her identity. She's a 10) _____ woman but she's not going to take the punishment lying down. Later, the scarlet letter comes to stand not for the word adultery but for ableism that Hester Prynne is such an able woman. She can do anything that's awesome. Hester works hard and the townspeople recognize that they begin to admire her for her 11) _____ and charity, which begins to 12) _____ the meaning of the scarlet letter in their own minds.

The rosebush represents hope in the darkness of prison. It is strongly 13) _____ to represent strength and hope for the prisoners. It produces beauty and a soft scent for the incoming prisoners, and it represents the kindness of nature to those leaving the dark place. "It may serve, let us hope, to symbolize some sweet moral blossom, that may be found along the track, or relieve the darkening close of a tale of human 14) _____ and sorrow."

The brook or stream in Chapter 19 represents the likeness of Pearl. It stands as 15) _____ between Dimmesdale or Hester and Pearl, listing that they are on opposite sides. But it also shows how they are tied together. When it forms the quiet pool, it shows the beauty of Pearl's figure and charm. It shows 16) _____ to cross it just like how Pearl is hard to comprehend sometimes. It is the boundary or bridge between two worlds where all three can be together in 17) _____ in the real world where they are separated because of the adultery. The brook has mysterious roots much like Pearl. "This brook is the boundary between two worlds and that thou can never meet pearl again. Pearl resembled the brook in as much as the current of her life gushed from a wellspring as mysteriously and flowed through the scenes shadowed as heavily with gloom."

Pearl is the daughter of the adulteress Hester Prynne and Minister Dimmesdale. She seems like a normal girl but she represents so much more than that. She is a constant 18) _____ for Hester of her sin that Pearl was born through. Like the scarlet letter, Pearl is another punishment that constantly reminds Hester of her sin. "God, as a direct consequence of the sin which man thus punished, has given her a lovely child." Even though Pearl symbolizes punishment for Hester, she also represents God's grace and redemption. She symbolizes Hester's hope and redemption even in the midst of pain and 19) _____.

The reflection in the armor at governor Bellingham's mansion was a convex mirror. This means that the reflection is disproportionate and unclear. In other words, it makes a certain area of something bigger than the rest of the area. When Hester looks into the reflection, the scarlet letter was represented in exaggerated and gigantic proportions so as to be greatly the most 20) _____ feature of her appearance. This symbolizes the way Puritan society looks at Hester. They only focus on who she was in scarlet letter, and not who she actually is.

Part Ⅳ Finding Emily Dickinson in the Power of Her Poetry

Watch the video and answer the following questions.
1. How could poetry lovers find Emily Dickinson in the power of her poetry?
2. Where is the poet Emily Dickinson getting even more attention and a new

look now?

3. What is the title of the exhibition about the most known and most mysterious American cultural figures, Emily Dickinson, at the Morgan Library and Museum in New York?

4. What is the comment on Emily Dickinson by Marta Werner from D'Youville College?

5. Why is this exhibition so special according to Jeffrey Brown?

6. According to Carolyn Vega, the curator, what has really stuck to her?

7. How did Emily Dickinson engage with her times, including the Civil War years by Jeffrey Brown?

8. Who is Susan Howe?

9. What is the comment on the significance of Dickinson's poems by poet Susan Howe?

10. When did the first editions of Dickinson's poetry come out?

11. How many poems did Dickinson write during her lifetime?

12. What was Dickinson's attitude towards her own work and her public image?

13. How do scholars and everyday fans access to Dickinson's original manuscripts?

Part V Projects and Presentations

Choose one of the following projects, or design one of your own that closely related to the theme of the unit. Finish the project by giving a presentation in class and leading a discussion afterwards.

1. In the 1920s, G. M. Weaver did solid spadework in reviving Herman Melville. Since then, Melville has been on the pedestal in American literature. Can you think of the significance of Herman Melville's works in literature, especially for readers leading modern life of the West? How do his works relate to the dilemma of the modern life? Work in groups and have a discussion. Each group summarize the viewpoints of members and reports your discussion results in class.

2. Edgar Allan Poe is listed at the bottom of 19th century American romantics. It is largely due to the reason that he was the last in chronological order or the least in importance. He usually stands alone when being talked about. Think about his unique position in the history of American literature, and give a short talk titled "Some Category: A Unique Poe".

3. As it is known to all, the largest portion of Emily Dickinson's poetry concerns death and immortality, themes at the center of Dickinson's world. Have a group

discussion on the questions: "Why was Dickinson so obsessed with death and immortality? Is there any connection between these poems and Dickinson's nature poems?"

Part VI　Vocabulary and Notes

Video 1

Walt Whitman 沃尔特·惠特曼（1819—1892），出生于纽约州长岛，美国著名诗人、人文主义者，创造了诗歌的自由体（free verse），其代表作品是诗集《草叶集》（*Leaves of Grass*）

voracious [vəˈreɪʃəs] *adj.* wanting a lot of new information and knowledge（对信息、知识）渴求的；求知欲强的

volatile [ˈvɒlətaɪl] *adj.* of a person or one's mood changing easily from one to another（人或其情绪）易变的；无定性的；无常性的

Leaves of Grass《草叶集》，19世纪美国作家惠特曼的浪漫主义诗集，从1855年初版的12首发展到1891—1892年"临终版"的401首，记录着诗人一生的思想和探索历程，也反映出他的时代和国家的面貌。诗集得名于其中这样一句诗："哪里有土，哪里有水，哪里就长着草。"

the Civil War 美国内战，美国南北战争（1861—1865年）

paymaster [ˈpeɪmɑːstə(r)] *n.* an official who pays the wages in the army, a factory, etc.（军队、工厂等）工薪出纳员

atrocity [əˈtrɒsəti] *n.* (*pl. -ies*) a cruel and violent act, especially in a war（尤指战争中的）残暴行为

Drum Taps《桴鼓集》，于1865年秋天出版，惠特曼表达了对北方军队和政权进行统一战争之正义性的肯定和对为祖国统一而战之军人的激励和歌颂，也表达了对士兵逝去生命的深切哀悼

Democratic Vistas《民主的远景》，由美国作者惠特曼于1871年出版，被认为是比较政治学和文学的早期经典著作

Passage to India《印度之行》，是惠特曼于1871年出版的诗集。第一版有120页，收录了74首诗，其中23首或24首诗歌为首次发表。惠特曼还将这些诗歌作为当年版本《草叶集》的一部分

bard [bɑːd] *n.* (literary) a person who writes poems 诗人

disgraceful [dɪsˈɡreɪsfl] *adj.* very bad or unacceptable; that people should feel ashamed about 不光彩的；可耻的；丢脸的

Video 2

The Scarlet Letter《红字》，由美国作家纳撒尼尔·霍桑所著，对清教徒进行了

尖酸的讽刺

symbolism [ˈsɪmbəlɪzəm] *n.* the use of symbols to represent ideas, especially in art and literature（尤指文艺中的）象征主义，象征手法

symbol [ˈsɪmb(ə)l] *n.* (of something) a person, an object, an event, etc., that represents a more general quality or situation 象征

scaffold [ˈskæfəʊld] *n.* a platform used when executing criminals by cutting off their heads or hanging them from a rope 断头台；绞刑架

redemption [rɪˈdempʃn] *n.* (formal) the act of saving or state of being saved from the power of evil; the act of redeeming 拯救；救赎

hither [ˈhɪðə(r)] *adv.* (old use) to this place 在这里

impulse [ˈɪmpʌls] *n.* a sudden strong wish or need to do something, without stopping to think about the results 冲动；心血来潮；一时的念头

remorse [rɪˈmɔːs] *n.* the feeling of being extremely sorry for something wrong or bad that you have done 懊悔；非常遗憾；自责

Dimmesdale 丁梅斯代尔，是《红字》中的男主人公，是霍桑忏悔意识的集中体现者

myriad [ˈmɪriəd] *n.* (literary) an extremely large number of something 无数；大量

exaggerated [ɪɡˈzædʒəreɪtɪd] *adj.* made to seem larger, better, worse or more important than it really is or needs to be 夸张的；夸大的；言过其实的

gigantic [dʒaɪˈɡæntɪk] *adj.* extremely large 巨大的；庞大的

Hester 海丝特，《红字》中的女主人公

adultery [əˈdʌltəri] *n.* sex between a married person and somebody who is not their husband or wife 通奸

adulterer [əˈdʌltərə(r)] *n.* (formal) a person who commits adultery 通奸者

identity [aɪˈdentəti] *n.* (abbr. ID) who or what somebody/something is 身份；本身；本体

ableism [ˈeɪblɪzəm] *n.* unfair treatment of disabled people by giving jobs or other advantages to able-bodied people （针对残疾人的）残障歧视

frailty [ˈfreɪlti] *n.* weakness in a person's character or moral standards （性格或道德上的）弱点，懦弱，软弱

brook [brʊk] *n.* a small river 溪；小河；小川

Pearl 海丝特与丁梅斯代尔的女儿

complexity [kəmˈpleksəti] *n.* the state of being formed of many parts; the state of being difficult to understand 复杂性；难懂

comprehend [ˌkɒmprɪˈhend] *v.* (often used in negative sentences, formal) to understand something fully （常用于否定句）理解；领悟；懂

boundary [ˈbaʊndri] *n.* a real or imagined line that marks the limits or edges of something and separates it from other things or places; a dividing line 边界；界限；分界线

grace [greɪs] *n.* the kindness that God shows towards the human race 恩宠；恩典

armor [ˈɑːmə(r)] *n.* special metal clothing that soldiers wore in the past to protect their bodies while fighting 盔甲；甲胄

Bellingham《红字》中的贝灵汉总督

convex [ˈkɒnveks] *adj.* (of an outline or a surface) curving out（外形或表面）凸出的；凸面的

disproportionate [ˌdɪsprəˈpɔːʃənət] *adj.* too large or too small when compared with something else 不成比例的；不相称的；太大（或太小）的

Puritan [ˈpjʊərɪtən] *n.* a member of a Protestant group of Christians in England in the 16th and 17th centuries who wanted to worship God in a simple way 清教徒（属于16世纪和17世纪的英国教会）

Video 3

exhibition [ˌeksɪˈbɪʃn] *n.* the act of showing something, for example, works of art, to the public 展览；展出

Morgan Library and Museum 摩根图书馆与博物馆，位于纽约市曼哈顿区的中心

iconic [aɪˈkɒnɪk] *adj.* acting as a sign or symbol of something 符号的；图标的；图符的；偶像的

remnant [ˈremnənt] *n.* a part of something that is left after the other parts have been used, removed, or destroyed, etc. 残余部分；剩余部分

International Women's Day 国际妇女节

summons [ˈsʌmənz] *n.* an order to come and see somebody 召唤

preciseness [prɪˈsaɪsənɪs] *n.* clarity as a consequence of precision 准确，一丝不苟

resume [rɪˈzuːm] *v.* if you resume an activity, or if it resumes, it begins again or continues after an interruption 重新开始；（中断后）继续

circumscribed [ˈsɜːkəmskraɪbd] *adj.* if someone's life is circumscribed, it is limited or restricted 受限制的

sibling [ˈsɪblɪŋ] *n.* a brother or sister 兄；弟；姐；妹

daguerreotype [dəˈgerətaɪp] *n.* a photograph taken using an early process that used a silver plate and mercury gas（早期的）达盖尔银版照片

authenticated [ɔːˈθentɪkeɪtɪd] *adj.* to be proved that something is genuine, real or true 被证明是真实的

auburn [ˈɔːbən] *adj.* (of hair) reddish-brown in colour（毛发）红褐色的

replica [ˈreplɪkə] *n.* a very good or exact copy of something 复制品；仿制品

botanical [bəˈtænɪkl] *adj.* connected with the science of botany 植物学的

specimen [ˈspesɪmən] *n.* a small amount of something that shows what the rest of it is like 样品；样本；标本

retreat [rɪˈtriːt] *n.* to escape to a place that is quieter or safer 隐退；逃避；躲避

stereotype [ˈsteriətaɪp] *n.* a fixed idea or image that many people have of a particular type of person or thing, but which is often not true in reality 模式化观念（或形象）；老一套；刻板印象

recluse [rɪˈkluːs] *n.* a person who lives alone and likes to avoid other people 隐居者；喜欢独处的人

verses [vɜːs] *n.* [复数] (old-fashioned) poetry（旧时）诗

vacuum [ˈvækjuːm] *n.* a situation in which somebody/something is missing or lacking 真空状态；空白

seclusion [sɪˈkluːʒn] *n.* the state of being private or of having little contact with other people 清静；隐居；与世隔绝

correspondence [ˌkɒrəˈspɒndəns] *n.* (with somebody) the letters a person sends and receives 来往信件；往来书信

stanza [ˈstænzə] *n.* a group of lines in a repeated pattern that form a unit in some types of poem（诗的）节，段

document [ˈdɒkjumənt] *n.* to record the details of something 记录，记载（详情）

beacon [ˈbiːkən] *n.* a light that is placed somewhere to guide vehicles and warn them of danger（指引车船等的）灯标，灯塔；立标

verbal [ˈvɜːbl] *adj.* relating to words 文字的；言语的；词语的

manuscript [ˈmænjuskrɪpt] *n.* a copy of a book, piece of music, etc., before it has been printed 手稿；原稿

acoustic [əˈkuːstɪk] *n.* related to sound or to the sense of hearing 声音的；音响的；听觉的

hinder [ˈhɪndə(r)] *v.* (from something/from doing something) to make it difficult for somebody to do something or something to happen 阻碍；妨碍；阻挡

stumble [ˈstʌmb(ə)l] *v.* to make a mistake or mistakes and stop while you are speaking, reading to somebody or playing music（不顺畅地）说，读，演奏

idiosyncrasy [ˌɪdiəˈsɪŋkrəsi] *n.* a person's particular way of behaving, thinking, etc., especially when it is unusual; an unusual feature（个人特有的）习性；特征；癖好

format [ˈfɔːmæt] *v.* to arrange text in a particular way on a page or a screen 安

排……的版式

conventional [kən'venʃənl] *adj.* following what is traditional or the way something has been done for a long time 传统的；习惯的

unsigned [ˌʌn'saɪnd] *adj.* of something not to write your name on a document, letter, etc. 未签（名）；没署（名）；未签字；未签署

anonymous [ə'nɒnɪməs] *adj.* written, given, made, etc., by somebody who does not want their name to be known or made public 匿名的；不具名的

chloroform ['klɒrəfɔːm] *n.* (symbol $CHCl_3$) a clear liquid used in the past in medicine, etc., to make people unconscious, for example, before an operation 氯仿，三氯甲烷（旧时医用麻醉剂）

reticent ['retɪs(ə)nt] *adj.* (about something) unwilling to tell people about things 寡言少语；不愿与人交谈；有保留

star [stɑː(r)] *v.* to have one of the main parts in a film/movie, play, etc. 主演；担任主角

fascination [ˌfæsɪ'neɪʃn] *n.* a very strong attraction, that makes something very interesting 魅力；极大的吸引力

marathon ['mærəθən] *n.* an activity or a piece of work that lasts a long time and requires a lot of effort and patience 马拉松式的活动（或工作）

the Library of Congress 国会图书馆

restoration [ˌrestə'reɪʃn] *n.* the work of repairing and cleaning an old building, a painting, etc., so that its condition is as good as it originally was 整修；修复

enduring [ɪn'djʊərɪŋ] *adj.* lasting for a long time 持久的；耐久的

Chapter 3 Realism

Part I Warm-up

Discuss the following questions in pairs or groups.
1. What are the main features of realist literature?
2. How is Realism different from Romanticism in literary sense?
3. What do you know about the historical background of American Realism?
4. Who are the representative realist writers in America?
5. What do you know about *Adventures of Huckleberry Finn*?

Part II Mark Twain: Father of American Literature

Watch the video. Write *T* for true or *F* for false for each statement.
1. (   ) Mark Twain is considered one of the most influential writers in American literature.
2. (   ) Mark Twain was born Samuel Langhorne Clemens on November 30, 1835.
3. (   ) Mark Twain served in the Confederate military for many years.
4. (   ) Mark Twain worked as a steamboat pilot on the Mississippi River.
5. (   ) Mark Twain's first bestseller was *The Adventures of Tom Sawyer*.
6. (   ) Mark Twain wrote 38 books, numerous stories, lectures, and essays.
7. (   ) Mark Twain's *Huckleberry Finn* was published in 1885.
8. (   ) Mark Twain received honorary degrees from Harvard and Cambridge.
9. (   ) Mark Twain's lecture tour in 1895 and 1896 was a failure.
10. (   ) Mark Twain died at his Connecticut home on April 21, 1910.

Part III Henry James and American Painting

Watch the video and answer the following questions.
1. Where and when will the show *Henry James and American Painting* be on view according to the speaker?
2. What did the painter John La Farge introduce Henry James to?

3. What did the painter John Singer Sargent have in common with Henry James?

4. How many letters did Henry James write to the young sculptor Hendrik Andersen?

5. Other than normal letters, what important information does Henry James convey in these letters?

6. How many novels of James does the drama of Lizzie Boott's love with American painter Frank Duveneck go into? What are they?

7. Who painted the portrait of Henry James?

8. Where does the portrait of Henry James make its way into?

Part Ⅳ William Dean Howells, Dime Novels, and Realism

Watch the first part of the video and answer the following questions.

1. What was the dominant American aesthetic for literature in the second half of the 19th century?

2. What were Americans in love with in the second half of the 19th century?

3. What were they fascinated about in the 1930s and 1940s?

4. What and who were "dime novels" arranged and presented for?

5. Children of what ages were enthusiastic about these novels?

6. What kind of stories do the young readers expect in dime novels?

7. Why do we say *Huck Finn* and Tom Sawyer were greatly influenced by dime novels?

8. What do American parents today blame the screen time for?

9. What did American parents of mid-1800s blame dime novels for?

10. What did writers and editors do to resist the mania for dime novels among children?

Watch the second part of the video and fill in the blanks.

One of these editors was William Dean Howells. Howells himself was a novelist, though he is far better remembered as the editor of *The Atlantic Monthly*, one of the most important magazines in the country, as the 1) _____ of Realism began to grow. He was hired by *The Atlantic* in 1866 as an 2) _____ editor, and by 1871, he was named the head editor, where he supported and wrote essays about a new wave of American Realist writers, such as Mary Wilkins Freeman, Frank Norris, and Mark Twain.

Much later in his life, to explain the political choices he had made in promoting writers of Realism over writers of Romanticism, he wrote an essay on novel-writing and novel-reading. I'll read you part of this, and also, I'll talk you through it as well. But to better understand the following excerpt, you should know that William Dean Howells was writing to a 3) _____ of readers who were familiar with two essential types of fiction: the earlier mode, Romanticism, which he calls "the romance", which told 4) _____ tales about unrealistic characters, and the more recently developed Realism, which featured authentic locations filled with realistic, often middle-class, characters. Add into this maybe one more thing: all of those dime novels that eventually produced stories of pirates, detectives, Western 5) _____, all of them featuring characters who had little connection to the people that Howells knew in his real life. Howells' argument was that too much Romantic fiction, like too much TV, might warp the minds of its readers and lead them to unrealistic expectations later in life. Through Realistic fiction, he believed readers could better understand themselves and the situations around them. In short, he believed that good art should imitate real life, and that a serious writer has a responsibility to represent what he or she knew.

But he also had a practical problem. By 1899, when he wrote this essay, Nathaniel Hawthorne has become 6) _____ in the American school system. Pretty much all schoolkids look to Nathaniel Hawthorne as the person who started serious American literature. Instead of two categories, then, William Dean Howells decides to create three categories. The top category is for Realistic fiction. He refers to this as the novel. Today, we call all fictions over 200 pages a novel. But in Howells' time, the romance was a category for fiction of unusual events, while the novel was the category for more 7) _____ events with realistic characters. In general, Realists tended to describe their works as novels, essentially the new stories. The middle category in Howells' 8) _____ was the romance. These were writers who tried to work towards art, but as fiction was in its early stages of development, couldn't yet achieve that goal. In short, these writers tried, but were limited by the traditions of their time.

I should point out, though, that all of the examples that Howells gives for the romance were written by Hawthorne. It might be reasonable, then, to 9) _____ that for Howells, the only American fiction writer that exists in this category is Nathaniel Hawthorne. And at the very bottom of this list is romantic fiction. This is the 10) _____ category of unusual tales that warp the mind, like those of Edgar Allan Poe, or fiction that pretends to portray real life, but dresses it up to make it more exciting, strange, or intriguing, thereby giving readers unusual ideas about how life elsewhere in the States might work.

Part V *Huckleberry Finn* and the N-word

Watch the video and answer the following questions.

1. According to the host, why does Mark Twain's *Adventures of Huckleberry Finn* cause controversy since its publication?

2. When was this news report made?

3. What did a publishing company in Alabama do to make the classic book more suitable for students?

4. How many times does Mark Twain use the n-word in *Adventures of Huckleberry Finn*?

5. What are the two-sided opinions about Twain's using of n-word in *Adventures of Huckleberry Finn*?

Part VI Projects and Presentations

Choose one of the following projects, or design one of your own closely related to the theme of the unit. Finish the project by giving a presentation in class and leading a discussion afterwards.

1. According to the news report, race is still a controversial issue in American literature. What's your opinion towards the controversy caused by *Adventures of Huckleberry Finn*? What do you think of the book's reflection of the slavery system? Work in groups and have a discussion. Each group summarize the viewpoints of members and report your discussion results in class.

2. When white authors write about the black, they are often accused of cultural appropriation, which takes place when members of a majority group adopt cultural elements of a minority group in an exploitative, disrespectful, or stereotypical way. Do you think there is any cultural appropriation in *Adventures of Huckleberry Finn*? What other texts which may have such a problem can you think of? Do you think these writers deal with the racial issue appropriately? Discuss with your group members and give a short talk titled "How should authors write about cross-racial matters?"

3. Cultural appropriation is prevalent not only in literature, but also in music, movies and other fields. For example, cultural appropriation is a creative strategy of Disney's *Mulan*. In 1998, the animated film *Mulan* produced by Walt Disney was officially released. The director and screenwriter modified the content of the basic

structure of the original story to a certain extent. Have a group discussion on the question "Is cultural appropriation good or bad for cultural exchange?"

Part Ⅶ Vocabulary and Notes

Video 1

palpable ['pælpəbl] *adj.* able to be touched or felt; so intense as to seem almost tangible 明显的；可触摸的；可感知的

pneumonia [njuː'məʊniə] *n.* a lung inflammation caused by bacterial or viral infection 肺炎

cub [kʌb] *n.* a young bear, fox, lion, etc.; (informal) a junior member of a group (e.g., Cub Scouts) 幼兽（如小熊、幼狮）；童子军成员

full-fledged [ˌfʊl 'fledʒd] *adj.* completely developed or established; having full status 成熟的；完全合格的；羽翼丰满的

bestseller [ˌbest 'selə] *n.* a product (often a book) that sells in very large numbers 畅销书；畅销商品

folly ['fɒli] *n.* lack of good sense; foolishness; a costly, foolish building or project 愚蠢；蠢事；华而不实的建筑

prolific [prə'lɪfɪk] *adj.* producing much fruit, work, or offspring; highly productive 多产的；丰富的

celebrity [sə'lebrəti] *n.* a famous person; the state of being famous. 名人；名流；名声

Video 2

John La Farge 约翰·拉·法尔热，是一位美国画家、彩色玻璃制作家和作家

masterpiece ['mæstərpiːs] *n.* a work of art such as a painting, film/movie, book, etc., that is an excellent, or the best, example of the artist's works 代表作；杰作；名著

John Singer Sargent 约翰·辛格·萨金特，美国艺术家，因为描绘了爱德华时代的奢华，所以被称为"当代领军肖像画家"

sculptor ['skʌlptər] *n.* a person who makes sculptures 雕刻家；雕塑家

Hendrik Andersen 亨德里克·安德森，挪威裔美籍雕塑家

Lizzie Boott 全名伊丽莎白·布特·杜维尼克（Elizabeth Boott Duveneck），美国作家亨利·詹姆斯多部作品中的人物原型。布面油画《伊丽莎白·布特·杜维尼克》为美国艺术家杜韦内克于 1888 年所作，现收藏于美国辛辛那提艺术博物馆

Frank Duveneck 弗兰克·杜韦内克（1848—1919），美国画家、蚀刻家和教育家。他将 19 世纪 70 年代在慕尼黑流行的现实主义绘画风格引进美国

magisterial [mædʒɪˈstɪriəl] *adj.* (especially of a person or their behaviour) having or showing power or authority （尤指人或行为）权威的；威严的；傲慢的

commission [kəˈmɪʃn] *n.* a formal request to somebody to design or make a piece of work such as a building or a painting （请某人作建筑设计或作一幅画等的）正式委托

Video 3

aesthetic [esˈθetɪk] *n.* the aesthetic qualities and ideas of something 美感；审美观

highbrow [ˈhaɪbraʊ] *adj.* concerned with or interested in serious artistic or cultural ideas 关于正统艺术（或文化）思想的；对正统的艺术（或文化）感兴趣的

authentic [ɔːˈθentɪk] *adj.* true and accurate 真实的；真正的

nickel [ˈnɪkl] *n.* a coin of the US and Canada that worths 5 cents （美国和加拿大的）5 分镍币

dime [daɪm] *n.* a coin of the US and Canada that worths 10 cents （美国、加拿大的）10 分硬币，10 分钱

inflation [ɪnˈfleɪʃn] *n.* a general rise in the prices of services and goods in a particular country, resulting in a fall in the value of money; the rate at which this happens 通货膨胀；通胀率

reminisce [ˌremɪˈnɪs] *v.* (about something/somebody) to think, talk or write about a happy time in your past 回忆，追忆，缅怀（昔日的快乐时光）

advent [ˈædvent] *n.* the coming of an important event, person, invention, etc. （重要事件、人物、发明等的）出现，到来

triumphant [traɪˈʌmfənt] *adj.* showing great satisfaction or joy about a victory or success 欢欣鼓舞的；洋洋得意的；耀武扬威的

rendezvous [ˈrɒndɪvuː] *n.* a place where people have arranged to meet 约会地点

bandit [ˈbændɪt] *n.* a member of an armed group of thieves who attack travellers 土匪

pirate [ˈpaɪrət] *n.* (especially in the past) a person on a ship who attacks other ships at sea in order to steal from them （尤指旧时的）海盗

warp [wɔːrp] *v.* (something) to become, or make something become, twisted or bent out of its natural shape, for example, when it is too hot, too damp, etc. （使）扭曲，弯曲，变形

Video 4

astray [əˈstreɪ] to go in the wrong direction or to have the wrong result 走错方向；误入歧途

abusive [əˈbjuːsɪv] *adj.* (of speech or of a person) rude and offensive; criticizing rudely and unfairly（言语或人）辱骂的；恶语的；毁谤的

censor ['sensər] *v.* to remove parts of a book, film/movie, etc., that are considered to be offensive, immoral or a political threat 删剪（书籍、电影等中被认为犯忌、违反道德或具政治威胁的内容）

sanitize ['sænɪtaɪz] *v.* (disapproving) to remove parts of something that could be considered unpleasant 去除……中使人不快的内容；净化

divisive [dɪ'vaɪsɪv] *adj.* causing people to be split into groups that disagree with or oppose each other 造成不和的；引起分歧的；制造分裂的

monstrous ['mɑːnstrəs] *v.* considered to be shocking and unacceptable because it is morally wrong or unfair 丑恶的；道德败坏的；骇人的

dilemma [dɪ'lemə] *n.* a situation which makes problems, often one in which you have to make a very difficult choice between things of equal importance （进退两难的）窘境，困境

repetitive [rɪ'petətɪv] *adj.* repeated many times 多次重复的

callous ['kæləs] *adj.* not caring about other people's feelings or suffering 冷酷无情的；无同情心的；冷漠的

preposterous [prɪ'pɑːstərəs] *adj.* completely unreasonable, especially in a way that is shocking or annoying 荒唐的；极不合情理的

Chapter 4 Naturalism

Part I Warm-up

Discuss the following questions in pairs or groups.
1. What do you know about Naturalism as a literary movement?
2. Do you know some representative works of naturalistic style?
3. What do you know about the historical background of American Naturalism?
4. Who are the representative naturalistic writers in America?
5. How is Naturalism different from Realism as a literary genre?

Part II Progressive Era—The Muckrakers

Watch the video. Write *T* for true or *F* for false for each statement.
1. ( ) This video is part of an online course on US history.
2. ( ) The Muckraker could be a cartoonist.
3. ( ) The goal of the muckrakers is to bring the social problems to the attention of public officials in government in hopes of trying to solve some of these problems.
4. ( ) The name "Muckraker" was given to some journalists by president Franklin Roosevelt.
5. ( ) Thomas Nast was contributive to exposing economic corruption.
6. ( ) The famous book *The Octopus* by Frank Norris is a fictional account about the struggle that farmers were engaged in with railroad monopolies.
7. ( ) Lewis Hine helped pave the way for child labor laws in different states and across the country as a whole through his camera.
8. ( ) Ida Tarbell's damaging articles led to the split-up of the Standard Oil Company of John Rockefeller.
9. ( ) Danish immigrant Jacob Riis exposed the housing problems of the city's poor through his articles.
10. ( ) *The Jungle* by Upton Sinclair investigates the dangerous working conditions and unsanitary procedures in the meatpacking industry of New York.

Part III Jack London and Sustainable Agriculture

Watch the video and answer the following questions.

1. What was more important than his writing to Jack London?
2. What was Jack London determined to change the Valley of the Moon into?
3. Why did Jack London despair of the wasteful California pioneer farmers?
4. What did Jack London do by putting innovative ideas learned from his Asian journey into action?
5. What did Jack London do to enrich his soil?
6. What was Jack London famous for in addition to his prize-winning livestock?
7. What innovative methods did Jack London provide for his bulls?
8. What failures did Jack London meet in experimenting plants?
9. Why do we say Jack London was a visionary ahead of his time?
10. Why did Jack London want to revolutionize agriculture?

Part IV Pure Pessimism: A Reading, Summary, and Analysis of Crane's *A Man Said to the Universe*

Watch the video and fill in the blanks with the right information.

In a mere 24 words, Stephen Crane 1) _____ one of humankind's greatest fears. Welcome to a reading summary and analysis of *A Man Said to the Universe*.

    A man said to the universe:
     "Sir I exist!"
   "However," replied the universe,
    "The fact has not created in me
     A sense of obligation."

So, this is one of those poems that is so short that you can probably 2) _____ it in just a couple of minutes. However, that doesn't mean we should ignore one of the golden rules of reading poetry, that you need to understand every word in the poem, especially for shorter poems. So, make sure you check out the definitions, if there's anything you're unfamiliar with.

In terms of poetic devices there's not a whole lot, I guess you get a rhyme with universe and universe, but it's just a repeated word, so it's not much of a rhyme. However, we see line breaks 3) _____ here, and in fact I have another video specifically on line breaks, and this is one of the poems that I 4) _____ in it,

Chapter 4   Naturalism

because there's not much that Crane's working with outside of line breaks. And usually when we're studying poetic devices, we're gonna see that 5) _____ sort of thing, so the poet is using this device, because it supports the meaning behind the poem.

And one of the things that jumps right out at me is that, one of these lines, the second line is 6) _____ short, and this line is the quote from the man. The man in this poem represents all of humanity. We shout into the universe but the universe doesn't need to care. Just because we have a voice doesn't mean that the universe is listening, is another way to think about it.

Now again, this is Stephen Crane's world view here, or at least in this poem the world view that he's 7) _____. Crane comes from an 8) _____ of literature in the United States known as Realism and Naturalism, and you see a lot of Nihilism in that. You look at some of Stephen Crane's other works—*The Open Boat*, *Red Badge of Courage* are two examples that come right to mind and they're not necessarily encouraging or 9) _____. Even if you jump back into like the sort of 10) _____ and depressing works of Romanticism and Dark Romanticism with Poe and Hawthorne and Melville, there's still like a 11) _____ at play.

And there's this idea that there is some justice in the universe. The murderer gets caught, ambition is punished, the terrible things people do out of sight are brought to the light. You don't see that with Stephen Crane. At least not with this piece. I think it's also worth pointing out that the whole poem is short, and obviously Crane realizes this it's one thought there's no real room for 12) _____. "However," replied the universe, "the fact that you exist has not created in me—the universe—a sense of obligation." I'm not obliged to care for you or even really 13) _____ you.

So, I think when we shout into the 14) _____, when we want to think that we're important, that we're significant, that there is a higher power, perhaps we want a reply. We think, wow! I want a reply to confirm my beliefs. Wouldn't it be great if God just spoke back to me? Or whatever higher power you subscribe to or don't subscribe to, whatever it is you worship, wouldn't it be great if something just spoke back? And here, the higher power of the universe, the entity as a whole does speak back, but what a depressing thing to have spoken back to us: "I'm not obliged to care for you." It's really the 15) _____ to what most religions 16) _____.

So, you can see how this would be a controversial poem when it comes out, and I'm not saying that Stephen Crane or the speaker in this poem is correct. In the 17) _____ _____ sense here, it is not the world view that I personally subscribe to, as a God-fearing Christian, but that doesn't mean I reject the poem 18) _____ or don't think that it has merit or value. In many ways the universe is unfair. It's not obliged to care for you. And I think if you examine most ideas of religion, you'll find that the world that we live in very much like the universe here is not obliged to care for us. The idea of care comes from our fellow humans or from God. So, I think even all these years later, *A Man Said to the Universe* is still a rather shocking poem. It 19) _____ exactly what Crane 20) _____ do.

And whether you believe that this is all there is or not, you still have to do something about it. You still have to move forward. I think the sequel to this poem what Crane's asking us here, is what do we do with this? And one answer is to continue to learn and grow and search for answers. And I think if you're watching this video, you're probably the type of person who does that. So, I wish you luck in finding, whatever it is you're searching for. And I want to encourage you that I truly believe that even if the universe as a whole doesn't care for you, there are people in this universe that do. That might have been a little deep if you were just here to figure out something for your homework. But anyway, that's what it was. Happy reading. I hope to see you in the next video. Thank you so much for watching.

Part V Dreiser's Cities—Chicago and New York in Late 19th Century

Watch the video and answer the following questions.

1. Which novel of Dreiser's do Chicago and New York provide settings for?
2. What was the religious belief of Dreiser's family?
3. When and why did Dreiser leave for Chicago?
4. What kind of life did Dreiser's sister Emma live in Chicago?
5. What naive ambition did Dreiser have when he came to Chicago?
6. What lay beneath the few stories of stupendous fortunes in the Gilded Age?
7. What was the Factory Chicago most known for?
8. How much did one American working-class family spend for food, rents and other necessities in 1891?
9. What did the completion of Erie Canal in 1825 mean?
10. What was most responsible for the growth of Chicago in 1850, 1860, and 1870?
11. Who was the incredible vast railway system of Chicago constructed mostly by?
12. What were the Irish people regarded as in the 19th century?
13. How many people were left homeless by the Great Chicago Fire in 1871?
14. How many people lived in cities by 1920 in America?
15. What influenced Dreiser's use of the city as the setting for Carrie's early failures

in the novel?

Watch the video and choose the best answer for the following questions.

1. What did Dreiser do in New York?
   A. Worker and writer.
   B. Photographer and writer.
   C. Journalist and writer.
   D. Journalist and worker.

2. New York City has a long history as a famous _____.
   A. railway hub
   B. airport
   C. highway transport center
   D. business harbor

3. What influenced Dreiser's choice of Chicago as the setting for Carrie's early failures in the novel?
   A. His success in finding employment in Chicago.
   B. His lack of familiarity with Chicago's commercial workings.
   C. His preference for a city with rapid growth and development.
   D. His intimate familiarity with Chicago's commercial workings and his own problems finding employment there.

4. "But he did make note of the abundant beaver population. Beaver pelts were in fashion in Europe…" What does "beaver" possibly mean?
   A. An economic crop.
   B. A furry animal.
   C. Native people.
   D. An eatable bird.

5. New York was at the beginning founded as a colony by _____.
   A. Spain   B. Portugal   C. Holland   D. Denmark

6. Central Park, the first landscaped park in an American city, resulted from a _____.
   A. governmental project
   B. design company
   C. engineer seminar
   D. design contest

7. What similar social problem did New York and other American cities have during that time?
   A. Economic inequality.
   B. Racial discrimination.
   C. Gender inequality.
   D. Increasing immigration.

8. What was Jacob Riis able to expose in his famous book *How the Other Half Live*?
   A. The sufferings of immigrants.
   B. The working condition of the urban poor.
   C. The living conditions of the urban poor.
   D. The sufferings of the working women.

9. What other technique did Riis use in exposing the social problem?

A. Photograph.　　B. Movie.　　C. Cartoon.　　D. Advertisement.

10. What is the major theme of literary naturalism according to the video?

A. Object depiction of the character.

B. Idealism about life.

C. Life determined by environment and heredity.

D. Mental damage by the war.

Part VI　Projects and Presentations

Choose one of the following projects, or design one of your own closely related to the theme of the unit. Finish the project by giving a presentation in class and leading a discussion afterwards.

1. Setting means the context in a scene or story that describes the elements in which a story is taking place, including time, place, and environment. Elements making up a setting may include: 1) the actual geographical location, its topography, scenery, and such physical arrangements. 2) the occupations and daily manner of living of the characters. 3) the time and period in which the action takes place. 4) the general environment of the characters. Discuss with your partner on "The Best Settings in American Naturalist Literature". Why do they impress you so much? How are these settings interrelated with the literary works?

2. City is a key motif in British and American literature. However, to writers of different literary schools, the space of city may be presented differently in their works. Compare the city images in representative literary works of Romanticism, Realism and Naturalism and discuss in groups on their different functions and significance.

Part VII　Vocabulary and Notes

Video 1

Progressive Era The Progressive Era in the United States was a period of reform which lasted from the 1880s to the 1920s. In response to industrialization Progressives advocated a wide range of economic, political, social, and moral reforms. 美国的进步时代是从19世纪80年代到20世纪20年代的改革时期。作为对工业化的回应，进步主义者主张进行广泛的经济、政治、社会和道德改革

muck [mʌk] *n.* dirt or mud 脏东西；泥浆；淤泥

Monopolies [məˈnɒpəli] *n.* the complete control of trade in particular goods or the supply of a particular service; a type of goods or a service that is controlled in this way 垄断；专营服务；被垄断的商品（或服务）

Northern Securities 北方证券公司，20 世纪美国反托拉斯垄断的第一枪——北方证券公司诉美国案（1904 年）

ruthless ['ruːθləs] *adj.* hard and cruel; determined to get what you want and not caring if you hurt other people 残酷无情的；残忍的

tactics ['tæktɪks] *n.* the methods that you choose to use in order to achieve what you want in a particular situation 战术；策略；招数

McClure's Magazine was an illustrated American magazine that published literature and journalism in the 19th and early 20th centuries.《麦克卢尔杂志》，是一本带有插图的美国杂志，在 19 世纪和 20 世纪初出版文学和新闻

Standard Oil in full Standard Oil Company and Trust, an American company and corporate trust that from 1870 to 1911 was the industrial empire of John D. Rockefeller and associates, controlling almost all oil production, processing, marketing, and transportation in the United States. 标准石油，全称标准石油公司和信托，是约翰·洛克菲勒及其合伙人的工业帝国，从 1870 年到 1911 年这家公司控制了美国几乎所有的石油生产、加工、销售和运输

tenements ['tenəmənts] *n.* a large building divided into flats/apartments, especially in a poor area of a city （尤指城市贫困区的）经济公寓，廉租公寓

unsanitary [ʌnˈsænətri] *adj.* dirty and likely to spread disease 不卫生的；不洁的

ingredients [ɪnˈɡriːdiənts] *n.* things that are used to make something, especially all the different foods you use when you are cooking a particular dish 成分；（烹调的）原料

regulate ['reɡjuleɪt] *v.* to control something by means of rules （用规则条例）约束，控制，管理

Video 2

despair [dɪˈspeə(r)] *v.* (of something/somebody or of doing something) to stop having any hope that a situation will change or improve 绝望；失去希望；丧失信心

utilizing ['juːtəlaɪzɪŋ] *v.* to use something, especially for a practical purpose 使用；利用；运用；应用

cover cropping ['kʌvə(r) 'krɒpɪŋ] to grow a crop for the protection and enrichment of the soil 覆盖作物栽培

crop rotation [krɒp rəʊˈteɪʃn] *n.* the practice of growing different crops in succession on the same land chiefly to preserve the productive capacity of the soil 轮作

terracing ['terəsɪŋ] *n.* a slope or the side of a hill that has had flat areas like steps cut into it 阶梯状坡地；阶梯形山坡

liquid ['lɪkwɪd] *n.* a substance that flows freely and is not a solid or a gas, for example, water or oil 液体

manures [mə'njʊəz] *n.* the waste matter from animals that is spread over or mixed with the soil to help plants and crops grow 粪肥；肥料

livestock ['laɪvstɒk] *n.* the animals kept on a farm, for example, cows or sheep 牲畜；家畜

optimum ['ɒptɪməm] *adj.* the best possible; producing the best possible results 最佳的；最适宜的

Duroc jersey pigs 杜洛克泽西猪，产于美国，于19世纪60年代在美国东北部由美国纽约的红毛杜洛克猪、新泽西州的泽西红毛猪和康万狄格州的红毛巴克夏猪育成

carbolic acid [kɑː'bɒlɪk 'æsɪd] *n.* or carbolic, is a liquid that is used as a disinfectant and antiseptic （用作消毒和防腐的）石炭酸；（苯）酚

trough [trɒf] *n.* a long narrow open container for animals to eat or drink from 槽；饲料槽；饮水槽

shredded ['ʃredɪd] *adj.* prepared by cutting 碎的

stalks [stɔːks] *n.* a thin stem that supports a leaf, flower or fruit and joins it to another part of the plant or tree; the main stem of a plant （叶）柄；（花）梗；（果实的）柄；（植物的）茎，秆

ferment [fə'ment] *v.* to experience a chemical change because of the action of yeast or bacteria, often changing sugar to alcohol; to make something change in this way （使）发酵

eucalyptus [ˌjuːkə'lɪptəs] *n.* a tall straight tree with leaves that produce oil with a strong smell, that is used in medicine. There are several types of eucalyptus and they grow especially in Australasia. 桉树（产于澳大拉西亚）

spineless ['spaɪnləs] *adj.* having no spines (= sharp parts like needles) 无刺的

cactus ['kæktəs] *n.* a plant that grows in hot dry regions, especially one with thick stems covered in spines but without leaves. There are many different types of cactus. 仙人掌科植物；仙人掌

Video 3

Nihilism ['naɪɪlɪzəm] *n.* the belief that nothing has any value, especially that religious and moral principles have no value 虚无主义

The Open Boat is based on the real-life ordeal that Crane endured, when the boat he was taking to Cuba ran aground and sank off the Florida coast. 《海上扁舟》，是来源于现实生活中克莱恩所经历的磨难，他乘坐去往古巴的船在佛罗里达州海岸搁浅并

沉没

Red Badge of Courage is a war novel by American author Stephen Crane (1871—1900). 《红色英勇勋章》,是美国作家斯蒂芬·克莱恩(1871—1900)所著的一部战争小说

Dark Romanticism is a literary subgenre that emerged from the Transcendental philosophical movement popular in 19th century America. 黑色浪漫主义,是从 19 世纪美国流行的先验哲学运动中产生的一个文学流派

subscribe to [səbˈskraɪb tu] *v.* If you subscribe to an opinion or belief, you are one of a number of people who have this opinion or belief. 同意;赞成

Video 4

vibrating [vaɪˈbreɪtɪŋ] *vt.* (vibrate 的现在分词) to move or make something move from side to side very quickly and with small movements (使)振动,颤动,摆动

vexed [vekst] *adj.* a problem that is difficult to deal with (指问题等)棘手的,伤脑筋的

disreputable [dɪsˈrepjətəbl] *adj.* that people consider to be dishonest and bad 名声不好的;不名誉的;不光彩的

infatuated [ɪnˈfætʃueɪtɪd] *adj.* having a very strong feeling of love or attraction for somebody/something so that you cannot think clearly and in a sensible way 热恋的;痴情的

marquees [mɑːˈkiːz] *n.* a cover over the entrance of a building, for example, a hotel or a theatre (饭店、剧院等入口处的)遮篷,遮檐

dispiriting [dɪˈspɪrɪtɪŋ] *adj.* making somebody lose their hope or enthusiasm 令人沮丧的;使人气馁的

the Gilded Age period of gross materialism and blatant political corruption in U S history during the 1870s that gave rise to important novels of social and political criticism 镀金时代,19 世纪 70 年代美国历史上极度物质主义和公然政治腐败的时期,催生了重要的社会和政治批评小说

glitter [ˈɡlɪtə(r)] *n.* bright light consisting of many little flashes 灿烂的光辉;闪烁;闪耀

sham [ʃæm] *n.* a situation, feeling, system, etc., that is not as good or true as it seems to be 假象;假情假义;伪善;伪装

stupendous [stjuːˈpendəs] *adj.* extremely large or impressive, especially greater or better than you expect 极大的;令人惊叹的;了不起的

grinding [ˈɡraɪndɪŋ] *adj.* that never ends or improves 没完没了的;无休止的;无改进的

monotonous [məˈnɒtənəs] *adj.* never changing and therefore boring 单调乏味的
exponentially [ˌekspəˈnenʃəli] *adv.* in an exponential manner 迅速增长地；成指数倍增地
the Erie Canal 伊利运河
navigable [ˈnævɪɡəbl] *adj.* wide and deep enough for ships and boats to sail on 通航的；可航行的
drizzle [ˈdrɪzl] *n.* light fine rain 毛毛细雨
lampposts [ˈlæmpˌpəʊsts] *n.* posts supporting a usually outdoor lamp or lantern 路灯柱
territorial [ˌterəˈtɔːriəl] *adj.* connected with the land or sea that is owned by a particular country 领土的
infrastructure [ˈɪnfrəstrʌktʃə(r)] *n.* the basic systems and services that are necessary for a country or an organization to run smoothly, for example, buildings, transport, water and power supplies （国家或机构的）基础设施，基础建设
impetus [ˈɪmpɪtəs] *n.* something that encourages a process or activity to develop more quickly 动力；推动；促进；刺激
multiplied [ˈmʌltɪplaɪd] *v.* （multiply 的过去分词）to increase or make something increase very much in number or amount 成倍增加；迅速增加
Henry Hudson 亨利·哈德逊（16 世纪下半叶—约 1611 年）是一位英国探险家与航海家，以搜寻西北航道而闻名
westerly [ˈwestəli] *adj.* in or towards the west 西方的；向西的；西部的
aristocracy [ˌærɪˈstɒkrəsi] *n.* (in some countries) people born in the highest social class, who have special titles （某些国家的）贵族
edifices [eˈdɪfɪsɪz] *n.* a large impressive building 大厦；宏伟建筑
Central Park largest and most important public park in Manhattan, New York City 中央公园，是位于美国纽约市曼哈顿中心的一个大型都会公园
unsavory [ʌnˈseɪvəri] *adj.* unpleasant to taste or smell 难吃的；难闻的
lodger [ˈlɒdʒəz] *n.* a person who pays money to live in someone else's house 寄宿者；租住者；房客
negatives [ˈneɡətɪvz] *n.* in photography, a negative is an image that shows dark areas as light and light areas as dark. Negatives are made from a camera film, and are used to print photographs. （摄影的）负片，底片

Chapter 5　Modernist Poetry

Part Ⅰ　Warm-up

Discuss the following questions in pairs or groups.
1. What do you know about the historical background of Modernism?
2. How is Modernism different from Realism in literary sense?
3. What are the striking features of modernist poetry?
4. What do you know about the Imagist Movement?
5. Who is your favorite American modernist poet?

Part Ⅱ　What is Imagism?

Watch the video. Write *T* for true or *F* for false for each statement.
1. (　) Imagism was born in England in the early 20th century.
2. (　) Imagism is a reactionary movement against Romanticism and Elizabethan poetry.
3. (　) Imagism emphasized simplicity, clarity of expression, and precision through the use of exacting visual images.
4. (　) The Imagist Movement was rooted in ideas first developed by English philosopher and poet T. E. Hulme.
5. (　) It was Hulme who first introduced the term into the literary lexicon during a meeting with Hilda Doolittle.
6. (　) Ezra Pound used the term "Imagiste" in print for the first time in November 1908.
7. (　) Imagism aimed to replace abstractions with concrete details that could be further expounded upon through the use of figuration.
8. (　) Japanese Haiku is a kind of poetic form that focuses much on images rather than fixed meter and moral reflections.
9. (　) Pound defined image as something that presents an intellectual and emotional complex in an instant of time.
10. (　) The tenets of imagist poetry were first proposed by F. S. Flint.

Part III What Makes a Poem a Poem?

Watch the video and fill in the blanks.

Muhammad Ali spent years training to become the greatest boxer that the world had ever seen, but only spent a few moments to create the shortest poem. Ali 1) _____ Harvard's graduating class in 1975 with his message of unity and friendship. When he finished, the audience wanted more. They wanted a poem. Ali 2) _____ what is considered the shortest poem ever. "Me, we." Or is it "me, weeee"? No one is really sure. Regardless, if these two words are a poem, then what exactly makes a poem a poem? Poets themselves have struggled with this question, often using metaphors to 3) _____ a definition. Is a poem a little machine? A firework? An echo? A dream? Poetry generally has certain 4) _____ characteristics:

One, poems emphasize language's musical qualities. This can be achieved through rhyme, rhythm, and meter. From the sonnets of Shakespeare, to the odes of Confucius, to the Sanskrit Vedas.

Two, poems use 5) _____ language, like literature with all the water wrung out of it.

Three, poems often feature intense feelings, from Rumi's spiritual poetry to Pablo Neruda's "Ode to an Onion".

Poetry, like art itself, has a way of challenging simple definitions. While the 6) _____ patterns of the earliest poems were a way to remember stories even before the 7) _____ of writing, a poem doesn't need to be lyrical. Reinhard Döhl's "Apfel" and Eugen Gomringer's "Silencio" toe the line between 8) _____ art and poetry. Meanwhile, E. E. Cummings wrote poems whose shapes were as important as the words themselves, in this case 9) _____ the sad loneliness of a single leaf falling through space. If the visual nature of poetry faded into the background, perhaps we'd be left with music, and that's an area that people love to debate. Are songs poems? Many don't regard songwriters as poets in a literary sense, but lyrics from artists like Paul Simon, Bob Dylan, and Tupac Shakur often hold up even without the music. In rap, poetic elements like rhyme, rhythm, and imagery are 10) _____ from the form. Take this lyric from the Notorious B. I. G.

"I can hear sweat trickling
down your cheek

Your heartbeat sound
like Sasquatch feet

Thundering, shaking the concrete."

So far, all the examples we've seen have had line breaks. We can even imagine the two words of Ali's poem organizing in the air—Me, We. Poetry has a shape that we can usually recognize. Its line breaks help readers 11) ＿＿＿＿＿＿ the rhythms of a poem. But what if those line breaks disappeared? Would it lose its 12) ＿＿＿＿＿＿ as a poem? Maybe not. Enter the prose poem. Prose poems use vivid images and wordplay but are 13) ＿＿＿＿＿＿ like paragraphs. When we look at poetry less as a form and more as a concept, we can see the poetic all around us: spiritual hymns, the speeches of 14) ＿＿＿＿＿＿ like Martin Luther King, Jr., John Fitzgerald Kennedy, and Winston Churchill, and surprising places like social media. In 2010, journalist Joanna Smith tweeted updates from the earthquake in Haiti.

"Was in b-room getting dressed
when heard my name.

Tremor. Ran outside through sliding door.

All still now. Safe. Roosters crowing."

Smith uses language in a way that is powerful, direct, and filled with vivid images. Compare her language to a Haiku, the ancient Japanese poetic form that emphasizes 15) ＿＿＿＿ of brief intensity with just three lines of five, seven, and five syllables. The waters of poetry run wide and deep. Poetry has 16) ＿＿＿＿ over time, and perhaps now more than ever, the line between poetry, prose, song, and visual art has 17) ＿＿＿＿. However, one thing has not changed. The word poetry actually began in verb form, coming from the ancient Greek *poiēsis*, which means to create. Poets, like craftsmen, still work with the raw materials of the world to 18) ＿＿＿＿ new understandings and comment on what it is to be human in a way only humans can. Dartmouth researchers tested this idea by asking robots to pen poetry. A panel of judges sorted through stacks of 19) ＿＿＿＿＿＿ to see if they could distinguish those made by man and machine. You may be happy to know that while scientists have successfully used artificial intelligence in manufacturing, medicine, and even 20) ＿＿＿＿＿＿

journalism, poetry is a different story. The robots were caught red-handed 100% of the time.

Part Ⅳ What is Modernity? —T. S. Eliot's Context

Watch the video and answer the following questions.
1. What have the previous videos discussed?
2. What does Modernity include and what is Eliot's attitude towards Modernity?
3. What was modern life like visually during the time of Eliot?
4. What was the modern landscape like in Eliot's eyes?
5. What is the paradox in Eliot's poetry?
6. What do we see in all of Eliot's poems?
7. Why is nighttime significant in Eliot's poetry?
8. What does the light in the quote signify?

Part Ⅴ Can a Computer Write a Poem?

Watch the video and decide which poem is written by human and which one is written by computer. Write *H* if it is composed by a human, and *C* if it is composed by a computer.

1. (　) Little Fly / Thy summer's play, /My thoughtless hand / Has brushed away. / Am I not / A fly like thee? / Or art not thou / A man like me?

2. (　) We can feel / Activist / through your life's / morning / Pauses to see, pope I hate the / Non all the night to start a / great otherwise (…)

3. (　) A lion roars and a dog barks. It is interesting / and fascinating that a bird will fly and not / roar or bark. /Enthralling stories about animals are in my dreams and I will sing them all if I / am not exhausted or weary.

4. (　) Oh! Kangaroos, sequins, chocolate sodas! / You are really beautiful! Pearls, / harmonicas, jujubes, aspirins! All / the stuff they've always talked about (…)

5. (　) Red flags the reason for pretty flags. / And ribbons. Ribbons of flags / And wearing material / Reasons for wearing material. (…)

6. (　) A wounded deer leaps highest, / I've heard the daffodil/ I've heard the flag to-day / I've heard the hunter tell; / 'Tis but the ecstasy of death, / And then the brake is almost done (…)

Part VI Projects and Presentations

Choose one of the following projects, or design one of your own closely related to the theme of the unit. Finish the project by giving a presentation in class and leading a discussion afterwards.

1. If you read a poem and feel moved by it, but then find out it was actually written by a computer, would you feel differently about the experience? Would you think that the computer had expressed itself and been creative, or would you feel like you had fallen for a cheap trick? Have a group discussion and share your opinion with your group members.

2. By Ezra Pound, an "image" in a poem is that which presents an intellectual and emotional complex in an instant of time. Pound and his contemporaries agreed on Imagist principles in the early 1910s. The three main principles were: (1) Direct treatment of the "thing" whether subjective or objective. (2) To use absolutely no word that does not contribute to the presentation. (3) As regarding rhythm: to compose in the sequence of the musical phrase, not in sequence of a metronome. Do you agree with Pound's poetics? Why or why not?

3. One of the influences on American Modernist poetry is Chinese ancient poetry. Many of Pound's poems are the recreation of some Chinese classical verses based on translation which is a very controversial topic. Discuss with your classmates on the English translation of Chinese ancient poetry. Do you think there is something that is untranslatable in it?

Part VII Vocabulary and Notes

Video 1
Victorian [vɪkˈtɔːriən] *adj.* connected with the period from 1837 to 1901 when Queen Victoria ruled Britain（英国）维多利亚女王时代（1837—1901）的

verbiage [ˈvɜːbiɪdʒ] *n.* the use of too many words, or of more difficult words than needed, to express an idea 冗词；赘语；晦涩

adapt [əˈdæpt] *v.* to change something in order to make it suitable for a new use or situation 使适应，使适合（新用途、新情况）

earnest [ˈɜːnɪst] *adj.* very serious and sincere 非常认真的；真诚的

strand [strænd] *n.* one of the different parts of an idea, a plan, a story, etc. （观点、计划、故事等的）部分，方面

expound [ɪkˈspaʊnd] *v.* to explain something by talking about it in detail 详解；详述；阐述

Haiku [ˈhaɪkuː] *n.* a poem with three lines and usually 17 syllables, written in a style that is traditional in Japan 俳句（日本传统诗体，三行为一首，通常有 17 个音节）

lyricist [ˈlɪrɪsɪst] *n.* a person who writes the words of songs 歌词作者

Video 2

Muhammad Ali 穆罕默德·阿里，出生于美国肯塔基州路易斯维尔，美国著名拳击运动员、拳王

Sanskrit [ˈsænskrɪt] *n.* An ancient language of India belonging to the Indo-European family, in which the Hindu holy texts are written and on which many modern languages are based 梵语（古印度语，属于印欧语系，用于印度教经文撰写，也是很多现代语言的基础）

Veda [ˈveɪdə] *n.* an ancient holy text of Hinduism《吠陀》（印度教古经文）

Rumi 鲁米，全名莫拉维·贾拉鲁丁·鲁米，1207 年生于巴尔赫（今阿富汗境内）

Pablo Neruda 巴勃鲁·聂鲁达，智利当代著名诗人

Reinhard Döhl 赖因哈德·多尔（1934—2004）德国文学与传媒研究者、作家、艺术家

Eugen Gomringer 瑞士诗人尤金·冈姆林格

Tupac Shakur 图派克·夏库尔，美国说唱歌手、演员，拥有超过 7500 万的全球唱片销量纪录，这使他成为有史以来最畅销的嘻哈音乐艺术家

Notorious B. I. G 原名克里斯托弗·华莱士（Christopher Wallace, 1972—1997），美国说唱歌手、嘻哈音乐人，他的歌曲轻松、流畅，有半自传性的歌词与优异的叙事能力

John Fitzgerald Kennedy 约翰·菲茨杰尔德·肯尼迪（1917—1963，也被称为约翰·F. 肯尼迪/John F. Kennedy、杰克·肯尼迪/Jack Kennedy），出生于美国马萨诸塞州布鲁克莱恩，爱尔兰裔美国政治家、军人，第 35 任美国总统

tweet [twiːt] *v.* make a posting on the social media Twitter 发推特

Video 3

implicate [ˈɪmplɪkeɪt] *v.* to show or suggest that something is the cause of something bad 表明（或意指）……是起因

encapsulate [ɪnˈkæpsjuleɪt] *v.* to express the most important parts of something in a few words, a small space or a single object 简述；概括；压缩

backdrop [ˈbækdrɒp] *n.* the general conditions in which an event takes place, which sometimes help to explain that event （事态或活动的）背景

omnipresence [ˌɒmnɪˈprezns] *n.* the state of being everywhere at once (or seeming to be everywhere at once) 无所不在；全在；无所不至；遍在

critique [krɪˈtiːk] *v.* to write or give your opinion of, or reaction to, a set of ideas, a work of art, etc. 写评论；对……发表评论；评判

disparate [ˈdɪspərət] *adj.* (of two or more things) so different from each other that they cannot be compared or cannot work together 迥然不同的；无法比较的

dismantle [dɪsˈmænt(ə)l] *v.* to end an organization or system gradually in an organized way （逐渐）废除，取消

cramped [kræmpt] *adj.* a cramped room, etc., does not have enough space for the people in it 狭窄的；狭小的

persona [pəˈsəʊnə] *n.* the aspects of a person's character that they show to other people, especially when their real character is different 伪装；假象；人格面具

forebode [fɔːˈbəʊd] *v.* implying or seeming to imply that something bad is going to happen 预示将发生不祥之事

Video 4

William Blake 威廉·布莱克，英国第一位重要的浪漫主义诗人、版画家，英国文学史上最重要的伟大诗人之一，主要诗作有诗集《纯真之歌》《经验之歌》等

algorithm [ˈælɡərɪðəm] *n.* (especially computing) a set of rules that must be followed when solving a particular problem 算法；计算程序

Frank O'Hara 弗兰克·奥哈拉，美国作家、诗人和艺术评论家

regenerate [rɪˈdʒenəreɪt] *v.* to make an area, institution, etc., develop and grow strong again 使振兴；使复兴；发展壮大

Gertrude Stein 格特鲁德·斯泰因（1874—1946），美国作家与诗人

grapple with 努力克服；扭打；与……搏斗；抓住；尽力克服

existential [ˌeɡzɪˈstenʃəl] *adj.* connected with human existence 关于人类存在的；与人类存在有关的

Chapter 6　Modernist Fiction

Part Ⅰ　Warm-up

Discuss the following questions in pairs or groups.
1. Who were the prominent authors associated with the Lost Generation literature?
2. What were the key themes and characteristics of the Lost Generation literature?
3. How did the literary scene in the 1920s reflect the social and cultural milieu of the United States?
4. Who was Gertrude Stein and what was her contribution to literature?

Part Ⅱ　The Introduction of the Lost Generation

Watch the video. Write *T* for true or *F* for false for each statement.
1. (　) The Lost Generation refers to the people whose hopes and dreams had been crushed by the Second World War.
2. (　) Many Americans moved to Paris during the 1920s because they were not satisfied with some social values and phenomenon in their country.
3. (　) Although under high economic pressure, American writers and artists in Paris could embrace more artistic freedom.
4. (　) Ernest Hemingway had quoted from Gertrude Stein and created the term "the Lost Generation" in his novel *The Sun Also Rises*.
5. (　) In a careless way, the authors like James Joyce and Aldous Huxley could also be included in the category of the Lost Generation.
6. (　) The Lost Generation writers usually wrote about their own lives and their experiences revolving the war.
7. (　) The common themes of the writers were about the absurdly wealthy lives of the upper class people, the awakening of new gender roles, and the striving for the American dream.
8. (　) Eventually, all Americans who had been through the war and lost faith in the new way of life could be categorized as the Lost Generation.

Chapter 6　Modernist Fiction

Part Ⅲ　Gertrude Stein, the Enigma

Watch the video. Answer the following questions.

1. What did the speaker in the video describe about Gertrude Stein?
2. What was controversial about Gertrude Stein as a writer?
3. What was Stein mainly writing about in her *Tender Buttons*?
4. What was Stein's purpose of writing these things? Why was the book so monumental?
5. What was the critical response to the book at that time?
6. Why was Stein's *The Autobiography of Alice B. Toklas* so different from anything she had written before?
7. What was the another thing that perplexed readers in the autobiography according to the video? How did it work?
8. Why was Alice made both an insider and an outsider in the modernist world?
9. What did Gertrude Stein try to tell readers through challenging their expectations of a linear series of event?
10. What was Stein's modernist writing trying to encourage readers to do?

Part Ⅳ　Ernest Hemingway — So Ugly, So Beautiful

Watch the video. Answer the following questions for the main ideas.

1. What does it mean by saying Hemingway is "so ugly, so beautiful"?
2. What was Hemingway mainly presenting in his novels?
3. What did Hemingway learn from the impressionist painters and apply into his own novels?
4. What are the valuable lessons we can learn from reading Hemingway?

Watch the video again. Rearrange the following statements in the same order as they appear in the speech.

_____ Hemingway's masculinity was fully practiced by him and was presented by all kinds of authentic achievements in life.

_____ Hemingway wrote about many things such as Paris and Spain, the Great War, and some stories related to the activities he pursued.

_____ Hemingway gives us lessons about how to live according to our values and forces us to consider what we may become, which is why he endures and why we still teach him.

_____ Hemingway's masculinity became representative and was famous among some people, as he had established an image of a contested man that was not ordinary at the time.

_____ One of the reasons for Hemingway's greatness can be related to Cezanne, whose impressionist painting skill had an influence on Hemingway's writing.

_____ The changing gender roles at the time did not influence Hemingway's performance of masculinity.

_____ Hemingway applied motion to show how everything in the natural world was connected.

_____ We might read Hemingway for some reasons not articulable, but the troubled world depicted in his novels would catch our attention once we had dropped into them.

_____ Hemingway learned from the short, repetitive, concentrated brushstrokes, as were the techniques used by impressionist painters, and applied it as repetition of images and words to present the interconnectedness of the natural world.

_____ Ernest Hemingway was the most famous American writer, but there were also flaws in his personality; therefore it will be a question to ponder over of why we still teach Hemingway.

_____ For students, they read Hemingway for his realistic lessons that revealed a cold and treacherous world of adults.

Part V   F. Scott Fitzgerald's *The Great Gatsby*

Watch the video. Answer the following questions.

1. Why did Fitzgerald want to go to Europe? What was he trying to find there?
2. What did Fitzgerald think of *The Great Gatsby* in his conception of the book?
3. What was the theme of *The Great Gatsby*?
4. What were the questions related to the theme?
5. Why did one of the speakers in the video refuse to be an English teacher as was expected by his teacher? What did he learn from Gatsby?
6. What did Fitzgerald see of the opportunities America offered to people?
7. What was Fitzgerald's attitude towards those who pushed beyond limits to pursue their dreams? And what did he see from them?
8. What was the symbolic meaning of the valley of ashes in *The Great Gatsby*?
9. What was the thing people like George Wilson could never truly understand about the rich like Tom Buchanan?

10. What was Gatsby's relation with those rich and entitled people like Tom?

11. Who was Myrtle? What kind of person was she?

12. What was Tom's attitude towards Myrtle?

13. Why did Fitzgerald insist on writing in detail the death scene of Myrtle?

14. What are the two kinds of rebellions according to Fitzgerald?

15. According to the last monologue of Nick in the video, what was truly to be blamed for the death of Gatsby?

Part VI Projects and Presentations

Choose one of the following projects, or design one of your own closely related to the theme of the unit. Finish the project by giving a presentation in class and leading a discussion afterwards.

1. Gertrude Stein wrote in modernist ways, as she absorbed the new techniques such as automatic writing and those from painting to replicate abstract painting in literary form. But this truly disturbed her readers, and through the voice of her Alice B. Toklas the perplexity and difficulty of modern art for normal person was expressed. Van Gogh, for instance, was also misunderstood by people at his time, though his contribution to modernist styles like expressionism and impressionism was well recognized later. What is your feeling about modernism? Work in groups and have a discussion. Give a presentation titled "My Understanding about Modernism".

2. The life of Hemingway always shows ugliness and beauty at the same time, but this is proof that he was being frank to himself and authentic to what came in his life. What do you think of Hemingway? Could you make some comments on him combined with one or two of his novels? Each group summarize the viewpoints of members and report the results in class.

3. In *The Great Gatsby*, Gatsby was murdered in the way of chasing his dream, and Nick Carraway, the narrator of the story, was trapped into a deep misanthropy and cynicism. What is your opinion about those people like Tom and Daisy? Are they worthy of their position and power? What do you think of George's vengeance? Is he worth sympathy or merely pathetic? The conflict between the two kinds of people was heated at that time in America. Reflect on the questions with your knowledge about the society and the novel. Give a brief talk to the class.

Part Ⅶ　Vocabulary and Notes

Video 1

Lost Generation 迷惘的一代，又称迷失的一代，通常指西方世界在第一次世界大战期间成年的一代人，出生于 1883 年至 1900 年

institutionalized [ˌɪnstɪˈtuːʃənəlaɪzd] *adj.* that has become established as part of the normal systems, practices, etc., of an organization, society or culture 约定俗成的；成惯例的

riot [ˈraɪət] *n.* a situation in which a group of people behave in a violent way in a public place, often as a protest 暴乱；骚乱

xenophobia [ˌzenəˈfəʊbiə] *n.* a strong feeling of dislike or fear of people from other countries 仇外，惧外（对外国人的厌恶或惧怕）

censorship [ˈsensərʃɪp] *n.* the act or policy of censoring books, etc. 审查；审查制度

materialism [məˈtɪriəlɪzəm] *n.* the belief that money, possessions and physical comforts are more important than spiritual values 实利主义；物质主义

franc [fræŋk] *n.* the unit of money in Switzerland and several other countries (replaced in 2002 in France by the euro) 法郎（瑞士等国的货币单位，在法国于 2002 年被欧元所取代）

expatriate [ˌeksˈpeɪtriət] *n.* a person living in a country that is not their own 居住在国外的人；侨民

Ernest Hemingway 欧内斯特·海明威（1899—1961），美国人、古巴记者和作家，20 世纪最著名的小说家之一

The Sun Also Rises 《太阳照常升起》，是欧内斯特·海明威于 1926 年创作的小说

Gertrude Stein 格特鲁德·斯泰因（1874—1946），美国作家、诗人，后居住于法国

F. Scott Fitzgerald 弗朗西斯·斯科特·菲茨杰拉德（1896—1940），美国长篇小说、短篇小说作家

T. S. Eliot 托马斯·斯特恩斯·艾略特（1888—1965），美国英国诗人、评论家、剧作家

lump [lʌmp] *v.* to put or consider different things together in the same group, even when they are actually quite different 把……归并一起

James Joyce 詹姆斯·乔伊斯（1882—1941），爱尔兰作家和诗人，20 世纪最

Chapter 6　Modernist Fiction

重要的作家之一

Sherwood Anderson 舍伍德·安德森（1876—1941），美国小说家

John Dos Passos 约翰·多斯·帕索斯（1896—1970），美国小说家、艺术家

John Steinbeck 约翰·斯坦贝克（1902—1968），20 世纪的美国作家、战地记者，1962 年度的诺贝尔文学奖得主

William Faulkner 威廉·福克纳（1897—1962），美国小说家、诗人和剧作家，是美国文学历史上最具影响力的作家之一，意识流文学在美国的代表人物

Aldous Huxley 奥尔德斯·赫胥黎（1894—1963），英格兰作家

Isadora Duncan 伊莎多拉·邓肯（1877—1927），美国舞蹈家，现代舞的创始人

Alan Seeger 阿兰·西格（1888—1916），美国诗人

Aaron Copland 阿隆·科普兰（1900—1990），美国古典音乐作曲家、指挥家和钢琴家

materialistic [məˌtɪəriəˈlɪstɪk] *adj.* caring more about money and possessions than anything else 物质享乐主义的；贪图享乐的

The Great Gatsby 《了不起的盖茨比》，出版于 1925 年，是美国作家弗朗西斯·斯科特·菲茨杰拉德所写的一部以 20 世纪 20 年代的纽约市及长岛为背景的中篇小说

Video 2

enigma [ɪˈnɪɡmə] *n.* a person, thing or situation that is mysterious and difficult to understand 神秘的人；费解的事物

modernism [ˈmɑːdərnɪzəm] *n.* a style and movement in art, architecture and literature popular in the early 20th century in which modern ideas, methods and materials were used rather than traditional ones 现代派，现代主义（盛行于 20 世纪中期的艺术、建筑和文学风格）

polarize [ˈpəʊləraɪz] *v.* to separate or make people separate into two groups with completely opposite opinions （使）两极化，截然对立

salon [səˈlɑːn] *n.* (in the past) a regular meeting of writers, artists and other guests at the house of a famous or important person 沙龙（旧时作家、艺术家等在名流家中定期举行的聚会）

modernist [ˈmɑːdərnɪst] *n.* an artist, architect or writer who works in the style of modernism （尤指艺术）现代主义者

The Autobiography of Alice B. Toklas 《爱丽丝·B·托克拉斯的自传》是格特鲁德·斯坦因的自传，写于 1932 年 10 月和 11 月，出版于 1933 年

connoisseur [ˌkɑːnəˈsɜːr] *n.* an expert on matters involving the judgement of beauty, quality or skill in art, food or music 鉴赏家；鉴定家

patron ['peɪtrən] *n.* a person who gives money and support to artists and writers （艺术家的）赞助人，资助者

Pablo Picasso 巴勃罗·毕加索（1881—1973），西班牙著名的艺术家、画家、雕塑家、版画家、舞台设计师、作家

Paul Cézanne 保罗·塞尚（1839—1906），著名画家，其风格介于印象派和立体主义画派之间

Henri Matisse 亨利·马蒂斯（1869—1954），法国画家，野兽派的创始人及主要代表人物

controversy ['kɑːntrəvɜːrsi] *n.* (over/about/surrounding somebody/something) public discussion and argument about something that many people strongly disagree about, think is bad, or are shocked by 争论，争议

laud [lɔːd] *v.* to praise somebody/something 赞扬；赞美

Tender Buttons《软纽扣》，是美国作家格特鲁德·斯坦因于1914年出版的诗集

portrait ['pɔːrtrət] *n.* a detailed description of somebody/something 详细的描述；描绘

replicate ['replɪkeɪt] *v.* to copy something exactly 复制；（精确地）仿制

automatic writing [ˌɔːtəˈmætɪk ˈraɪtɪŋ] *n.* writing that is believed to have been done in an unconscious state or under a supernatural influence （无意识状态或在超自然力影响下的）自书动作

proclaim [prəˈkleɪm] *v.* to publicly and officially tell people about something important 宣布；声明

populace ['pɑːpjələs] *v.* all the ordinary people of a particular country or area 平民百姓；民众

autobiography [ˌɔːtəbaɪˈɑːgrəfi] *n.* the story of a person's life, written by that person; this type of writing 自传；自传体写作

gossipy ['gɑːsɪpi] *adj.* enjoying talking about other people's private lives 闲聊式的，谈论私人生活的

Fanny Butcher 芬妮·布彻，《芝加哥论坛报》(*Chicago Tribune*)的长期撰稿人和文学评论家

Chicago Tribune《芝加哥论坛报》，是美国重要报纸之一，在美国第三大城市芝加哥出版，创办于1847年

critic ['krɪtɪk] *n.* a person who expresses opinions about the good and bad qualities of books, music, etc. 批评家；评论家

subvert [səbˈvɜːrt] *v.* to challenge somebody's ideas or expectations and make them consider the opposite 颠覆；策反

ideology [ˌaɪdiˈɑːlədʒi] *n.* a set of beliefs, especially one held by a particular group, that influences the way people behave 意识形态；观念形态

linearity [ˌlɪniˈærəti] *n.* the fact that something goes from one thing to another in a single series of stages 线性；平铺直叙

exemplify [ɪɡˈzemplɪfaɪ] *v.* to give an example in order to make something clearer 举例说明；例示

destabilize [ˌdiːˈsteɪbəlaɪz] *v.* to make a system, country, government, etc., become less well-established or successful 使动摇；使不稳定

ventriloquist [venˈtrɪləkwɪst] *n.* a person who entertains by speaking without moving their lips and making it look as if their voice is coming from a puppet or another person 腹语者

subversion [səbˈvɜːrʒn] *n.* an act of changing something to its opposite, especially when this challenges fixed ideas or expectations 颠覆；策反

upheaval [ʌpˈhiːvl] *n.* a big change that causes a lot of worries and problems 剧变；动荡

Video 3

misogynist [mɪˈsɑːdʒɪnɪst] *n.* a person who hates or dislikes women or believes they are not as good as men 厌女者

narcissist [ˈnɑːrsɪsɪt] *n.* a person who admires himself or herself too much, especially their appearance 自恋者

unflattering [ʌnˈflætərɪŋ] *adj.* making somebody/something seem worse or less attractive than they really are 贬损的；有损形象的

journalism [ˈdʒɜːrnəlɪzəm] *n.* the work of collecting and writing news stories for newspapers, magazines, radio, television or online news sites; the news stories that are written 新闻业；新闻工作

Italian Front 意大利战线，是在第一次世界大战中的 1915 年到 1918 年期间，在意大利北部进行的战事

Ambulance Corps 此处指一战期间的救护队，海明威一战时作为美国红十字的救护车驾驶员在意大利活动

valor [ˈvælər] *n.* great courage, especially in war 英勇；勇气

Great War 指第一次世界大战

A Farewell to Arms 《永别了，武器》，是美国作家海明威于 1929 年写成的半自传体小说

bullfight [ˈbʊlfaɪt] *n.* a traditional public entertainment, popular especially in

Spain, in which bulls are fought and usually killed（尤指盛行于西班牙的）斗牛表演

Death in the Afternoon《午后之死》，是海明威撰写的关于西班牙斗牛仪式和传统的非小说类书籍，出版于 1932 年

Green Hills of Africa《非洲的青山》，是海明威的四部随笔作品之一

Spanish Civil War 西班牙内战，是在西班牙发生的一场内战，由西班牙共和军和人民阵线等代表西班牙第二共和国对抗以弗朗西斯科·佛朗哥为核心的西班牙国民军和西班牙长枪党。西班牙内战被认为是第二次世界大战的前奏

For Whom the Bell Tolls《丧钟为谁而鸣》，是海明威于 1940 年出版的小说

The Old Man and the Sea《老人与海》，是海明威生前最后一部主要作品，于 1952 年出版

D-Day D 日，即诺曼底登陆（Normandy landing），发生于 1944 年，是第二次世界大战西方盟军在欧洲西线战场发起的一场大规模攻势

Battle of the Bulge 突出部之役，或称阿登战役，发生于 1944 年 12 月 16 日到 1945 年 1 月 25 日

masculinity [ˌmæskjəˈlɪnəti] *n.* the qualities that are considered to be typical of men 男子气概

manufacture [ˌmænjuˈfæktʃər] *v.* to make goods in large quantities, using machines 大量生产，成批制造

shrapnel [ˈʃræpnəl] *n.* small pieces of metal that are thrown out with a lot of force when a bomb explodes 飞溅的弹片

safari [səˈfɑːri] *n.* a trip to see or hunt wild animals, especially in east or southern Africa（尤指在东非、非洲南部的）观赏（或捕猎）野兽的旅行；游猎

kudu [ˈkuːduː] *n.* a large grey or brown African antelope with white stripes (=narrow lines) on its sides. The male kudu has long, curly horns. 捻角羚（见于非洲）

eBay [ˈiːbeɪ] *n.* a website on the Internet where people can sell goods to other users of the website, usually to the one who offers the most money 易趣（网站）

marlin [ˈmɑːrlɪn] *n.* a large sea fish with a long, sharp nose, that people catch as a sport 枪鱼

post-traumatic stress disorder 创伤后应激障碍（PTSD），指的是人们在经历过或目睹了一场威胁到自己（或周围其他人）生命或安全的创伤性事件后可能产生的一系列反应

glossy [ˈɡlɑːsi] *adj.* smooth and shiny 光滑的；有光泽的

slick [slɪk] *adj.* done or made in a way that is clever and efficient but often does not seem to be sincere or lacks important ideas 华而不实的；虚有其表的

contest [kənˈtest] *v.* to take part in a competition, election, etc., and try to win it 争取获胜（比赛、选举等）

cynical [ˈsɪnɪkl] *adj.* believing that people only do things to help themselves rather than for good or honest reasons 愤世嫉俗的

Frederic 弗瑞德里克·亨利（Frederic Henry），《永别了，武器》中的美国青年

Catherine 凯瑟琳·巴克莉（Catherine Barkley），《永别了，武器》中年轻漂亮的英国护士

incorporate [ɪnˈkɔːrpəreɪt] *v.* (in/into/within something) to include something so that it forms a part of something 将……包括在内；包含

post-impressionist [ˌpəʊst ɪmˈpreʃənɪst] *adj.* in the style of post-impressionism; painting in this style 后印象派的

interconnectedness [ˌɪntərkəˈnektɪdnəs] *n.* the state of being connected to similar things 关联性

echo [ˈekəʊ] *v.* if a sound echoes, it is reflected off a wall, the side of a mountain, etc., so that you can hear it again 回响；回荡

navigate [ˈnævɪɡeɪt] *v.* to sail along, over or through a sea, river etc. 航行；横渡

treacherous [ˈtretʃərəs] *adj.* dangerous, especially when seeming safe 有潜在危险的

obnoxious [əbˈnɑːkʃəs] *adj.* extremely unpleasant, especially in a way that offends people 极度讨厌的；可憎的

Video 4

acute [əˈkjuːt] *adj.* very serious or severe 十分严重的

dismal [ˈdɪzməl] *adj.* causing or showing the feeling of being sad 忧郁的；凄惨的

wagon [ˈwæɡən] *n.* (= station wagon here) a car with a lot of space behind the back seats and a door at the back for loading large items 旅行车

deterioration [dɪˌtɪriəˈreɪʃn] *n.* the fact or process of becoming worse 恶化

Gloria Swanson 格洛丽亚·斯旺森（1899—1983），美国电影演员，也是默片时期最著名的女演员

extravagance [ɪkˈstrævəɡəns] *n.* something that is impressive or likely to attract attention because it is unusual or extreme 富丽堂皇；奢华

clamor [ˈklæmər] *n.* a loud noise, especially one that is made by a lot of people or animals 叫嚷，喧嚣

dwell [dwel] *v.* to live somewhere 居住；栖身

hectic [ˈhektɪk] *adj.* very busy; full of activity 忙碌的；繁忙的

superlative [suːˈpɜːrlətɪv] *adj.* excellent 极佳的；卓越的

intricately [ˈɪntrɪkətli] *adv.* with a lot of different parts and small details that fit together 杂乱地；复杂地

Zelda 泽尔达·菲茨杰拉德（Zelda Fitzgerald）（1900—1948），本名泽尔达·塞尔（Zelda Sayre），是一位美国小说家、社交名流和美国作家弗朗西斯·斯科特·菲茨杰拉德的妻子

Gatsby 杰伊·盖茨比（Jay Gatsby），《了不起的盖茨比》中的主人公

glamour [ˈglæmər] *n.* the attractive and exciting quality that makes a person, a job or a place seem special, often because of wealth or status 吸引力，魅力

constraint [kənˈstreɪnt] *n.* a thing that limits something, or limits your freedom to do something 限制；约束

impediment [ɪmˈpedɪmənt] *n.* something that delays or stops the progress of something 阻碍；障碍

glittering [ˈglɪtərɪŋ] *adj.* shining brightly with many small flashes of light 灿烂夺目的；闪闪发光的

George Wilson 乔治·威尔逊，《了不起的盖茨比》中的机修工，修理厂老板

custodian [kʌˈstəʊdiən] *n.* a person who takes responsibility for taking care of or protecting something 监护人；看守人

Tom Buchanan 汤姆·布坎南，《了不起的盖茨比》中的一位富豪，黛西的丈夫

uncanny [ʌnˈkæni] *adj.* strange and difficult to explain 异常的；难以解释的

Myrtle 默特尔·威尔逊（Myrtle Wilson），《了不起的盖茨比》中乔治·威尔逊的妻子

vulgar [ˈvʌlgər] *adj.* not having or showing good taste; not polite, pleasant or well behaved 庸俗的；粗野的

brutally [ˈbruːtəli] *adv.* in a violent and cruel way 残忍地；野蛮地

presumably [prɪˈzuːməbli] *adv.* used when you think that something is probably true 大概，可能

Daisy 黛西·布坎南（Daisy Buchanan），《了不起的盖茨比》中汤姆·布坎南的妻子

mutilation [ˌmjuːtɪˈleɪʃn] *n.* severe damage to somebody's body, especially when part of it is cut or torn off; the act of causing such damage （肢体）残缺；毁伤（形）

proletarian [ˌprəʊləˈteriən] *n.* connected with ordinary people who earn money by working, especially those who do not own any property 无产阶级者

rebellion [rɪˈbeljən] *n.* opposition to authority within an organization, a political party, etc. （对权威的）反抗，不服从

sullen [ˈsʌlən] *adj.* in a bad mood and not speaking, either on a particular occasion or because it is part of your character 阴沉的；闷闷不乐的

resentment [rɪˈzentmənt] *n.* a feeling of anger or unhappiness about something that you think is unfair 愤恨；怨恨

revolver [rɪˈvɑːlvər] *n.* a small gun that has a container for bullets that turns around so that shots can be fired quickly without having to stop to put more bullets in 左轮手枪

riotous [ˈraɪətəs] *adj.* noisy, exciting and fun 狂欢的；纵情欢闹的

excursion [ɪkˈskɜːrʒn] *n.* a short period of trying a new or different activity （短期的）涉足，涉猎

abortive [əˈbɔːrtɪv] *adj.* (of an action) not successful; failed 不成功的；失败的

elation [ɪˈleɪʃn] *n.* a feeling of great happiness and excitement 兴高采烈；欢欣鼓舞

Chapter 7   Literature of the 1930s

Part I   Warm-up

Discuss the following questions in pairs or groups.

1. How did American literature in the 1930s reflect the social and cultural climate of the time?

2. What were some significant literary movements or themes in American literature during the 1930s?

3. What are some notable works of Willa Cather?

4. What are some major themes explored in *The Grapes of Wrath*?

Part II   Sinclair Lewis — The Conscience of His Generation

Watch the video. Answer the following questions.

1. What were Sinclair Lewis's achievements in literary history?

2. How did some people think about Lewis as the first American to receive the Nobel Prize?

3. Why did Lewis become really famous in early 20th century?

4. What was Lewis mainly writing about at his time?

5. What does it mean by "finger on the pulse of the culture"?

6. What was *Elmer Gantry* mainly about?

7. What was the vision of Lewis in his novel *Babbitt*?

8. What was the theme of Lewis's *Main Street*?

9. What was the place Sauk Centre, which was called Gopher Prairie in his novel?

10. What gave Lewis the stature in literary history? And what made him nearly fall out of the canon?

Part III   Sherwood Anderson's Camden

Watch the video. Answer the following questions for the main ideas.

1. What was Camden? What was it for Anderson?

2. What was the symbolic meaning of Anderson's Camden?
3. What was his relation with other writers?
4. What did Anderson mean by saying "we are all small-towners"?

Watch the video again. Fill in the following blanks.

Anderson's Camden was a place of mystery — the home of romance, a 1) _____ town tucked in among the hills and cut off from the modern world. Sherwood Anderson was born in Camden, Ohio in 1876 just as summer was fading away. His most famous work *Winesburg, Ohio* tells the story of many people living in a small town. Anderson uses literary 2) _____, giving a pessimistic observation of the human condition. When leaving Winesburg, the final character looked out of the car window: the town of Winesburg had disappeared, and his life there had become but a background on which to paint the dreams of his 3) _____.

Anderson developed relationships with Ernest Hemingway and William Faulkner, becoming a vital 4) _____ in the development of their writing. Anderson said, "In Faulkner, you feel an inner sympathy with the fact of life itself, but not in Hemingway; in him there was the desire always to kill."

Camden was always alive inside Anderson. His Camden was full of citizens who were honest, hard-working people, who planted their corns by hand and harvested wheats—people that Anderson felt he could understand. Camden 5) _____ ideals the Andersons celebrated and strove for as a writer and as a man. It was full of people who worked with their hands, who recognized human worth—a 6) _____, a democracy at work. In his 64 years, he would live in countless places but none could compare with Camden. It was his favorite. And for a very simple reason he did not remember a thing about it.

His family moved away when he was only one year old. Anderson was free to make of it what he would and could retreat there whenever he desired to do so. And in 1934, he and his fourth wife Eleanor set out to visit many towns, including Camden. The ideal community he had 7) _____ as Camden had not come into being. In fact, it might have seemed it never would. But Anderson still heard how strong and decent people were. Although Camden was never the perfect community, it still sits tucked in among the hills with continuing life. And in writing his own 8) _____, Anderson says, "Life, not death, is the great adventure." In 1938, Thomas Wolfe wrote, "I think you are one of the most important writers of this century, that you have 9) _____ another deep furrow in American earth, revealing to us another 10) _____ that we knew was there, but no one else had spoken." "I think of you with Whitman and Twain, that is, with men who have seen America with a poet's vision and with a 11) _____ vision of life, which to my mind is the only way 12) _____ it can be seen." In 1958, Faulkner expressed his view that Anderson had never been given his rightful place in American literature. He said, "In my opinion, he is the father of all my generation."

Anderson's widow Eleanor visited Camden again in 1962. She visited Anderson's birthplace as well as the building where his father owned a 13) _____ shop. She spent most of her visit at the local library and was highly impressed with what they had done to 14) _____ the memory of her husband. And later in 1969, his daughter, Marion, visited Camden in their library. The visit gave Marion a good sense of her roots, which she said was a nice feeling.

Sherwood Anderson once wrote, "We are all small-towners." The small-town boy hungers to see the wonders of the world, to be an important figure out there. During all his life in the city, the small town of his boyhood had remained home to him. Every house in the town, the faces of people seen on the street in his boyhood have all remained sharp in his mind. The city man returning to his hometown has always a feeling of sadness. He 15) _____ the change in the town, the fact that people of the town have grown older as he has, that strangers have come in. He is shocked, half wishing he hadn't come, and he thinks it would have been better to leave my dream alone.

Part IV   John Steinbeck's *The Grapes of Wrath*

Watch the video. Write *T* for true or *F* for false for each statement.

1. (   ) *The Grapes of Wrath* is a classic for the themes of endurance, sacrifice and family, and are less powerful today than when it was published.

2. (   ) The Joads are sharecroppers in Oklahoma, and they are pushed out of their land by the Depression and drought and head for California, the Golden State.

3. (   ) Many of the farmers in the Central Plains were forced to move, and even with the help of the banks, the population had dropped 40%.

4. (   ) The "Joad moment" represents a spirit to fight against the unjust and rise up for human decency and one's own values.

5. (   ) Ma Joad is a stoic type of person, which means she will hardly be crushed by the challenges and is always ready for anything that could happen; but it does not mean she is indifferent and cold.

6. (   ) At the end of the journey, the Joads encountered one of the largest Hoovervilles in America, east of the Mississippi; it was at that time the single worst example of poverty in

America.

7. (　) Rose of Sharon delivers a child in a desperate situation and offers her milk laden breast to the child; the milk represents life, suffering from pain and anguish, human kindness and strivings of common people.

8. (　) Steinbeck insisted that the Civil War should be placed on the book's covers, for the important American values are contained within: the spirit of persistence that all of us cling to as human beings; the spirit of family and community to take care of each other at times of hardship.

Part V　Willa Cather's *My Antonia* and *The Professor's House*

Watch the video. Answer the following questions.

1. What was Cather's initial conception of Antonia before she wrote the novel?
2. According to the lecture, what does Antonia mean to Americans?
3. What was the property of Annie Pavelka that Cather admired when she took her as the prototype of Antonia?
4. What were the conditions of the frontier in Nebraska for immigrants like Pavelka at that time?
5. Why is such hardship in the frontier a very American theme?
6. How does Antonia face her hardship?
7. What has been revealed by the striving of Antonia and her children in the family?
8. What did Cather know when she saw the cruelty of war from those returned soldiers?
9. What was Cather's understanding of the world? And what was the choice she made that was so different from many of others in the face of the change?
10. What was Cather facing at her age of 52? What did she do?
11. What did Cather write in her book that very few people wrote about?
12. What are the situations the professor is facing with in the novel?
13. Why does Tom Outland's story touch the professor so deeply?
14. What was the fear haunting the professor?
15. How does the accident of nearly getting killed by the toxic fumes change the professor's life?

Part VI Projects and Presentations

Choose one of the following projects, or design one of your own closely related to the theme of the unit. Finish the project by giving a presentation in class and leading a discussion afterwards.

1. In *Babbitt*, Sinclair Lewis was visionary on what effects mass culture and new inventions, represented by the automobile particularly at that time, would have on a country. Our time is also deeply attached to technology, as the Internet culture for example, is taking over almost every aspect of our life. These new technologies are shaped by the western minds from the late 20th century like Bill Gates and Steve Jobs. Could you find out what are some aspects in your life shaped by Western culture today? What should we do to carry forward the spirit of Chinese culture in this situation? Have a discussion with your group members. Each group summarize the viewpoints of members and report the results in class.

2. Sherwood Anderson said, "We are all small-towners." His small town Camden carried his ideal and dream, and was a place human labors were recognized. Are you a small-towner? Do you buy into Anderson's idea about human values and community? What is an ideal community or society for you? Have a discussion with your group members. Give a brief talk titled "What Is An Ideal Community?"

3. Willa Cather knew that the world was entering a century of displacement, pain and suffering when she saw those soldiers returning from World War I, and she chose to retreat to the old world and the old values instead of stepping to the side of the new. The reaction also influenced the themes of her writing, as is presented in *My Antonia* and *The Professor's House*. What is your opinion about her choice? You can compare Cather's values with other writers such as Hemingway, who also wrote a lot about war. Have a discussion with your group members and share the results in class.

Part VII Vocabulary and Notes

Video 1

Sinclair Lewis 辛克莱·刘易斯（1885—1951），美国小说家、短篇故事作家、剧作家，是第一个获得诺贝尔文学奖的美国人

conscience [ˈkɑːnʃəns] *n.* the part of your mind that tells you whether your actions are right or wrong 良心；良知

rolling [ˈrəʊlɪŋ] *adj.* （of hills or countryside）having gentle slopes 起伏的，延绵的

launching pad [ˈlɔːntʃɪŋ pæd] a platform from which a spacecraft, etc., is sent into the sky 发射台

Jazz Age 爵士时代，指 20 世纪 20 年代和 30 年代，当时流行爵士乐与舞蹈，主要出现在美国，但是法国、英国与其他地区也有这种现象

Main Street 《大街》，是辛克莱·刘易斯写的讽刺小说，于 1920 年出版

satirical [səˈtɪrɪkl] *adj.* using satire to criticize somebody/something 讽刺的；讥讽的

smugness [ˈsmʌgnəs] *n.* the fact of looking or feeling too pleased about something you have done or achieved 洋洋自得；自视甚高

eloquently [ˈeləkwəntli] *adv.* in a way that uses language and expresses your opinions well, especially when you are speaking in public 善辩地；富有表现力地

foibles [ˈfɔɪb(ə)lz] *n.* ［复数］a silly habit or a strange or weak aspect of a person's character that is not considered serious by other people （性格上无伤大雅的）怪癖，缺点

visionary [ˈvɪʒəneri] *n.* a person who has the ability to think about or plan the future in a way that is intelligent and shows imagination 有眼力的人；有远见卓识的人

pulse [pʌls] *n.* （usually singular）the regular beat of the heart as it sends blood around the body, that can be felt in different places, especially on the inside part of the wrist; the number of times the heart beats in a minute 脉搏；脉率

satirize [ˈsætəraɪz] *v.* to use satire to show the faults in a person, an organization, a system, etc. 讽刺；讥讽

Elmer Gantry 《埃尔默·甘特利》，是辛克莱·刘易斯在 1926 年写的一部讽刺小说

Burt Lancaster 伯顿·兰开斯特（1913—1994），是一位美国电影演员，出演过电影《埃尔默·甘特利》

evangelist [ɪˈvændʒəlɪst] *n.* a person who tries to persuade people to become Christians, especially by travelling around the country holding religious meetings or speaking on radio or television （基督教）布道者；传播福音者

Amy Semple McPherson 艾米·森坡·麦克弗森（麦艾梅），是 20 世纪 20 年代至 30 年代在加拿大、美国五旬节运动（Pentecostalism）的传福音者和大众媒体名流，为《埃尔默·甘特利》中的角色

televangelist [ˌtelɪˈvændʒəlɪst] *n.* （especially in the US）a person who appears regularly on television to try to persuade people to become Christians and to give money 电

视福音布道者

feet of clay the bad quality that you keep hidden（看似完美的人的）缺陷，弱点

theological [ˌθiːəˈlɑːdʒɪkl] *adj.* connected with the study of religion and beliefs 神学的

seminary [ˈsemɪneri] *n.* a college where priests, ministers or rabbis are trained 神学院；修院

deacon [ˈdiːkən] *n.* a religious leader just below the rank of a priest 执事，会吏

sermon [ˈsɜːrmən] *n.* a talk on a moral or religious subject, usually given by a religious leader during a service 布道；讲道

Babbitt《巴比特》，是辛克莱·刘易斯在1922年发表的长篇小说

automobile [ˈɔːtəməbiːl] *n.* a car 汽车

phonograph [ˈfoʊnəɡræf] *n.* a piece of equipment for playing records in order to listen to the music, etc., on them 留声机

Victorian Era 维多利亚时代，指从19世纪30年代至20世纪初的英国历史时期，即维多利亚女皇统治时期

provincialism [prəˈvɪnʃəlɪzəm] *n.* the attitude of people who are unwilling to consider new or different ideas or things 胸襟狭隘；排外主义

conservative [kənˈsɜːrvətɪv] *adj.* opposed to great or sudden social change; showing that you prefer traditional styles and values 保守的；守旧的

Gopher Prairie 字面意思为"地鼠草原"，是《大街》中虚构的一个中产阶级社区，原型为辛克莱·刘易斯的家乡索克森特（Sauk Centre）

lowest common denominator [ˌloʊɪst ˌkɑːmən dɪˈnɑːmɪneɪtər]（disapproving）something that is simple enough to seem interesting to, or to be understood by, the highest number of people in a particular group 大众化的东西

crack down（**on sb/sth**）to try harder to prevent an illegal activity and deal more severely with those who are caught doing it 镇压；打击

lead with one's chin to behave very aggressively 鲁莽行事

newfangled [ˌnuːˈfæŋɡld] *adj.* used to describe something that has recently been invented or introduced, but that you do not like because it is not what you are used to, or is too complicated 新奇怪异的；时髦复杂的

bog sth/sb down（usually passive）to prevent somebody from making progress in an activity 使停滞，使陷入泥沼

canon [ˈkænən] *n.* a list of the books or other works that are generally accepted as the real work of a particular writer or as being important（作家的）真作，精品

transcend [trænˈsend] *v.* to be or go beyond the usual limits of something 超出，超越

Video 2

Sherwood Anderson 舍伍德·安德森（1876—1941），美国小说家

Camden 卡姆登，是美国俄亥俄州（Ohio）普雷布尔县（Preble County）的一个村庄

pristine [ˈprɪstiːn] *adj.* not developed or changed in any way; left in its original condition 未开发的；处于原始状态的

tuck [tʌk] *v.* to put something into a small space, especially to hide it or keep it safe or comfortable 把……塞进狭窄的空间；把……藏入

Winesburg, Ohio 《小镇畸人》，是美国作家舍伍德·安德森的代表作

naturalism [ˈnætʃrəlɪzəm] *n.* a style of art or writing that shows people, things and experiences as they really are 自然主义（文学艺术以反映现实为宗旨）

embody [ɪmˈbɑːdi] *v.* to express or represent an idea or a quality 具体表现，代表（思想或品质）

Eleanor 埃莉诺·科彭哈维尔·安德森（Eleanor Copenhaver Anderson），是一名社会工作者和活动家，舍伍德·安德森的妻子

epitaph [ˈepɪtæf] *n.* words that are written or said about a dead person, especially words on a gravestone 悼文；墓志铭

Thomas Wolfe 托马斯·伍尔夫（1900—1938），美国小说家

plow [plaʊ] *v.* (= plough) to dig and turn over a field or other area of land with a plough 耕，犁

furrow [ˈfɜːrəʊ] *n.* a long narrow cut in the ground, especially one made by a plough for planting seeds in 犁沟；车辙

Walt Whitman 沃尔特·惠特曼（1819—1892），美国诗人、散文家、新闻工作者及人文主义者

Mark Twain 马克·吐温（1835—1910），原名塞姆·朗赫恩·克莱门斯（Samuel Langhorne Clemens），是美国的幽默大师、小说家、作家，亦是著名演说家

harness [ˈhɑːrnɪs] *n.* a set of narrow pieces of leather and metal that is put around the head and body of an animal, especially a horse, so that the animal can be controlled and fastened to a carriage, etc. 马具；挽具

Video 3

The Grapes of Wrath 《愤怒的葡萄》，美国作家约翰·斯坦贝克于 1939 出版的长篇小说，是一部美国社会纪实文学

Joads 《愤怒的葡萄》中的乔德一家人

impoverished [ɪmˈpɑːvərɪʃt] *adj.* very poor; without money 赤贫的；不名一文的

Oklahoma 美国的俄克拉何马州

sharecropper [ˈʃerkrɑːpər] *n.* a farmer who gives part of their crops as rent to the owner of the land 佃农

Depression 大萧条（Great Depression），又称经济大危机、经济大恐慌，指 1929 年至 1933 年的全球经济大衰退，是第二次世界大战前最严重的全球经济衰退

battered [ˈbætərd] *adj.* old, used a lot, and not in very good condition 破旧不堪的

Golden State 金州，即加利福尼亚州（California），因其丰富的自然资源和气候得名

milestone [ˈmaɪlstəʊn] *n.* a very important stage or event in the development of something 重要阶段；里程碑

High Plains 美国高地平原，是大平原（Great Plains）的一部分，主要位于美国西部

panhandle [ˈpænhændl] *n.* a narrow piece of land that sticks out from the main part of a state, like the handle of a pan（美）柄状的狭长区域（如平底锅柄）

Boise City 博伊西城，是美国俄克拉何马州（Oklahoma）的一座城市，位于俄克拉何马州的柄状狭长区域

pull up stakes to take all the things that you own and go and live in a different place 迁离，搬离

Tom Joad 汤姆·乔德，《愤怒的葡萄》中的主人公

convict [ˈkɑːnvɪkt] *n.* a person who has been found guilty of a crime and sent to prison 已决犯；服刑囚犯

intolerance [ɪnˈtɑːlərəns] *n.* the fact of not being willing to accept ideas or ways of behaving that are different from your own 不容忍；偏狭

exploitation [ˌeksplɔɪˈteɪʃ(ə)n] *n.* a situation in which somebody treats somebody else in an unfair way, especially in order to make money from their work 剥削；压榨

Ma Joad 乔德妈，《愤怒的葡萄》中的角色，家庭女族长，为人务实、温良，她努力将全家团结在一起

stoicism [ˈstəʊɪsɪzəm] *n.* the fact of not complaining or showing what you are feeling when you are suffering 对痛苦泰然处之；坚忍

corrugated [ˈkɔːrəgeɪtɪd] *adj.* having the shape of a series of regular folds that look like waves 起皱的；波纹的

Hoovervilles 胡佛村，是大萧条期间美国无家可归者修建的棚户区，名字来源于大萧条初期时任美国总统的赫伯特·胡佛（Herbert Hoover），而大萧条也被广泛地归咎于他

Rose of Sharon 罗丝·莎伦，《愤怒的葡萄》中的一位 18 岁姑娘

stillborn [ˈstɪlbɔːrn] *adj.* born dead 死产的

anguish [ˈæŋɡwɪʃ] *n.* severe physical or mental pain, difficulty or unhappiness 剧痛；极度痛苦

Battle Hymn of the Republic 《共和国战歌》，是一首美国的爱国歌曲，由茱丽雅·沃尔德·何奥（Julia Ward Howe）作词，为南北战争期间十分流行的歌曲

Video 4

Willa Cather 薇拉·凯瑟（1873—1947），美国作家，作品以擅长描写女性及美国早期移民的拓荒开垦生活而闻名，为美国重要的乡土作者之一

My Antonia 《我的安东妮亚》，是美国作家薇拉·凯瑟于 1918 年出版的小说，被认为是她最好的作品之一

The Professor's House 《教授的房子》，是薇拉·凯瑟的小说，于 1925 年出版

Annie Pavelka 安娜·帕维尔卡，是薇拉·凯瑟的小说《我的安东妮亚》中人物安东尼娅·希默达（Antonia Shimerda）的现实生活灵感来源

Red Cloud 雷德克劳德，是一个位于美国内布拉斯加州（Nebraska）的城市

Bohemia 波希米亚，是古中欧地名，占据了古捷克地区西部三分之二的区域，现为包括布拉格在内的捷克共和国中西部地区

Nebraska 内布拉斯加州，位于美国

frontier [frʌnˈtɪr] *n.* (singular) the edge of land where people have settled and built towns, beyond which the country is wild and unknown, especially in the western US in the 19th century （尤指 19 世纪美国西部的）边缘地带，边远地区

unfold [ʌnˈfəʊld] *v.* to be gradually made known; to gradually make something known to other people （使）逐渐展现；展示

stove [stəʊv] *n.* a piece of equipment that can burn various fuels and is used for heating rooms 炉子，火炉

Czechoslovakia 捷克斯洛伐克，是一个存在于 1918 年至 1992 年的中东欧国家

towhead [ˌtoʊˈhɛd] *n.* someone who has very light blond hair, most common to describe blond children 金发的人（常用于金发的孩子）

veritable [ˈverɪtəbl] *adj.* a word used to emphasize that somebody/something can be compared to somebody/something else that is more exciting, more impressive, etc. 十足的；名副其实的

runaway [ˈrʌnəweɪ] *adj.* happening very easily or quickly, and not able to be controlled 难以控制的

H. L. Mencken H·L·孟肯，美国记者、讽刺作家、文化评论家

pier [pɪr] *n.* a long low structure built in a lake, river or the sea and joined to the land at one end, used by boats to allow passengers to get on and off （凸入湖、河、海

中的）码头

Jersey City 泽西市或泽西城，是美国新泽西州（New Jersey）的一个城市

gas [gæs] *v.* to kill or harm somebody by making them breathe poisonous gas 用毒气杀伤（或杀死）；使吸入毒气

displacement [dɪsˈpleɪsmənt] *n.* the act of forcing somebody/something away from their home or position 取代；移位

imposition [ˌɪmpəˈzɪʃn] *n.* the action or process of imposing something 强加；强迫接受

retreat [rɪˈtriːt] *n.* a quiet, private place that you go to in order to get away from your usual life 僻静处；隐居处

dismantle [dɪsˈmænt(ə)l] *v.* to take apart a machine or structure so that it is in separate pieces 拆开，拆卸

Godfrey St. Peter 戈弗雷·圣·彼得，是《教授的房子》中故事的主人公

cluttered [ˈklʌtərd] *adj.* (with sb/sth) covered with, or full of, a lot of things or people, in a way that is untidy 杂乱的；凌乱的

stuffy [ˈstʌfi] *adj.* (of a building, room, etc.) warm in an unpleasant way and without enough fresh air 闷热的；通风不畅的

Tom Outland 汤姆·奥特兰，是《教授的房子》中的角色

mesa [ˈmeɪsə] *n.* a hill with a flat top and steep sides that is common in the southwest of the US 桌子山，方山（常见于美国西南部）

Cliff City 崖边城市，是故事中汤姆·奥特兰发现的一座石城

cavern [ˈkævərn] *n.* a cave, especially a large one 大洞穴；大山洞

vacantly [ˈveɪkəntli] *adv.* in a way that shows no sign that a person is thinking of anything 茫然地；空虚地

tremendous [trəˈmendəs] *adj.* very great 巨大的；极大的

Chapter 8　Southern Literature

Part Ⅰ　Warm-up

Discuss the following questions in pairs or groups.

1. What was the Southern Renaissance in literature?
2. How did the Southern Renaissance reflect the social and cultural atmosphere of the American South in the early 20th century?
3. What is the concept of "Southern myth" in literature?
4. What do you think is William Faulkner's most famous novel and what makes it significant?

Part Ⅱ　Furious Fiction: Discussing William Faulkner's *Absalom, Absalom*

Watch the video. Write *T* for true or *F* for false for each statement.

1. (　) *Absalom, Absalom* is one of the classics of American southern literature.
2. (　) According to Diane, *Absalom, Absalom* is the greatest American novel of the 20th century.
3. (　) *Absalom, Absalom* is a beach read.
4. (　) All the five different narrators in *Absalom, Absalom* are sometimes misrepresenting, sometimes possibly lying, and definitely not knowing what really happened.
5. (　) Mark Mush was happy to read the chronology in the back of the book.
6. (　) *Absalom, Absalom* is a Civil War novel in Diane's opinion.
7. (　) *Gone with the Wind* was published in 1936.
8. (　) *Absalom, Absalom* is a novel against slavery.
9. (　) Every time when Diane reread *Absalom, Absalom*, somebody would stick pages that were never in my book before in her book.
10. (　) *Absalom, Absalom* is in Top Three American novels.

Part III Why Should You Read Flannery O'Connor?

Watch the video and choose the right answer for the following questions.

1. Flannery O'Connor enjoyed the company of _____ .
   A. cows   B. birds   C. dogs   D. cats
2. Most of O'Connor's stories take place in the US, specifically in _____ .
   A. Texas   B. New York   C. rural south   D. fantasy worlds
3. What is a characteristic of Flannery O'Connor's writing style?
   A. Straightforward and realistic descriptions.
   B. Sentimental and romantic language.
   C. Stinging language and offbeat humor.
   D. Minimalistic and sparse prose.
4. O'Connor claimed she incorporated ugly and unpleasant situations into her work ____ .
   A. to scare her readers
   B. to penetrate the human character
   C. to judge her characters
   D. to annoy her readers
5. O'Connor had mostly been confined to her farm in Georgia since she was ____ .
   A. 27   B. 29   C. 37   D. 39
6. How does Flannery O'Connor challenge her readers in her writing?
   A. By creating predictable and formulaic characters.
   B. By avoiding controversial subjects and sensitive topics.
   C. By exploring the nuance and variety of human character.
   D. By conforming to the conventions of the Southern Gothic genre.

Part IV *To Kill a Mockingbird* and the Southern Gothic Tradition

Watch the video and answer the following questions.

1. Which literary tradition does *To Kill a Mockingbird* belong to?
2. Where does the southern Gothic genre derive tension?
3. Whose works have attributes of southern Gothic novels?
4. Where did the Gothic genre originate from?
5. What is special about the Gothic novels?
6. How do we know that familiar southern Gothic elements exist in *To Kill a*

Mockingbird?

Watch the video again and fill in the blanks.

To Kill a Mockingbird arrived at the end of southern Gothic's initial flourishing. William Faulkner, the author of novels including *As I Lay Dying* and *The Sound and the Fury*, was one of its earliest and best-known 1) _____. His stories take place in rural Mississippi and feature characters grappling with the racial and economic anxieties of the post-civil war south. 2) _____ houses and characters, taboo themes such as incest, and suppressed 3) _____ and violence feature prominently in his stories. Faulkner's famous quote "the past is never dead" is not even past, 4) _____ how the characters in his books and in southern Gothic writing in general cannot move beyond the sins of their forefathers. Flannery O'Connor is another writer associated with the genre, even though she 5) _____ the term southern Gothic. She's best known for her short stories, including *A Good Man Is Hard to Find* and *Everything That Rises Must Converge*. O'Connor's works are renowned for their 6) _____ outlook, their 7) _____ characters called grotesques, and their complex treatment of race in the segregated south. Shocking acts of violence remind the reader that dark 8) _____ drives lurk beneath the surface of a small-town life.

While *To Kill a Mockingbird* has many similarities with other southern Gothic works, it also has differences. Its family 9) _____ tone contrasts with the more 10) _____ subject matter and language of other southern Gothic works. Since it's told from the 11) _____ of a young girl who doesn't understand many of the adult topics being mentioned, it 12) _____ less on sex, violence and evil than other southern Gothic works. The humor in *To Kill a Mockingbird* is also gentler than other southern Gothic works, whose humor is typically dark and at the expense of the characters. It's also more 13) _____. Instead of ending in murder and hopelessness, we see good represented by Boo Radley and the Finch's 14) _____ over Bob Ewell's evil. We still see violence rooted in the past, but it's 15) _____ by hope for reconciling with history and learning from past sins. Some characters are driven by typical repressed torments, but others are motivated by desire to do good and enact 16) _____ change. Secrets lose their power to haunt in the light of day, as when Boo finally emerges from his house to be seen. The novel's final words, "Most people are nice when you finally see them", evoke hope for a less 17) _____, more 18) _____ future.

Part V Why Is William Faulkner So Difficult to Read?

Watch the video and answer the following questions.

1. What was the purpose of William Faulkner's intentional use of confusion in his novels?

2. Where are many of Faulkner's novels set, and what does this setting represent?

3. How does Faulkner's use of multiple perspectives contribute to the reader's understanding of his characters and their biases?

4. In what ways does Faulkner's fiction challenge rigid Jim Crow policies and the region's history of genocide and slavery?

5. How does Faulkner captivate readers with his writing style?

6. What is the significance of the title *The Sound and the Fury* in relation to Faulkner's exploration of confusion and perception?

Part VI Projects and Presentations

Choose one of the following projects, or design one of your own closely related to the theme of the unit. Finish the project by giving a presentation in class and leading a discussion afterwards.

1. Gothic genre has been mentioned several times in the lectures of this unit. Please work in groups and discuss with your partners about the characteristics of the Gothic genre, its embodiment in works as well as its social meaning. Each group summarize the viewpoints of members and reports your discussion results in class.

2. Female characters in American southern literature are of great value and unique style. Please find some research articles about them and give a brief talk on "The Female Characters in American Southern Literature".

3. Give a brief talk on the cultural significance of southern literature. Your talk may include the following parts: the impact and legacy of southern literature on American literary tradition; the role of southern literature in challenging stereotypes and addressing social issues; the representation of the South's diverse voices and perspectives.

Chapter 8 Southern Literature

Part VII Vocabulary and Notes

Video 1

chronology [krəˈnɒlədʒi] *n.* the order in which a series of events happened; a list of these events in order 按事件发生的年代排列的顺序；年表

doom [duːm] *v.* to make somebody/something certain to fail, suffer, die, etc. 使……注定失败（或遭殃、死亡等）

plug hat [plʌɡ hæt] *n.* a felt hat that is round and hard with a narrow brim 高礼帽；男式帽

crinoline [ˈkrɪnəlɪn] *n.* a frame that was worn under a skirt by some women in the past in order to give the skirt a very round full shape （旧时的）裙衬，裙撑，裙架

The Antigone 《安蒂冈妮》，是1988年书林出版有限公司出版的图书，作者是苏弗克里兹

gentry [ˈdʒentri] *n.* (old-fashioned) people belonging to a high social class 绅士阶层；上流社会人士

cod liver oil [ˌkɒd lɪvər ˈɔɪl] a thick yellow oil from the liver of cod (= a type of fish), containing a lot of vitamins A and D and often given as a medicine 鱼肝油

epic poem [ˈepɪk ˈpəʊɪm] a long narrative poem telling of a hero's deeds 史诗；叙事诗；英雄史诗

compelling [kəmˈpelɪŋ] *adj.* that makes you pay attention to it because it is so interesting and exciting 引人入胜的；扣人心弦的

Video 2

garrulous [ˈɡærələs] *adj.* talking a lot, especially about unimportant things （尤指在琐事上）饶舌的，唠叨的，喋喋不休的

roaming [ˈrəʊmɪŋ] *v.* (roam 的现在分词) to walk or travel around an area without any definite aim or direction 徜徉；闲逛；漫步

handyman [ˈhændimæn] *n.* a man who is good at doing practical jobs inside and outside the house, either as a hobby or as a job 善于做室内外杂活的人；杂活工

scribble [ˈskrɪbl] *v.* to write something quickly and carelessly, especially because you do not have much time 草草记下，匆匆书写（尤指因时间仓促）

outcast [ˈaʊtkɑːst] *n.* a person who is not accepted by other people and who sometimes has to leave their home and friends 被抛弃者；被排斥者

misfit [ˈmɪsfɪt] *n.* a person who is not accepted by a particular group of people, especially because their behaviour or their ideas are very different 与别人合不来的人；

行为（或思想）怪异的人

stinging [ˈstɪŋɪŋ] v. (sting 的现在分词) If someone's remarks sting you, they make you feel hurt and annoyed. （言谈）刺痛，刺伤，惹恼

offbeat [ˌɒfˈbiːt] adj. different from what most people expect 不寻常的；不落俗套的；标新立异的

brim [brɪm] v. to be full of something; to fill something （使）满，盛满

caricature [ˈkærɪkətʃʊə(r)] n. a funny drawing or picture of somebody that exaggerates some of their features 人物漫画

urn [ɜːn] n. a tall decorated container, especially one used for holding the ashes of a dead person 瓮；（尤指）骨灰缸

sly [slaɪ] adj. acting or done in a secret or dishonest way, often intending to trick people 诡诈的；狡诈的

self-assured [ˌselfəˈʃʊəd] adj. having a lot of confidence in yourself and your abilities 自信的；胸有成竹的

scheming [ˈskiːmɪŋ] adj. often planning secretly to do something for your own advantage, especially by cheating other people 惯搞阴谋的；诡计多端的；狡诈的

rattle [ˈrætl] v. to make a series of short loud sounds when hitting against something hard; to make something do this （使）发出咔嗒咔嗒的声音

off limits [ɒf ˈlɪmɪts] If you say that an activity or a substance is off limits for someone, you mean that they are not allowed to do it or have it. 不得从事的；禁止使用（或拥有）的

devout [dɪˈvaʊt] adj. believing strongly in a particular religion and obeying its laws and practices 笃信宗教的；虔诚的

grapple [ˈɡræpl] v. to take a firm hold of somebody/something and struggle with them 扭打；搏斗

prophet [ˈprɒfɪt] n. (in the Christian, Jewish and Muslim religions) a person sent by God to teach the people and give them messages from God （基督教、犹太教和伊斯兰教的）先知

compromising [ˈkɒmprəmaɪzɪŋ] adj. if something is compromising, it shows or tells people something that you want to keep secret, because it is wrong or embarrassing 有失体面的；不宜泄露的

attune [əˈtjuːn] v. to adjust or accustom (a person or thing); acclimatize 使（人或事物）协调

bigotry [ˈbɪɡətri] n. the state of feeling, or the act of expressing, strong, unreasonable beliefs or opinions 顽固盲从；偏执

exempt [ɪɡˈzempt] v. to give or get somebody's official permission not to do something or not to pay something they would normally have to do or pay 免除；豁免

scrutiny ['skruːtəni] *n.* careful and thorough examination 仔细检查；彻底的审查

close in [kləʊz ɪn] If a group of people close in on a person or place, they come nearer and nearer to them and gradually surround them. 包围；逼近

balk [bɔːk] *v.* to be unwilling to do something or become involved in something because it is difficult, dangerous, etc. 畏缩；回避

nuance ['njuːɑːns] *n.* a very slight difference in meaning, sound, colour or somebody's feelings that is not usually very obvious （意义、声音、颜色、感情等方面的）细微差别

insularity [ˌɪnsjuˈlærəti] *n.* the state of being isolated or detached 绝缘性；岛国性质；孤立

superstition [ˌsuːpəˈstɪʃn] *n.* the belief that particular events happen in a way that cannot be explained by reason or science; the belief that particular events bring good or bad luck 迷信；迷信观念（或思想）

lupus ['luːpəs] *n.* a disease that affects the skin or sometimes the joints 狼疮

flit [flɪt] *v.* to move lightly and quickly from one place or thing to another 轻快地从一处到另一处；掠过

revulsion [rɪˈvʌlʃn] *n.* a strong feeling of disgust or horror 嫌恶；恶心；惊恐

revelation [ˌrevəˈleɪʃn] *n.* the act of making people aware of something that has been secret 披露；揭露

Video 3

Gothic ['ɡɒθɪk] *adj.* (of a novel, etc.) written in the style popular in the 18th and 19th centuries, which described romantic adventures in mysterious or frightening surroundings 哥特派的，哥特风格的（流行于18至19世纪，描述神秘或恐怖气氛中的爱情故事）

macabre [məˈkɑːbrə] *adj.* unpleasant and strange because connected with death and frightening things 可怕的，恐怖的（尤指与死亡等相联系的）

tranquil ['træŋkwɪl] *adj.* (formal) quiet and peaceful 安静的；平静的；安宁的

erupt [ɪˈrʌpt] *v.* to start happening, suddenly and violently 突然发生；爆发

on the wane [ɒn ðə weɪn] becoming weaker, less vigorous, or less extensive 正在减弱，正在衰弱，正在减少

repressed [rɪˈprest] *adj.* not expressed openly 受压抑的；被抑制的

monstrous ['mɒnstrəs] *adj.* considered to be shocking and unacceptable because it is morally wrong or unfair 丑恶的；道德败坏的；骇人的

genteel [dʒenˈtiːl] *adj.* (of people and their way of life) quiet and polite, often in an exaggerated way; from, or pretending to be from, a high social class 显得彬彬有礼的；假斯文的；上流社会的；装体面的；装出绅士派头的

underscore [ˌʌndəˈskɔː(r)] *v.* another term for underline 强调；在……下面画线；着重说明

loath [ləʊθ] *adj.* (formal) not willing to do something 不情愿；不乐意；勉强

grotesque [grəʊˈtesk] *n.* a person who is extremely ugly in a strange way, especially in a book or painting（尤指书画中的）奇形怪状的人，丑陋的人

segregated [ˈsegrɪgeɪtɪd] *adj.* segregated buildings or areas are kept for the use of one group of people who are the same race, sex, or religion, and no other group is allowed to use them（因种族、性别、宗教不同而）隔离的，分开的

dwell [dwel] *v.* (formal or literary) to live somewhere 居住；栖身

temper [ˈtempə(r)] *v.* to make something less severe by adding something that has the opposite effect 使缓和；使温和

reconcile [ˈrekənsaɪl] *v.* to find an acceptable way of dealing with two or more ideas, needs, etc., that seem to be opposed to each other 使和谐一致；调和；使配合

torment [ˈtɔːment] *n.* extreme suffering, especially mental suffering; a person or thing that causes this（尤指精神上的）折磨，痛苦；苦难之源

evoke [ɪˈvəʊk] *v.* to bring a feeling, a memory or an image into your mind 引起，唤起（感情、记忆或形象）

Video 4

perplexing [pəˈpleksɪŋ] *adj.* confusing, often because you do not know how to solve something 令人迷惑的

hilarious [hɪˈleəriəs] *adj.* extremely funny 极其滑稽的

labyrinth [ˈlæbərɪnθ] *n.* (formal) a complicated series of paths, which it is difficult to find your way through 迷宫；曲径

Jim Crow [ˌdʒɪm ˈkrəʊ] the former practice in the US of using laws that allowed black people to be treated unfairly and kept separate from white people, for example, in schools 种族歧视，种族隔离

spurn [spɜːn] *v.* to reject or refuse somebody/something, especially in a proud way（尤指傲慢地）拒绝

dupe [djuːp] *v.* (into doing something) to trick or cheat somebody 诈骗；哄骗；欺骗

disjointed [dɪsˈdʒɔɪntɪd] *adj.* not communicated or described in a clear or logical way; not connected 不连贯的；支离破碎的；杂乱无章的

bewildering [bɪˈwɪldərɪŋ] *adj.* making you feel confused because there are too many things to choose from or because something is difficult to understand 令人困惑的；使人糊涂的

ambiguity [ˌæmbɪˈɡjuːəti] *n.* the state of having more than one possible meaning 歧义；一语多义

spellbind [ˈspelˌbaɪnd] *v.* to cause to be spellbound; entrance or enthral 使入迷；迷住

acrobatics [ˌækrəˈbætɪks] *n.* acts and movements acrobatic 杂技

haggle [ˈhæɡl] *v.* (with somebody) (over something) to argue with somebody in order to reach an agreement, especially about the price of something 争论；（尤指）讲价

conflate [kənˈfleɪt] *v.* (formal) to put two or more things together to make one new thing 合并；合成；混合

contemplate [ˈkɒntəmpleɪt] *v.* to think about whether you should do something, or how you should do something 考虑；思量；思忖

Chapter 9　Drama

Part Ⅰ　Warm-up

Discuss the following questions in pairs or groups.

1. How did the emergence of American realism in the late 19th and early 20th centuries impact the development of American drama?

2. Who is considered the father of American drama, and what are some key characteristics of his plays?

3. How did the Theatre of the Absurd movement influence American drama in the mid-20th century?

4. What are some recurring themes in the plays of Tennessee Williams?

Part Ⅱ　Susan Glaspell's *A Jury of Her Peers*

Watch the video. Answer the following questions.

1. What did Amy think about the life of the pioneer woman in America?
2. What were Amy's descriptions of the life in the frontier for women?
3. What did Leon see in the story?
4. Why did Leon think that Amy's opinion revealed something stark on the frontier?
5. What was another thing that was quintessentially American in the story mentioned by Leon?
6. What was the vigilante justice of the westerns?
7. What did the law mean to the westerns in the frontier?
8. What was the reading from the ideas of Lincoln?
9. What is Martin Luther King's idea Diana talked about?
10. What is the relation between the ideas of Lincoln, Glaspell and King? Could you explain it in more details?

Chapter 9   Drama

Part Ⅲ   Clifford Odets's *Waiting for Lefty*

Watch the video. Choose the best answer to each question.

1. Which of the following is **incorrect** on the relation between Clifford Odets and the Group Theatre?
   A. Odets represented the voice of the Group.
   B. The atmosphere and the spirit of the Group had influenced Odets.
   C. It was an accident for the Group to discover Odets's gift.
   D. Odets could never have been a playwright without the Group.

2. What is the common theme between the Group theatre and Clifford Odets?
   A. The optimism about the future of the society.
   B. American dream.
   C. The true human desire.
   D. The social climate of America.

3. Which of the following is **correct** about *Waiting for Lefty*?
   A. It is about a taxi company.
   B. It uses flashbacks.
   C. It was finished 6 weeks after *Awake and Sing*.
   D. It uses merely street language for the voice of American people.

4. What does the scene of *Waiting for Lefty* in the video imply?
   A. The social need of health care for children.
   B. Children at that time went sick easily.
   C. The exploitation and inequality of the society.
   D. The scarcity of fruits for the fruit trees were rare.

5. What happened for the first production of *Waiting for Lefty*?
   A. The audience was shocked because the actors no longer performed.
   B. The audience had become part of the play in the end.
   C. The audience was wild and the theatre became chaotic.
   D. The balcony of the theatre fell down for the audience was stomping their feet.

6. What was Odets trying to convey to the audience through his works according to the narrator?
   A. Criticism on an over-materialistic society.
   B. Criticism on dollar bills and money.
   C. Criticism on the spirit of revolt.
   D. Criticism on the wasting of life.

7. What was the social background of *Waiting for Lefty* according to the video?

A. World War I had greatly depressed people.

B. People had become aggressive and radical.

C. The whole country went mad and desperate.

D. There was no answer for the social problems.

8. What was the prevailing sentiment among many Americans during the 1930s, as described by Phoebe Brand and Tony Kraber?

A. A longing for financial stability and prosperity.

B. A belief in the power of capitalism to solve societal issues.

C. A rejection of communism and socialism as viable options.

D. A desire for radical change and a solution to the country's desperate situation.

Part Ⅳ An Interview on Edward Albee

Watch the video. Write *T* for true or *F* for false for each statement.

1. (　) In his play *Seascape*, Albee makes the long speech of one of his characters as an aria.

2. (　) In his career as a playwright, Albee accidentally finds out the analogy between a piece of music and a play, which gradually leads to his absorption with classical music.

3. (　) Albee only takes his characters as instruments to make analogy to a piece of music, since ideas and themes in a play are not related.

4. (　) For Albee, a play can also have an allusion of a quartet even though the characters are not speaking simultaneously.

5. (　) When trying to make something loud, a composer of a piece of music can highlight it by composing a forte, while a playwright can do so by italicizing.

6. (　) Among Albee's plays, *Seascape* and *The Zoo Story* are set outdoors, whereas *Who's Afraid of Virginia Woolf* and *A Delicate Balance* are set indoors.

7. (　) The inspiration of his setting indoors, according to Albee himself, comes partly from T. S. Eliot, a great playwright in Albee's words.

8. (　) Albee is rebellious in a sense; and because of his family background, he is interested in exposing the naked truth beneath the masks of those so-called cultivated but prejudiced people who are controlling society.

9. (　) For Albee, serious art is no better than staying home and watching network TV. It is a waste of time going to the theatre.

10. (　) Albee's plays are more easily to be accepted by cultures from other countries than that of Tennessee Williams's, because the settings and themes of Albee's works are

more related to common life, which can easily be understood by people from other cultures.

Part V Eugene O'Neill

Watch the video. Answer the following questions.
1. What is the first thing to understand about Eugene O'Neill?
2. Where did all the ideas of O'Neill's come from?
3. What was O'Neill's contribution to American drama?
4. What was O'Neill's reaction to his fame?
5. Why O'Neill could overturn the frivolous Broadway?
6. What was necessary for O'Neill to involve in something protean and invent American theatre? Give some examples.
7. Where did O'Neill want to take his audience?
8. What did the inner turmoil of his characters mirror?
9. What happened to O'Neill's family life?
10. What is the function of "masks" O'Neill was pursuing?
11. Why did O'Neill become obsessed with masks?
12. As to O'Neill's consciousness of his own limitations, the term "pseudo-genius" is applied. What does it mean?
13. What was the relation between O'Neill's obsession with illusions and dreams and the dream of America?
14. Why was a failing theatre a perfect metaphor of a central question of life for O'Neill?
15. What was the function of a theatre in the sense of illusion and dream?

Part VI Arthur Miller's *Death of a Salesman*

Watch the video. Answer the following questions for the main ideas.
1. What was Arthur Miller's opinion about the theme of the play?
2. What were the different themes Miller had discussed in the interview?
3. What did the title "The Inside of His Head" reveal on the technique of the play?

Watch the video again. Fill in the following blanks.
The Theme of the Play:
1. It is about a salesman and his death. It's hard to 1) _____ that play.

That's about the United States; it's about a man, about an economic situation, about a family; it's about a life. And to try to 2) _____ it down to a sentence is beyond me.

2. Some say it is a play about the 3) _____ of capitalism.

3. It depends what 4) _____ you're on, as to what it means to you. And in that case it was quite the 5) _____ of what I had originally intended. It's about coming to 6) _____ with the reality of your own life.

4. From Willy's point of view, it's a love story basically, between the father and the son. It's about the loss of love and the finding of love again. One of the great moments in the play is when Willy realizes he is loved. The 7) _____ of that play is that both he and Biff, his son, a lost person, find themselves more or less at the end, by 8) _____ their love for one another. And that's 9) _____ what the story is.

5. Willy kills himself because he realizes he is more valuable dead than alive for some other reasons. He wants to give of himself, he wants to 10) _____ himself, he wants to 11) _____ out his love for his son. And in his circumstances, he knows there's no way in this life to do that. And so his great 12) _____ will be his giving his 13) _____ money to his son.

The Techniques of the Play:

1. The original title was "The Inside of His Head", but it was very awkward, and I dropped it soon after I thought of it. But the original set, as I saw it, would be a 14) _____, the 15) _____ of a skull, and the whole thing would be played in there.

2. Jo Mielziner, who was one of the great set designers of America, designed this 16) _____ set for it, and it was by no means the inside of a skull. It was a very wispy house and looked like it could be blown away by a 17) _____. To make that happen on the stage, it took a lot of writings over the years working through straight 18) _____, through poetic theatre, even some 19) _____ plays that I was writing, until I came upon that form.

3. The play, formally speaking, is a kind of invention. The idea was to make everything happen at the same time—that is the past and the present working together, instead of stopping a play and going back. There are no 20) _____ in the play, and yet the past is always with us, just as it is in life when you're talking to somebody and you think of something 35 years ago.

Part VII Projects and Presentations

Choose one of the following projects, or design one of your own closely related to the theme of the unit. Finish the project by giving a presentation in class and leading a discussion afterwards.

1. Give a short talk or write an essay on the connections between Eugene O'Neill and Taoism. Research and familiarize yourself with the works of Eugene O'Neill, particularly his plays that showcase themes related to existentialism, spirituality, and the human condition. Study the basic principles and concepts of Taoism, an ancient Chinese philosophy that emphasizes harmony, balance, and the interconnectedness of all things. Reflect on the potential connections and influences between Eugene O'Neill's works and Taoist philosophy.

2. Edward Albee mentions in the interview that serious arts should be something to keep us awake and make us think differently about things. If an art piece fails to bring changes after an experience, it will be a waste of time, being more worthless even than network TV. In fact, Internet has taken an important place in people's entertainment and leisure time today. Prepare a speech to talk about your ideas about art and literature today. What should be their functions? What challenges are they facing with today?

3. Reality is the state of the world of how it really is, whereas an illusion is an erroneous or created interpretation of reality. The conflict between them is usually presented in literature with a lost or an innocent character and a cruel reality that is devastating and suffocating. The tragedy of Icarus, for instance, can be a metaphor for dream and disillusionment. Think about the meaning of them and give a short talk titled "The Relation Between Reality and Illusion".

4. In *Death of a Salesman*, Arthur Miller presents multiple themes from different perspectives taken by the characters in the story, and some of them are still not outdated. Combined with your own reading (or watching) experience and thinking, what stance will you take for this story? Share your opinions with your group members and report the results in class.

Part VIII Vocabulary and Notes

Video 1

Susan Glaspell 苏珊·格拉斯佩尔（1876—1948），美国剧作家、小说家、记者和女演员

A Jury of Her Peers 《同命人审案》，是格拉斯佩尔于 1917 年创作的短篇小说

law-abidingness [ˌlɔː əˈbaɪdɪŋnəs] *n.* the quality or action of obeying and respecting the law 守法；守法行为

practicality [ˌpræktɪˈkæləti] *n.* the quality of being suitable, or likely to be successful 可行性；适用性

quintessentially [ˌkwɪntɪˈsenʃəli] *adv.* in a way that represents the perfect example of something 典型地；标准地

probe [prəʊb] *v.* (into something) a complete and careful investigation of something 调查；探究

haunt [hɔːnt] *v.* if something unpleasant haunts you, it keeps coming to your mind so that you cannot forget it（不快的事）萦绕于脑际，难以忘却

Alexis de Tocqueville 亚历克西·德·托克维尔（1805—1859），法国思想家、政治学家、历史学家、政治家、外交家，法国第二共和时期的外交部部长、众议院议员

Democracy in America 《论美国的民主》，是托克维尔最出名的著作

pioneer [ˌpaɪəˈnɪr] *n.* one of the first people to go to a particular place, especially in order to live and work there 开发者；拓荒者

frontier [frʌnˈtɪr] *n.* (singular) the edge of land where people have settled and built towns, beyond which the country is wild and unknown, especially in the western US in the 19th century（尤指 19 世纪美国西部的）边缘地带，边远地区

piggyback [ˈpɪɡibæk] *v.* (on somebody/something) to use something that already exists as a support for your own work; to use a larger organization, etc., for your own advantage 借助；攀附利用

stark [stɑːrk] *adj.* unpleasant; real, and impossible to avoid 严酷的；赤裸裸的

partake [pɑːrˈteɪk] *v.* (of something) to eat or drink something especially something that is offered to you 吃，喝，享用

sheriff [ˈʃerɪf] *n.* (in the US) an elected officer responsible for keeping law and order in a county or town（在美国的）县治安官，城镇治安官

vigilante [ˌvɪdʒɪˈlænti] *n.* a member of a group of people who try to prevent crime or punish criminals in their community, especially because they think the police are not doing this（尤指由于认为警方不发力而自发组织的）治安会会员

rectitude [ˈrektɪtuːd] *n.* the quality of thinking or behaving in a correct and honest way 公正；正直

Abraham Lincoln 亚伯拉罕·林肯（1809—1865），美国政治家、军事家、律师，是美国第16任总统（1861—1865）

Martin Luther King 马丁·路德·金（1929—1968），是一位美国牧师、社会运动者、人权主义者和非裔美国人民权运动领袖

array [əˈreɪ] *n.* a group or collection of things or people, often one that is large or impressive 大堆；大量

Video 2

Clifford Odets 克利福德·奥德茨（1906—1963），美国现代著名剧作家，20世纪30年代美国左翼戏剧的代表人物

Waiting for Lefty《等待老左》，是1935年由美国剧作家奥德茨创作的剧本

Group Theatre 组合剧院，是由哈罗德·克勒曼、谢丽尔·克劳福德和李·斯特拉斯伯格于1931年成立于美国纽约市的剧团

intensity [ɪnˈtensəti] *n.*（不可数名词）the state or quality of being intense 强烈；紧张；剧烈

fervor [ˈfɜːrvər] *n.* very strong feelings about something 热情；激情

belligerence [bəˈlɪdʒərəns] *n.* aggressive or warlike behaviour 好斗，好战

coincide [ˌkəʊɪnˈsaɪd] *v.* (of ideas, opinions, etc.) to be the same or very similar 相同；相符

playwright [ˈpleɪraɪt] *n.* a person who writes plays for the theatre, television or radio 剧作家

simultaneously [ˌsaɪmlˈteɪniəsli] *adv.* at the same time as something else 同时地

Awake and Sing!《醒来歌唱!》，是由美国剧作家克利福德·奥德茨创作的戏剧。该剧最初由 The Group Theatre 在1935年制作

one-act play 独幕剧，戏剧作品的一种形式。全剧情节在一幕内完成

strike [straɪk] *n.* a period of time when an organized group of employees of a company stop working because of an argument over pay or conditions 罢工

flashback [ˈflæʃbæk] *n.* a part of a film, play, etc., that shows a scene that happened earlier in time than the main story （电影或戏剧的）闪回，倒叙

crooked [ˈkrʊkɪd] *adj.* not in a straight line; bent or twisted 不直的；弯曲的

grapefruit [ˈɡreɪpfruːt] *n.* a large round yellow citrus fruit with juice that has a slightly sharp bitter taste 柚子；西柚

Eva Le Gallienne 伊娃·列·高丽安（1899—1991），是一名英裔美国舞台女演员、制作人、导演和作家

tidal [ˈtaɪdl] *adj.* connected with tides (= the regular rise and fall of the sea) 潮汐的；有潮的

exultancy [ɪgˈzʌltənsi] *n.* a feeling of great happiness 大喜；狂悦

sensational [senˈseɪʃənl] *adj.* causing great surprise, excitement, or interest 轰动的；引起哗然的

inhibition [ˌɪnhɪˈbɪʃn] *n.* a shy or nervous feeling that stops you from expressing your real thoughts or feelings 拘谨；拘束感

pandemonium [ˌpændəˈməʊniəm] *n.* a situation in which there is a lot of noise and activity with a great lack of order, especially because people are feeling angry or frightened 骚动；群情沸腾

Jamaica 这里应该指美国纽约在1913年开张的Jamaica Theater，属于百老汇"地铁巡回"的剧院之一

Subway Circuit "地铁巡回"，当时百老汇的一种在剧院间的巡回演出形式

CIO-AFL (The American Federation of Labor and Congress of Industrial Organizations, officially AFL-CIO) 美国劳工联合会和产业工会联合会，简称劳联－产联，是美国最大的工会组织

indictment [ɪnˈdaɪtmənt] *n.* (of/on somebody/something) a sign that a system, society, etc. is very bad or very wrong（制度、社会等的）衰败迹象，腐败迹象

veteran [ˈvetərən] *n.* a person who has been a soldier, sailor, etc., in a war 退伍军人；老兵

Herbert Hoover 赫伯特·克拉克·胡佛（1874—1964），美国第31任总统

maras 马拉（mara）是起源于美国的帮派形式，并蔓延到萨尔瓦多，洪都拉斯和危地马拉等中美洲国家

radical [ˈrædɪkl] *n.* a person with radical opinions 激进分子

Video 3

Edward Albee 爱德华·阿尔比（1928—2016），美国剧作家

Seascape《海景画》，是美国剧作家爱德华·阿尔比的两幕剧

quartet [kwɔːˈtet] 四重奏，是合奏的一种，指使用四种不同的乐器演奏的乐曲

A Delicate Balance《优美的平衡》，是爱德华·阿尔比于1965年和1966年创作的三幕剧

Tobias《优美的平衡》中的退休商人

aria [ˈɑːriə] *n.* a song for one voice, especially in an opera or oratorio（尤指歌剧

或清唱剧中的）咏叹调

simultaneity [ˌsaɪmltəˈniːəti] *n.* the fact of something happening or being done at the same time as something else 同时发生；共时性

notate [nəʊˈteɪt] *v.* to write (especially music) in symbols （尤其在音乐中）以符号表示

composer [kəmˈpəʊzər] *n.* a person who writes music, especially classical music 作曲者；作曲家

enormous [ɪˈnɔːrməs] *adj.* extremely large 巨大的；庞大的

Who's Afraid of Virginia Woolf? 《谁害怕弗吉尼亚·伍尔夫?》，是美国爱德华·阿尔比创作的一部话剧

The Lady from Dubuque 《来自杜布克的女士》，是爱德华·阿尔比的一部戏剧，该剧于1980年在百老汇首演了一段短暂的演出

The Sandbox 《沙盒》，是爱德华·阿尔比（Edward Albee）在1959年写的一部剧

The Zoo Story 《动物园故事》，是美国剧作家爱德华·阿尔比的一部独幕剧

Anton Pavlovich Chekhov 安东·帕夫洛维奇·契诃夫（1860—1904），19世纪末俄国的世界级短篇小说巨匠、作家，其剧作对20世纪戏剧产生了很大的影响

profoundly [prəˈfaʊndli] *adv.* in a way that has a very great effect on somebody/something 极大地；深刻地

The Family Reunion 《家庭聚会》，是由T.S.艾略特撰写的戏剧

The Cocktail Party 《鸡尾酒会》，是T.S.艾略特创作于1948年的三幕诗剧

ambience [ˈæmbiəns] *n.* the character and atmosphere of a place 环境；气氛

veneer [vəˈnɪr] *n.* (of something) an outer appearance of a particular quality that hides the true nature of somebody/something 虚假的外表，虚饰

maverick [ˈmævərɪk] *n.* a person who does not behave or think like everyone else, but who has independent, unusual opinions 独行其是者；言行与众不同者

iconoclast [aɪˈkɑːnəklæst] *n.* a person who criticizes popular beliefs or established customs and ideas 批判传统信仰的人；反传统者

reactionary [riˈækʃəneri] *adj.* opposed to political or social change 反动的，保守的

Republicans [rɪˈpʌblɪkənz] 共和党员

Tennessee Williams 托马斯·拉尼尔·威廉斯（Thomas Lanier Williams，1911—1983），以笔名田纳西·威廉斯（Tennessee Williams）闻名于世，20世纪美国最重要的剧作家之一

Video 4

Eugene O'Neill 尤金·奥尼尔（1888—1953），美国著名剧作家，表现主义文

学的代表作家

Beyond the Horizon 《天边外》，是美国剧作家尤金·奥尼尔创作的戏剧作品

unparalleled [ˌʌnˈpærəleld] *adj.* used to emphasize that something is bigger, better or worse than anything else like it 无比的；空前的

Broadway 百老汇，即纽约百老汇剧院，位于美国纽约市

Pulitzer Prizes 普利策奖，是表彰美国国内在报纸、杂志、数字新闻、文学及音乐创作等领域成就的奖项

Herman Melville 赫尔曼·梅尔维尔（1819—1891）是美国小说家、散文家和诗人

Nathaniel Hawthorne 纳撒尼尔·霍桑（1804—1864），19世纪美国小说家

Henry James 亨利·詹姆斯（1843—1916），英国、美国作家

gorgeous [ˈɡɔːrdʒəs] *adj.* very beautiful and attractive; giving great pleasure 非常漂亮的；令人愉快的

frivolous [ˈfrɪvələs] *adj.* having no useful or serious purpose 无聊的；不严肃的

protean [ˈprəʊtiən] *adj.* able to change quickly and easily 多变的；易变的

Emperor Jones 《琼斯皇》，是由美国剧作家尤金·奥尼尔在1920年创作的悲剧剧本

expressionist [ɪkˈspreʃənɪst] *adj.* in the style of expressionism in early 20th century art, theatre, cinema and music; working in this style 表现主义的

Hairy Ape 《毛猿》，是1922年由美国剧作家尤金·奥尼尔创作的表现主义戏剧

stylized [ˈstaɪlaɪzd] *adj.* drawn, written, etc., in a way that is not natural or realistic（绘画、写作等手法）非写实的

Anna Christie 《安娜·克里斯蒂》，是尤金·奥尼尔的四幕剧

desolate [ˈdesələt] *adj.* (of a place) empty and without people, making you feel sad or frightened 荒无人烟的；荒凉的

turmoil [ˈtɜːrmɔɪl] *n.* a state of great worry in which everything is confused and nothing is certain 骚动；焦虑

strain [streɪn] *n.* pressure on a system or relationship because great demands are being placed on it 紧张；压力

psychiatrist [saɪˈkaɪətrɪst] *n.* a doctor who studies and treats mental illnesses 精神病学家；精神科医生

ransack [ˈrænsæk] *v.* to make a place untidy, causing damage, because you are looking for something 洗劫；（为找东西）把……翻腾得乱七八糟

millennia [mɪˈleniə] *n.* (plural) a period of 1,000 years 一千年，千年期（尤指公元纪年）

nagging [ˈnæɡɪŋ] *adj.* continuing for a long time and difficult to cure or remove 纠缠不休的；难以摆脱的

pseudo- [ˈsuːdəʊ]（combining form）not what somebody claims it is; false or pretended 假的；冒充的

hound [haʊnd] *v.* to keep following somebody and not leave them alone, especially in order to get something from them or ask them questions 追踪；纠缠

artifice [ˈɑːrtɪfɪs] *n.* the clever use of tricks to cheat somebody 诡计；奸计

decompose [ˌdiːkəmˈpəʊz] *v.* to be destroyed gradually after death by natural processes 腐烂

intact [ɪnˈtækt] *adj.* complete and not damaged 完好无损的；完整的

disillusionment [ˌdɪsɪˈluːʒnmənt] *n.* (with something) the state of being disillusioned 幻灭；醒悟

Video 5

Arthur Miller 亚瑟·米勒（1915—2005），生于美国纽约，美国犹太裔剧作家

Death of a Salesman 《推销员之死》，是剧作家亚瑟·米勒的剧本，1949 年 2 月在百老汇剧院首演

The Man Who Had All the Luck 《鸿运高照的人》，是亚瑟·米勒的第二部主要作品

The Crucible 《萨勒姆的女巫》，是美国剧作家亚瑟·米勒创作于 1953 年的一部作品

A View from the Bridge 《临桥望景》，是美国剧作家亚瑟·米勒的一部单幕诗剧，演于 1955 年 9 月 29 日

capsulize [ˈkæpsjʊlaɪz] *v.* to express in a concise form; condense 简略表达，压缩

boil something down (to something) to make something, especially information, shorter by leaving out the parts that are not important 概括；压缩

capitalism [ˈkæpɪtəlɪzəm] *n.* an economic system in which a country's businesses and industry are controlled and run for profit by private owners rather than by the government 资本主义

variation [ˌveriˈeɪʃn] *n.* (on something) a thing that is different from other things in the same general group 变种；变体

CBS CBS 新闻，指美国电视联播网哥伦比亚广播公司（CBS）的新闻部门，也可以指其制作播出节目的总称

Willy Loman 威利·罗曼，是亚瑟·米勒的《推销员之死》中的虚构人物和主角

Biff Loman 比夫·罗曼,《推销员之死》中的虚构人物,威利·罗曼之子

gigantic [dʒaɪˈɡæntɪk] *adj.* extremely large 巨大的;庞大的

Jo Mielziner 乔·米辛纳(1901—1976),是美国戏剧界著名的布景设计师,曾参与舞台剧和音乐剧的创作

marvelous [ˈmɑːrvələs] *adj.* extremely good; wonderful 极好的;非凡的

wispy [ˈwɪspi] *adj.* consisting of small, thin pieces; not thick 小束状的;纤细的

Chapter 10　Post-war Fiction

Part Ⅰ　Warm-up

Discuss the following questions in pairs or groups.
1. Can you name some American novels written after World War Ⅱ?
2. Can you identify a few American novelists in the postwar period?
3. How would you describe the American novel after 1945?
4. Can you summarize the socio-historical background of the period?
5. How do the postwar novels relate to the background discussed above?

Part Ⅱ　The American Novel after 1945

Watch the video. Write *T* for true or *F* for false for each statement.
1. (　) The first reading of the term is about Richard Wright's *Black Boy*.
2. (　) Class shoppers will be asked to leave between the course induction and the first reading.
3. (　) The lecturer mentions war, love, identity and race as the thematic concerns of postwar novels.
4. (　) When it comes to love as a theme of postwar novels, the lecturer mentions John Barth and Philip Roth.
5. (　) The lecturer mentions a nervous breakdown in *Lolita*.
6. (　) In the second half of the 20th century, writers were thinking very hard about what to do stylistically with all the innovations in modernism.
7. (　) Don DeLillo and John Updike are included in the syllabus.

Part Ⅲ Celebrating J. D. Salinger: Fame, Outsider and *The Catcher in the Rye*

Watch Erica Wagner's interview with J. D. Salinger's son, Matt Salinger. Answer the following questions.

1. Who is Mark David Chapman, and what did he say about *The Catcher in the Rye*?

2. How many people does Matt reckon have read *The Catcher in the Rye*?

3. What is Matt's response to Erica's question that the book might inspire murderers?

4. The two speakers are going to do an event this evening with Penguin, a famous publishing house. What do you think it is about?

5. Matt quotes a line from *The Catcher in the Rye*. Can you try to paraphrase it?

Part Ⅳ An Evening with Joyce Carol Oates at Cornell University

Watch the video and fill in the blanks.

Good evening, and welcome to the last of the summer series. This is a special 1) _____, and I'm glad to have all of you here. Please silence all of your electronic devices. And I also want to thank Katherine Brewer, the Dean of the College of Agriculture and Life Sciences, for the use of this hall. She's been very generous this year. In the United States, one possible way to find out if you've made it is to check with *The Simpsons*. 11 years ago, Lisa Simpson dreamed she was in prison. And when a guard came around with a book cart, she asked, "Got any Joyce Carol Oates?" The guard replied, "Nope. It's all Danielle Steel." Does anyone know how Lisa 2) _____? Do you remember that? OK, go look it up. But it gets even better. In 2017, in an episode, "Pork and Burns", Joyce actually appears as herself and even voices her own character. But we're at Cornell. And for us, *The Simpsons* doesn't count as a particularly reliable and 3) _____ source of anything. So let's look at a far better one.

In the essay, *Reflecting on Joyce Carol Oates*, Joanne Creighton, an English professor, former president of Mount Holyoke College and the author of two books, and many reviews, and articles about the work of Joyce Carol Oates, 4) _____, "While Joyce Carol Oates was early called the Dark Lady of American 5) _____, that label is not right. She has a tremendous respect for the dark side of human experience, for the mysterious depth of the conscious, and for the primitive 6) _____ at the core of physical existence. Yet Joyce's vision is not dark. She is, in fact, optimistic about the possibilities of human 7) _____ and transcendence of a distinctly American variety. Despite the 8) _____ and duress that her characters typically endure, Joyce respects their tenacious attempt to, as she wrote in the preface to *Marya*, 'forge their own souls by way of the choices they make, large and small, conscious and half conscious'."

Professor Creighton continues, "But she sprints far ahead of those who would attempt to assess her body of work. I agree with Anne Tyler who is 9) _____ in a Washington Post article as saying, '100 years from now, people will laugh at us for sort of taking her for granted'." Professor Creighton then finishes, "This we know she is one of the most accomplished and significant American writers of our time." The dictionary definitions of the words productive and 10) _____ surely must have after them these words, as exemplified by Joyce Carol Oates. By my likely incomplete count, she has published at least 11) _____ novels, 12) _____ novellas, 13) _____ collections of short stories, 10 children's and young adult novels, 14) _____ plays, and 6 one-act plays, and 15) _____ collections of poetry. She has also written hundreds of essays and book reviews, in addition to longer non-fiction works on literary 16) _____ ranging from Emily Dickinson's poetry and the fiction of Dostoyevsky and James Joyce, to studies of the 17) _____ and horror genres, and on such non-literary subjects as the painter George Bellows and boxer Mike Tyson.

How does she do this? I've read — and she'll correct me if I'm wrong — but that she writes daily in longhand from 8:00 am to noon, and then she resumes her writing in the evening. Joyce is a native New Yorker, who attended the same one room school her mother did. While a student at Syracuse University, where she 18) _____ in English and was valedictorian of her class, she won the college short story contest, sponsored by *Mademoiselle* magazine. Some years ago, one of her Syracuse University's professors, Donald A. Dyke, commented that about once a term, "She'd drop a 400-page novel on my desk." He added, "She was the most brilliant student we've ever had here." Joyce earned a Master of Arts in English from the University of Wisconsin, Madison. She has won many, many 19) _____. She still runs, and she is an active hiker and bicyclist. And she is the Roger S. Berlin 52 professor of the 20) _____ emeritus and professor of creative writing emeritus at Princeton University.

Joyce Carol Oates was last here 9 years and 361 days ago. And it is a genuine pleasure to have her with us again tonight.

Part V A Lecture on John Updike

Watch the video and answer the following questions.

1. Which term does the speaker use to contrast with dirty realism and magical realism?
2. When was John Updike born and when did he die?
3. Where are Updike's most noted realist novels set?
4. Which university did Updike attend?
5. Which contemporary of Updike is mentioned when it comes to the silent generation?
6. Which party did Updike support lifelong?
7. What was Updike's attitude towards the Vietnam War?
8. Which "insider's game" does the speaker mention that Updike enjoyed playing?
9. Which writer does the speaker credit as the founder of American realism?

Part VI Projects and Presentations

Choose one of the following projects, or design one of your own closely related to the theme of the unit. Finish the project by giving a presentation in class and leading a discussion afterwards.

1. In the first mini lecture, the lecturer mentions the innovations that come in the powerful period known as modernism and asks a few questions as to how postwar American novels deal with those innovations. She says: "Are they abandoned? Are they embellished? Are they stretched? Are they rejected? What happens to those resources that the great modernist writers endowed language with so powerfully earlier in the century?" Discuss in groups, and then report your discussion results in class.

2. Joanne Creighton, a scholar of Joyce Carol Oates reflects that "While Joyce Carol Oates was early called the Dark Lady of American letters [...] Joyce's vision is not dark [...] Despite the violence and duress that her characters typically endure, Joyce respects their tenacious attempt to [...] 'forge their own souls by way of the choices they make'". Do you think Joyce's vision is dark or not? Have a debate and present your arguments.

3. The editors of the *Norton Anthology* say that John Updike is arguably the most significant transcriber or creator rather of middleness in American writing since William

Dean Howells. Have a group discussion on whether you agree with this statement.

Part Ⅶ Vocabulary and Notes

Video 1

Richard Wright 理查德·赖特（1908—1960），美国黑人小说家、评论家
Black Boy 《黑孩子》，是理查德·赖特的自传体小说
thematic [θɪˈmætɪk] *adj.* connected with the theme or themes of something 题目的；主题的；专题的
the Trojan War 特洛伊战争，荷马作品《伊利亚特》中所记载的希腊联军对特洛伊十年围城之战
the Mexican-American War 美墨战争，美国与墨西哥在1846年至1848年爆发的一场关于领土控制权的战争
guise [gaɪz] *n.* a way in which somebody/something appears, often in a way that is different from usual or that hides the truth about them/it 表现形式；外貌；伪装；外表
Lolita [ləʊˈliːtə] 《洛丽塔》，是弗拉基米尔·纳博科夫所著的小说
pedophiliac [ˌpiːdəˈfɪlɪək] *adj.* sexual perversion in which children are the preferred sexual object 恋童癖的
ideational [ˌaɪdɪˈeɪʃənəl] *adj.* being of the nature of a notion or concept 概念的；观念的；构想的；设想的
John Barth 约翰·巴思，美国后现代主义小说家，反讽、戏拟、元小说作家
The Human Stain 《人性的污点》，是美国小说家菲利普·罗斯代表作
Philip Roth 菲利普·罗斯（1933—2018），20世纪下半叶美国批判现实主义文学代表人物
interweave [ˌɪntərˈwiːv] *v.* [usually passive] to twist together two or more pieces of thread, wool, etc. 交织；交错编织
Franny and Zooey 《弗兰尼与佐伊》，是美国当代著名作家J. D. 塞林格继《麦田里的守望者》《九故事》之后出版的第三部作品，于1961年结集出版
vagrant [ˈveɪɡrənt] *n.* a person who has no home or job, especially one who begs (asks for money) from people 无业游民；流浪者；（尤指）乞丐
embellish [ɪmˈbelɪʃ] *v.* to make something more beautiful by adding decorations to it 美化；装饰；布置
Don DeLillo 唐·德里罗（1936— ），美国当代最优秀的小说家之一，代表作《白噪音》被誉为后现代主义文学的巅峰之作
John Updike 约翰·厄普代克（1932—2009），美国长篇小说、短篇小说作家、

诗人

substantive [ˈsʌbstəntɪv] *adj.* （formal）dealing with real, important or serious matters 实质性的；本质上的；重大的；严肃认真的

video 2

Mark David Chapman 马克·大卫·查普曼，1980 年枪杀前"披头士"乐队主唱约翰·列侬的凶手

John Lennon 约翰·列侬，英国男歌手、音乐家、诗人、社会活动家，著名摇滚乐队"披头士"的成员

The Catcher in the Rye《麦田里的守望者》，是美国作家 J·D·塞林格创作的长篇小说，发表于 1951 年

maniac [ˈmeɪniæk] *n.* a person who behaves in an extremely dangerous, wild, or stupid way 行为极其危险（或狂暴、愚蠢）的人；疯子；狂人

susceptibility [səˌseptəˈbɪləti] *n.* (to something) the state of being very likely to be influenced, harmed or affected by something 易受影响（或伤害等）的特性；敏感性；过敏性

outsider [ˌaʊtˈsaɪdər] *n.* a person who is not accepted as a member of a society, group, etc. 外人；局外人

sensibility [ˌsensəˈbɪləti] *n.* ［不可数名词］the ability to experience and understand deep feelings, especially in art and literature（尤指文艺方面的）感受能力，鉴赏力，敏感性

lunatic [ˈluːnətɪk] *n.* a person who does crazy things that are often dangerous 精神错乱者；狂人

bunch [bʌntʃ] *n.* a group of people 群体

misapprehension [ˌmɪsæprɪˈhenʃn] *n.* a wrong idea about something, or something you believe to be true that is not true 误解；误会

morass [məˈræs] *n.* an unpleasant and complicated situation that is difficult to escape from 困境；陷阱

including [ɪnˈkluːdɪŋ] *prep.* having something as part of a group or set 包括……在内

Video 3

The Simpsons《辛普森一家》，美国福克斯广播公司出品的一部动画情景喜剧，由马特·格勒宁创作

Lisa Simpson 丽莎·辛普森，动画片《辛普森一家》中的虚构人物

Joyce Carol Oates 乔伊斯·卡罗尔·奥兹，出生于 1938 年，美国当代著名女作家，美国小说家、诗人、评论家、剧作家

Danielle Steel 丹尼尔·斯蒂尔，出生于 1947 年，美国通俗文坛最具代表性的畅销书作家之一

primitive [ˈprɪmətɪv] *adj.* belonging to a very simple society with no industry, etc. 原始的；远古的

transcendence [trænˈsendəns] *n.* ［不可数名词］the quality of being able to go beyond normal limits or boundaries 超越；卓越；超然存在

tenacious [təˈneɪʃəs] *adj.* that does not stop holding something or give up something easily; determined 紧握的；不松手的；坚持的

preface [ˈprefəs] *n.* an introduction to a book, especially one that explains the author's aims （书的）前言，序言

Marya《玛丽亚》，乔伊斯·卡罗尔·奥兹作品，讲述了女主人公玛丽亚·科诺尔踏上寻母之路，实现自我价值的故事

forge [fɔːrdʒ] *v.* to put a lot of effort into making something successful or strong so that it will last 艰苦干成；努力加强

sprint [sprɪnt] *v.* to run or swim a short distance very fast 短距离快速奔跑（或游泳）；冲刺

novella [nəˈvelə] *n.* a short novel 中篇小说

Emily Dickinson 艾米莉·狄金森（1830—1886），美国著名女诗人

Dostoyevsky 陀思妥耶夫斯基（1821—1881），俄国作家，代表作有《罪与罚》《卡拉马佐夫兄弟》和《白痴》等

James Joyce 詹姆斯·阿洛伊修斯·乔伊斯（1882—1941），爱尔兰作家、诗人，后现代文学的奠基者之一，其"意识流"思想对世界影响巨大

George Bellows 乔治·贝洛斯（1882—1925），美国现实主义画家

Mike Tyson 迈克·泰森（1966— ），美国前重量级拳击职业运动员，演员，曾获世界最年轻重量级拳击冠军

longhand [ˈlɒŋhænd] *n.* ordinary writing, not typed or written in shorthand 普通书写（非打印或速记）

valedictorian [ˌvælɪdɪkˈtɔːriən] *n.* the student who has the highest marks/grades in a particular group of students and who gives the valedictory speech at a graduation ceremony （毕业典礼上）致告别辞的最优生

Mademoiselle《小姐》，是一本创办于 1935 年的关于时尚的女性杂志

emeritus [iˈmerɪtəs] *adj.* used with a title to show that a person, usually a university teacher, keeps the title as an honour, though he or she has stopped working （常指大学教师）退休后保留头衔的，荣誉退休的

Video 4

dirty realism 肮脏现实主义，20 世纪 80 年代源于美国的一种写作风格，该风

格对日常生活的肮脏面或世俗面进行了大量细节描绘

magical realism 魔幻现实主义，将现实主义叙述和自然主义技巧与超现实的梦幻元素融为一体

Raymond Carver 雷蒙德·卡佛（1938—1988），美国当代著名短篇小说家、诗人

Louise Erdrich 路易丝·厄德里克（1954— ），是美国当代创作最盛、得奖最多且声望最高的印第安女作家之一

Zadie Smith 扎迪·史密斯（1975— ），英国青年一代作家的代表

August Wilson 奥古斯特·威尔逊（1945—2005），美国著名编剧、制作人

fantastical [fænˈtæstɪkəl] *adj.* existing in fancy only 奇异的，虚构的

New Yorker《纽约客》，美国知识、文艺类的综合杂志

innumerable [ɪˈnjuːmərəbl] *adj.* too many to be counted; very many 多得数不清的；很多的

John Cheever 约翰·契弗（1912—1982），美国小说家、短篇故事作家

evocative [ɪˈvɒkətɪv] *adj.* (of something) making you think of or remember a strong image or feeling, in a pleasant way 引起记忆的；唤起感情的

minimalism [ˈmɪnɪməˌlɪzəm] *n.* [不可数名词] minimalism is a style in which a small number of very simple things are used to create a particular effect 简约风格

polarizing [ˈpəʊləraɪzɪŋ] *adj.* If something polarizes people or if something polarizes, two separate groups are formed with opposite opinions or positions. 两极分化的

Adrian Rich 艾德丽安·里奇（1929—2012），美国女诗人，被认为是美国最具影响力的作家之一

overtake [ˌəʊvəˈteɪk] *v.* to go past a moving vehicle or person ahead of you because you are going faster than they are 超过；赶上

elevated [ˈelɪveɪtɪd] *adj.* higher than the area around; above the level of the ground 高的；升高的；高出地面的

reproduction [ˌriːprəˈdʌkʃn] *n.* the act or process of producing babies, young animals or plants 生殖；繁殖

graphic [ˈɡræfɪk] *adj.* very clear and full of details, especially about something unpleasant 形象的，生动的，逼真的（尤指令人不快的事物）

James Baldwin 詹姆斯·鲍德温（1924—1987），美国黑人作家、散文家、戏剧家和社会评论家

Toni Morrison 托尼·莫里森（1931—2019），美国黑人女作家，其作品以美国的黑人生活为主要内容

entitlement [ɪnˈtaɪtlmənt] *n.* (to something) the official right to have or do something（拥有某物或做某事的）权利，资格

prosecute [ˈprɒsɪkjuːt] v. (somebody) (for something/doing something) to officially charge somebody with a crime in court 起诉；控告；检举

placidly [ˈplæsɪdli] adv. in a quiet and tranquil manner 平静地，沉着地

complacently [kəmˈpleɪsntli] adv. in a self-satisfied manner 满足地，得意地

frisson [friːˈsɔːn] n. a sudden strong feeling, especially of excitement or fear 强烈兴奋感；恐惧感；震颤

tingle [ˈtɪŋgl] v. a slight stinging or uncomfortable feeling in a part of your body 感到刺痛

juxtaposition [ˌdʒʌkstəpəˈzɪʃn] n. things are placed together or described together, so that the differences between them are emphasized 并列

carnality [kɑːˈnælɪti] n. feeling morbid sexual desire or a propensity to lewdness 淫荡

blandly [ˈblændlɪ] adv. If you do something blandly, you do it in a calm and quiet way 温和地；平静地

consummate [ˈkɒnsəmət] adj. extremely skilled; perfect 技艺高超的；完美的

anonymity [ˌænəˈnɪməti] n. the state of remaining unknown to most other people 匿名；不知姓名；名字不公开

Norton Anthology 《诺顿文选》，是由诺顿出版公司出版的文学批评选集

William Dean Howells 威廉·迪恩·豪威尔斯（1837—1920），小说家、文学批评家，美国现实主义文学奠基人

Chapter 11 Postmodernism I

Part I Warm-up

Discuss the following questions in pairs or groups.
1. What would pop in your mind when you see the word postmodernism?
2. Would you say American postmodernism accords with a certain period?
3. Can you name a few American postmodern novels?
4. Can you name some representative figures of American postmodernism?

Part II An Overview of American Postmodern Literature

Watch the video and answer the following questions.
1. When did the Internet go public?
2. Why does the speaker mention the case of O. J. Simpson?
3. According to the speaker, when was the postmodern period?
4. What techniques do the postmodernists use to create works without traditional structure or narrative?
5. What social issues do postmodernist works address?

Part III 1001 Nights with John Barth: *The Sot-weed Factor*

Watch the video and answer the following questions.
1. When was *The Sot-weed Factor* published?
2. Which works of Samuel Richardson are mentioned in the recording?
3. What is the epistolary form? Can you guess the meaning from the speaker's summary of *Pamela*'s plot?
4. Who wrote the parody *Shamela*?
5. How do the examples of *Pamela* and *Shamela* relate to the speaker's argument on John Barth?
6. Who is Ebenezer Cooke?
7. What does the speaker mean by "appropriations of identity"?

Chapter 11　Postmodernism I

Part IV　An Introduction to Vladimir Nabokov

Watch the video. Write *T* for true or *F* for false for each statement.

1. (　) Nabokov was raised bilingual, and spoke Russian and German fluently.
2. (　) Nabokov attended Cambridge University.
3. (　) Nabokov's last work of Russian fiction was a 1939 novella called *The Enchanter*, which later became *Lolita*.
4. (　) In 1950, Nabokov with his wife and son fled to the United States.
5. (　) Nabokov used to teach in Wellesley College and Cornell University.

Part V　A Lecture on Thomas Pynchon

Watch the video and fill in the blanks.

All right everybody. Welcome back to contemporary American literature. This will be a 1) _____ of our discussion of postmodern fiction for this week. The topic of today's lecture is probably the most 2) _____ or the most famous of postmodern fiction writers Thomas Pynchon, one of the most acclaimed but also challenging writers in postmodern American literature, comparable in the world of the novel to John Ashbery in the world of poetry I would say. They're both equally 3) _____ but also not always the easiest writers to engage with. Thomas Pynchon is a difficult writer to do a 4) _____ slide about, because there's not a lot of biography that we know. He's a famously 5) _____ writer who has 6) _____ all publicity for most of his writing life. There are very few even pictures of him that exist. I think very few recordings of his voice and one of the most notable is his appearance on *The Simpsons* in 2004, in which he appeared with a paper bag over his head but he did do the voice of his own character, so the image of Pynchon on *The Simpsons* and then this early photograph of him as a very young man that I have on the slide are the only images that we have of him.

He was born in 1937 on Long Island to a family whose roots go back to the puritan 7) _____ of New England, and that is a theme throughout his work, the theme of what America is, of its founding, its destiny, its history, is something that's very important to him. He majored in engineering physics at Cornell in the late 1950s and that's another very important aspect of his life, which is that he is a writer and one of the things that make his writing challenging for literary types like myself is that, he is an expert in and steeped in the sciences, and can write with great fluency and knowledge about science as he does throughout his work. But while he was at Cornell, he attended lectures by the postmodern Russian émigré novelist Vladimir Nabokov who was mentioned in the introduction to the Norton Anthology of American Literature that I had you read at the beginning of the semester. As a major kind of literary figure and major writer and also either a late modernist or a postmodernist novelist, depending on what you do with these terms, and so Pynchon did attend his lectures and then Pynchon went on professionally to work at Boeing in the early 1960s. And I think that one of the things about his work and the politics of his work that is not evident in this early short story is that, he's very worried about the 8) _____ of technology and power so he's working in the aerospace industry in the early 1960s and he's seeing you know some of the ways that 9) _____ technology is going, some of the ways that surveillance technology is going. There are these eerie 10) _____ even in his early work in the 1960s of the Internet because that's being developed as a military technology. There's also an 11) _____ throughout his work which again is not evident in this short story of the lingering, the lingering presence of Nazism over modern life. Well because he has worked in the aerospace industry, he knows the American space program is being worked on by men who were former Nazis, who were brought out of Germany to do it.

We don't know a lot about his life but we can infer from his not only being steeped in the sciences in the abstract but in the practical applications of science and the 12) _____ industry that the experience is going to shape some of the concerns that we see come back again and again throughout particularly his later works. I mentioned he's a very reclusive writer. He doesn't teach. He refuses media appearances with the exception of his appearance on *The Simpsons*, which will tell you something. He's a very funny writer and his writing has been very influential on popular culture despite the fact that he is a difficult writer. So yes he has influenced some of the later writers we'll read in this course like Don Delillo, David Foster Wallace and George Saunders.

Part VI Projects and Presentations

Choose one of the following projects, or design one of your own closely related to the theme of the unit. Finish the project by giving a presentation in class and leading a discussion afterwards.

1. In the first lecture, the speaker states that modernism is about objectivity and postmodernism is about subjectivity; that modernism seeks a singular truth and postmodernism seeks the multiplicity of truths. Have a group discussion on whether you agree with this statement.

2. Amy Tan writes: "My work might only be words, but behind the words there's a lot of contemplation about human nature." Postmodernism comes with diversity and multiculturalism. Discuss in groups examples of postmodernist works that celebrate diversity and multiculturalism.

3. *The Sot-weed Factor* can be seen as a parody of history and historiography. How would you understand this statement? Share your views with your group members and then present in class.

Part VII Vocabulary and Notes

Video 1
unprecedented [ʌnˈpresɪdentɪd] *adj.* that has never happened, been done or been known before 前所未有的；空前的；没有先例的

saturation [ˌsætʃəˈreɪʃn] *n.* the state or process that happens when no more of something can be accepted or added because there is already too much of it or too many of them 饱和；饱和状态

usher [ˈʌʃə(r)] *v.* to take or show somebody where they should go 把……引往；引导；引领

singular [ˈsɪŋɡjələ(r)] *adj.* connected with or having the singular form 单数的；单数形式的

narrative [ˈnærətɪv] *n.* a description of events, especially in a novel （尤指小说中的）描述，叙述

multiplicity [ˌmʌltɪˈplɪsəti] *n.* [不可数名词] a great number and variety of something 多样性；多种多样

absurdity [əbˈsɜːdəti] *n.* the quality or state of being ridiculous or wildly unreasonable 荒谬；荒唐

multiculturalism [ˌmʌltiˈkʌltʃərəlɪzəm] *n.* [不可数名词] the practice of giving importance to all cultures in a society 多元文化主义（重视社会中各种文化）

confessional [kənˈfeʃənəl] *adj.* admitting to bad or embarrassing things that you have done 忏悔的

regionalism [ˈriːdʒənəlɪzəm] *n.* a feature of a language that exists in a particular part of a country, and is not part of the standard language （语言的）地域特征，地域性

alienation [ˌeɪljəˈneɪʃn] *n.* a state or experience of being isolated from a group or an activity to which one should belong or in which one should be involved 离间；疏远

Video 2

Samuel Richardson 塞缪尔·理查逊（1689—1761），18 世纪英国著名小说家，保守派作家，英国小说的创始人之一

Clarissa《克拉丽莎》，是塞缪尔·理查逊创作的书信体小说

Pamela《帕米拉》，是塞缪尔·理查逊首部书信体小说，英国早期的心理小说

crib [krɪb] *v.* (~ something) (from somebody) to dishonestly copy work from another student or from a book（学生在考试或做作业时）抄袭，剽窃

Ian Watt 伊恩·瓦特（1917—1999），斯坦福大学文学评论家、文学史学家，代表作《小说的兴起》

The Rise of the Novel《小说的兴起》，主要讲述英国小说兴起的历史原因、经济条件、社会语境、特色及其对世界文学的贡献

epistolary [ɪˈpɪstələri] *adj.* written or expressed in the form of letters 书信的；用书信表达的；书信体的

virtuous [ˈvɜːtʃuəs] *adj.* behaving in a very good and moral way 品行端正的；品德高的；有道德的

lech [letʃ] *n.* a man who shows an unpleasant sexual interest in somebody 好色之徒；色鬼

premise [ˈpremɪs] *n.* a statement or an idea that forms the basis for a reasonable line of argument 前提；假定

Tom Jones《汤姆·琼斯》，是作家亨利·菲尔丁创作的现实主义长篇小说

Henry Fielding 亨利·菲尔丁（1707—1754），18 世纪杰出的英国小说家、戏剧家

Shamela《莎美拉》，是亨利·菲尔丁针对理查逊的《帕米拉》仿写而成的小说，情节类似，但结局相反

crook [krʊk] *n.* a dishonest person 骗子

immersive [ɪˈmɜːsɪv] *adj.* used to describe a computer system or image that seems to surround the user（计算机系统或图像）沉浸式虚拟现实的

vernacular [vəˈnækjələ(r)] *n.* the language spoken in a particular area or by a particular group, especially one that is not the official or written language 方言；土语

go ape (slang) to become extremely angry or excited 暴跳如雷；激动异常

Video 3

slacks [slæks] *n.* trousers/pants for men or women, which are not part of a suit 便裤；宽松的长裤

abdication [ˌæbdɪˈkeɪʃn] *n.* a formal resignation and renunciation of powers 辞职；退位

The Enchanter 《魅人者》，小说家弗拉基米尔·纳博科夫最后一部中篇俄国小说

entomologist [ˌentəˈmɑːlədʒɪst] *n.* a zoologist who studies insects 昆虫学者

lepidopterist [ˌlepɪˈdɒptərɪst] *n.* a person who studies butterflies and moths 鳞翅目昆虫学家（研究蝴蝶和飞蛾的人）

Ruth Bader Ginsburg 鲁斯·巴德·金斯伯格（1933—2020），德裔犹太人，美国法学家，女权主义者

Video 4

Thomas Pynchon 托马斯·品钦（1937— ），美国后现代主义文学代表作家

John Ashbery 约翰·阿什贝利（1927—2017），美国后现代诗歌代表人物

esteemed [ɪˈstiːmd] *adj.* someone who you greatly admire and respect 受尊敬的

publicity [pʌbˈlɪsəti] *n.* the attention that is given to somebody/something by newspapers, television, etc. （媒体的）关注，宣传，报道

steeped [stiːpt] *adj.* If a place or person is steeped in a quality or characteristic, they are surrounded by it or deeply influenced by it 充满……的色彩；深受……浸淫的

émigré [ˈemɪɡreɪ] *n.* a person who has left their own country, usually for political reasons （通常因政治原因移居外国的）流亡者，逃亡者

confluence [ˈkɒnfluəns] *n.* the fact of two or more things becoming one （事物的）汇合，汇聚，汇集

infer [ɪnˈfɜː(r)] *v.* (from something) to reach an opinion or decide that something is true on the basis of information that is available 推断；推论；推理

reclusive [rɪˈkluːsɪv] *adj.* a reclusive person or animal lives alone and deliberately avoids the company of others 独处的；隐居的

David Foster Wallace 戴维·福斯特·华莱士（1962—2008），美国小说家

George Saunders 乔治·桑德斯（1958— ），美国小说家，代表作有《林肯在中阴界》

Chapter 12   Postmodernism II

Part I   Warm-up

Discuss the following questions in pairs or groups.

1. What is the nature of truth, relative or absolute? How do postmodernists generally view truth?
2. Do you find it challenging to read a postmodernist novel?
3. Does postmodernism mean anti-modernism? Why or why not?
4. Suppose you are going to write a postmodernist novel. Where would you begin?

Part II   Unboxed: Lyotard, Postmodernism and the Metanarrative

Watch the video. Write *T* for true or *F* for false for each statement.

1. (   ) According to Lyotard, the story of the Renaissance and the Age of Reason remains the metanarrative of today.
2. (   ) According to Lyotard, all cultures tend to tell and retell stories that give cultures purpose and meaning.
3. (   ) Lyotard compares the story of democracy and science to the similar metanarratives of Christianity.
4. (   ) According to Lyotard, many would have little idea what their lives or our culture mean without faith and trust in Christianity.
5. (   ) According to Lyotard, people are encouraged to question the way of the ancestors and doubt the practices of democracy and science.
6. (   ) Jack Kerouac wrote of the "lost generation", the beatnik youth of the fifties who turned from American conformity, tired and doubtful of consumerism and the Korean War.
7. (   ) The Civil Rights Movement of the sixties called for revolutionary changes to American democracy, at the same time protesting the Vietnam War.
8. (   ) Lyotard argues that Postmodernism is a playful engagement with many conflicting micronarratives, while the metanarrative of the progress of the West is dead.

9. ( ) For many, the dominance of wealthy nations, the environmental impact of technology on the world's poor is untrue and the Western metanarrative is out of date.

10. ( ) Critics of Lyotard reckon that postmodernism might be a cure for the condition and merely another symptom.

Part III Why should you read Kurt Vonnegut?

Watch the video and answer the following questions.

1. In what sense has Billy Pilgrim become "unstuck" in time?
2. How to understand "the shapes of stories" generated by Kurt Vonnegut?
3. According to Kurt Vonnegut, what kind of story is the truest to real life?
4. What is the purpose of life that Vonnegut tried to seek in most of his novels?
5. What do you believe is the hallmark of Vonnegut's novels?
6. Since Vonnegut holds a bleak view of the human condition, are hopes all dashed in his assessments?

Watch the video again and fill in the blanks.

Billy Pilgrim can't sleep because he knows aliens will arrive to abduct him in one hour. He knows the 1) _____ are coming because he has become "unstuck" in time, causing him to experience events out of 2) _____ order.

Over the course of Kurt Vonnegut's *Slaughterhouse-Five*, he hops back and forth between a childhood trip to the Grand Canyon, his life as a middle-aged optometrist, his captivity in an intergalactic zoo, the 3) _____ he endured as a war prisoner, and more.

The title of *Slaughterhouse-Five* and much of its source material came from Vonnegut's own experiences in World War II. As a prisoner of war, he lived in a former slaughterhouse in Dresden, where he took 4) _____ in an underground meat locker while allied forces bombed the city. When he and the other prisoners finally emerged, they found Dresden utterly 5) _____. After the war, Vonnegut tried to make sense of human behavior by studying an unusual aspect of anthropology: the 6) _____ of stories, which he insisted were just as interesting as the shapes of pots or spearheads. To find the shape, he graphed the main character's 7) _____ from the beginning to the end of a story. The zany curves he generated revealed common types of fairy tales and myths that echo through many cultures. But this shape can be the most interesting of all. In a story like this, it's impossible to distinguish the character's good fortune from the bad.

Vonnegut thought this kind of story was the 8) _____ to real life, in which we are all the victims of a series of accidents, unable to predict how events will impact us in the long term. He found the tidy, satisfying arcs of many stories at 9) _____ with this reality, and he set out to explore the 10) _____ between good and bad fortune in his own work.

When Vonnegut ditched clear-cut fortunes, he also 11) _____ straightforward chronology. Instead of proceeding tidily from the beginning to the end, in his stories "All 12) _____, past, present and future always have existed, always will exist." Tralfamadorians, the aliens who crop up in many of his books, see all moments at once. They "can see where each star has been and where it is going, so that the heavens are filled with rarefied, luminous spaghetti." Although they can see all of time, they don't try to change the course of events. While the Trafalmadorians may be at peace with their lack of 13) _____, Vonnegut's human characters are still getting used to it.

In *The Sirens of Titan*, when they seek the meaning of life in the vastness of the universe, they find nothing but "empty heroics, low 14) _____, and pointless death." Then, from their vantage point within a "chrono-synclastic infundibulum", a man and his dog see devastating futures for their earthly 15) _____ but can't change the course of events.

Though there aren't easy answers available, they eventually conclude that the purpose of life is "to love whoever is around to be loved." In *Cat's Cradle*, Vonnegut's characters turn to a different source of meaning: Bokonism, a religion based on harmless lies that all its adherents recognize as lies. Though they're aware of Bokonism's lies, they live their lives by these 16) _____ anyway, and in so doing develop some genuine hope.

They join together in groups called Karasses, which consist of people we "find by accident but [...] stick with by choice" — 17) _____ linked around a shared purpose. These are not to be confused with Granfalloons, groups of people who appoint significance to actually meaningless 18) _____, like where you grew up, political parties, and even entire nations.

Though he held a bleak view of the human condition, Vonnegut believed strongly that "we are all here to help each other get through this thing, whatever it is."

We might get pooped and demoralized, but Vonnegut 19) _____ his grim assessments with more than a few morsels of hope. His fictional alter ego, Kilgore Trout, supplied this parable: two yeast sat "discussing the possible purposes of life as they ate sugar and suffocated in their own excrement. Because of their limited intelligence, they never came close to guessing that they were making champagne." In spite of his insistence that we're all here to fart around, in spite of his deep concerns about the course of human existence, Vonnegut also advanced the possibility, however 20) _____, that we might end up making something good.

And if that isn't nice, what is?

Part Ⅳ *Catch-22* by Joseph Heller: How to Read It

Watch the video and answer the following questions.
1. Why does the speaker say that *Catch-22* has passed into common parlance?
2. What does "catch" refer to in the book title?
3. In what way does the speaker describe the war?
4. How are Joseph Heller's own experiences reflected in the novel *Catch-22*?
5. Why did Joseph Heller begin writing the novel eight years after the war?
6. According to the speaker, what should we bear in mind regarding the historical background?
7. Should we approach the novel *Catch-22* as "a 'Vietnamization' of World War Ⅱ"?
8. How does the author organize the chapters in *Catch-22*?
9. How to understand the character "Yossarian" in the story?
10. What is the main plot of *Catch-22*?
11. How to describe the linguistic style of the novel?
12. Is the novel a work of "absurdism"?
13. Why did the speaker say that the frustration in reading the novel is a key element of the novel's success?
14. According to the speaker, what else can we expect from reading the novel beyond its astute commentary on war?

Part Ⅴ Projects and Presentations

Choose one of the following projects, or design one of your own closely related to the theme of the unit. Finish the project by giving a presentation in class and leading a discussion afterwards.

1. Lyotard talked about postmodernism as a playful engagement with many conflicting micronarratives, alternatives that have emerged in the space created by the questioning of the grand metanarrative. Do you agree? What do you think are the notable literary devices of taking a postmodern approach to literature? Have a group discussion and

report your discussion results in class.

2. Some critics have argued that postmodern literature is all style and has no substance. Do you agree? To what extent do you think this is true/untrue? Exchange your thoughts with members in your group.

3. Joseph Heller revealed the influence of certain wars in his writing of *Catch-22*, a classic in postmodern literature, what do you know about these wars that gave rise to postmodern literature? Form a research group and share your findings in class.

Part Ⅵ Vocabulary and Notes

Video 1

Lyotard 利奥塔（Jean-François Lyotard，1924—1998），法国哲学家，文学理论家，后现代思潮理论家，解构主义哲学的杰出代表

European Enlightenment 欧洲启蒙运动，指17—18世纪欧洲资产阶级和人民大众反封建的思想文化运动，是文艺复兴之后近代人类的第二次思想解放

Age of Reason 理性时代，指17—18世纪末欧洲启蒙主义哲学盛行、以理性和常识占优势为特征的时期

metanarrative [ˈmetənærətɪv] *n.* (in postmodernist literary theory) a narrative about a narrative or narratives（后现代文学理论）元叙事

Marxism [ˈmɑːksɪzəm] *n.* the political and economic theories of Karl Marx (1818—1883) which explain the changes and developments in society as the result of opposition between the social classes 马克思主义

genocide [ˈdʒenəsaɪd] *n.* the murder of a whole race or group of people 种族灭绝；大屠杀

Auschwitz [ˈauʃˌvits] *n.* 奥斯维辛（波兰城市名）

authoritarian [ɔːˌθɒrɪˈteəriən] *adj.* believing that people should obey authority and rules, even when these are unfair, and even if it means that they lose their personal freedom 专制的

Jack Kerouac 杰克·凯鲁亚克（1922—1969），极具反叛精神的小说家，他于1957年创作的小说《在路上》（*On the Road*）成了20世纪60年代嬉皮士运动的经典之作，开创了影响至今的嬉皮士文化

beatnik [ˈbiːtnɪk] *n.* a young person in the 1950s and early 1960s who rejected the way of life of ordinary society and showed this by behaving and dressing in a different way from most people "垮掉的一代"的青年（20世纪50年代及60年代初摈弃传统生活与衣着的年轻人）

conformity [kənˈfɔːməti] *n.* (to/with something) behaviour or actions that follow the accepted rules of society（对社会规则的）遵从，遵守

Civil Rights Movement （美国）民权运动，20 世纪 50 年代和 60 年代非裔美国人争取平等权利的运动

supremacist [suːˈpreməsɪst] *n.* a person who believes that their own race is better than others' and should be in power 种族优越论者

valve [vælv] *n.* a device for controlling the flow of a liquid or gas, letting it move in one direction only 阀；阀门

accommodate [əˈkɒmədeɪt] *v.* to consider something, such as somebody's opinion or a fact, and be influenced by it when you are deciding what to do or explaining something 考虑到；顾及

disenchanted [ˌdɪsɪnˈtʃɑːntɪd] *adj.* (with somebody/something) no longer feeling enthusiasm for somebody/something; not believing something is good or worth doing 不再着迷的；不再抱幻想的

Video 2

abduct [æbˈdʌkt] *v.* to take somebody away illegally, especially using force 劫持；绑架

chronological [ˌkrɒnəˈlɒdʒɪkl] *adj.* (of a number of events) arranged in the order in which they happened（许多事件）按发生时间顺序排列的

Kurt Vonnegut 库尔特·冯内古特（1922—2007），美国黑色幽默文学的代表人物，与马克·吐温并称。其代表作《第五号屠宰场》（*Slaughterhouse-Five*, 1969）是黑色幽默的反战作品中的经典

Grand Canyon [grænd ˈkænjən] 大峡谷，全称大峡谷国家公园（Grand Canyon National Park），是美国西南部的国家公园，在 1979 年被列为世界自然遗产

optometrist [ɒpˈtɒmətrɪst] *n.* someone whose job is to test people's eyesight to see if they need glasses, and how strong their glasses should be 验光师

captivity [kæpˈtɪvəti] *n.* the state of being kept as a prisoner or in a confined space 监禁；关押；困住

intergalactic [ˌɪntəɡəˈlæktɪk] *adj.* existing or happening between galaxies of stars 星系际的

humiliation [hjuːˌmɪliˈeɪʃn] *n.* an occasion or a situation in which you feel embarrassed and ashamed 丢脸的事；丢脸的场合

Dresden [ˈdrezdən] *n.* 德累斯顿（东德的城市）

demolish [dɪˈmɒlɪʃ] *v.* to pull or knock down a building 拆毁，拆除（建筑物）

anthropology [ˌænθrəˈpɒlədʒi] *n.* the study of the human race, especially of its origins, development, customs and beliefs 人类学

spearhead ['spɪəhed] *n.* the sharp-pointed head of a spear 矛头

zany ['zeɪni] *adj.* strange or unusual in an amusing way 古怪的；滑稽可笑的

arc [ɑːk] *n.* (geometry) part of a circle or a curved line （几何）弧

ditch [dɪtʃ] *v.* to get rid of something/somebody because you no longer want or need it/them 摆脱；抛弃；丢弃

crop up If something crops up, it appears or happens, usually unexpectedly. 意外出现；突然发生

rarefied ['reərɪfaɪd] *adj.* (of air) containing less oxygen than usual （空气）稀薄的；含氧量低的

luminous ['luːmɪnəs] *adj.* shining in the dark; giving out light 夜光的；发光的；发亮的

The Sirens of Titan 《泰坦的警笛》，是 Kurt Vonnegut 创作的漫画科幻小说，于 1959 年首次出版

vantage ['vɑːntɪdʒ] *n.* a state, position, or opportunity affording superiority or advantage 优势

Cat's Cradle 《猫的摇篮》，是美国作家 Kurt Vonnegut 的科幻小说，初版于 1963 年

adherent [əd'hɪərənt] *n.* a person who supports a political party or set of ideas （政党、思想的）拥护者，追随者，信徒

tenet ['tenɪt] *n.* one of the principles or beliefs that a theory or larger set of beliefs is based on 原则；信条；教义

bleak [bliːk] *adj.* (of a situation) not encouraging or giving any reason to have hope （状况）不乐观的；无望的；暗淡的

poop [puːp] *v.* ~ somebody (out) to make somebody very tired 累垮（某人）；使筋疲力尽

demoralize [dɪ'mɒrəlaɪz] *v.* to make somebody lose confidence or hope 使泄气；使意志消沉

intersperse [ˌɪntə'spɜːs] *v.* to put something in something else or among or between other things 散布

morsel ['mɔːsl] *n.* a small amount or a piece of something 少量

alter ego [ˌæltə 'egəʊ] a person whose personality is different from your own but who shows or acts as another side of your personality 第二自我

parable ['pærəbl] *n.* a short story that teaches a moral or spiritual lesson, especially one of those told by Jesus as recorded in the *Bible* （尤指《圣经》中的）寓言故事

suffocate [ˈsʌfəkeɪt] *v.* to die because there is no air to breathe （使）窒息而死

excrement [ˈekskrɪmənt] *n.* solid waste matter that is passed from the body through the bowels 粪便；排泄物

Video 3

Catch-22 《第 22 条军规》（1961），是美国作家 Joseph Heller 的代表作，通常被认为是 20 世纪最重要的小说之一。该词已经进入英语词典之中，象征人们处在一种荒谬的两难之中

parlance [ˈpɑːləns] *n.* a particular way of using words or expressing yourself, for example, one used by a particular group 说法；术语；用语

anglophone [ˈæŋɡləʊfəʊn] *adj.* anglophone communities are English-speaking communities in areas where more than one language is commonly spoken 讲英语的

bureaucracy [bjʊəˈrɒkrəsi] *n.* (often disapproving) the system of official rules and ways of doing things that a government or an organization has, especially when these seem to be too complicated 官僚主义；官僚作风

exasperation [ɪɡˌzæspəˈreɪʃ(ə)n] *n.* an exasperated feeling of annoyance 恼怒

squadron [ˈskwɒdrən] *n.* a group of military aircraft or ships forming a section of a military force （空军或海军的）中队

sanity [ˈsænəti] *n.* the state of having a normal healthy mind 精神健全；神志正常

protagonist [prəˈtæɡənɪst] *n.* the main character in a play, film/movie or book （戏剧、电影、书的）主要人物，主人公，主角

axis [ˈæksɪs] *n.* an agreement or alliance between two or more countries 国与国之间的协议或联盟

Italian peninsula 意大利半岛，又名亚平宁半岛，是南欧洲三大半岛之一，位居三大半岛的中间，在地中海之北

consign [kənˈsaɪn] *v.* ~ somebody/something to something to put somebody/something somewhere in order to get rid of them/it （为摆脱而）把……置于，把……交付给

Band of Brothers 《兄弟连》，是一部 2001 年的美国战争迷你剧，改编自历史学家史蒂芬·安布罗斯创作于 1992 年的同名非虚构书籍

paranoia [ˌpærəˈnɔɪə] *n.* fear or suspicion of other people when there is no evidence or reason for this （对别人的）无端恐惧，多疑

Forrest Gump 《阿甘正传》，是一部 1994 年的美国电影，改编自美国作家温斯顿·葛鲁姆于 1986 年出版的同名小说

tangent [ˈtændʒənt] *n.* a straight line that touches the outside of a curve but does not cross it 切线

emblematic [ˌembləˈmætɪk] *adj.* that is considered typical of a situation, an area of work, etc. 特有的；典型的；有代表性的

colonel [ˈkɜːnl] *n.* an officer of high rank in the army, the marines, or the US air force（陆军、海军陆战队或美国空军）上校

staggering [ˈstægərɪŋ] *adj.* so great, shocking or surprising that it is difficult to believe 令人难以相信的

feign [feɪn] *v.* to pretend that you have a particular feeling or that you are ill/sick, tired, etc. 假装，装作，佯装（有某种感觉或生病、疲倦等）

prescribe [prɪˈskraɪb] *v.* (of a doctor) to tell somebody to take a particular medicine or have a particular treatment; to write a prescription for a particular medicine, etc.（医生）给……开（药）；让……采用（疗法）；开（处方）

syndicate [ˈsɪndɪkət] *n.* a group of people or companies who work together and help each other in order to achieve a particular aim 辛迪加；企业联合组织

dalliance [ˈdæliəns] *n.* a sexual relationship that is not serious 调情；调戏

partake [pɑːˈteɪk] *v.* (in something) to take part in an activity 参加；参与

brazen [ˈbreɪzn] *adj.* (disapproving) open and without shame, usually about something that people find shocking 厚颜无耻的

discombobulate [ˌdɪskəmˈbɒbjuleɪt] *v.* to throw into confusion 使混乱

rambling [ˈræmblɪŋ] *adj.* (of a speech or piece of writing) very long and confused（讲话或文章）冗长而含糊的；不切题的

Kafkaesque [ˌkæfkəˈesk] *adj.* used to describe a situation that is confusing and frightening, especially one involving complicated official rules and systems that do not seem to make any sense 卡夫卡式的；恐怖而怪诞的

The Trial《审判》，是弗兰兹·卡夫卡在1914年至1915年写的一部长篇小说，于1925年发表

pedantic [pɪˈdæntɪk] *adj.* (disapproving) too worried about small details or rules 迂腐的；学究气的

astute [əˈstjuːt] *adj.* very clever and quick at seeing what to do in a particular situation, especially how to get an advantage 精明的；狡猾的

Chapter 13 Jewish American Literature

Part I Warm-up

Discuss the following questions in pairs or groups.
1. Can you name a few American novelists who have a Jewish ancestry?
2. Can you identify some representative works of Jewish American writers?
3. What are some recurring themes in Jewish American literature?
4. What is the concept of diaspora and how does it relate to literature?

Part II The Rise and Fall of Jewish American Literature

Watch the video and fill in the blanks.

I'm just wondering if I should give some introductory words but I won't. I'll just start. So part one, my title makes an achingly oblique reference to Irving Howe's famous 1976 cultural history *World of Our Fathers: The Journey of the Eastern European Jews to America and the Life They Found and Made*. And for those who don't know the book, the 1) _____ says it all, though I'm actually not going to spend any time at all talking about the book today. My argument is that Howe's key word "world" reveals the hegemonic legitimation of the Jewish American literary field as part of a larger 2) _____ project to tell the history of the Jews and the innovation of critical practices operating outside the dominion of sort of larger 3) _____ sphere of ethnohistory system. But first I need to take a few steps back; so I've just finished a new book on the history of the Jewish American literary field. I argue that the field central 4) _____, ethnography essentially, has a distinct history and is in fact largely residual now. Ask anyone who cares the dominant event of Jewish American literary history is emergence or breakthrough, right, these are in quotation marks, "the eruption in the 1950s of Jewish American writers like Bernard Malamud, Philip Roth, Saul Bellow, Grace Paley, into the heart of the American cultural scene". More to the point, the fact of breakthrough is the primal scene of the Jewish American literary field. The more or less formalized or academically 5) _____ study of Jewish American literature grew up around the consolidating self-evidence of the break through narrative, and the field's legibility has from the start been 6) _____ with it. The prevailing accounts of Jewish literature in the US inevitably orbit, even if only implicitly or inconspicuously, or once or twice removed in the gravitational field of this central event. The Jewish American literary study, unlike its brother and sister the US ethnic literary formations, has mostly resisted the urge to explicitly theorize itself, and its practices, the narrative of breakthrough has operated as a deputized proxy for the only real theory, however sporadically or insufficiently acknowledged, of Jewish American literature that has ever been able to carry any currency either professionally in the Academy or publicly among the readers of Jewish American writing, namely immigration. Thus if Jewish American writing before the war can be characterized by a parochial or provincial angst dependably fitting into the US literary historical departments, like immigrant writing or regionalism or urban fiction categories as durable as the dependability with which they are marked by decided second-order 7) _____, then within two decades of the war's end it had rapidly shed these marginalizing limitations and come to represent American literature at its most central and innovative and ascendant. Accordingly, as Jewish American literary study has tended certainly in some of its recent formations to become more diverse and focused and more sophisticated in scope, it often draws its warrant for these critical investments and it reproduces an image of its own intellectual responsibility in the name of the increasing diversity, sophistication and independence of Jews in America. Jewish American literary study persists in imagining itself as part of the enduring historical reality of breakthrough. Significantly in this narrative of socio-cultural movement from margin to Center, and rearguard to leading-edge, Jewish American literature dependably tracks the career of Jewish America. The breakthrough narrative of Jewish American literature normalizes itself as a straightforward and largely politically innocent reflection or representational lens, as a mode of access that suppresses critical theorization in the name of self-evident history, leveraging its hegemony on the assumption that literary history is itself neither theoretical nor historical.

My new book begins with a critical suspicion about the way in which professional academic formations including both English department-based literary study and Jewish studies-based 8) _____ have taken Jewish American literature for granted, and about the way in which Jewish American literary history has itself reflected these predispositions, taking for granted its own literary historical warrant. My critical targets are the disciplinary and intellectual modes in which the Jewish American literary field's Exceptionalist estrangement from the mainstream of humanistic critical self-regard has been carried out. By 9) _____ the practice of Jewish American literary study and destabilizing the assumption that Jewish American literary history operates entirely under the institutional authority of historical inquiry into the lives and times of Jews in America, I hope to make it easier for humanists to imagine and act on a critically self-aware intellectual practice. I certainly don't pretend that there was no institutionally house study of writing by Jews in America before the 1950s, or that the literary intellectuals of the breakthrough. People not only liked Howe but Leslie Fiedler, Irving Malin, Daniel Walden, Alfred Kazin, Sheldon Grebstein and Allen Guttmann for a few notable examples, invented the idea of thinking about what we now easily call Jewish American writing. To be sure before Wilbur—there was fiction being written by Jews in the United States, there were scholarly works written that is their object, the representation of Jews in English and American literature, and there was of course the persuasive historical tradition of 19th century German Jewish vision, the cultural 10) _____ logic of a trans historical unity of Jewish expression. But scholarship could not yet take for granted the field unity of a 11) _____ of literature organized, defined and indeed interpretable by the Jewish American identity of its authors. This was a post-war development and it has a history that itself cannot be extracted from the gravitational pull of the breakthrough narrative. The innovation of breakthrough was not simply to link inevitably and unimpeachably the Jewish authors and Jewish texts of Jewish American literature, but to reorient thinking about literary texts written by Jews in America around authors as representatives of Jewish American people and experiences. Jewish American literary study would professionalize over the following decades, as scholarly focus shifted from the object of literary representation to its subject, from Jews as a community written about, to Jews as a community writing. More pointedly, the elaboration of breakthrough was often framed in triumphalist terms if colored at times by the tragic, by critics for whom the narrative of emergence was also crucially and fundamentally bound up with a reflexive structure of self-recognition.

As Leslie Fiedler, one of the leading breakthrough intellectuals put it, in a late career reflection on his writing about Jewish American literature, "it was not I realize now a disinterested 12) _____, since I thought of myself at the beginning of my career as part of the movement that had carried such children of immigrant Jews from Eastern Europe from the periphery to the center of American literary culture, making their experience our experience, a part of the 13) _____ dream stuff, the myth that makes all Americans one whatever their ethnic origin". And the repetition of first-person pronouns like "our" and "us" in his writings is his marker. The Exceptionalist insiderism that breakthrough inherited from the Wissenschaft tradition matured in post-war writing and post-war thinking about Jewish American 14) _____ as well a legacy for the consolidation of professional Jewish Studies. The ethnic literary formations we often associate with the emergence of academic multiculturalism and ethnic studies arose from and as institutional arms of active political movements. And they still often identified themselves as part of this struggle in its institutional interdependence with a narrative of breakthrough, however, Jewish American literary study in a sense emerged as part of a perception that a political struggle was in fact over, and as a result to the extent that it continues to constitute itself as a technology for interpreting what Jews do say and write. Jewish American literary study reproduces the grounds of its own 15) _____ if not in fact its own obsolescence.

Part Ⅲ Remembering Philip Roth

Watch the video and answer the following questions.

1. How old was Philip Roth when he died?
2. How many books did Roth publish?
3. How long does it usually take for Roth to write a novel?
4. The interviewer says Roth is considered a provocateur. What does it mean in the context?
5. When did Roth come back to live in America?

Part Ⅳ Isaac Bashevis Singer, Not a Typical Yiddish Writer

Watch the video. Write T for true or F for false for each statement.

1. ( ) Singer liked the Yiddish secular world.
2. ( ) Singer had no respect for traditional Jewish life.
3. ( ) Singer enjoyed eating bacon and eggs.
4. ( ) Singer grew up in Warsaw.
5. ( ) Singer was a conservative in his politics.
6. ( ) The speaker mentions Singer's work *The Magician of Lublin*.

Part Ⅴ Zachary Leader on Saul Bellow, with Martin Amis

Watch the video and answer the following questions

1. What does it mean when Henry James said he bought a wheelbarrow after he published a new book?
2. When was *Herzog* published?

3. The speakers read out a paragraph from a book. What is that book?
4. How was *Herzog* received when it was published?
5. What does "21" refer to in the paragraph that the speakers read out?

Part VI　Projects and Presentations

Choose one of the following projects, or design one of your own closely related to the theme of the unit. Finish the project by giving a presentation in class and leading a discussion afterwards.

1. How do Jewish Americans perceive their identity? And how does the perception manifest itself in Jewish American writings? Choose a Jewish American writer and share your views with your group.

2. Philip Roth says: "I don't think about the reader. I think about the book [...] I think about the sentence; I think about the paragraph; I think about the page." What do you think of this statement? Discuss in groups and then present in class.

3. In the last video, a speaker says that "it was Henry James who complained that when Edith Wharton [...] wrote a new book, or published a new book, she bought a new house. When he wrote a new book [...] he bought a new wheelbarrow." What do you think of the relationship between literature and fame, especially in the context of American society? Share your views with your classmates.

Part VII　Vocabulary and Notes

Video 1

introductory [ˌɪntrəˈdʌktəri] *adj.* written or said at the beginning of something as an introduction to what follows 序言的；引导的；介绍的

oblique [əˈbliːk] *adj.* not expressed or done in a direct way 间接的；不直截了当的；拐弯抹角的

Irving Howe 欧文·豪 (1920—1993)，20 世纪美国社会文化批评家

World of Our Fathers: The Journey of the Eastern European Jews to America and the Life They Found and Made 《父辈的世界》，欧文·豪作品，描述东欧犹太人移居美国以及他们发现与创造生活的历程

hegemonic [ˌhedʒɪˈmɑːnɪk] *adj.* related to a leader, capable of command 霸权的；支配的

institutional [ˌɪnstɪˈtjuːʃənl] *adj.* connected with an institution 机构的；慈善机构的

dominion [dəˈmɪniən] *n.* (over somebody/something) authority to rule; control 统治（权）；管辖；支配

legitimate [lɪˈdʒɪtɪmət] *adj.* for which there is a fair and acceptable reason 正当合理的；合情合理的

ethnohistory [ˌeθnəʊˈhɪstri] *n.* a study of the development of cultures 人种历史学

paradigm [ˈpærədaɪm] *n.* a typical example or pattern of something 典范；范例；样式

residual [rɪˈzɪdjuəl] *adj.* remaining at the end of a process 剩余的；残留的

Bernard Malamud 伯纳德·马拉默德（1914—1986），美国小说家

Grace Paley 格蕾丝·佩利（1922—2007），美国短篇小说作家、诗人、教师和政治活动家

disciplined [ˈdɪsɪplɪnd] *adj.* someone who is disciplined behaves or works in a controlled way 有纪律的

legibility [ˌledʒəˈbɪləti] *n.* distinctness that makes perception easy 易读性；易辨认

articulate [ɑːˈtɪkjuleɪt] *v.* to express or explain your thoughts or feelings clearly in words 明确表达；清楚说明

formation [fɔːˈmeɪʃn] *n.* a thing that has been formed, especially in a particular place or in a particular way 组成物；形成物

deputize [ˈdepjutaɪz] *v.* (for somebody) to do something that somebody in a higher position than you would usually do 担任代表；充当代理人

proxy [ˈprɒksi] *n.* the authority that you give to somebody to do something for you, when you cannot do it yourself 代理权；代表权

sporadically [spəˈrædɪkəli] *adv.* not regularly or constantly 零星地；偶发地

parochial [pəˈrəʊkiəl] *adj.* connected with a church parish 教区的；堂区的

prestige [preˈstiːʒ] *n.* [不可数名词] the respect and admiration that somebody/something has because of their social position, or what they have done 威信；声望；威望

interdisciplinarity [ˌɪntərˌdɪsəplɪˈnærəti] *n.* interdisciplinarity involves the combining of two or more academic disciplines into one activity 跨学科性；多科性；跨领域

predispositions [ˌpriːdɪspəˈzɪʃn] *n.* (to/towards something) (to do something) a condition that makes somebody/something likely to behave in a particular way or to suffer from a particular disease 倾向；癖性；（易患某种病的）体质

exceptionalism [ɪkˈsepʃənəlɪzəm] *n.* an attitude to other countries, cultures, etc., based on the idea of being quite distinct from, and often superior to, them in vital ways 例外主义；对其他国家、文化等的一种态度，认为自己的国家或文化在很多重要方面不同并优越于其他国家或其文化

estrangement [ɪˈstreɪndʒmənt] *n.* (from somebody/something) (between A and B) the state of being estranged; a period of being estranged 疏远（的一段时间）；分居（期）

historicize [hɪsˈtɔːrəˌsaɪz] *v.* to give something the appearance of historical truth 历史化；使具历史真实性；运用史料

Leslie Fiedler 莱斯利·菲德勒，美国著名文学批评家、文化批评家，早期后现代主义代表人物之一

Irving Malin 欧文·马林，美国文学批评家

Daniel Walden 丹尼尔·瓦尔登，钢琴家，大键琴手，音乐理论家和音乐学家

Alfred Kazin 阿尔弗雷德·卡津，美国社会文化批评家，著名文学批评家

Sheldon Grebstein 谢尔登·诺曼·格雷布斯坦，文学评论家，作品主要关注20世纪美国文学

Allen Guttmann 艾伦·古特曼，美国阿默斯特学院教授，美国著名语言学家和社会学家

nationalist [ˌnæʃnəˈlɪstɪk] *adj.* having very strong feelings of love for and pride in your country, so that you think that it is better than any other 国家主义的；民族主义的

canon [ˈkænən] *n.* a generally accepted rule, standard or principle by which something is judged 原则；准则；标准

unimpeachably [ʌnɪmˈpiːtʃəbli] *adv.* without question 无可指责地；无懈可击地

reorient [riːˈɔːriɛnt] *v.* to adjust or align (something) in a new or different way 以新的或不同的方式适应（某事）；以新的或不同的方式公开支持（某事）

triumphalist [traɪˈʌmfəlɪst] *adj.* triumphalist behaviour is behaviour in which politicians or organizations celebrate a victory or a great success, especially when this is intended to upset the people they have defeated （尤指带炫耀性的）庆祝胜利的

disinterested [dɪsˈɪntrəstɪd] *adj.* not influenced by personal feelings, or by the chance of getting some advantage for yourself 客观的；无私的；公正的

venture [ˈventʃə(r)] *n.* a business project or activity, especially one that involves taking risks （尤指有风险的）企业，商业，投机活动，经营项目

periphery [pəˈrɪfəri] *n.* the outer edge of a particular area 边缘；周围；外围

communal [kəˈmjuːnl] *adj.* shared by, or for the use of, a number of people, especially people who live together （尤指居住在一起的人）共享的，共有的，共用的

Wissenschaft 指任何涉及系统研究和教学的研究或科学

constitute [ˈkɒnstɪtjuːt] *v.* to form a group legally or officially （合法或正式地）成

立，设立

redundancy [rɪˈdʌndənsi] *n.* the state of not being necessary or useful 多余；累赘

Video 2

congestive [kənˈdʒestɪv] *adj.* a congestive disease is a medical condition where a part of the body becomes blocked 充血的；充血性的

Nathan Zuckerman 内森·祖克曼，作家菲利普·罗斯在作品中创造的第二自我

raunchy [ˈrɔːntʃi] *adj.* intended to be sexually exciting 下流的

ensuing [ɪnˈsjuːɪŋ] *adj.* events happen immediately after other events 随后发生的

accolade [ˌækəˈleɪd] *n.* praise or an award for an achievement that people admire 赞扬；表扬；奖励；奖赏；荣誉

provocateur [prəˌvɒkəˈtɜː(r)] *n.* a secret agent who incites suspected persons to commit illegal acts 破坏分子，煽动者

enact [ɪˈnækt] *v.* to pass (a law) 通过（法律）

Video 3

live off [ˈlɪv ɔːf] *v.* if you live off another person, you rely on them to provide you with money 依赖（某人）生活

Yiddish [ˈjɪdɪʃ] *n.* a Jewish language, originally used in central and eastern Europe, based on a form of German with words from Hebrew and several modern languages 意第绪语，依地语（犹太人的语言，起源于欧洲中部和东部，以德语为基础，借用希伯来语和若干现代语言的词语）

The Magician of Lublin 《卢布林的魔术师》，美国作家艾萨克·巴什维斯·辛格的作品

synagogue [ˈsɪnəgɒg] *n.* a building where Jews meet for religious worship and teaching 犹太会堂；犹太教堂

Talmud [ˈtælmʊd] *n.* a collection of ancient writings on Jewish law and traditions 《塔木德》（犹太古代法典）

Ojai [ˈoʊhaɪ] *n.* 奥哈伊，美国加利福尼亚州文图拉县的小镇

Reagan 罗纳德·威尔逊·里根，政治家，美国第四十任总统

Video 4

Henry James 亨利·詹姆斯（1843—1916），英籍美裔小说家，文学批评家，剧作家和散文家

Edith Wharton 伊迪丝·华顿（1862—1937），美国女作家，主要作品有长篇

小说《高尚的嗜好》《纯真年代》等

Herzog《赫索格》，美国作家索尔·贝娄的作品

plebeian [pləˈbiːən] *adj.* connected with ordinary people or people of the lower social classes 平民的，百姓的，下层社会的

princeling [ˈprɪnslɪŋ] *n.* （usually disapproving）a prince who rules a small or unimportant country（小国的）国王，国君，大公

compact [ˈkɒmpækt] *adj.* （of a person or an animal）small and strong（人或动物）矮小而健壮的

Chapter 14　African American Literature

Part I　Warm-up

Discuss the following questions in pairs or groups.
1. How much do you know about the Harlem Renaissance?
2. What are the social factors leading to Harlem Renaissance?
3. What influences did the Harlem Renaissance have on African-Americans?
4. What are some common themes in African-American literature?

Part II　*Notes of a Native Son*: The World According to James Baldwin

Watch the video. Write *T* for true or *F* for false for each statement.

1. (　) In the 1960s, the FBI spent a lot of time and energy investigating James Baldwin.

2. (　) James Baldwin was the best-selling black author in the world.

3. (　) James Baldwin agreed with the Church on racial inequality and homosexuality.

4. (　) James Baldwin published his first novel, *Go Tell it on the Mountain*, in Harlem in 1953.

5. (　) *Notes of a Native Son* gathered James Baldwin's thoughts on race, class, culture and exile.

6. (　) During the Civil Rights Movement, the blacks enjoyed the same rights with the whites in the workplace.

7. (　) James Baldwin believed that racism hurt both the blacks and the whites.

8. (　) James Baldwin was deeply involved in the Civil Rights Movement.

9. (　) James Baldwin liked the label that Kennedy gave him, i.e. an ambassador for black Americans.

10. (　) James Baldwin's words have helped generations of people improve their understanding of the society.

Part III Why should you read Toni Morrison's *Beloved*?

Watch the video and choose the right answer for the following questions.

1. Which of the following is NOT a symbol of a haunted house?
   A. A trail of cracker crumbs strewn across the floor.
   B. A mirror that stands in a corner.
   C. A tiny handprint that appears on a cake.
   D. A book that flies in the sky.
2. Who does Sethe live with at 124 Bluestone Road?
   A. Her mother-in-law Baby Suggs.
   B. Her daughter Denver.
   C. Her husband Halle.
   D. Stamp Paid, who helped Sethe escape to freedom.
3. Who does Sethe believe the ghost is?
   A. Her grandmother.
   B. Her husband.
   C. Her eldest daughter.
   D. Her former neighbor.
4. What is one of the main themes explored in *Beloved*?
   A. Love and trauma in African-American history.
   B. The role of religion in the lives of enslaved people.
   C. The most important battles of the Civil War.
   D. Segregation and anti-miscegenation laws.
5. According to Morrison, slavery is harmful to _____.
   A. love
   B. enslavers
   C. enslaved people
   D. all the above
6. How does Sethe cope with the trauma of the past?
   A. By dissociating and forgetting.
   B. By drinking excessively.
   C. By talking about it with Halle.
   D. By remaining mired in it.
7. One of the literary techniques Morrison uses is _____.
   A. onomatopoeia
   B. stream-of-consciousness
   C. allusion
   D. foreshadowing
8. In *Beloved*, Morrison asks people to _____.

A. consider hope in the dark
B. question what hope really means
C. ponder the power they have over each other
D. use the power wisely

Part IV Can Love and Independence Coexist?

Watch the video and answer the following questions.
1. What did the hurricane of 1928 bring to Janie Crawford?
2. Who wrote *Their Eyes Were Watching God* and what was it about?
3. What were Janie's neighbors most curious about?
4. What kind of form did the novel *Their Eyes Were Watching God* take in untangling Janie's life story?
5. What similarities are there between Janie and Hurston?
6. Where did Hurston write most of *Their Eyes Were Watching God*?
7. How did Hurston bring readers into the intimate spaces of Black southern life in *Their Eyes Were Watching God*?
8. What effects does the third-person have in *Their Eyes Were Watching God*?

Watch the second part of the video and fill in the blanks.

Perhaps more than any specific details, Hurston's experiences of being a black woman in America at this time are more 1) _____ in the novel's themes. Over the course of one long evening, Janie and Pheoby discussed the nature of family, marriage, 2) _____ and more. But their conversation always comes back to Janie's 3) _____ desire: to live honestly and be truly loved in return. As a teenager, Janie resents an 4) _____ marriage, despite the safety it offers her and the wishes of her loving grandmother. When her family becomes well-respected in Eatonville, she struggles with the 5) _____ eyes of strangers and a husband who wants her to be something she's not.

Throughout her life, Janie frequently feels she is at the whim of natural and spiritual forces that can shift the course of her existence without warning. And when she finally does find true love, these 6) _____ powers continue to act on her, 7) _____ to destroy the life she has so painstakingly built.

The story takes place during a time where women had little to no agency, and Janie's life is full of 8) _____ characters who demand different kinds of love and submission. But despite the loneliness of her situation, Janie 9) _____ these trials with defiance and curiosity. Her questions and commentary push back in subtle, clever ways. And as the reader follows Janie's journey from childhood to middle age, her confidence becomes 10) _____.

Just like Hurston, Janie defies the 11) _____ expectations for a woman in her time. Early in the novel, Hurston writes that "there are years that ask questions and years that answer," suggesting that life can only truly be understood by living it. But through her 12) _____ storytelling, Hurston invites us into Janie's life, her life, and the lives of so many other women.

Part V Langston Hughes: Leading Voice of the Harlem Renaissance

Watch the video and fill in the blanks.

—Langston Hughes was a great author because he spoke to, for and about black people in America.

(Poet, novelist and playwright, Langston Hughes was the 1) _____ voice of the Harlem Renaissance.)

—America was changing during the time that Langston Hughes was so popular. Black Consciousness was becoming more and more public, more 2) _____. I think that Langston Hughes was important because he was one of the early figures to show the 3) _____ and the beauty of ordinary black life.

—He was one of the most 4) _____ of the younger black poets, a new generation that described themselves as the New Negro. They covered new topics, took on new poetic forms and sought a wider audience, and Langston Hughes was at the 5) _____ of that.

(James Mercer Langston Hughes was born in Joplin Missouri on February 1st, 1902.)

—He wrote a lot about being 6) _____ when he was young, and I think that was a tremendous part of the product of moving around so much.

(After graduating from high school, Hughes published his first and most famous poem *The Negro Speaks of Rivers*.)

—It is the first poem that 7) _____ Africa and dignifies the image of Africa in American literature.

—*The Negro Speaks of Rivers* was published in a popular black journal, and so he was really rather widely read from the beginning. His poetry and his prose actually had access to 8) _____ people.

(While studying at Columbia University, Hughes discovered the Harlem art scene, spending hours in jazz and blues clubs, 9) _____ the rhythms of music into his work.)

—Jazz and blues had great influences on Langston Hughes. He sought to capture the energy and 10) _____ of the music of his poetry.

—He was very familiar with the Harlem nightlife. He knew the musicians and later in this life he would even 11) _____ with some of the key figures at that time such as Duke Ellington.

(Hughes was a 12) _____ writer and one of the first African-American authors who could support himself through his writing.)

—Langston Hughes wrote plays. He edited 13) _____ of poets of African descent across the Diaspora. He wrote short stories. One of his most famous series of short stories center around Jessie Be Simple. These are tales told by a resident of Harlem to an 14) _____ writer who is a stand-in for Langston Hughes.

—He was one of the most widely published young poets of the period. He was also among the better 15) _____. He really worked hard to promote the careers of other young writers in Harlem and also throughout the rest of his life. That's also one of his big 16) _____.

(Langston Hughes died of cancer on May 22nd, 1967. His Harlem residence was given landmark status, a fitting 17) _____ for a legendary writer.)

—His influence, his ambition as a creative writer, his success and accessibility. He wrote for the 18) _____ person. He was not writing for college classrooms. He was not writing for the elite. All of those things, I think, require that we recognize and acknowledge him as a great American literary voice of the 20th century.

Part VI Projects and Presentations

Choose one of the following projects, or design one of your own closely related to the theme of the unit. Finish the project by giving a presentation in class and leading a discussion afterwards.

1. It has been pointed out that many of the works by African-American authors reflect their struggle for identity. Could you use one or two literary texts you have read as examples and give a brief talk on how racial or cultural identity is constructed in the works.

2. African-American literature has been studied a lot in China. Please turn to CNKI

and other databases to find some research articles about African-American literature. Share with your group members or classmates about your summary of the African-American literature studies in China.

3. Slave narratives are an important part of African-American literature from the very beginning to the present. What is the significance of slave narratives in African-American literature?

Part VII Vocabulary and Notes

Video 1

amass [ə'mæs] *v.* to collect something, especially in large quantities（尤指大量）积累，积聚

fraction ['frækʃn] *n.* a small part or amount of something 小部分；少量；一点儿

loom [luːm] *v.* to appear important or threatening and likely to happen soon 显得突出；逼近

homophobia [ˌhəʊmə'fəʊbiə] *n.* a strong dislike and fear of homosexual people 对同性恋者的厌恶和恐惧

disillusioned [ˌdɪsɪ'luːʒnd] *adj.* disappointed because the person you admired or the idea you believed to be good and true now seems without value 大失所望的；不再抱幻想的；幻想破灭的

incremental [ˌɪŋkrə'mentl] *adj.* increasing gradually by regular degrees or additions 增加的；递增的

spiral ['spaɪrəl] *v.* to move in continuous circles, going upwards or downwards 螺旋式上升（或下降）；盘旋上升（或下降）

incarceration [ɪnˌkɑːsə'reɪʃn] *n.* the state of being imprisoned 监禁，下狱，禁闭

arresting [ə'restɪŋ] *adj.* attracting a lot of attention; very attractive 引人注意的；很有吸引力的

inextricably [ˌɪnɪk'strɪkəbli] *adv.* if two things are inextricably linked, etc., it is impossible to separate them 不可分开地；密不可分地

enmesh [ɪn'meʃ] *v.* to involve somebody/something in a bad situation that it is not easy to escape from 使陷入，使卷入（困境等）

liaison [li'eɪzn] *n.* a person whose job is to make sure there is a good relationship between two groups or organizations 联络员；联系人

faculty ['fæklti] *n.* a particular ability for doing something 才能；能力

rampant ['ræmpənt] *adj.* (of something bad) existing or spreading everywhere in a way that cannot be controlled 泛滥的；猖獗的

Video 2

strew [struː] *v.* to cover a surface with things 把……布满（或散布在）；在……上布满（或散播）

barbaric [bɑːˈbærɪk] *adj.* cruel and violent and not as expected from people who are educated and respect each other 残暴的；野蛮的；没有文化的

wrought [rɔːt] *v.* （work 的古体过去式和过去分词）caused something to happen, especially a change 使发生了，造成了（尤指变化）

in its wake used to say what is left behind by someone or something 随后

dissolve [dɪˈzɒlv] *v.* to officially end a marriage, business agreement or parliament 解除（婚姻关系）；终止（商业协议）；解散（议会）

specter [ˈspektə(r)] *n.* (literary) a ghost 鬼；幽灵

shun [ʃʌn] *v.* to avoid somebody/something 避开；回避；避免

fugitive [ˈfjuːdʒətɪv] *adj.* lasting only for a very short time 短暂的；易逝的

diminish [dɪˈmɪnɪʃ] *v.* to become or to make something become smaller, weaker, etc. 减少；（使）减弱，缩减；降低

mire [ˈmaɪə(r)] *v.* 〈figurative〉 (mire someone/something in) involve someone or something in (difficulties) 〈喻〉使陷入（困境）；使受困扰

dissociate [dɪˈsəʊʃieɪt] *v.* to say or do something to show that you are not connected with or do not support somebody/something; to make it clear that something is not connected with a particular plan, action, etc. 否认同……有关系；声明不支持；表明无关

irreparably [ɪˈrepərəblɪ] *adv.* in an irreparable manner or to an irreparable degree 不能恢复地；不能挽回地

ripple [ˈrɪpl] *v.* (of water) form or flow with small waves on the surface （水）起涟漪；起微波

delve [delv] *v.* to try hard to find out more information about something 探索；探究；查考

align [əˈlaɪn] *v.* to arrange something in the correct position, or to be in the correct position, in relation to something else, especially in a straight line 排整齐；校准；（尤指）使成一条直线

vulnerability [ˌvʌlnərəˈbɪləti] *n.* the state of being vulnerable or exposed 弱点；脆弱性；易伤性

subjugation [ˌsʌbdʒʊˈɡeɪʃn] *n.* the act of conquering 征服；镇压；屈服；服从

redeeming [rɪˈdiːmɪŋ] *adj.* bringing about salvation or redemption from sin 弥补

的；补偿的

heed [hiːd] *v.* to pay careful attention to somebody's advice or warning 留心，注意

Video 3

baritone [ˈbærɪtəʊn] *adj.* lower in range than tenor and higher than bass 男中音的

snarling [ˈsnɑːlɪŋ] （snarl 的现在分词）to show the teeth and make a deep angry noise in the throat （动物）龇牙低吼；（人）咆哮

consuming [kənˈsjuːmɪŋ] *adj.* so strong or important that it takes up all your time and energy 强烈的；重要的；令人着迷的

downpour [ˈdaʊnpɔː(r)] *n.* a sudden and unexpected heavy fall of rain 倾盆大雨；暴雨；骤雨

agency [ˈeɪdʒənsi] *n.* a business or an organization that provides a particular service especially on behalf of other businesses or organizations 服务机构；（尤指）代理机构，经销机构

shroud [ʃraʊd] *v.* to cover or hide something 覆盖；隐藏；遮蔽

span [spæn] *v.* to last all through a period of time or to cover the whole of it 持续；贯穿

untangle [ˌʌnˈtæŋgl] *v.* to undo string, hair, wire, etc., that has become twisted or has knots in it 解开，松开（结子等）

scandalous [ˈskændələs] *adj.* shocking and unacceptable 可耻的；不可原谅的

specifics [spəˈsɪfɪks] *n.* the details of a subject that you need to think about or discuss 详情；细节

garner [ˈgɑːnə(r)] *v.* to obtain or collect something such as information, support, etc. 获得，得到，收集（信息、支持等）

omniscient [ɒmˈnɪsiənt] *adj.* knowing everything 无所不知的；全知全能的；博闻广识的

unleash [ʌnˈliːʃ] *v.* to suddenly let a strong force, emotion, etc., be felt or have an effect 发泄；突然释放；使爆发

whim [wɪm] *n.* a sudden wish to do or have something, especially when it is something unusual or unnecessary 心血来潮；一时的兴致；突发的奇想

painstakingly [ˈpeɪnzteɪkɪŋli] *adv.* in a fastidious and painstaking manner 精心地，刻苦地

infectious [ɪnˈfekʃəs] *adj.* an infectious disease can be passed easily from one person to another, especially through the air they breathe 传染性的，感染的（尤指通过呼吸）

defy [dɪˈfaɪ] *v.* to be impossible or almost impossible to believe, explain, describe, etc. 不可能，无法（相信、解释、描绘等）

empathetic [ˌempəˈθetɪk] *adj.* showing empathy or ready comprehension of others' states 移情的；有同感的；能产生共鸣的

Video 4

dignify [ˈdɪɡnɪfaɪ] *v.* to make somebody/something seem impressive 使有尊严；使崇高；使显贵；使增辉

weaving [ˈwiːvɪŋ] （weave 的现在分词）to put facts, events, details, etc., together to make a story or a closely connected whole （把……）编成，编纂成，编造（故事等）

prolific [prəˈlɪfɪk] *adj.* producing many works, etc. 多产的；创作丰富的

the Diaspora [daɪˈæspərə] *n.* the movement of the Jews leaving their own country to live and work in other countries （犹太人的）大流散

stand-in [ˈstænd ɪn] *n.* a person who does somebody's job for a short time when they are not available 代行职务者

tribute [ˈtrɪbjuːt] *n.* an act, a statement or a gift that is intended to show your respect or admiration, especially for a dead person （尤指对死者的）致敬，颂词；悼念；致哀；吊唁礼物

Chapter 15   Asian American Literature

Part I   Warm-up

Discuss the following questions in pairs or groups.

1. Can you name some Asian American authors?
2. Who is your favorite Asian American writer? Why?
3. Do you believe reading Asian American literature is a good way for westerners to know about Asia? Why?
4. How does Asian American literature contribute to the broader field of American literature?

Part II   Celeste Ng and Maxine Hong Kingston answer your questions about *The Woman Warrior*

Watch the video. Write *T* for true or *F* for false for each statement.

1. (   ) Taboos, the adventures, the lives of people who had to keep their lives secret are told in the bestselling novel *Little Fires Everywhere*.

2. (   ) Maxine Hong Kingston created a new way of storytelling, so that people can't tell whether she is writing fiction or nonfiction.

3. (   ) According to Celeste Ng, reading *The Woman Warrior* sort of made clear to her things about her parents' lives.

4. (   ) *Little Fires Everywhere* is Celeste Ng's first book published.

5. (   ) Celeste Ng believes it's the writer's impulse that, when there is a secret, there is a power.

6. (   ) Jeffrey Brown thinks that there is the power of influence between the two authors.

7. (   ) Maxine Hong Kingston had been to China and collected all the information before she wrote her stories.

8. (   ) Celeste Ng worked hard to mentor so that the voice of America can be heard.

9. (   ) Celeste Ng thinks that there is more space for writers with Asian heritage to talk about their particular ethnicity.

10. (   ) Maxine Hong Kingston feels that Asian-American, Pacific Islander, literature

did not exist as part of American literature 40 years ago.

Part Ⅲ   Philosophies of Self: East-West Distinctions

Watch the video and answer the following questions.
1. How do people describe "self" in the United States?
2. What kind of "self" do people have in Asia?
3. How do people define and measure "difference" in the East?
4. Why do people show sign of anxiety in making choices in the West?
5. How are people in the East viewed in the eyes of westerners?
6. What views are held by people from the West and the East respectively with regards to taking care of the elderly?

Watch the video again and fill in the blanks.

In the United States, generally we have a mode of self where the self is kind of like an avocado. We have a 1) _____ inside of us. The pit is ourselves, our 2) _____, our identity. It is the thing to which we must above all be true. And, of course, very importantly we see that pit as 3) _____. So that everything we do we want to show, to 4) _____ that pit. We like that self and we want it to be unique.

In Asia, people frequently have a "flexi-self". So it's a different kind of self. It is a self that's oriented more to 5) _____ than to rights for instance. And very importantly, it does not have a cultural 6) _____ to be different and to be unique. People in the East are not all 7) _____. So if you looked at my family, believe me, every single person is very, very different. That is true, of course, throughout Asia.

The difference is not, "How different are we from each other?" The difference is, "How much 8) _____ do we attach to that difference?" In other words, do we think it's very important to differentiate ourselves from others? So if you're asking, "Are they individuals?" Of course they're individuals. You know, are they different? Of course they're different. But of course for them it's like, "Well of course I'm different. Why would I make a big deal about that?" And they think it is very 9) _____ that in the West that we feel that we must differentiate ourselves from others 10) _____.

So one of the ways that we do that of course is through 11) _____, you know. Choice in the West is, very important. Everyone is always making choices. And honestly a lot of those choices make us a little 12) _____. If you do a study where

Chapter 15　Asian American Literature

you are just sitting in an empty room and you're making a choice and you come from a more 13) _____ culture, you actually show signs of a little anxiety. Every little choice that you make—even in private, because it's defining of who you are—is a little 14) _____. They feel like they just choose. In other words, when they make those choices, it doesn't have this 15) _____.

And that's one of the reasons they feel that actually we are less free than they are. So they think that we are the ones who are kind of in this prison where, you know, like I say every moment we must 16) _____ ourselves. Well isn't that awful? And of course the way that we live, we feel that we want to be 17) _____ electing to live the way that we live, right?

And so, even when we're doing things like taking care of the elderly, for example, we want to feel that it's an 18) _____ of our great love and the nature of our being to be able to take care of the elderly. The other day I was having dinner with somebody and he said, "You know, I just don't feel that, and it's just very, very hard." So somebody from a more flexi-self or 19) _____ culture would say, "It's just your duty." And so for them it's like, you know, they help their elderly parents, they just go take care of their elderly parents because that's their duty. For them this is really 20) _____. You just go do it and you don't expect that to be an expression of yourself. It's just what people do. From their point of view, we have made things very hard for ourselves to demand that everything should be an expression of our inner nature.

Part Ⅳ　Why Should You Read *The Joy Luck Club* by Amy Tan

Watch the video and choose the best answer for the following questions.

1. What game serves as both the center of *The Joy Luck Club* and a model for the novel's structure?
　　A. Ping-pong.　　B. Mahjong.　　C. Tennis.　　D. Chess.

2. Who are the main characters of *The Joy Luck Club*?
　A. Four Chinese immigrant mothers and their American-born daughters.
　B. Four Chinese immigrant fathers and their American-born sons.
　C. Four friends who grew up in San Francisco's Chinatown.
　D. Four members of a Chinese-American family.

3. In what corner did Jing-Mei's mother, and now Jing-Mei, sit at the mahjong table?
　　A. North.　　B. South.　　C. West.　　D. East.

4. What year was *The Joy Luck Club* published?
   A. 1945.　　　B. 1949.　　　C. 1989.　　　D. 2001.
5. What is the central theme of the novel?
   A. The role of entertainment in different cultures.
   B. The need to be understood.
   C. The power of storytelling.
   D. The fear of war.

Watch the video again and answer the following questions.
1. What is the significance of the mahjong table gathering in *The Joy Luck Club*?
2. How is the structure of *The Joy Luck Club* influenced by the game of mahjong?
3. Why does Jing-Mei struggle to fill her mother's place in *The Joy Luck Club*?
4. Why do the mothers in the novel feel divided from their daughters?

Part V　Projects and Presentations

Choose one of the following projects, or design one of your own closely related to the theme of the unit. Finish the project by giving a presentation in class and leading a discussion afterwards.

1. According to Gish Jen, one major East-West culture gap lies in how people define "self", be it a "flexi-self" in the East or a unique "self" in the West. Do you agree with her on the two end points or want to provide a different viewpoint? How would you define your "self"? Since we are living in a globalized society, do people still care about understanding this divide? Work in groups and have a discussion. Each group summarize the viewpoints of members and report your discussion results in class.

2. Celeste Ng talked about the great influence of the novel *The Woman Warrior*, written by Maxine Hong Kingston, in her own writing of a bestselling novel *Little Fires Everywhere*, saying that the former has provided her with a reading experience that she never had. Share one novel that has refreshed you in the same way, and give a brief talk titled "I Recommend This Book".

3. Asian-American, Pacific Islander literature, according to Maxine Hong Kingston, came into existence just 40 years ago. Novels like *The Joy Luck Club* by Amy Tan, *Little Fires Everywhere* by Celeste Ng, became instant hits when they were first published, and were later adapted into movies and television series in the US. Have a group discussion on the question "Why do Asian American novels get so popular in the US?"

Chapter 15　Asian American Literature

Part VI　Vocabulary and Notes

Video 1

Gish Jen 任碧莲（1955 —　），华裔第二代美国作家，其著作《典型美国人》(*Typical American*) 在 1991 年已成为英美文学专业主要的论文题目之一

pit [pɪt] *n.* the hare seed (in fruit) 核

orient [ˈɔːrient] *v.* [usually passive] (to/towards somebody/something) to direct somebody/something towards something 朝向；面对

mandate [ˈmændeɪt] *n.* given the authority to do something 授权

individualistic [ˌɪndɪˌvɪdʒuəˈlɪstɪk] *adj.* like to think and do things in one's own way, rather than imitating other people 个人主义的；利己主义的

loaded [ˈləʊdɪd] *adj.* having more meaning than you realize at first and intended to make you think in a particular way 意味深长的；含蓄的

overlay [ˌəʊvəˈleɪ] *n.* a thing that is laid on top of or covers something else 覆盖物

elect [ɪˈlekt] *v.* (formal) to choose to do something 选择，决定（做某事）

extension [ɪkˈstenʃn] *n.* (of something) the act of increasing the area of activity, group of people, etc., that is affected by something 扩大；延伸

liberate [ˈlɪbəreɪt] *v.* ~ somebody (from something) to free somebody from something that restricts their enjoyment of life 使自由；使摆脱约束（或限制）

Video 2

Maxine Hong Kingston 汤婷婷（1940 —　），美籍华裔女作家，成名作是回忆录式小说《女勇士》(*The Woman Warrior: Memoirs of a Girlhood Among Ghosts*, 1976)，融入了中国的传统故事，获评美国《现代》周刊 20 世纪 70 年代最佳作品奖

Celeste Ng 伍绮诗（1980 —　），美籍华裔女作家，处女作为《无声告白》(*Everything I Never Told You*, 2014)，获美国亚马逊年度最佳图书第一名

jolt [dʒəʊlt] *v.* to move or to make somebody/something move suddenly and roughly （使）震动，摇动，颠簸

mythology [mɪˈθɒlədʒi] *n.* ancient myths in general; the ancient myths of a particular culture, society, etc. （统称）神话；某文化（或社会等）的神话

memoir [ˈmemwɑː(r)] *n.* an account written by somebody, especially somebody famous, about their life and experiences （尤指名人的）回忆录；自传

deport [dɪˈpɔːt] *v.* to force somebody to leave a country, usually because they have broken the law or because they have no legal right to be there 把（违法者或无合法居留

权的人）驱逐出境，递解出境

opaque [əʊˈpeɪk] *adj.* (of speech or writing) difficult to understand; not clear（说话或写作）难懂；模糊；隐晦；不清楚

filter [ˈfɪltə(r)] *v.* (of information, news, etc.) to slowly become known（信息、新闻等）慢慢传开；走漏

mentor [ˈmentɔː(r)] *v.* serve as a teacher or trusted counselor 给予培训

heritage [ˈherɪtɪdʒ] *n.* the history, traditions and qualities that a country or society has had for many years and that are considered an important part of its character 遗产（指国家或社会长期形成的历史、传统和特色）

ethnicity [eθˈnɪsəti] *n.* the fact of belonging to a particular race 种族渊源；种族特点

syllabus [ˈsɪləbəs] *n.* a list of the topics, books, etc., that students should study in a particular subject at school or college 教学大纲

Video 3

Amy Tan 谭恩美（1952— ），美国华裔女作家，她的作品多以表现母女关系和讲述美国华人经历为主。她的小说《喜福会》（1989）在 1993 年被导演王颖改编为电影

Joy Luck Club 《喜福会》，一部由美籍华裔作家谭恩美所著的小说，讲述了四位华裔母亲和她们的美籍华裔女儿之间的故事

wonton [ˌwɒnˈtɒn] *n.* (from Chinese) a small piece of food wrapped in dough, often served in Chinese soup or as dim sum 馄饨

vignette [vɪnˈjet] *n.* a short piece of writing or acting that clearly shows what a particular person, situation, etc., is like（清晰展示人物特征、局势等的）短文，片段，小品

alternately [ɔːlˈtɜːnətli] *adv.* in a way that involves two things happening or existing one after the other repeatedly 交替地；轮流地

matriarch [ˈmeɪtriɑːk] *n.* a woman who is the head of a family or social group 女家长；女族长

dire [ˈdaɪə(r)] *adj.* (formal) very serious 极其严重的；危急的

weigh down to make a person feel worried and unhappy because of problems, responsibilities, and duties 使（某人）焦虑，使负荷太重

interrogation [ɪnˌterəˈgeɪʃn] *n.* a process of asking someone a lot of questions for a long time in order to get information, sometimes by threatening or using violence 审问，质问

captivate [ˈkæptɪveɪt] *v.* to keep somebody's attention by being interesting, attractive, etc. 迷住；使着迷

Chapter 16　Native American Literature

Part Ⅰ　Warm-up

Discuss the following questions in pairs or groups.
1. Can you name some Native American writers and their representative works?
2. What is the significance of the oral tradition in Native American literature?
3. How does Native American literature often portray the relationship between humans and the natural world?
4. How has contemporary Native American literature evolved compared to traditional forms?

Part Ⅱ　Samson Occom: The Father of Native American Literature

Watch the video and choose the best answer for the following questions.
1. When was Samson Occom born?
A. 1713.　　　B. 1723.　　　C. 1772.　　　D. 1792.
2. What is Samson Occom known as?
A. Father of Native American rights.
B. Father of Native American literature.
C. Father of the Great Awakening.
D. Father of Native American education.
3. What movement did the Great Awakening counter?
A. Age of Enlightenment.
B. Industrial Revolution.
C. Renaissance.
D. Scientific Revolution.
4. Where did Samson Occom teach Native Americans and minister to them?
A. New Hampshire.
B. New Jersey.
C. Pennsylvania.

D. Long Island.

5. What did Samson Occom oppose due to his concern for Native American rights?
A. Slavery.
B. Alcohol consumption.
C. European colonization.
D. Religious conversion.

6. What was the title of the first book published in English by a Native American?
A. *Sinners in the Hands of an Angry God.*
B. *The Diary of Samson Occom.*
C. *Sermon Preached at Execution of Moses Paul.*
D. *The Great Awakening.*

7. What caused Samson Occom to lose support from his denomination?
A. His heavy drinking habits.
B. His opposition to slavery.
C. His involvement in politics.
D. His relocation to Wisconsin.

8. What is Samson Occom's significance in Native American literature?
A. He wrote the first Native American novel.
B. He introduced Native American folklore to the world.
C. He fought for Native American language preservation.
D. He is considered the father of Native American literature.

Part III   New Erdrich Novel Deals with Crime and Jurisdiction

Watch the video and answer the following questions.

1. What is the title of Louise Erdrich's novel that has been nominated for a National Book Award?
2. Where is the story set in *The Round House*?
3. What issue does Louise Erdrich explore in her novel?
4. What is the jurisdictional problem discussed in the book?
5. What is *The Violence Against Women Reauthorization Act*?
6. Who is the main character in *The Round House*?
7. Why did Louise Erdrich choose to focus the novel on Joe's voice?
8. What does the Round House symbolize in Native American culture?

Chapter 16 Native American Literature

Part Ⅳ   Leslie Marmon Silko: How to Connect to Nature, Even in the City

Watch the video. Write *T* for true or *F* for false for each statement.

1. (   ) The author wrote *The Turquoise Ledge* to preserve and document different ways of living from her childhood.
2. (   ) The landscapes have not changed much thanks to the establishment of reservations.
3. (   ) The destruction of natural elements is driven by a lack of understanding, rather than greed.
4. (   ) Developing a better appreciation for nature in urban environments requires an open heart and openness to other beings.
5. (   ) The author's relationship with the land and animals is primarily based on fear and avoidance.
6. (   ) The author wrote about her relationship with animals to highlight the need for their protection.
7. (   ) Tucson is a welcoming and integrated city with equal opportunities for all.
8. (   ) The author believes that wild creatures can provide sustenance and hope to humans.

The following passage is a summary of the interview. Watch the video again and select one word for each blank from a list of choices given in the word bank following the passage. Do not use any of the words in the bank more than once.

In this interview, the author discusses the inspiration behind writing *The Turquoise Ledge* and the urgency to document the disappearing ways of life from her childhood. She expresses 1) _____ about the rapid changes in the world and the need to preserve the knowledge of different ways of living. The author emphasizes that 2) _____ is driving the shocking and heartbreaking transformations in the landscapes she knows. She 3) _____ the destruction of centuries-old saguaro cactuses and foothill palomero days due to poorly built houses driven by profit.

To develop a better appreciation for nature, the author suggests cultivating an open heart and connecting with other beings, even in 4) _____ environments. By finding moments of solitude and observing the natural world, one can establish a connection and understand the consciousness shared with other living beings.

The author highlights her relationship with the land and animals, particularly in Tucson. She describes the city as lonely and 5) _____, with newcomers often

139

feeling unwelcome. However, she found friendship and affection from wild animals like rattlesnakes, pack rats, bees, and hummingbirds. These creatures became her longest friends, and she wanted to protect their lives and 6) _____ from destruction.

In writing *The Turquoise Ledge*, the author aimed to convey the depth of friendship and connection she received from wild animals. She wanted to raise 7) _____ about the importance of 8) _____ their lives and emphasize their ability to provide sustenance and hope when human connections fail.

Overall, the interview 9) _____ the author's motivation to capture and share the disappearing ways of life, the 10) _____ impact of greed on landscapes, the possibility of connecting with nature in any environment, and the profound relationship between the author and the land and its creatures.

approaches	awareness	concern	destructive	environmental
establishment	greed	habitats	interrogation	laments
preserving	segregated	rural	underscores	urban

Part V Projects and Presentations

Choose one of the following projects, or design one of your own closely related to the theme of the unit. Finish the project by giving a presentation in class and leading a discussion afterwards.

1. Choose a Native American literary work to read. After the reading, engage in a group discussion, sharing your insights, interpretations, and reflections on the chosen work. Explore the significance of the work within the context of Native American literature and its broader social and cultural implications.

2. Native American tribes or cultural groups (e.g. Navajo, Cherokee, Lakota) are known for their rich oral tradition. Do some research and prepare a presentation on the oral tradition within a tribe or cultural group. Explore the significance of storytelling, myths, legends, and oral history in their culture, as well as the role of oral tradition in preserving and passing down cultural knowledge.

3. The last video touches upon the motif of land and nature in Native American literature. Give a presentation on the portrayal of land and nature in a literary work or an author's body of work. Share your findings, incorporating excerpts from the literary work,

visual aids, and examples of how Native American literature emphasizes the importance of respecting and preserving the natural world.

Part VI Vocabulary and Notes

Video 1

reverend [ˈrevərənd] *adj.* [只用于名词前]（abbr. Rev.）the title of a member of the clergy that is also sometimes used to talk to or about one（尊称神职人员）尊敬的，可敬的

Presbyterian [ˌprezbɪˈtɪəriən] *n.* a member of a branch of the Christian Protestant Church that is the national church of Scotland and one of the largest churches in the US. It is governed by elders who are all equal in rank. 长老派成员（长老会为苏格兰国教及美国最大教会之一）

quota [ˈkwəʊtə] *n.* an amount of something that somebody expects or needs to have or achieve 定量；定额；指标

Mohegan [məʊˈhiːɡən] *n.*（原住康涅狄格州的印第安人）莫希干族人

convert [kənˈvɜːt] *n.* a person who has changed their religion, beliefs or opinions 改变宗教（或信仰、观点）的人；皈依者

the Great Awakening（美国）大复苏；大觉醒；十三州大悔悟

revitalization [ˌriːˌvaɪtəlaɪˈzeɪʃn] *n.* the state or process of making something stronger, more active or more healthy 更强壮；恢复生机（或健康）

deliverance [dɪˈlɪvərəns] *n.* (from something)（formal) the state of being rescued from danger, evil or pain 解救；拯救；解脱

denomination [dɪˌnɒmɪˈneɪʃn] *n.* a branch of the Christian Church（基督教）教派，宗派

coalition [ˌkəʊəˈlɪʃn] *n.* a group formed by people from several different groups, especially political ones, agreeing to work together for a particular purpose（尤指多个政治团体的）联合体，联盟

Video 2

jurisdiction [ˌdʒʊərɪsˈdɪkʃn] *n.* (over somebody/something) (of somebody/something) (to do something) the authority that an official organization has to make legal decisions about somebody/something 司法权；审判权；管辖权

diatribe [ˈdaɪətraɪb] *n.* (against somebody/something) (formal) a long and angry speech or piece of writing attacking and criticizing somebody/something（无休止

的）指责；（长篇）抨击，谴责

underpinning [ˌʌndəˈpɪnɪŋ] *n.* (formal) the act of supporting or forming the basis of an argument, a claim, etc. 加强，巩固，构成（……的基础等）

sovereignty [ˈsɒvrənti] *n.* complete power to govern a country or a place 主权；最高统治权；最高权威

nonfiction [nɒnˈfikʃn] *n.* the writing that gives information or describes real events, rather than telling a story 纪实文学

unravel [ʌnˈrævl] *v.* to explain something that is difficult to understand or is mysterious; to become clearer or easier to understand 阐释；说明；澄清；变得清楚易懂

kiva [ˈkiːvə] *n.* a Pueblo Indian ceremonial structure that is usually round and partly underground 大地穴，地下礼堂 [普韦布洛印第安人（美国西部和墨西哥等地印第安人）用于宗教活动的地下或半地下建筑]

tepee [ˈtiːpiː] *n.* a type of tall tent shaped like a cone, used by Native Americans in the past（美洲印第安人旧时使用的）圆锥形帐篷

Video 3

mortgage [ˈmɔːɡɪdʒ] *n.* (also informal home loan) a legal agreement by which a bank or similar organization lends you money to buy a house, etc., and you pay the money back over a particular number of years; the sum of money that you borrow 按揭（由银行等提供房产抵押借款）；按揭贷款

transient [ˈtrænziənt] *adj.* staying or working in a place for only a short time, before moving on 暂住的；过往的；临时的

rattlesnake [ˈrætlsneɪk] *n.* a poisonous American snake that makes a noise like a rattle with its tail when it is angry or afraid 响尾蛇（产于美洲）

hummingbird [ˈhʌmɪŋbɜːd] *n.* a small brightly coloured bird that lives in warm countries and that can stay in one place in the air by beating its wings very fast, making a continuous low sound (= a humming sound) 蜂鸟（快速扇动翅膀发出声音，能原位停留）

Key to Exercises and Transcripts

Chapter 1

Appendix 1 Key to Exercises

Part I Warm-up

Discuss the following questions in pairs or groups.

1. Washington Irving played a significant role in the development of American literature during the early 19th century. He was one of the first American writers to achieve international acclaim, gaining recognition in both Europe and the United States. Irving's works, such as *Rip Van Winkle* and *The Legend of Sleepy Hollow*, blended elements of European folklore and American settings, creating a distinctive American literary voice. He also helped to establish a sense of national identity in American literature by drawing on American history and folklore. Irving's storytelling style, characterized by wit, humor, and vivid descriptions, influenced subsequent generations of American writers and contributed to the emergence of a distinct American literary tradition.

2. James Fenimore Cooper made a significant contribution to the development of the historical novel genre through his works, particularly his "Leatherstocking Tales" series. These novels blended historical events with fictional narratives, creating a vivid depiction of early American history. Cooper's meticulous research and attention to historical detail, combined with his storytelling skills, helped popularize the historical novel genre in the United States. His novels, including *The Last of the Mohicans*, introduced readers to the rich historical past of the American frontier and influenced subsequent historical novelists by demonstrating the potential of using history as a backdrop for compelling storytelling.

3. American Transcendentalist literature is characterized by several key characteristics. First, it emphasizes the inherent goodness of both nature and humanity, promoting the belief in the inherent divinity of the individual and the interconnectedness of all things. Second, Transcendentalist literature often explores the concept of intuition and the idea that individuals can access higher truths through introspection and self-reliance. Third, it rejects societal conventions and promotes nonconformity, encouraging individuals to follow their own beliefs and values. Finally, Transcendentalist literature often incorporates vivid descriptions of nature and employs poetic language to convey spiritual and philosophical ideas.

4. Several prominent American writers were associated with the Transcendentalist movement. Ralph Waldo Emerson, often considered the leading figure of Transcendentalism, wrote essays and delivered lectures that promote self-reliance, individualism, and the importance of nature. Henry David Thoreau,

another influential Transcendentalist writer, is known for his book *Walden*, which documents his experiences living in solitude in nature and emphasizes simplicity and self-sufficiency. Margaret Fuller, an important female Transcendentalist, advocated for women's rights and wrote influential works on women's rights and feminism. These writers, among others, contributed to the development of Transcendentalist literature by expressing its core ideas and inspiring future generations of writers and thinkers.

Part II   Tracing the Haunting Roots of *The Legend of Sleepy Hollow*

Watch the video. Write *T* for true or *F* for false for each statement.

1. F   2. T   3. F   4. F   5. T   6. T   7. F   8. F   9. F   10. T

答案解析：

1. 不是 by Will Rogers，而是 by Washington Irving。

3. 如今大多数人不知道它在那里。

4. 她不是 an expert on the horseman，而是 on the man who first told of the horseman, Washington Irving。

7. 任何人不得进入。

8. 这个观点不正确。

9. 原文为 "The cemetery even features a bridge, not unlike one that figures prominently in the legend."。

Part III   James Fenimore Cooper

Watch the video and answer the following questions.

1. It was used to describe the inherent privilege held by Americans to explore and lay claims to the western frontier.

2. It was a remarkably desirable place, despite the obvious dangers it presented.

3. Through the works of James Fenimore Cooper.

4. His influence on future novelists combined with his work in shaping the American identity.

5. It was characterized by intense nationalism and a common sense of pride in the civic fledgling United States.

6. To prove that even after his death, Cooper's impact is still felt.

Watch the video again and fill in the blanks.

1) patriot   2) acclaim   3) established
4) romance   5) nationalistic   6) Incidentally
7) possession   8) mark   9) chronicling
10) portrayed   11) resourceful   12) individualists
13) introduced   14) embodied   15) populate
16) impact   17) democratic   18) landslide
19) likability   20) altering

Part IV   Ralph Waldo Emerson

Watch the video and answer the following questions.

1. He fundamentally changed the way that America viewed its cultural and artistic possibilities.

2. America's intellectual declaration of independence.

3. A remarkable aunt of Emerson's, Mary Moody Emerson, strongly influenced him. She, through self-taught, had read everything from Shakespeare to the romantics and had formed a unique religious perspective based on piety, nature, and literature that would resonate powerfully in the life and work of her nephew.

4. The first was that he went to the famous Jardin des Plantes and had an epiphany there. The second was that he met the English romantic poets Samuel Taylor Coleridge and William Wordsworth, and found them rather ordinary, dry and conservative men.

5. Nature is in us, a part of us, and not just its higher forms, but in all its grotesquery and wildness.

6. The insight that he drew was that if great men could be so ordinary, why ordinary men could not be great?

7. The two ideas were that man and nature are one and that everyone can recognize that they are a uniquely significant human being.

8. The importance of American originality.

9. America needed to stop looking back to its European heritage, and start looking at itself. No past moment was more important than the present moment; no tradition was more important than novelty; no generation was better than the current generation. Everything that matters is here now, insisted Emerson, and that here was America.

10. Because they were all too busy being what they were supposed to be.

11. History is an impertinence and an injury, we have not chosen our religion but society has chosen for us, and society everywhere is in conspiracy against the manhood of every one of its members.

12. The integrity of our own mind.

13. It's the surrender to the force that Emerson recognized back in the Jardin des Plantes, an obedience to nature itself.

14. God.

15. A pantheist is someone who believes that God exists in every part of creation, from the smallest grain of sand to the stars, but also crucially that the divine spark is in each of us.

16. It is the sublime, great mountains, rushing torrents and dark forests.

17. An essential connection between nature, God and man.

18. The emphasis on the value of being ordinary.

19. Because for Emerson, the Transcendentalist God is everywhere, and it's the poet's job to reveal this.

20. They all looked around and wrote about what they saw and how they lived, transforming the everyday into a vital symbol of something higher and more elusive.

Part V Henry David Thoreau

Watch the video and answer the following questions.

1. He was known for his transcendentalism and abolitionism.

2. Four.

3. Yes.

4. Ralph Waldo Emerson.

5. Individual and nature.

6. He should on above materialistic needs as much as possible and focus on the spiritual aspects of life.

7. Abolitionism was a movement during the 1830s up until 1865, when the Civil War ended. It advocated for the abolishment of slavery.

Watch the video again and fill in the blanks.

1) transcendental	2) consisted	3) discontinued
4) simplicity	5) accounts	6) luxuriously
7) personal	8) slavery	9) mentored
10) evils	11) passage	12) nonviolent
13) justifies	14) disregarding	15) approve
16) rebel	17) exposed	18) challenge

Appendix 2　Transcripts

Part II　Tracing the Haunting Roots of *The Legend of Sleepy Hollow*

The Legend of Sleepy Hollow was popular enough nearly a hundred years ago for one of Hollywood's biggest stars at the time, Will Rogers, took a stab at bringing the ghost story to the big screen. It was first published 200 years ago by Washington Irving, considered by many to be the father of the American short story. *Sleepy Hollow* may be America's all-time great ghost story, and two centuries later is still linked forever to Halloween. Today we visit the history of this classic tale in the spot where it all began.

Most people passing by these days don't even know it's there. But 25 miles north of New York City, in a place overlooking the Hudson river, the legend of the headless horseman took off.

"I can't think of a more iconic Halloween character than the headless horseman."

"He really is the one. He's kind of the original American ghost story and he's our arch villain."

Elizabeth Bradley is an author, an expert on the man who first told of the horseman 200 years ago, Washington Irving.

"He wrote here?"

"He did, and he wrote in that room right there. That was his study room."

We spoke to Bradley at Irving's famed sunny side estate.

"The stories he wrote were witty, mischievous, anarchic, and they have really formed the foundation for so much of of American literature."

"Mischievous is a good word for it."

"Definitely, definitely."

Set shortly after the American Revolution, Irving's *The Legend of Sleepy Hollow* unspools the story of Ichabod Crane, an oddball outsider who arrives in town and pursues a beautiful young woman, Katrina Van Tassel. He is then himself pursued by a local phantom known as the headless horseman. As the legend goes, the horseman was a Hessian soldier who lost his head to a cannonball while fighting for the

British. He was buried but it said he rises from his grave every night in search of his missing skull. The original tale, just 24 pages long, seems to grow more famous each year.

"*The Legend of Sleepy Hollow* was popular when it was first published, but it was not the iconic story that we know it today. Nobody had heard of the headless horseman. He... the headless horseman was Irving's really to invent in the form in which it took in that story."

The story has spawned countless adaptations, most notably Disney's 1949 classic *The Adventures of Ichabod and Mr. Toad...* and the 1999 Tim Burton film *Sleepy Hollow* starring Johnny Depp.

"When people revisit *The Legend of Sleepy Hollow* today, what should they think?"

"I think they should take the time to appreciate the imagery and the way in which it's inspired, all of the adaptations. There is something about the mystery and the way in which Irving describes the landscape as being one of contagion that I think really describes our own obsession with Halloween today."

"That contagion takes on an even more eerie relevance these days. Guess what else was happening a little more than 200 years ago?"

"Washington Irving fled from a pandemic?"

"He did, he did. He came to this region first as a teenager and the reason he did so is because New York was experiencing an epidemic of yellow fever."

"So people were trying to get out of a major city into the suburbs."

"Very much as they are today."

"Irving's sunny side is still open to visitors. But because of our current pandemic, no one is allowed inside or near his writing desk, and the bedroom where he died in 1859 have been preserved. People of all ages come to hear the stories about the legend and its author whose penchant for mischief is on full display."

"1656 is just a date that Irving put up for the fun of it. This is a little touch of the ways in which Irving liked to play with ideas of authenticity, with the notion of history being fixed."

"So people walk by here and say 1656 and like what that mean."

"They think that the house, as we see it today, must have all been built in 1656, and I think Irving would have loved that."

"Which is not true at all."

"It's not true, otherwise, there would have been a very small farmhouse here."

"Not far away from the house, the graveyard at the old Dutch Church where the horseman is said to roam is also a tourist attraction today."

"So he just hangs around here."

"That is what they say. We can come back after dark."

"Irving is buried in the adjacent Sleepy Hollow Cemetery."

"Part of what makes this region feel so charmed and possibly haunted is that not only is his home here, but his gravesite is here, and they're both accessible to anyone who wants to come and see them."

"The cemetery even features a bridge, not unlike one that figures prominently in the legend."

"People know it as the horsemen."

"They know it. They insist this must be the bridge. You know, at the base of this bridge is where they were meant to have found a shattered pumpkin, and the saddle of the horse nearby."

"At least on the pages of Irving's story."

"What's your favorite version of the story?"

"I'd say Irving's, because there's so much magic in it, and there are so many details and mysteries to be mined, and there's a lot of comedy too that people tend to lose sight of."

"But the ending in Irving's version remains nebulous."

"Yes, it's purposefully vague, I think, and that's part of Irving's genius."

"That means that the headless horseman then could still be."

"Oh yes."

"Out here."

"Absolutely, he is ageless, so yeah, just you know, don't look behind you."

"Shout out to Seth Fox, his first producer piece there. He did it, he did a great job. A couple of other notes: North Tarrytown actually renamed itself Sleepy Hollow 25 years ago to capitalize on the story's fame which is interesting, and the interesting thing about the book and the story in general, the first 24 pages, is so pliable that there's a version you can find for kids and adults. I mean Tim Burton's *Sleepy Hollow* is not for kids."

"My favorite, I just love Tim Burton's version."

"It's a very good movie, but not for kids. *Ichabod and Mr. Toad* is for kids."

"Totally for kids."

"Right."

Part Ⅲ James Fenimore Cooper

In 1845, journalist John O'Sullivan used the term "Manifest Destiny" to describe the inherent privilege had by Americans to explore and lay claims to the western frontier. Well, the validity of this belief is somewhat questionable. It also exposes a rather curious reality about the national perception of the West in the mid-1800s. As evidenced in O'sullivan's remarks, the frontier was a remarkably desirable place, despite the obvious dangers it presented. The vast majority of Americans were quite taken by it. However, the West had not been transformed into this romantic idyll overnight. It had been rendered so through the work of James Fenimore Cooper. Cooper is widely credited with inventing the Great American Novel, and his influence on future novelists combined with his works in shaping the American identity secure him a place in the American Public University System (APUS) history Hall of Fame. James Fenimore Cooper's legacy began following the war in 1812, often referred to as the era of good feelings. This time period was characterized by intense nationalism and a common sense of civilian pride in fledgling United States. However, the country had yet to find a truly representative set of values to define itself.

Cooper's debut novel *The Spy*, published in 1821, told the story of a heroic patriot fighting alongside George Washington in the Revolutionary War. Being the first American novel to achieve worldwide acclaim, it catapulted Cooper onto the national scene and established him as the first American to write with a style distinctly different from that seen in Europe. The specific genre employed by Cooper was called historical romance and it dramatized the events surrounding the American Revolution in a pious nationalistic vein. This mirrored the national psyche at the time, and was therefore very well received by the public. Incidentally, the writing itself was highly praised, with Victor Hugo calling it the greatest writing of the century.

At last, the United States was in possession of a talented writer who is distinctly American, but Cooper had only just begun to make his mark on the national identity. In response to the fame he achieved by *The Spies* romanticism, Cooper began working on *The Pioneers*, a novel chronicling a family's journey into the New York State frontier. Utilizing a similar style to his previous work, Cooper's first leatherstocking tale portrayed frontiersman as American nobility and thus galvanized the American public. Showcasing the power of the common man in his natural environment, Cooper painted Americans as bold, daring and resourceful man, and his popularity ensured that they would be seen as such throughout the world. Moving farther and farther from its British roots, the United States had become a society of ardent individualists, and James Fenimore Cooper was at the center of it.

In addition, *The Pioneers* introduced the character Natty Bumpo, who quickly became the archetypal American hero. He embodied the qualities Cooper so staunchly advocated and other characters modeled of Bumbo continued to populate American literature. In Melville, Thoreau and Twain, Cooper's writings and characters are clearly emulated, leaving no doubt to his impact on American literature. Still, Cooper's influence didn't end with his writing. As the American identity became increasingly associated with democratic ideas, such as that of the common man, so too did American politics. In 1828, Cooper's message had become so popular in American society that Andrew Jackson, running on a platform of agrarian individualist democracy, won in a landslide. While it was Jackson's beliefs and likability that endeared him to voters, it was Cooper's romanticism of democratic ideals that made such popularity possible. Without Cooper, the American identity may have been vastly different, altering social and political structures for generations.

After living briefly as an expatriate in France as well as studying naval history in the United States, Cooper returned to writing in the genre he knew the best. In the 1840s, he wrote two more leatherstocking tales, including his masterpiece *The Last of the Mohicans*, thereby cementing his legacy as the champion of the great American novel. By the late 1840s, Cooper's career was winding down and his health had begun to fail as well. In 1851, Cooper died and was memorialized in an event attended by Daniel Webster, William Cullen Bryant, and Washington Irving among others.

Even after his death though, Cooper's impact is still felt. In the same year, Nathaniel Hawthorne published *The Scarlet Letter*, a novel that many hailed as a continuation of Cooper's established American identity. At the same time, Herman Melville published *Moby Dick*, a highly romanticized sea novel similar to those first made popular by Cooper. Even in the 20th century, novels such as *Gone with the Wind*, *The Grapes of Wrath* and *To Kill a Mockingbird*, owe their existence to the great American novel that Cooper made possible.

Ultimately, Cooper's impact is not measured in economic upheaval or shocking political turmoil. It isn't measured in radical protests or brutal military feats. It is measured in how American Society came to be defined in the early 1800s, and how in the span of a single lifetime one man altered the identity of a nation from one strictly European to something uniquely American. That man is James Fenimore Cooper, and for these accomplishments, he deserves your vote to the APUS History Hall of Fame. Thank you.

Part Ⅳ Ralph Waldo Emerson

Ralph Waldo Emerson is the father of American literature. In a series of strikingly original essays written in the mid-19th century, he fundamentally changed the way that America saw its cultural and artistic possibilities, and he enabled a separation from transatlantic literary traditions. We have listened too long, he wrote, to the courtly muses of Europe. Emerson's ejection of cultural traditions brought about what one contemporary called America's intellectual declaration of independence, and he established generational conflict and transformation as commanding ideas in American literature.

Emerson himself hardly seemed destined to fit a revolutionary mold. He was born in 1803, the son of a Boston preacher, and was descended from a line of New England ministers that went back to the bedrock of the 17th-century Puritanism. When his father died in 1811, his mother took in lorders to pay the rent. Still, she sent her son to Harvard in 1817, and then Harvard Divinity School to train for the priesthood in 1825. As a young man, Emerson was strongly influenced by a remarkable aunt of his, Mary Moody Emerson, who through self-education had read everything from Shakespeare to the romantics and had formed a unique religious perspective based on piety, nature, and literature that would resonate powerfully in the life and work of her nephew. So when Emerson was ordained in 1829, marrying the love of his life, Ellen Tucker, in the same year, he was already unsatisfied with the formal nature of New England religious orthodoxy. When Ellen died of tuberculosis just two years later, he resigned from the church and soon after embarked on a trip to Europe, leaving on Christmas Day in 1832.

Two crucial things happened to Emerson on his tour of Europe. In Paris, he went to the famous Jardin des Plantes, a botanical and zoological garden. There, he had an epiphany, writing in his journal that "I feel the centipede in me, the caiman, carp, eagle and fox; I am moved by strange sympathies; I say continually I will be a naturalist." Emerson's insight was that nature is in us, a part of us, and not just its higher forms, but in all its grotesqueries and wildness. The second thing that happened on the tour was that Emerson met the English romantic poets Samuel Taylor Coleridge and William Wordsworth, and found them rather ordinary, dry and conservative men. The insight that Emerson drew from this was that if great men could be so ordinary, why should not ordinary men be great? As he would write a few years later, meek young men grow up in libraries, believing it their duty to accept the views, which Cicero, Locke, Bacon have given; forgetful that Cicero, Locke, Bacon were only young men in libraries when they wrote these books. Emerson had found two ideas that would guide his life's work: that man and nature are one and that everyone can recognize that they are a uniquely significant human being.

On his return to America in 1833, Emerson became a professional lecturer, giving talks on natural history and literature in halls around New England. He remarried and had several children, presenting a solid bourgeois appearance to the world. But his inner life was full of turbulence and originality. In his 1836 essay *Nature*, Emerson outlined the germ of a new philosophy. A key element of this was the importance of American originality. In its opening lines, Emerson wrote:

Our age is retrospective. It builds the sepulchers of the fathers. It writes biographies, histories and criticisms. The foregoing generations beheld God and nature face to face; we see through their eyes. Why should we not also enjoy an original relation to the universe?

America needed to stop looking back to its European heritage, and start looking at itself. No past moment was more important than the present moment; no tradition was more important than novelty; no previous generation was better than the current generation. Everything that mattered is here now, Emerson insisted, and that here was America.

This was an extension of Emerson's ideas about the significance of the individual that came under the heading of what he called self-reliance. Everywhere Emerson looked, he saw people leading lives that were based on tradition, and that were limited by religious forms and social habits. No one could be themselves, Emerson thought, because they were all too busy being what they were supposed to be. Emerson wanted to get rid of each of these burdens, including the past, religion and social forms, so that each person could find out who they truly were. As he put it, history is an impertinence and an injury, our religion is what we have not chosen but society has chosen for us, and society everywhere is in conspiracy against the manhood of every one of its members. We must, he argued, live from within, trusting nothing but our own intuitions. For as he concluded, nothing is at last sacred but the integrity of your own mind. This leaves open a vital question: what is your nature once you have rid yourself of history, tradition and religion? What can be said is that it isn't necessarily self-indulgence, hedonism or narcissism. Rather it's the surrender to that force which Emerson recognized back in the Jardin des Plantes, an obedience to nature itself. By nature, Emerson seemed to mean the natural world, plants, animals, rocks and sky, but what he really meant was God. Emerson was a pantheist, that is someone who believed that God exists in every part of creation, from the smallest grain of sand to the stars, but also crucially that the divine spark is in each of us. In following ourselves, we are therefore not merely being fickle or selfish. We are rather releasing a divine will that history, society and organized religion normally hide from us. The individual, as Emerson writes, is a God in ruins. But we have it within us by casting off all custom to rebuild ourselves. Emerson makes this pantheist connection explicit in what are perhaps his most famous lines:

Crossing a bare common, in snow puddles, at twilight, under a clouded sky, without having in my thoughts any occurrence of special good fortune, I have enjoyed a perfect exhilaration. I am glad to the brink of fear... Standing on the bare ground, my head bathed by the blithe air, and uplifted into infinite space, all mean egotism vanishes. I become a transparent eyeball; I am nothing; I see all; the currents of the universal being circulate through me; I am part or particle of God.

In the romantic tradition on which Emerson draws, it is the sublime, great mountains, rushing torrents, dark forests which release the inner vision as we find ourselves in all of them. For Emerson, it's a perfectly dull walk across an ordinary common on a dark winter's evening that brings him to the brink of fear. Emerson's God is in the snow puddles too. Standing there on the common, he disappears, becoming nothing as the currents of God flow through him. What is left is just a transparent eyeball. Such transcendent moments are rare, but they reveal an essential connection between nature, God and man. They are one. They also give Emerson a proper sense of each individual's importance as a part of God. Transcendentalism became the name of the movement that grew up around Emerson at this time.

Another aspect of the epiphany that was to have a profound effect on American literature was the emphasis on the value of the ordinary. What Emerson put forward in essays like *The American Scholar* and *The Poet* was that the American everyday was a proper subject for literature. This was because for Emerson, the transcendentalist God is everywhere, and it's the poet's job to reveal this. There is no object, he wrote, so foul that intense light will not make it beautiful. Even the corpse has its own beauty, this coming from a man, who had opened his first wife's tomb a year after her death to take a look.

The great American writers who followed Emerson were liberated by his works, to look around and write about what they saw and how they lived, transforming the everyday into a vital symbol of something higher and more elusive. Henry David Thoreau's two years at Walden Pond became a book that showed the cosmos reflected in the depths of the waters of a mere pond. The poet Walt Whitman said, "I was simmering simmering simmering. Emerson brought me to a boil". Emily Dickinson heard a fly and could write of the other side of death. The novelist, Herman Melville, took a whaling voyage and made it an allegory of American imperialism and the defiance of nature. In the 20th century, the American critic Harold Bloom looked back at Emerson's originality and saw in it the origin of the strong tradition of American poets, from Robert Frost and Wallace Stevens to John Ashbery. Emerson's legacy to American literature and culture and indeed to the world was one of the ceaseless inventions and forward momentum. As he put it, I unsettle all things, no facts are to me sacred, none are profane. I simply experiment, an endless seeker, with no past at my back.

Part V Henry David Thoreau

Henry David Thoreau was an author, poet, journalist and teacher, who became known for his transcendental beliefs, and had worked as a dedicated abolitionist in the reform against slavery. He was born in Concord, Massachusetts, on July 12, 1817 to parents John Thoreau and Cynthia Dunbar Thoreau. John Thoreau worked as a small businessman and shopkeeper. Henry David Thoreau, being the third child, had two older siblings, Helen, the oldest and John Jr. He also had a younger sister, Sophia. In 1818, the family moved from Concord to Chelmsford and Boston, where they moved for John Thoreau's work purposes. In 1823, the Thoreau family moved back to Concord, Massachusetts. It was here that John Thoreau began operating a pencil factory that eventually brought the family to financial stability.

Growing up, Henry David Thoreau was sent to Concord Academy in 1828, where he impressed his teachers. After he graduated from the Academy, he attended Harvard in 1833. He studied Greek, Latin and German as well as courses in mathematics and mental, natural and intellectual philosophy. Partway through his education, Thoreau had to drop out of Harvard due to financial and health-related concerns. But he did go on to graduate in the middle ranks of his class from Harvard in 1837. After college, Thoreau and his brother opened a grammar school which unfortunately closed three years later due to John's illnesses. He then worked for his father and for Ralph Waldo Emerson, who Thoreau saw as a guide, father and friend. He spent the following years of his life as a part of nature, following his transcendental views, and he wrote essays in his spare time. He published *Walden*, his main work, in 1854. He then wrote *Civil Disobedience* in May of 1849, which was fueled from a night he spent in jail after refusing to pay a poll-tax. He spent the last few years of his life as less of a transcendentalist and more of an abolitionist in the fight against slavery. Unfortunately, Thoreau's health grew poor as time went on, and he died of tuberculosis in 1862.

Ralph Waldo Emerson taught Thoreau about the ideas and purpose of transcendentalism. The transcendentalist movement was one of the greatest literary movements of the 19th century. It combined romanticism with reform and focused on the individual. Transcendentalism also put a large focus on nature in which Thoreau found solace in and enjoyed since he was a young boy. In order to be successful in a transcendental world, one must live above materialistic needs as much as possible and focus on the spiritual aspects of life. One of the fundamental principles of transcendentalism was the belief in the reliability of the human conscience, which was based upon the conviction of the human immanence of God in the soul of the individual.

Most importantly, Thoreau was also an avid abolitionist. Abolitionism was a movement during the 1830s up until 1865, when the Civil War ended. It advocated for the abolition of slavery. The movement focused on abolishing slavery completely in the United States, and was mainly supported by Northerners. Many of the Northerners believed that slavery was a sin, and a racial prejudice. However, many of the Southerners who had slaves strongly opposed these views in the abolitionist movement. The clashing of these views became increasingly important during the time period, leading up to the Civil War. Eventually, this conflict would lead to the Civil War in 1861.

Thoreau's literature was his main contribution to the transcendental movement. With the help of Ralph Waldo Emerson, he wrote *The Dial*. *The Dial* was a magazine led by Emerson that supported the transcendentalist writers as well as their ideas and consisted of many of Thoreau's poems and essays. One of Thoreau's first chapter essays, *Natural History of Massachusetts*, was published in *The Dial* as a book review, and with this he proved his calling as a nature style author. The magazine discontinued publication in April, 1844.

In 1845, Thoreau experimented with his view of transcendentalism by living in full simplicity and leisure, which inspired the creation his work *Walden*, consisting of 18 essays which described the things he saw, smelt, touched, heard and tasted on his journey to live self-sufficiently. Thoreau spent two years living at Walden Pond, but his work only accounts for one year. The work was written in the first person as he stressed his beliefs on how society should live with simplicity and not luxuriously. The work was eventually published in 1854. After leaving Walden Pond in 1849, Thoreau wrote *A Week on the Concord and Merrimack Rivers* which reflected a boating trip that he and his brother John took on 1839. Many of Thoreau's works consisted of personal experiences as well as his views on a simple way of life.

Henry David Thoreau was a key player in the fight against slavery. After he left Walden Pond, Thoreau's transcendentalist beliefs faded and he turned his focus on being an abolitionist in his later life. John Brown, an abolitionist, mentored Thoreau, and Thoreau thought of him as an idol. Thoreau wrote many papers on the evils of slavery, including one of his most important works, known as *Slavery in Massachusetts*. These papers were one of his contributions to the abolitionist movement. Also, Thoreau helped many slaves escape through a secret passage known as the Underground Railroad. One of Thoreau's most important contributions, however, was advocating for nonviolent resistance and protests in the fight for abolishing slavery. In one of his most famous works, *Civil Disobedience*, Thoreau justifies that it is okay to intentionally break unjust laws in order to better the government. Also known as resistance to the government, *Civil Disobedience* showed the power of the role of the individual to determine what is right versus what is wrong, while disregarding what society says is right or wrong. These views paralleled to slavery in that even though society may approve of slavery, it was not necessarily just. Thus, like with his previous work *Slavery in Massachusetts*, Thoreau used literature to rebel against the government and support the fight against slavery.

Henry David Thoreau's impact on society was immense because of his talent and achievements. As a result of his literature such as *Walden*, people of the 19th century were exposed to transcendental writing at its best. His focus on simplicity and balance between man and nature showed people another way to live their lives as the country was industrializing. His literature, as a whole, affected the people, because it made them think about and challenge their intentions.

In the movement against slavery, Thoreau helped slaves escape on the Underground Railroad, and he thus impacted the lives of those he helped on the road to freedom. In the long run of history, Thoreau's civil disobedience has motivated many notable figures and peaceful protest movements. The peaceful way of resisting politics and society motivated activists such as Martin Luther King Jr., Gandhi and others.

Henry David Thoreau showed a way to peacefully, intellectually rebel against the government. He also helped in the fight to free the slaves. Above all, he is proved to be a transcendentalist, an abolitionist whose literature and actions changed history.

Chapter 2

Appendix 1　Key to Exercises

Part I　Warm-up

Discuss the following questions in pairs or groups.

1. American Romanticism in literature is characterized by several key features. Firstly, it emphasizes the individual and celebrates the power of imagination and intuition. Romantic writers often explore the beauty of nature and its connection to the human spirit. They reject societal conventions and advocate for personal freedom and individualism. Additionally, American Romanticism is known for its exploration of the supernatural, the mysterious, and the sublime. Romantic writers often employ vivid imagery, emotional intensity, and poetic language to convey their ideas and evoke strong emotions in readers. Overall, American Romanticism seeks to capture the essence of human experience, emphasizing passion, idealism, and the pursuit of individual truths.

2. Several notable American Romantic writers made significant contributions to the movement. Ralph Waldo Emerson, a prominent figure, championed transcendentalism, emphasizing the inherent goodness of both nature and humanity. His essays, such as *Self-Reliance* and *Nature*, inspired

individuals to trust their own instincts and seek spiritual connections with the natural world. Another influential writer was Henry David Thoreau, known for his book *Walden*, which documents his experiences living in solitude in nature. Thoreau's work promoted self-reflection, simplicity, and a deep appreciation for the natural environment. Margaret Fuller, a feminist writer, advocated for women's rights and social equality, challenging societal norms through her writings. These writers, among others, played pivotal roles in shaping American Romanticism by exploring themes of individualism, nature, and social reform.

3. American Romanticism had a profound impact on the development of American literature. It marked a shift away from the prevailing neoclassical ideals of reason and restraint towards a focus on individualism, emotion, and imagination. The Romantic writers rejected the strict rules of literary composition and explored new forms of expression. They celebrated the beauty of nature, delved into the depths of human emotions, and challenged societal norms. This emphasis on personal experience and the exploration of inner thoughts and feelings paved the way for the development of various literary genres, such as the personal essay, the short story, and the poetic form. American Romanticism also laid the foundation for later literary movements, influencing transcendentalism, realism, and even modernism.

4. American Romanticism emerged during the 19th century, a time of significant cultural and social changes in the United States. The movement reflected the growing sense of American identity and the desire to establish a unique literary tradition separate from European influences. Romantic writers sought to capture the essence of the American experience, exploring themes of individualism, frontier life, and the vastness of the American landscape. They questioned traditional social and religious institutions, advocating for personal freedom and social reform. American Romanticism also reflected the tensions and conflicts of the era, including the ongoing debates over slavery, women's rights, and the impact of industrialization. It offered a platform for expressing dissent, challenging societal norms, and envisioning a more idealistic and egalitarian society.

Part II   Walt Whitman Revolutionized American Poetry

Watch the video. Write *T* for true or *F* for false for each statement.

1. T   2. F   3. F   4. F   5. T   6. F   7. T   8. T   9. F   10. F

答案解析：

2. 不是 May 13th，而是 May 31st。
3. 不是 largely received education at schools，而是 was largely self-taught。
4. 不是 men's property rights，而是 women's property rights。
6. 不是 local people，而是 soldiers。
9. 不是 good，而是 disgraceful。
10. 不是 really received，而是 never really received。

Part III   Symbolism in *The Scarlet Letter*

Watch the video and answer the following questions.

1. Symbolism.

2. The scaffold, the scarlet letter, the rosebush, the brook or stream, Pearl, and the reflection in the armor at governor Bellingham's mansion.

3. It symbolizes the way Puritan society looks at Hester. They only focus on her once in the scarlet letter, and not who she actually is.

4. Yes. Later, the scarlet letter comes to stand not for the word adultery but for ableism that Hester Prynne is such an able woman. She can do anything that's awesome. Hester works hard and the townspeople recognize that they begin to admire her for her grace and charity, which begins to alter the meaning of the scarlet letter in their own minds.

5. The likeness of Pearl. It stands as separation between Dimmesdale / Hester and Pearl, listing they are on opposite sides. But it also shows how they are tied together. When it forms the quiet pool, it shows the beauty of Pearl's figure and charm. It shows complexity to cross it just how Pearl is hard to comprehend sometimes. It is the boundary / bridge between two worlds where all three can be together in harmony in the real world where they are separated because of the adultery.

Watch the video again and fill in the blanks.

1) symbolism   2) redemption   3) scaffold   4) punishment
5) salvation   6) title   7) myriad   8) shame
9) adulterer   10) marked   11) grace   12) alter
13) rooted   14) frailty   15) separation 16) complexity
17) harmony   18) reminder   19) suffering   20) prominent

Part Ⅳ Finding Emily Dickinson in the Power of Her Poetry

Watch the video and answer the following questions.

1. By a new exhibition at the Morgan Library and Museum in New York when taking a closer look at the iconic American cultural figure through her poems and the remnants of her life, and finding a less reclusive woman than we thought.

2. In books, online, on film, and in a major museum exhibition.

3. "I'm Nobody! Who Are You?" the first line of one of her most famous poems.

4. She is a constant summons to me to think about language and its preciseness, and not only its preciseness, but its power.

5. This exhibition, with some 100 rarely seen items, is eager to present a different, fresh take on Dickinson.

6. The stereotype that was attached to her very early on of this total recluse, of this woman in white who never left her bedroom, who penned these amazing verses, like, in a vacuum almost, in total seclusion, has really stuck to her.

7. Through her reading and a constant correspondence with friends, leading thinkers, and others.

8. A leading contemporary poet and Dickinson scholar.

9. She broke the glass ceiling in poetry. And Emily Dickinson is like a beacon of verbal power that will not be silenced. She breaks down the barriers between poetry, prose, ear and eye.

10. Only after her death in 1886.

11. She wrote some 1,800 poems, but only 10 were published in newspapers during her lifetime.

12. Dickinson was thought to be reticent about seeing her work, as well as her image in public, so we can only wonder what she would think of *A Quiet Passion*, a film due in April starring Cynthia Nixon.

13. And now both scholars and everyday fans have access to a trove of original manuscripts and more online, digitized from the collections of Amherst College, Harvard University and the Boston Public Library.

Appendix 2   Transcripts

Part II   Walt Whitman Revolutionized American Poetry

Walt Whitman was the man who revolutionized American poetry. He invented a whole new poetic form and he opened up topics to a wide range that nobody else would touch. Walt Whitman was born on May 31st, 1819 in West Hills, New York. His parents were of modest means and he had seven siblings. At the age of 11, Walt Whitman was pulled from school so that he could help the family support itself in the printing industry. As a result, Whitman was largely self-taught. He became a voracious reader. He read widely, especially novels.

When he was 17, Whitman turned to teaching and his first job was in a one-room schoolhouse. He taught for 5 years, and then in 1841 he set his sights on journalism. Walt Whitman was a volatile editor and writer. He had strong ideas about women's property rights, about immigration and about the major issue of the day-slavery. From 1848 to 1855, Whitman began what was to become his greatest work—*Leaves of Grass*. His free verse is stitching together of encyclopedic lists, completely broke with poetic and literary convention and vastly influenced poets ever after across the world. It began as a book of very few poems and grew to one over the years to contain almost 300 poems. Over his lifetime, he had seven editions of the book.

During the Civil War, Whitman moved to Washington, DC to attend his wounded brother George. He stayed in DC several years, working in the paymaster's office, and volunteered visiting wounded soldiers. When he went to the hospitals, there were limbs piled outside. He spoke with young soldiers who had witnessed the most astonishing atrocities. From his experience with the wounded during the war, he produced a small book of poems called *Drum Taps*. This is one of the only two accounts of the Civil War written by people who actually experienced it.

Whitman published two new collections of poems in 1870, *Democratic Vistas* and *Passage to India*. Whitman was called the bard of democracy, because all of his poems are based on the notion of a universal brotherhood. He thought that the possibility of America was to achieve a brotherhood that no other culture had yet had been able to achieve.

Whitman suffered a stroke in 1873, leaving him partially paralyzed. He moved to Camden, New Jersey where he remained until his death on March 26, 1892. In his lifetime, *Leaves of Grass* was considered by many people to be a disgraceful book. But by the end of his life, he acquired the name "the good grey poet" as if America was finally ready in the later years to accept him as a poet.

Whitman never really received the attention that he deserved during his lifetime. It was only in the 20th century that we learned how to read his poetry and understand what he accomplished.

Part III   Symbolism in *The Scarlet Letter*

There are a lot of different things going on in *The Scarlet Letter*. One of the main topics of the book is symbolism. We will explore some examples of symbolism in the book.

The scaffold plays a vital role in *The Scarlet Letter*. In the novel, it's both the symbol of sin and shame as well as the site of ultimate redemption. Dimmesdale finally decided to act upon his guilt since he had been driven hither to the scaffold by the impulse that remorse which dogged him everywhere. And the scaffold as this punishment comes full circle, a process that begins with shame and ends with salvation for himself, for Dimmesdale, and for their daughter Pearl.

Ah, *The Scarlet Letter*, since it's the title of the book, you know it's got to be important and it is, the scarlet letter, is a symbol for a myriad of things like identity, shame, sin, and grace. Hester wears it on her chest throughout the novel, so naturally it's going to have a lot of meanings. The scarlet letter was represented in exaggerated and gigantic proportions so as to be the most prominent feature of her appearance. At first, the scarlet letter is symbolic of Hester's sin and shame. She commits adultery and has a child as a result. The letter A is sewn into her clothing, literally marking her as an adulterer. She takes ownership of that letter which makes it sort of a cool symbol for her identity. She's a marked woman but she's not going to take the punishment lying down. Later, the scarlet letter comes to stand not for the word adultery but for ableism that Hester Prynne is such an able woman. She can do anything that's awesome. Hester works hard and the townspeople recognize that they begin to admire her for her grace and charity, which begins to alter the meaning of the scarlet letter in their own minds.

The rosebush represents hope in the darkness of prison. It is strongly rooted to represent strength and hope for the prisoners. It produces beauty and a soft scent for the incoming prisoners, and it represents the kindness of nature to those leaving the dark place. "It may serve, let us hope, to symbolize some sweet moral blossom, that may be found along the track, or relieve the darkening close of a tale of human frailty and sorrow."

The brook / stream in Chapter 19 represents the likeness of Pearl. It stands as separation between Dimmesdale / Hester and Pearl, listing they are on opposite sides. But it also shows how they are tied together. When it forms the quiet pool, it shows the beauty of Pearl's figure and charm. It shows complexity to cross it just how Pearl is hard to comprehend sometimes. It is the boundary / bridge between two worlds where all three can be together in harmony in the real world where they are separated because of the adultery. The brook has mysterious roots much like Pearl. "This brook is the boundary between two worlds and that thou can never meet Pearl again. Pearl resembled the brook in as much as the current of her life gushed from a wellspring as mysteriously and flowed through the scenes shadowed as heavily with gloom." The scarlet letter was represented in exaggerated and gigantic proportions so as to be greatly the most prominent feature of her appearance.

Pearl is the daughter of the adulteress Hester Prynne and Minister Dimmesdale. She seems like a normal girl but she represents so much more than that. She is a constant reminder for Hester of her sin that Pearl was born through. Like the scarlet letter, Pearl is another punishment that constantly reminds Hester of her sin. "God, as a direct consequence of the sin which man thus punished, has given her a lovely child." Even though she symbolizes punishment for Hester, she also represents God's grace and redemption. She symbolizes Hester's hope and redemption even in the midst of pain and suffering.

The reflection in the armor at governor Bellingham's mansion was a convex mirror. This means that it is disproportionate and unclear. In other words, it makes a certain area of something bigger than the rest of the area. When Hester looks into the reflection, the scarlet letter is represented in exaggerated and gigantic proportions so as to be greatly the most prominent feature of her appearance. This symbolizes the way Puritan society looks at Hester. They only focus on who she was in scarlet letter, and not who she actually is.

Part IV Finding Emily Dickinson in the Power of Her Poetry

Finding Emily Dickinson in the power of her poetry.

Who was Emily Dickinson? A new exhibition at the Morgan Library and Museum in New York takes a closer look at the iconic American cultural figure through her poems and the remnants of her life, and finds a less reclusive woman than we thought we knew, Jeffrey Brown reports.

Read the Full Transcript

JUDY WOODRUFF:

Finally tonight, on this International Women's Day, she is as beloved as ever. And now, the poet Emily Dickinson is getting even more attention and a new look, in books, online, on film, and in a major museum exhibition.

Jeffrey Brown reports from New York.

JEFFREY BROWN:

She is at once among the most known of and most mysterious American cultural figures, Emily Dickinson, subject of an exhibition at the Morgan Library and Museum in New York titled, "I'm Nobody! Who Are You?" the first line of one of her most famous poems.

Who was Emily Dickinson? Scholar Marta Werner offers this:

MARTA WERNER, D'Youville College:

She is a constant summons to me to think about language and its preciseness, and not only its preciseness, but its power.

WOMAN:

These are the days when skies resume the old.

JEFFREY BROWN:

Here, visitors can listen to readings of the poems, while examining remnants of a circumscribed 19th century life lived almost completely in one town, Amherst, Massachusetts, the only known painting of Dickinson as a child with her siblings, a daguerreotype of her as a young woman, the only authenticated photo of the poet.

There's also a lock of her auburn hair, a replica of cut and pressed botanical specimens, and another of the rose wallpaper in the bedroom to which she retreated in her later years.

This exhibition, with some 100 rarely seen items, is eager to present a different, fresh take on Dickinson.

CAROLYN VEGA, Curator:

The stereotype that was attached to her very early on of this total recluse, of this woman in white who never left her bedroom, who penned these amazing verses, like, in a vacuum almost, in total seclusion, has really stuck to her.

JEFFREY BROWN:

You're fighting that?

CAROLYN VEGA:

Yes, we're fighting that, or just bringing it into context a little bit.

JEFFREY BROWN:

Emily Dickinson engaged with her times, including the Civil War years, through her reading and a constant correspondence with friends, leading thinkers, and others.

Often, she sent poems, sentences, stanzas and entire poems written on scraps of paper and envelopes, even chocolate wrappers, a new book, *Envelope Poems*, as well as the recent *The Gorgeous Nothings*, document this aspect of her work.

SUSAN HOWE, Poet:

By God, she broke the glass ceiling in poetry. And Emily Dickinson is like a beacon of verbal power that will not be silenced.

JEFFREY BROWN:

For Susan Howe, a leading contemporary poet and Dickinson scholar, the powerful voice of Dickinson is best heard and seen in these original manuscripts, the unusual line breaks, alternative word choices, poems as virtual works of art.

SUSAN HOWE:

Ultimately, she leads me to the fundamental mystery of all poetry, which is the relation between the ear and the eye. Every mark on paper is an acoustic mark. Dickinson breaks down the barriers between poetry, prose and ear and eye.

JEFFREY BROWN:

Marta Werner, a leading expert on Dickinson's manuscripts, showed me an example.

MARTA WERNER:

She talks about wanting to hinder time.

And as the poem unfolds, the way that the writing almost stumbles, right, performs that hindering of time, but you're seeing, to some extent, the mind thinking.

JEFFREY BROWN:

The first edition of Dickinson's poetry came out only after her death in 1886, and, from the beginning, editors ignored her idiosyncrasies and formatted her writings into a more conventional style.

She wrote some 1,800 poems, but only 10 were published in newspapers during her lifetime.

MARTA WERNER:

It's unsigned. It's anonymous. Her name, you know, never appeared in print during her lifetime with any of her poems. It's dropped in, in the middle of this other column. What comes after it is a little piece on how to use chloroform.

(LAUGHTER)

JEFFREY BROWN:

Dickinson was thought to be reticent about seeing her work, as well as her image in public, so we can only wonder what she would think of *A Quiet Passion*, a film due in April starring Cynthia Nixon.

But there's no denying the continuing fascination with the woman and love of her work, as at marathon readings put on by the Library of Congress, and the restoration under way of her Amherst home.

And now both scholars and everyday fans have access to a trove of original manuscripts and more online, digitized from the collections of Amherst College, Harvard University and the Boston Public Library.

Marta Werner offered a personal story that drove home the connection many feel, how her dying father, a scientist, shared his favorite poems.

MARTA WERNER:

It was his idea. He started to write me letters. And then he would ask me to send back my list of poems. This was a very extraordinary thing.

I think there's a lot of people like my father who love her and can't quite say why.

JEFFREY BROWN:

The enduring power and mystery of one of America's greatest poets.

From the Morgan Library and Museum in New York, I'm Jeffrey Brown for the PBS NewsHour.

Chapter 3

Appendix 1 Key to Exercises

Part I Warm-up

Discuss the following questions in pairs or groups.

1. In realist literature, authors describe things as they are without embellishment or fantastical plots. Works of literary Realism shun flowery language, exotic settings and characters, and epic stories of love and heroism. Instead, they focus on everyday lives and people in ordinary times and places.

2. In art and literature, Realism expresses a message that depicts situations realistically, whereas Romanticism illustrates messages by using fiction. Romanticism focuses on plot, hyperbole, metaphor and feeling. In contrast, Realism focuses on character, detail, objectivity and separation of author and narrator. Romanticism rebels against prior forms of writing and art by picking apart feeling, belief, imagination and fantasy.

3. American Realism began as a reaction to and a rejection of Romanticism, with its emphasis on emotion, imagination, and the individual. The movement began as early as in the 1830s but reached prominence and held sway from the end of the Civil War to around the end of the 19th century.

4. William Dean Howells, Henry James, and Mark Twain. Other names may include Hamlin Garland, Bret Harte, Edith Wharton and so on.

5. *Adventures of Huckleberry Finn* (often shortened to *Huck Finn*) is a novel written by American humorist Mark Twain. It is commonly used and accounted as one of the first Great American Novels. It is also one of the first major American novels written using Local Color Regionalism, or vernacular, told in the first person by the eponymous Huckleberry (Huck) Finn, best friend of Tom Sawyer and hero of

three other Mark Twain books.

Part Ⅱ   Mark Twain: Father of American Literature

Watch the video. Write *T* for true or *F* for false for each statement.

1. T   2. T   3. F   4. T   5. F   6. F   7. T   8. F   9. F   10. T

答案解析：

3. 是 very briefly served，不是 for many years。

5. 他的第一本畅销书是 *Innocents Abroad*，出版于 1869 年。

6. 文中表示他创作并出版了 28 本书和很多其他作品。

8. 是 Yale and Oxford，不是 Harvard and Cambridge。

9. 马克·吐温 1895 年至 1896 年的巡回演讲是成功的。

Part Ⅲ   Henry James and American Painting

Watch the video and answer the following questions.

1. At the Morgan Library Museum between June 9th and September 10th, 2017.

2. Not only to painting but to European literature.

3. Both wandered in Europe with their parents as a child. Both were bachelors who moved easily between France, Italy and England. Both of them were intrigued by fashionable women.

4. 70.

5. What James saw as the role of the artist, or what the artists must do in the world or the artist's relationship to the audience.

6. Three. They are *Washington Square*, *Portrait of a Lady*, and *The Golden Bowl*.

7. John Singer Sargent.

8. National Portrait Gallery in London.

Part Ⅳ   William Dean Howells, Dime Novels, and Realism

Watch the first part of the video and answer the following questions.

1. Realism.

2. The book and the magazine.

3. Films.

4. Entertainment and young readers.

5. Between the ages of 10 and 15.

6. Stories about bandits and pirates.

7. They want to imitate lives of outlaws without even understanding what the stories are actually describing.

8. Screen time will rot their kids' minds, give them unrealistic ideas about how life will work in their future, damage their creativity and hurt their eyes.

9. Give their kids strange ideas about how life really works, limit their creativity, and hurt their eyes.

10. Strengthen the trend of Realism.

Watch the second part of the video and fill in the blanks.

1) aesthetic   2) assistant   3) community   4) fanciful

5) adventures 6) canonized 7) commonplace 8) scheme
9) assume 10) junk

Part V *Huckleberry Finn* and the N-word

Watch the video and answer the following questions.

1. It challenged authority, poked fun at religion and was accused of leading children astray.

2. In the year 2010.

3. Their newly released edition removes the n-word and replaces it with "slave".

4. 219 times.

5. To some, the word gets in the way of the story's powerful message against slavery. To others, Twain was simply capturing the way people talked back then.

Appendix 2 Transcripts

Part II Mark Twain: Father of American Literature

Mark Twain really is one of the most incredible and influential writers in American literature and his influence is still very much palpable in writing today. Called by many "the Father of American Literature", Mark Twain was born Samuel Langhorne Clemens on November 30th 1835 in Missouri. When Samuel was 12, his father died of pneumonia. At the age of 15, he got a job working for his brother Orion's newspaper *The Hannibal Western Union*. Mark Twain became a cub pilot on a steamboat on the Mississippi River. He later became a full-fledged pilot and he thought it was the best time of his life. But in 1861 when the Civil War broke out the steamboat trade absolutely came to an end and he was out of job. Twain very briefly served in the Confederate military that did not work out, so he then headed west with his brother. He eventually made his way to San Francisco and really began his career again as a journalist. Twain's first big literary break came in 1865 with the publication of *Jim Smiley and His Jumping Frog*. It was a huge success and was printed and reprinted all over the country. His first bestseller was *Innocents Abroad* which was published in 1869 and is still very much one of the most successful and widely renowned travel narratives of American literature. Mark Twain's best-known and best loved books *The Adventures of Tom Sawyer* published in 1876 and *Huckleberry Finn* published in 1885 are probably the reason that Ernest Hemingway famously said in 1935 that all American literature comes from Mark Twain. *Huck Finn* shows the possibility of making genuine moral changes in a world that's dominated by racism and other forms of human folly. It also was a book that was able to capture the vernacular speech of different classes along the Mississippi. Twain was the first person to put this kind of vocabulary into American writing. Twain was an immensely prolific writer; he wrote 28 books, a vast number of stories, lectures, and essays. In his last 15 years, Mark Twain was probably the most celebrated American around the world. He received honorary degrees from Yale and from Oxford and in 1895 and 1896 in order to pay off debts he did a lecture tour around the world which drew huge crowds. Mark Twain is now thought of as America's first celebrity because he was so good at capturing the public imagination and it became important to him to have a public image he always went on book tour wearing a white suit and he only wanted to be photographed in that white suit he tended that image very carefully. At the age of 74, Mark Twain died at his Connecticut home on April 21st 1910. I think Mark Twain was one of these towering figures in American literature because he was funny and smart and willing to sort of shoot arrows at the most powerful and I think that there's something deeply in the American character that responds to that.

Part III Henry James and American Painting

The show *Henry James and American Painting* will be on view at the Morgan Library Museum from June 9th to September 10th, 2017. James became very close to a painter who was a few years older than him and had lived in Europe called John La Farge, and it was La Farge who introduced James, not only to painting, but to European literature. And that began a relationship between James, as a writer and James as someone who really studied painting. The early letters are all about the paintings he was looking at, the masterpieces, and what he actually thought of them.

He then became friendly with a figure who was almost a mirror image of himself, John Singer Sargent. And in this show, we have some masterpieces, including a portrait of James, but also paintings that James himself had seen and admired. Singer Sargent, like James, had wandered in Europe, with his parents as a child, and was a bachelor who moved easily between France, Italy and England. Both of them were intrigued by fashionable women. Indeed, James wrote some of his best novels about women.

James met the young sculptor Hendrik Andersen. He became fascinated by him. He wrote him 70 letters, and these letters that he wrote Andersen are, I think, among James's—not only his most important letters, but his most important versions of what he saw as the role of the artist, or what the artists must do in the world or the artist's relationship to the audience.

What was actually happening at the time that James was writing *The Portrait of a Lady*, was that Lizzie Boott had fallen in love with the American painter Frank Duveneck. Her father deeply disapproved. Duveneck was the sort of man who sat in taverns. He was from Cincinnati. He was not part of the social world of the Bootts. But now he began to study this man who was in love with a woman, who was his social senior as it were. This drama made its way into *Washington Square*, into *The Portrait of a lady*. When Lizzie Boott married Frank Duveneck, it made its way into James's novel *The Golden Bowl*. Frank Duveneck's work, including the magisterial portrait of his father-in-law, was done in the old-style. Lizzie died early on in their marriage and Frank Duveneck made a wonderful tomb for her. And we also have that tomb that he made in the show.

People were fascinated by James's face, by James's pose and by James's presence in the world. Friends of him commissioned the painter John Singer Sargent to actually paint his portrait. And I think, for him, it's not hard to imagine how proud he must have been, when he was the most famous novelist of the age, being painted by the most famous portrait painter of the age, a painting that would eventually make its way into the National Portrait Gallery in London. He wrote many letters about being painted, but he was painted by many others as well, and indeed, photographed a great deal. It's not only the paintings he was looking at, or the painters and sculptors he was writing about, as a critic and as a novelist, but also the idea that he himself was a great subject. His great head was a great subject for painters and for photographers.

Part IV William Dean Howells, Dime Novels, and Realism

Welcome to the lecture on William Dean Howells, dime novels, and their relationship to American

Realism. As we discussed in the previous lecture, Realism was the dominant American aesthetic for literature in the second half of the 19th century. But it wasn't the only type of storytelling happening on the page in the country. Realism was the highbrow aesthetic that sought to present and preserve authentic American culture for decades to come.

But America was deep inside of a love affair with the book and with the magazine, much in the same way that America would fall in love with films in the 1930s and 1940s, and then TV in the 1950s and 1960s, and then later the Internet, and so on. Outside of these works of literature, some authors continued Romantic trends of presenting unlikely stories and out of the ordinary characters. In books and magazines arranged for entertainment, many of these novels, called nickel novels, or later, dime novels, with inflation, were presented for young readers. And in the late 1800s, they were enthusiastically read by older children between, say, the ages of 10 and 15. They were also purchased more by boys than by girls. Today, in terms of reading fiction, far more women purchase novels than men. But at the end of their lives, many of these boy readers grew up to write about how much they loved reading these dime novels when they were young.

Charles Harvey, in 1907, reminisced about his great love for them in an article called *The Dime Novel in American Life*. He said, "What boy of the 1860s can ever forget Beadle's dime novels? To the average youngster of that time, the advent of each of these books seemed to be an event of world consequence. How the boys swarmed into and through stores and newsstands to buy copies as they came hot off the press. And the fortunate ones, who got there before the supply gave out, how triumphantly they carried them off to the rendezvous, where eager groups awaited their arrival."

And what do you suppose was in these dime novels? Well, there were stories about bandits and pirates. There was a whole sub-genre of dime novels about European settlers who lived with or were kidnapped by Native Americans. Buffalo Bill and other figures of the American West were featured in dime novels, and Beadle's, the publisher of many of these dime novels, grew the mystery story, with its murders and crimes, into a profitable genre as well. In *Huck Finn*, you can see that Tom Sawyer and the other boys in his gang have been deeply influenced by these dime novels. So they want to imitate lives of outlaws without even understanding what the stories are actually describing.

Today, parents often say that their kids have spent too much time staring at the screen, either video games, or TV, or the Internet. Parents say that screen time will rot their kids' minds, that things on TV and on the Internet might give them unrealistic ideas about how life will work in their future, that too much screen time will damage their creativity, and also, it will hurt their eyes. It might be humorous now to consider this, but in the mid-1800s, American parents told their children the same thing about spending too much time reading these dime novels. These dime novels would do the same things to them: give them strange ideas about how life really worked, limit their creativity, even hurt their eyes. Many parents wanted their kids to put down these books, with their violence and alternative sense of morality, and go outside and play.

In response to this, some editors joined writers in strengthening the trend of Realism. Some editors of some large circulation and high-paying magazines said, essentially, that they wouldn't publish fiction unless it confined to the ideals of Realism.

One of these editors was William Dean Howells. Howells himself was a novelist, though he is far better remembered as the editor of *The Atlantic Monthly*, one of the most important magazines in the country, as the aesthetic of Realism began to grow. He was hired by *The Atlantic* in 1866 as an assistant editor, and by 1871, he was named the head editor, where he supported and wrote essays about a new wave of American Realist writers, such as Mary Wilkins Freeman, Frank Norris, and Mark Twain.

Much later in his life, to explain the political choices he'd made in promoting writers of Realism over writers of Romanticism, he wrote an essay on novel-writing and novel-reading. I'll read you part of this, and also, I'll talk you through it as well. But to better understand the following excerpt, you should know that William Dean Howells was writing to a community of readers who were familiar with two essential types of fiction: the earlier mode, Romanticism, which he calls "the romance", which told fanciful tales about unrealistic characters, and the more recently developed Realism, which featured authentic locations filled with realistic, often middle-class, characters. Add to this maybe one more thing: all of those dime novels that eventually produced stories of pirates, detectives, Western adventures, all of them featuring characters who had little connection to the people that Howells knew in his real life. Howells' argument was that too much Romantic fiction, like too much TV, might warp the minds of its readers and lead them to unrealistic expectations later in life. Through Realistic fiction, he believed readers could better understand themselves and the situations around them. In short, he believed that good art should imitate real life, and that a serious writer has a responsibility to represent what he or she knew.

But he also had a practical problem. By 1899, when he wrote this essay, Nathaniel Hawthorne has become canonized in the American school system. Pretty much all schoolkids look to Nathaniel Hawthorne as the person who started serious American literature. Instead of two categories, then, William Dean Howells decided to create three categories. The top category is for Realistic fiction. He refers to this as the novel. Today, we call all fiction over 200 pages a novel. But in Howells' time, the romance was a category for fiction of unusual events, while the novel was the category for more commonplace events with realistic characters. In general, Realists tended to describe their works as novels, essentially the new story. The middle category in Howells' scheme was the romance. These were writers who tried to work toward art, but as fiction was in its early stages of development, couldn't yet achieve that goal. In short, these writers tried, but were limited by the traditions of their time.

I should point out, though, that all of the examples that Howells gives for the romance were written by Hawthorne. It might be reasonable, then, to assume that for Howells, the only American fiction writer that exists in this category is Nathaniel Hawthorne. And at the very bottom of this list is romanticist fiction. This is the junk category of unusual tales that warp the mind, like those of Edgar Allan Poe, or fiction that pretends to portray real life, but dresses it up to make it more exciting, strange, or intriguing, thereby giving readers unusual ideas about how life elsewhere in the States might work.

Part V *Huckleberry Finn* and the N-word

From the moment it was published in 1885, Mark Twain's *Adventures of Huckleberry Finn* caused controversy. It challenged authority, poked fun at religion, and was accused of leading children astray. What's surprising is that 125 years later, *Huckleberry Finn* is still making news. Today, there are school districts in America that banned this American classic, for one reason, the word—nigger, a word that is so offensive thus it's usually called the n-word. As we first reported in March, a publishing company in Alabama says that schools don't have to change their reading list, because they have changed *Huckleberry Finn*. Their newly-released edition removes the n-word and replaces it with slave—a bold move, for what's considered one of the greatest works in American literature. The story will continue in a moment.

Mark Twain's *Huckleberry Finn* is a classic, set before the Civil War. The stories told by Huck—a white boy escaping an abusive father, and his adventures with a black man named Jim, escaping slavery. Their journey takes place along the Mississippi River. In the book, Twain used the n-word 219 times. To some, the word gets in the way of the story's powerful message against slavery. To others, Twain is simply capturing the way people talked back then.

"Are you censoring Twain?"

"We certainly are accused of censoring Twain."

Brenda Williams is a co-owner and editor of New South Books, the publisher of the sanitized edition of *Tom Sawyer and Huckleberry Finn* that replaces the n-word with "slave". It's aimed at schools that have already banned the book, though no one knows how many have. William says they are not trying to replace Twain's original, n-word included.

"If you can have the discussion and you're comfortable having the discussion, have it, have it with it in there. But if you're not comfortable with that, then here's an alternative for you to use. And I would argue to you that, it's still powerful."

The new edition drew powerful reactions from Twain scholars, the press and ordinary readers. And it's worth noting most of the articles don't spell out the word either.

"What does it say that people have been so passionate about it?"

"I think it says that race continues to be a volatile and divisive subject."

In this passage, Huck says the word three times in two sentences. Jim was monstrously proud of it, and he got so he couldn't hardly notice the other niggers—niggers came miles to hear Jim tell about he was more looked up to than any nigger in that country.

"What do you think of *Huckleberry Finn*?"

"It's a great book. It's one of the greatest books in American literature."

Author David Bradley teaches at the University of Oregon. He says the key to understanding *Huckleberry Finn* is through Twain's use of language as the friendship between Huck and Jim unfolds. "When Huck comes back to that raft, he says they're after us. He doesn't say they are after you. He says they're after us, and that's the moment when it becomes about the American dilemma, becomes about whether we are gonna get along?"

School districts struggling to teach *Huckleberry Finn* have called in David Bradley. He believes strongly in teaching Twain's original text.

"One of the first things I do is that I make everybody say it out loud about six or seven times."

"The n-word?"

"Yeah, nigger. Get over it. Now let's talk about the book."

Students at Woodbury High School in Minnesota read the original book this past school year, but there are differences in how their teachers approach it. Nora Weiss says the word out loud in class. Karen Morrill does not.

"What happens when we or when I say the n-word? And I don't pronounce NIGGER."

"People are scared to talk about race."

"Are you scared to talk about it in class?"

"No. But you will not say out loud the n-word."

"That's just such a minor part."

"Aren't you giving the word more power than it deserves by not saying it?"

"I didn't give the word its power. It came into my classroom with that power."

"I might not always reach and nourish and nurture every single student, but I can certainly do my best not to harm them."

When Nora Weiss says the word, she feels its impact on students is worth it. It makes sense in this novel to teach it with the controversy.

"It makes sense to bring up all of the hard emotions. They come with it. It's not just a classic book. It's not just a way the words are written. It's the ideas."

11th graders Melvin Alvasoho, Joseph Joadiho, and Ryhan Ferro confronted the controversial word and their feelings about it.

"I feel like that word is in there for a reason. Twain put the word in there to get our attention and every time we read it, it does exactly that it gets our attention."

"If you replace that with the word slave, of course people would be less bothered, but I think Twain wants people to be a little bit bothered."

"Melvin, you smiled."

"I smiled because I just kind of think that constant use of the n-word and there it's to me it feels unnecessary."

"Why? What is it about? It's just a word, right? What is it about this word?"

"It reflects on African-American history back then and like I said, it's like, it's a history that nobody wants to relive."

"Do you think that discomfort starts and stops with the n-word, or the discomfort extends to a conversation about race?"

"In this specific instance, it is the word itself that is the problem. People are not coming it up and saying we can't teach this book, because it's got discussion about slavery. What they're saying is we can't teach the book, because it's got all these repetitive instances of the offensive n-word in there and therefore we're not gonna use it."

"The publisher says they're providing a service."

"They are."

"There's school district that won't deal with *Huckleberry Finn* and they remove this word and now they're able to have their students read and deal with *Huckleberry Finn*."

"No, it's not *Huckleberry Finn* anymore. We're talking about students. What are we teaching them? This may be their first encounter with slavery. It shouldn't be their only one, but that's one of the reasons we can't mess around with it. There is a reality there that you cannot avoid."

"But do you lose their reality when you take out the n-word and replace it with slave?"

"Yeah. Slave is a condition. I mean anybody can be a slave, and it's nothing for anybody to be ashamed of, but nigger has to do with shame. Nigger has to do with calling somebody something. Nigger was what made slavery possible."

"It is not a positive word."

"Do you use the word?"

"Oh, I used to. I grew up saying the word. It was on one ear. I never gave it any thought."

Williams runs New South Books in Montgomery Alabama, cradle of the Confederacy and where Jim Crow was once King. Williams, a son of Alabama, says the civil rights movement changed him, as it did the rest of the South. For him, the subject of race and the n-word goes beyond any debate about the book. It's also about how far the South has come.

"We learn to think differently about it, and thank God we did. I mean the movement didn't just free, you know, black southerners. I mean it freed white southerners too."

"Freed you from?"

"Freed us from the sand of, you know, this this was a big sand."

"Kids use it, you know that, the rap artists use it, the black rap artists use it, as you know. As I well know, brothers use it all the time they talked to each other."

"I love it."

"Sorry?"

"I love it."

"You love it?"

"Yeah. Oh yeah. You're my nigger, man. Look! In every group there are words that you use. There are inflections. There is knowledge about what a word means to you or to me or how I mean it when I say it. That is not an insult. I think one of the things that offends white people about it is that they can't say it. Is that what is it because of my inflection or is it because it's not because you're not us. Jeff Foxy says you know you can't make jokes about a redneck unless you are one. You can't say nigger unless you are one, unless you are willing to accept everything that goes with it, which is a lot of good stuff, you know and that's what they worry about that good stuff."

"What's the good stuff that goes with that word?"

"Having an awareness that you have overcome centuries of oppression, the pride of saying yeah you can say anything you want and it won't slow me down one bit."

"But the word is hurtful."

"The word is not hurtful. How it is used is hurtful. The person who is saying is hurtful."

17-year old Jeremy Richardson wrestled with how to react to the word, especially as the only black student in Nora Weiss's English class.

"Having the teacher read it out loud to everyone, then everyone is looking at me like, oh, she just said that. What are you gonna do about it? Like I didn't really have a reaction. I just I basically..."

"You didn't have an external reaction?"

"Yeah. Internally, though, what was going on?"

"Internally, I just thought about it like this is wrong, like I don't think that she should be saying this out loud or..."

"Why didn't you say something at that moment?"

"I don't know maybe because I didn't want anyone to see that I was having a problem with her reading the word."

"Hmm."

"That may be it but I definitely did have a problem with it."

"That's an uncomfortable conversation for students."

"It's uncomfortable for me too."

Weiss spent three days in class talking about race even before starting *Huckleberry Finn*.

"How do you balance your strong conviction about using the words that are in the book with the notion that some of your students may be pained by the words?"

"Hmm I don't have a callous view about the pain. I don't. But on the other hand, I do feel like any time, you come up against something that creates tension or creates discomfort, it is a point at which you could grow. And I think that life in general has many many moments like that. And I don't think that teaching kids to step away from that is healthy."

"Is the argument that these kids should be subjected to pain? I mean you know I don't see the point of that."

New South Books says it sold all 7,500 copies of the edited version of *Huckleberry Finn*, and plans to print more in the fall.

"The only thing missing from their, you know, reading of this, will be the word itself. Have we taken every bit of the value of Twain now? Oh, that's a preposterous argument. Yeah, I just I can't even see that argument."

"What the publisher is saying, by introducing this new edition, they can still have the teachable moment and have the conversation about race. You look puzzled?"

"Well, you use the term teachable moment, and that's what nigger gives you. That's why it's important to keep it there. I call *Huckleberry Finn* a power tool when it comes to education. There are so many things that pry things open. It's like the jars of life. You said teachable moment, that teachable moment is when that word hits the table in a classroom, everybody ooh... OK, let's talk about it. Let's talk about where it came from. Let's talk about why you all say ooh. Well, you don't go ooh about anything else. When you all don't go ooh, when it's blasting around in the parking lot and what you all call music. If you take out everything in a book that causes the teachable moment, you have no teachable moments."

Chapter 4

Appendix 1 Key to Exercises

Part I Warm-up

Discuss the following questions in pairs or groups.

1. Naturalism is a literary movement beginning in the late 19th century, similar to literary realism in its rejection of Romanticism, but distinct in its embrace of determinism, detachment, scientific objectivism, and social commentary. Literary naturalism emphasizes observation and the scientific method in the fictional portrayal of reality.

2. *Maggie: A Girl of the Streets* by Stephen Crane: This novella portrays the life of Maggie, a young girl living in the slums of New York City, and explores the themes of poverty, urban decay, and moral degradation. *Sister Carrie* by Theodore Dreiser: The novel tells the story of Carrie Meeber, a young woman who moves to Chicago and faces the challenges of poverty, ambition, and the exploitative nature of urban life.

3. The post-bellum decades witnessed the emergence of Modern America. Industrialism produced financial giants, but at the same time created an industrial proletariat entirely at the mercy of external forces beyond their control. On the other hand, new ideas about man and man's place in the universe began to take root in America. Darwin's ideas of evolution and especially those of Herbert Spencer and his vogue in America helped to change the outlook of many rising authors and intellectuals, and produced an attitude of gloom and despair which characterized American literature of this period.

4. Stephen Crane, Frank Norris, and Theodore Dreiser. Other names include Jack London, Edwin Arlington Robinson, O. Henry, Upton Sinclair and so on.

5. Realism is a literary movement that is characterized by the representation of real life. Naturalism is an outgrowth of realism that is influenced by scientific theories. Realism portrays the everyday life of common or ordinary people. Naturalism portrayed how heredity, environment, and social conditions control human beings.

Part II Progressive Era—The Muckrakers

Watch the video. Write *T* for true or *F* for false for each statement.

1. T 2. T 3. T 4. F 5. F 6. T 7. T 8. T 9. F 10. F

答案解析：

4. 不是 Franklin Roosevelt，而是 Theodore Roosevelt。
5. 不是 economic corruption，而是 political corruption。
9. 不是 articles，而是 in photos and through stories。
10. 不是 New York，而是 Chicago。

Part III Jack London and Sustainable Agriculture

Watch the video and answer the following questions.

1. His connection to the land and his belief in sustainable agriculture.

2. A model California ranch.

3. Because they cultivated the land until the soil was exhausted and then moved on to another property.

4. To rebuild worn-out hillside lands.

5. Utilizing methods such as cover cropping, crop rotation, terracing and the use of liquid manures.

6. Unique farm structures and willingness to experiment with modern agricultural techniques.

7. Their own exercise equipment.

8. The wood twisted and split when cured.

9. He recognized that chemical fertilizers would destroy the earth.

10. He wanted to revolutionize agriculture so that it would sustain the soil and the people who depended on it forever.

Part Ⅳ Pure Pessimism: A Reading, Summary, and Analysis of Crane's *A Man Said to the Universe*

Watch the video and fill in the blanks with the right information.

1) summed up	2) memorize	3) on display	4) cite
5) form fits function	6) incredibly	7) exploring	8) era
9) uplifting	10) melancholy	11) moral	12) interpretation
13) acknowledge	14) void	15) antithesis	16) preach
17) ultimate	18) outright	19) accomplishes	20) set out to

Part Ⅴ Dreiser's Cities—Chicago and New York in Late 19th Century

Watch the video and answer the following questions.

1. *Sister Carrie*.

2. Catholics.

3. He left for Chicago when he was 16 to escape the poor farm on which his family resided.

4. A fairly disreputable life. She has numerous affairs.

5. He could earn enough to shake the dispiriting existence he had been enduring.

6. The 60 hours plus work weeks of men and women who labored at a grinding pace in dangerous factories day after sweat-filled day for miserable wages.

7. Its meatpacking factories.

8. 28 dollars and 1 cent.

9. Goods from the center of the continent could be sent directly to New York City where they could be speedily exported to Europe and elsewhere.

10. Chicago's place in the railroad lines.

11. Irish immigrants.

12. Non-white and subhuman.

13. 90,000.

14. Nearly half of the population.

15. His intimate familiarity with Chicago's commercial workings, and his own problems finding employment there.

Watch the video and choose the best answer for the following questions.
1. C 2. D 3. D 4. B 5. C 6. D 7. A 8. C 9. A 10. C

Appendix 2   Transcripts

Part II   Progressive Era—The Muckrakers

Hello and welcome to another US history online lesson. Today we're gonna continue with our unit on the Progressive Era, by examining the muckrakers. So, what is a muckraker? Well, a muckraker is a journalist, who could be someone writing an article, could be someone writing a book, could be someone taking pictures, could be someone drawing cartoons, and all in an effort to bring awareness to the dirt or the muck in society. Their goal is to bring it to the attention of public officials in government in hopes of trying to address some of these problems, and it's also bringing awareness to American people that may not know about some of these problems. The name "Muckraker" was given to these journalists by president Theodore Roosevelt, because they were always bringing up the muck in American society. In fact, you've already learned about one of the muckrakers — Thomas Nast and his efforts to expose political corruption.

The first muckraker that we're gonna talk about today is Frank Norris. Frank Norris wrote a book called *The Octopus* in 1901, which is a fictional account about the struggle that farmers were engaged in with railroad monopolies, during the age of industrialization, and it helps lead to the breakup of these monopolies, like what takes place in the Supreme Court case Northern Securities vs. the US in 1904.

Another influential muckraker was Lewis Hine. Lewis Hine was a photojournalist that was able to capture child labor. He was able to show kids working in coal mines, and in factories, in every other working condition imaginable. This helped pave the way for child labor laws in different states and across the country as a whole. Ida Tarbell was a writer who was able to expose the ruthless business tactics of the Standard Oil Company in a series of articles in *McClure's Magazine*, published together in 1904. These articles were so damaging that they led to the Supreme Court case Standard Oil vs. the US in 1911—the same Supreme Court case that would split up the Standard Oil Company of John Rockefeller.

In his book, *How the Other Half Lives* written in 1890, Danish immigrant Jacob Riis was able to expose the living conditions of the urban poor, focusing primarily on tenements, all in an effort to show the middle-class, literally how the other half lives. He was able to do this in photos and through stories, and as a result New York City passed building codes to promote safety and health.

Last and certainly not least is the book *The Jungle* written by Upton Sinclair in 1906. In the book *The Jungle*, it investigates the dangerous working conditions and unsanitary procedures in the meatpacking industry of Chicago. This will lead to a couple of different pieces of legislation to reform the food industry. The first coming in 1906 was the Pure Food and Drug Act, which required all food and medicines to have labels with ingredients, side effects and other things. This Act still exists and is regulated by the FDA—the Food and Drug Administration. And it also led the way for the Meat Inspection Act of 1906, which required all meat products to be inspected by the government before, during and after processing.

So, there you have it. This gives you a glimpse at just some of the works of some of the muckrakers during the Progressive Era. We'll explore the works of these five more in class. Next time, we'll focus on social reforms, including what happens when you take away America's alcohol.

Part III Jack London and Sustainable Agriculture

Jack London famously wrote, "I am a sailor on horseback! Watch my dust! Oh, I shall make mistakes of many; but watch my dreams come true—try to dream with me of my dreams of fruitful acres." Jack London wanted Beauty Ranch to be his true legacy. Though famous for his literature, it was his connection to the land and his belief in sustainable agriculture that mattered the most to Jack. In renewing the land, Jack renewed himself. In the Valley of the Moon, he and Charmian found their paradise. Jack was determined to transform the property into a model California ranch. He despaired of the wasteful California pioneer farmers who cultivated the land until the soil was exhausted and then moved on to another property. Influenced by his travels in Korea and Japan, Jack put innovative ideas into action to rebuild worn-out hillside lands. He enriched his soil utilizing methods such as cover cropping, crop rotation, terracing and the use of liquid manures. He was also known for his prize-winning livestock, unique farm structures and willingness to experiment with modern agricultural techniques. The stone piggery, dubbed by the press says London's Palace Hotel for Pigs, was one of Jack's most ambitious projects. A marvel of innovation in animal care, it provided sanitary and optimum health conditions for Duroc jersey pigs. It cost a fortune, but his pigs turned out prime. Visitors to the ranch had to walk through a carbolic acid trough before entering areas where animals were kept, maintaining his strict sanitation standards. His bulls had their own exercise equipment. His silos were built to store shredded corn stalks that would later ferment and to feed for livestock. Jack thought eucalyptus trees would be a successful lumber crop. He planted 100,000 seedlings, but his experiment failed—the wood twisted and split when cured. No one could use it. He also experimented with growing spineless cactus to feed his cattle, but that didn't work either. Jack riley called the farm, "the ranch of good intentions" since despite some of his best efforts, he met with some notable failures. Yet Jack never let failure stop him. Jack was a visionary. Well ahead of his time, he recognized that chemical fertilizers would destroy the earth. Jack wanted to revolutionize agriculture so that it would sustain the soil and the people who depended on it forever. He was California's first true organic farmer.

Part IV Pure Pessimism: A Reading, Summary, and Analysis of Crane's *A Man Said to the Universe*

In a mere 24 words, Stephen Crane summed up one of humankind's greatest fears. Welcome to a reading summary and analysis of *A Man Said to the Universe*.

A man said to the universe:
"Sir I exist!"
"However," replied the universe,
"The fact has not created in me
A sense of obligation."

So, this is one of those poems that is so short that you can probably memorize it in just a couple of minutes. However, that doesn't mean we should ignore one of the golden rules of reading poetry, that you need to understand every word in the poem, especially for shorter poems. So, make sure you check out the definitions, if there's anything you're unfamiliar with.

In terms of poetic devices there's not a whole lot, I guess you get a rhyme with universe and universe, but it's just a repeated word, so it's not much of a rhyme. However, we see line breaks on display here, and in fact I have another video specifically on line breaks, and this is one of the poems that I cite in it, because there's not much that Crane's working with outside of line breaks. And usually when we're studying poetic devices, we're gonna see that form fits function sort of thing, so the poet is using this device, because it supports the meaning behind the poem.

And one of the things that jumps right out at me is that, one of these lines, the second line is incredibly short, and this line is the quote from the man. The man in this poem represents all of humanity. We shout into the universe but the universe doesn't need to care. Just because we have a voice doesn't mean that the universe is listening, is another way to think about it.

Now again, this is Stephen Crane's world view here, or at least in this poem the world view that he's exploring. Crane comes from an era of literature in the United States known as Realism and Naturalism, and you see a lot of Nihilism in that. You look at some of Stephen Crane's other works—*The Open Boat*, *Red Badge of Courage* are two examples that come right to mind and they're not necessarily encouraging or uplifting. Even if you jump back into like the sort of melancholy and depressing works of Romanticism and Dark Romanticism with Poe and Hawthorne and Melville, there's still like a moral at play.

And there's this idea that there is some justice in the universe. The murderer gets caught, ambition is punished, the terrible things people do out of sight are brought to the light. You don't see that with Stephen Crane. At least not with this piece. I think it's also worth pointing out that the whole poem is short, and obviously Crane realizes this it's one thought there's no real room for interpretation. "However," replied the universe, "the fact that you exist has not created in me—the universe—a sense of obligation." I'm not obliged to care for you or even really acknowledge you.

So, I think when we shout into the void, when we want to think that we're important, that we're significant, that there is a higher power, perhaps we want a reply. We think, wow! I want a reply to confirm my beliefs. Wouldn't it be great if God just spoke back to me? Or whatever higher power you subscribe to or don't subscribe to, whatever it is you worship, wouldn't it be great if something just spoke back? And here, the higher power of the universe, the entity as a whole does speak back, but what a depressing thing to have spoken back to us: "I'm not obliged to care for you." It's really the antithesis to what most religions preach.

So, you can see how this would be a controversial poem when it comes out, and I'm not saying that Stephen Crane or the speaker in this poem is correct. In the ultimate sense here, it is not the world view that I personally subscribe to, as a God—fearing Christian, but that doesn't mean I reject the poem outright or don't think that it has merit or value. In many ways the universe is unfair. It's not obliged to care for you. And I think if you examine most ideas of religion, you'll find that the world that we live in very much like the universe here is not obliged to care for us. The idea of care comes from our fellow humans or from God. So, I think even all these years later, *A Man Said to the Universe* is still a rather shocking poem. It accomplishes exactly what Crane set out to do.

And whether you believe that this is all there is or not, you still have to do something about it. You still have to move forward. I think the sequel to this poem what Crane's asking us here, is what do we do with this? And one answer is to continue to learn and grow and search for answers. And I think if you're watching this video, you're probably the type of person who does that. So, I wish you luck in finding, whatever it is you're searching for. And I want to encourage you that I truly believe that even if the universe as a whole doesn't care for you, there are people in this universe that do. That might have been a little deep if you were just here to figure out something for your homework. But anyway, that's what it was. Happy reading. I hope to see you in the next video. Thank you so much for watching.

Part V Dreiser's Cities—Chicago and New York in Late 19th Century

Theodore Dreiser was intimately familiar with both Chicago and New York, the settings for his novel *Sister Carrie*. Born in Indiana into a poor Catholic home vibrating with three boys and four girls, he left for Chicago when he was 16 to escape the poor farm on which his family resided. His sister Emma, whose vexed life was the model for Carrie Meeber, was already living in Chicago, where she engaged in a fairly disreputable life, having numerous affairs. Regardless, once arrived, Dreiser grew infatuated with city life. He was excited by the bustling traffic on the sidewalks and streets. He enjoyed marquees or theatres, the noise inside and outside restaurants, the music from stage productions, and of course he naively believed that he could earn enough to shake the dispiriting existence he had been enduring. He failed to miss ambition however. Good jobs as he soon learned, were not plentiful in Chicago.

Here's some context that will be helpful. The late 19th century was the Gilded Age in America, when a few men made vast fortunes from the tremendous growth of industrial enterprises. The glitter associated with the age was a sham of sorts however. Beneath the few stories of stupendous fortunes lay the 60 hours plus work weeks of men and women who labored at a grinding pace in dangerous factories day after sweat-filled day for miserable wages. The factory Chicago became most known for, well, its meatpacking factories, earning it the nickname hog butcher to the world. Pulling from the livestock of the surrounding countryside, the factories often had workers repeat a single monotonous aspect of slaughtering, cleaning or packaging meat, in a process that would directly inspire Henry Ford's approach to industrial assembly. For many workers in the factories and elsewhere, earnings barely kept pace with their expenses. In 1891 for example, the monthly expenses of one family—a laborer, his wife and a child—total 28 dollars and one cent for food, rents and other necessities. His monthly income was 23 dollars and 67 cents.

Yet, even if it was unkind to many of its inhabitants, Chicago had been growing exponentially for decades, and would continue to do so. Why? First, you have to remember that in 1825, the Erie Canal was completed. It was a waterway in New York that runs about 363 miles from Albany on the Hudson River to Buffalo at Lake Erie, completing a navigable water route from the Atlantic Ocean to the Great Lakes. This meant that goods from the center of the continent—crops, meat, timber, no longer had to be sent down the Mississippi to New Orleans and beyond. Instead, materials could be sent directly to New York City where they could be speedily exported to Europe and elsewhere. Chicago became the major gathering place for these goods, largely because some of Chicago's businessmen had connived to have the country's railroad system focused on Chicago. Considering the growth of the city, in 1850, 1860, and 1870, just before the Great Chicago Fire hit in 1871, this growth was made possible only by virtue of Chicago's place in the railroad lines.

The incredible vast railway system was, in the East at least, constructed by mostly Irish immigrants. Railroad work is incredibly hard and the system became crucial to the prosperity of Chicago in the United States more generally. Yet the Irish immigrants who worked on it were treated horribly by the native population. Few Americans realized that in the 19th century, the Irish were perceived to be non-white and subhuman. The wealthy and middle-class Americans sought to distance themselves from these immigrants. Cities always involve conflicts of proximity. As the Irish settled in lands around the railroad, they were led ever closer to the very neighborhoods in which the city's wealthiest citizens lived.

On October 8th, 1871, a fire started in a barn owned by Patrick and Catherine and O'Leary. Winds picked up and as most of the city was made of wood, the fire spread rapidly. Eventually, the fire reached the central business district where it destroyed hotels, department stores, Chicago City Hall, the Opera House and theaters, churches and printing plants. The fire finally burned itself out, aided by diminishing winds, and a light drizzle that began following late on Monday night. Once the fire ended, the smoldering remains were still too hot for a survey of the damage to be completed for days. Eventually it was determined that the fire destroyed an area about 4 miles long, encompassing more than 2,000 acres. It destroyed more than 73 miles of roads, 120 miles of sidewalks, 2,000 lampposts, 17,000 buildings and over 200 million dollars in property, about a third of the city's valuation. Of the 300,000 inhabitants, 90,000 were left homeless.

Yet in subsequent decades, a rebuilt Chicago rose dramatically from the ashes. In 1890 when the novel begins, the territorial confines of Chicago stretched to 165 square miles. Infrastructure and industry guaranteed that it would grow, even more in the decades to follow. As industries continued to grow, young men and women poured into Chicago and other major cities from rural communities across the Midwest, hoping to earn their fortunes. The railroads provided the major impetus for growth. In 1860, there were only 60,000 miles of track in the United States, but by 1900 that figure had multiplied to 250,000, leaving hardly a single major community outside the railroad system. Supporting the rise of industry was an increase in non-agricultural jobs. About 4.6 million Americans worked in factories and 3 million in construction and transportation by the end of the century. The industrial workforce was fed by a steady stream of emigration, which brought 5 million people to the United States between 1880 and 1890 alone. Meanwhile, there was a major internal migration of workers from rural areas to urban centers. By 1920, nearly half of the population in the United States was living in cities. The main attraction of the cities was employment. Chicago was home to many large enterprises, including major weaving and cloth production facilities, an enormous meatpacking industry and countless clothing and shoe factories. Dreiser's interest in this rapid growth is presented in one of *Sister Carrie*'s early chapters. Dreiser's arrived in Chicago and circumstance is very similar to Carrie's, seeking work at a variety of industries, all with limited success. His intimate familiarity with Chicago's commercial workings, and his own problems finding employment there, most certainly influenced his use of the city as the setting for Carrie's early failures, and feelings of alienation and desperation.

The second half of the novel takes place in New York City, where Dreiser's career as a journalist and writer eventually took him. Unlike Chicago, New York City was established as a major trading post, not in the mid-19th century, but more than 200 years before, in 1609 when Englishman Henry Hudson sailed through the Narrows into upper New York Bay. Hudson was looking for a westerly passage to Asia and never found one. But he did make note of the abundant beaver population. Beaver pelts were in fashion in Europe, and Hudson's report of the beaver population in New York area served as the impetus for the founding of Dutch trading colonies in the New World, among them New Amsterdam which would become New York City.

Over the next 250 years, the city became the most populous and richest city in America, the place where the goods of the New World made their way to the old world, and vice versa. This process made some very rich indeed, and this wealth could be seen in the splendid architecture of the city. The city planners developed an expanded city grid that encompassed all Manhattan and the old merchant aristocracy pressed for a central park, which was opened to a design competition in 1857. It would become the first landscaped park in an American city. New York came to boast signs of incredible prosperity—gorgeous tall edifices, numerous theaters and places of entertainment, a complex public transit system, and numerous bridges. In many ways, however, places like the Central Park and the incredibly wealthy neighborhoods that surrounding it to the east and west, represented a counterpoint to the much poorer neighborhoods of the south. As in other American cities during this period, enormous gulfs and income and wealth existed side-by-side.

In the neighborhoods closer to the docks lived thousands of immigrants from regions far and wide. While many of these immigrants were Irish, as was the case in Chicago, New York was a true world city, even in these years. Life here, however, was in sharp contrast to life for the merchant aristocracy. Another journalist of the period Jacob Riis, a Dutch immigrant himself, documented the squalid living conditions common in these neighborhoods in his famous book *How the Other Half Live*. Riis had been a reporter in these areas for many years before he wrote this book, and his articles were always quite open about his sympathies for the poor. One day in 1888, we read of the use of flash powder to take 9 pictures and within weeks he was taking camera equipment into unlit tenement quarters and up foul alleyways at night, shooting pictures to portray the unsavory living conditions of the poor.

Riis put the pictures to work without delay. Later he wrote, "I recall a midnight expedition to the Mulberry Bend, with a sanitary police, that had turned up a couple of characters two cases of overcrowding. In one instance, two rooms that should at most have held 4 or 5 sleepers were found to contain 15 a-week-old baby among them. Most of them were lodgers and slept there for 5 cents a spot, there was no pretense of beds. When the report was submitted to the Health Board the next day, it did not make much of an impression. These things rarely do, put in mere words, until my negatives still dripping from the darkroom, came to reinforce them. From them, there was no appeal, neither the landlord's protest, nor the tenants' plea went in the face of the camera's evidence, and I was satisfied."

As we'll discuss in class, the life of the poor understood in terms of environmental and biological influences is a major theme of literary naturalism, movement with which Dreiser is most closely associated. Dreiser's novel shows us this same aspect of city life, as well as the glitter and prosperity, the yearning for success that was on display elsewhere in the city.

Chapter 5

Appendix 1 Key to Exercises

Part I Warm-up

Discuss the following questions in pairs or groups.

1. World War I had an important influence on the development of modernist literature. The war brought about a general feeling of pessimism, leading to the breakdown of old values and beliefs, as well as a sense that society was entering new phases. This led to a general feeling that life was pointless and meaningless.

2. In realism, that preceded modernism, the main thought was that the reality in everyday life is the ultimate truth. It is not dependent on the power of observers and so, it must be depicted as it is, in arts and literature. Modernism challenged realism, as it focused on inner self-consciousness and the power of scientific experimentation to challenge and consequently change reality.

3. Modern poetry is a style of writing that is defined by two distinct characteristics. The first is technical innovation in the writing, exemplified by the liberal use of free verse. The second is a departure from the Romantic idea of an unproblematic poetic "self" speaking directly to an equally unproble matic ideal reader or audience.

4. Imagism was a literary movement of the early 20th century. The proponents were interested in the use of precise imagery and clear language.

5. Ezra Pound, T. S. Eliot, William Carlos Williams, Wallace Stevens, Carl Sandburg, Robert Frost and so on.

Part II What is Imagism?

Watch the video. Write *T* for true or *F* for false for each statement.

1. F   2. F   3. T   4. T   5. F   6. F   7. T   8. T   9. T   10. F

答案解析：

1. 不是 England，而是 England and America。

2. 不是 Elizabethan，而是 Victorian。

5. 不是 Hulme，而是 Pound。

6. 不是 1908，而是 1912。

10. 不是 F. S. Flint，而是 Pound。

Part III What Makes a Poem a Poem?

Watch the video and fill in the blanks.

1) captivated   2) delivered   3) approximate   4) recognizable
5) condensed   6) rhythmic   7) advent   8) visual

9) amplifying	10) inseparable	11) navigate	12) essence
13) formatted	14) orators	15) bursts	16) evolved
17) blurred	18) forge	19) sonnets	20) journalism

Part IV What is Modernity? — T. S. Eliot's Context

Watch the video and answer the following questions.

1. The interrelationship between World War I and how that implicates the writing of T. S. Eliot's poetry.

2. The rise of modern life experience. Eliot is ambivalent toward modernity.

3. Urban landscapes were being erected and population is increasing. On the other hand, the development of the train line, the use of coal in industry, had the effect of really darkening the modern landscape.

4. The landscape was being dirtied by urban mindset.

5. He is in some ways optimistic about the possibility of what the urban landscape might bring in terms of connecting individuals, but he sees the geographical landscape as in itself dismantling the ability for people to live together and connect on an emotional level.

6. A persona on his own roaming through the landscape.

7. Nightfall and darkness are quite symbolic of that foreboding force of death.

8. The light signifies the inevitability of death.

Part V Can a Computer Write a Poem?

Watch the video and decide which poem is written by human and which one is written by computer. Write *H* if it is composed by a human, and *C* if it is composed by a computer.

1. H   2. C   3. C   4. H   5. H   6. C

Appendix 2 Transcripts

Part II What is Imagism?

Imagism was born in England and America in the early 20th century. A reactionary movement against Romanticism and Victorian poetry, imagism emphasized simplicity, clarity of expression, and precision through the use of exact visual images.

Though Ezra Pound is noted as the founder of Imagism, the movement was rooted in ideas first developed by English philosopher and poet T. E. Hulme, who, as early as in 1908, spoke of poetry based on an absolutely accurate presentation of its subject, with no excess verbiage. In his essay *Romanticism and Classicism*, Hulme wrote that the language of poetry is a "visual concrete one... Images in verse are not mere decoration, but the very essence".

Pound adapted Hulme's ideas on poetry for his imagist movement, which began in earnest in 1912, when he first introduced the term into the literary lexicon during a meeting with Hilda Doolittle. After reading her poem *Hermes of the Ways*, Pound suggested some revisions and signed the poem *H. D., Imagiste* before sending it to *Poetry* magazine in October of that year. That November, Pound himself used the term "Imagiste" in print for the first time when he published Hulme's Complete Poetical Works.

A strand of modernism, imagism aimed to replace abstractions with concrete details that could be further expounded upon through the use of figuration. These typically short, free verse poems—which had clear precursors in the concise, image-focused poems of ancient Greek lyricists and Japanese Haiku poets—moved away from fixed meters and moral reflections, subordinating everything to what Hulme once called the "hard, dry image".

Pound's definition of the image was "that which presents an intellectual and emotional complex in an instant of time". He said, "It is the presentation of such a 'complex' instantaneously which gives the sense of sudden liberation; that sense of freedom from time limits and space limits; that sense of sudden growth, which we experience in the presence of the greatest works of art." In March 1913, Poetry published *A Few Don'ts by an Imagiste*. In it, imagist poet F. S. Flint, quoting Pound, defined the tenets of imagist poetry.

Part III What Makes a Poem a Poem?

Muhammad Ali spent years training to become the greatest boxer that the world had ever seen, but only spent a few moments to create the shortest poem. Ali captivated Harvard's graduating class in 1975 with his message of unity and friendship. When he finished, the audience wanted more. They wanted a poem. Ali delivered what is considered the shortest poem ever. "Me, we." Or is it "me, weeee"? No one is really sure. Regardless, if these two words are a poem, then what exactly makes a poem a poem? Poets themselves have struggled with this question, often using metaphors to approximate a definition. Is a poem a little machine? A firework? An echo? A dream? Poetry generally has certain recognizable characteristics:

One, poems emphasize language's musical qualities. This can be achieved through rhyme, rhythm, and meter. From the sonnets of Shakespeare, to the odes of Confucius, to the Sanskrit Vedas.

Two, poems use condensed language, like literature with all the water wrung out of it.

Three, poems often feature intense feelings, from Rumi's spiritual poetry to Pablo Neruda's "Ode to an Onion".

Poetry, like art itself, has a way of challenging simple definitions. While the rhythmic patterns of the earliest poems were a way to remember stories even before the advent of writing, a poem doesn't need to be lyrical. Reinhard Döhl's "Apfel" and Eugen Gomringer's "Silencio" toe the line between visual art and poetry. Meanwhile, E. E. Cummings wrote poems whose shapes were as important as the words themselves, in this case amplifying the sad loneliness of a single leaf falling through space. If the visual nature of poetry faded into the background, perhaps we'd be left with music, and that's an area that people love to debate. Are songs poems? Many don't regard songwriters as poets in a literary sense, but lyrics from artists like Paul Simon, Bob Dylan, and Tupac Shakur often hold up even without the music. In rap, poet elements like rhyme, rhythm, and imagery are inseparable from the form. Take this lyric from the Notorious B. I. G.

"I can hear sweat trickling
down your cheek

Your heartbeat sound

like Sasquatch feet

Thundering, shaking the concrete."

So far, all the examples we've seen have line breaks. We can even imagine the two words of Ali's poem organizing in the air—Me, We. Poetry has a shape that we can usually recognize. Its line breaks help readers navigate the rhythms of a poem. But what if those line breaks disappeared? Would it lose its essence as a poem? Maybe not. Enter the prose poem. Prose poems use vivid images and wordplay but are formatted like paragraphs. When we look at poetry less as a form and more as a concept, we can see the poetic all around us: spiritual hymns, the speeches of orators like Martin Luther King, Jr., John Fitzgerald Kennedy, and Winston Churchill, and surprising places like social media. In 2010, journalist Joanna Smith tweeted updates from the earthquake in Haiti.

"Was in b-room getting dressed

when heard my name.

Tremor. Ran outside through sliding door.

All still now. Safe. Roosters crowing."

Smith uses language in a way that is powerful, direct, and filled with vivid images. Compare her language to a Haiku, the ancient Japanese poetic form that emphasizes bursts of brief intensity with just three lines of five, seven, and five syllables. The waters of poetry run wide and deep. Poetry has evolved over time, and perhaps now more than ever, the line between poetry, prose, song, and visual art has blurred. However, one thing has not changed. The word poetry actually began in verb form, coming from the ancient Greek *poiēsis*, which means to create. Poets, like craftsmen, still work with the raw materials of the world to forge new understandings and comment on what it is to be human in a way only humans can. Dartmouth researchers tested this idea by asking robots to write poetry. A panel of judges sorted through stacks of sonnets to see if they could distinguish those made by man and machine. You may be happy to know that while scientists have successfully used artificial intelligence in manufacturing, medicine, and even journalism, poetry is a different story. The robots were caught red-handed 100% of the time.

Part Ⅳ What is Modernity? —T. S. Eliot's Context

Hey guys! It's Leila from Ignite and this is my last video on context for T. S. Eliot. If you've watched the previous ones, we've looked at the interrelationship between World War One and how that implicates the writing of T. S. Eliot's poetry, in the sense that it connects to the exploration of psychoanalysis: How World War One implicates the subconscious, and how that interest in the subconscious filters through his poetry.

Today I'd like to look at Modernity, which encapsulates the rise of modern life experience and how Eliot is somewhat ambivalent towards this idea, but at the same time has a lot of concerns about the implications of modern life, particularly on our inability to connect to individuals, despite this bustle of modern life and experience. Okay! So just a flag. If you are a student studying the HSC, I will be connecting this contextual information to Module B. But if you're someone who's just interested in T. S. Eliot and the backdrop of his poetry, this is still highly relevant to you. As you know, if you have watched the previous videos, it's important to consider the context of Eliot, because that contextual backdrop, the ways of thinking at the time deeply influence what he exposes in his poetry in terms of his concerns during his context. But thinking more closely about Modernity, I've got a picture up here to show you quite visually what life was like during the time of T. S. Eliot. You had buildings, urban landscapes that were being erected, and you could see that this increase in population and this increase in the modern landscape, was quite anxiety—invoking for the individual. The development of the train line, the use of coal in industry, had the effect of really darkening the modern landscape. The omnipresence of thought, the blackness of the roads, had this implication that the world was dark. And you place that against the backdrop of war, you've got the experience of trauma, and now a landscape that was, through the eyes of Eliot, being dirtied by urban mindset. And you can see the description of the urban landscape within his poetry, really critiquing the urban landscape. Having said that though, I said earlier on that there is an ambivalence in his poetry. He is in some ways optimistic about the possibility of what the urban landscape might bring in terms of connecting individuals, but we don't see any physical connection in his poetry. Rather we see that the buildings of the urban landscape, the disparate ways that streets fail to connect, actually awoke, on a contextual level, the inability of the individual to connect with others. He sees the geographical landscape as in itself dismantles the ability for people to live together and connect on an emotional level. So, what I'd like you to look for in the poetry, is how the landscape, the construction of the landscape, delimit the individual's ability to connect with others, because in the ways that the streets follow on in a disconnected and disparate way, that also traces the disconnection of the population. So, there's an interrelationship between the environment and the mindset of people during this context. So, in this sense, while there was a development of industry and we see the development of buildings, there's a paradox associated with that, because in Eliot's eyes, more than benefiting society, the development of the urban landscape rather disconnected the individuals and failed to bring them together. So, while there was an absolute increase in the population during the time, he saw people as cramped together in this uncomfortable environment and unable to actually physically connect. So, what we see within his poetry is this interception between the environment and the mind of the individual, how psychoanalysis—the subconscious feeds into the description of the landscape, and there is a marriage between the external world and the internal insecurities of Eliot's personas. I've got a quote which illustrates this. I want you to have a look at how the environment is being described quite sincerely in Preludes. It reads, "The winter evening settles down/ with smell of steaks in passageways. / The burnt-out ends of smoky days / ' Grimy scraps ... withered leaves ... newspapers from/ vacant lots... broken blinds'. " So, we see in all of his poems really a persona on his own roaming through the landscape and it often occurs at night time. The significance of this occurring at night is nightfall and darkness is quite symbolic for that foreboding force of death. And the only places in his palms where light is dispersed, is often alongside memory. So, how light tries to bring back memories of the past—past being prior to modernity, which was for him a better state of living, and also how the light signifies the inevitability of death you will call the beating of the fatalistic drum which is a motif in his poetry. The point that I'm trying to convey here is it's within this grimy urban landscape, it's described as dirty as corrupted and as disconnected. And it's within this landscape that not only do we see a lack of connection, but how this external world awakens within the person a fear of life and an inevitability of death. So, take note of how the rise of modernity the implications of the modern landscape are evoked in his poetry through the imagery, the senses and the tones that they convey. And how they awaken the insecurities of the persona and how it's within this environment that not only is he unable to connect with others, but rather his mind is turned to the inevitability of his mortality, which means death as the end of his existence. I hope that you guys like this video and you can see the interrelationship between the three contextual frameworks we've gone through: World War I invoking trauma, inevitability of death, psychoanalysis bringing out to the fore the subconscious of the mind previous traumas and how they manifest in the present, and finally the urban landscape, and how the grimy nature of the external world awakens all of the fears of the individual, and it manifests in the form of isolation an inability to connect because of this disparate landscape. If you enjoy this video, guys, please do like and subscribe to our channel we'll have more content coming your way, but for now, thank you so much for watching!

Part V Can a Computer Write a Poem?

I have a question. Can a computer write poetry? This is a provocative question. You think about it for a minute, and you suddenly have a bunch of other questions like: What is a computer? What is poetry? What is creativity? But these are questions that people spend their entire lifetime trying to answer, not in a single TED Talk. So, we're going to try a different approach. So up here, we have two poems. One of them is written by a human, and the other one is written by a computer. I'm going to ask you to tell me which one is which. Have a go:

Poem 1: Little Fly / Thy summer's play, /
My thoughtless hand / Has brushed away.

Am I not / A fly like thee? /
Or art not thou / A man like me?

Poem 2: We can feel / Activist
through your life's / morning /

Pauses to see, pope I hate the /
Non all the night to start a / great otherwise (…)

Key to Exercises and Transcripts

Alright, time's up. Hands up if you think Poem 1 was written by a human. OK, most of you. Hands up if you think Poem 2 was written by a human. Very brave of you, because the first one was written by the human poet William Blake. The second one was written by an algorithm that took all the language from my Facebook feed on one day and then regenerated it algorithmically, according to methods that I'll describe a little bit later on. So, let's try another test. Again, you haven't got ages to read this, so just trust your gut.

Poem 1: A lion roars and a dog barks.
It is interesting / and fascinating

that a bird will fly and not / roar
or bark. Enthralling stories about animals

are in my dreams and I will sing them all
if I / am not exhausted or weary.

Poem 2: Oh! Kangaroos, sequins, chocolate
sodas! / You are really beautiful!

Pearls, / harmonicas, jujubes, aspirins!
All / the stuff they've always talked about (...)

Alright, time's up. So, if you think the first poem was written by a human, put your hands up. OK. And if you think the second poem was written by a human, put your hands up. We have, more or less, a 50/50 split here. It was much harder. The answer is, the first poem was generated by an algorithm called Racter, that was created back in the 1970s, and the second poem was written by a guy called Frank O'Hara, who happens to be one of my favorite human poets. So, what we've just done now is a Turing Test for poetry. The Turing Test was first proposed by this guy, Alan Turing, in 1950, in order to answer the question, can computers think? Alan Turing believed that if a computer was able to have a text-based conversation with a human, with such proficiency that the human couldn't tell whether they were talking to a computer or a human, then the computer can be said to have intelligence. So, in 2013, my friend Benjamin Laird and I, we created a Turing Test for poetry online. It's called Bot or Not, and you can go and play it for yourselves. But basically, it's the game we just played. You're presented with a poem. You don't know whether it was written by a human or a computer and you have to guess. So, thousands and thousands of people have taken this test online. So, we have results. And what are the results? Well, Turing said that if a computer could fool a human 30 percent of the time that it was a human, then it passes the Turing Test for intelligence. We have poems on the Bot or Not database that have fooled 65 percent of human readers into thinking it was written by a human. So, I think we have an answer to our question. According to the logic of the Turing Test, can a computer write poetry? Well, yes, absolutely it can. But if you're feeling a little bit uncomfortable with this answer, that's OK. If you're having a bunch of gut reactions to it, that's also OK because this isn't the end of the story. Let's play our third and final test. Again, you're going to have to read and tell me which you think is human.

Poem 1: Red flags the reason
for pretty flags. / And ribbons.

Ribbons of flags / And wearing material /
Reasons for wearing material. (…)

Poem 2: A wounded deer leaps
highest, / I've heard the daffodil

I've heard the flag to-day /
I've heard the hunter tell; /

'Tis but the ecstasy of death, /
And then the brake is almost done (…)

OK, time is up. So, hands up if you think Poem 1 was written by a human. Hands up if you think Poem 2 was written by a human. Whoa, that's a lot more people. So, you'd be surprised to find that Poem 1 was written by the very human poet Gertrude Stein. And Poem 2 was generated by an algorithm called RKCP. Now before we go on, let me describe very quickly and simply how RKCP works. So, RKCP is an algorithm designed by Ray Kurzweil, who is a director of engineering at Google and a firm believer in artificial intelligence. So, you give RKCP a source text, it analyzes the source text in order to find out how it uses language, and then it regenerates language that emulates the first text. So, in the poem we just saw before, Poem 2, the one that you all thought was human, it was fed a bunch of poems by a poet called Emily Dickinson. It looked at the way she used language, learned the model, and then it regenerated a model according to the same structure. But one important thing to know about RKCP is that it doesn't know the meaning of the words that it's using. The language is just a raw material, it could be Chinese, it could be Swedish, it could be the collected language from your Facebook feed for one day. It's just a raw material. And nevertheless, it's able to create a poem that seems more human than Gertrude Stein's poem, and Gertrude Stein is a human. So, what we've done here is, more or less, a reverse Turing Test. So, Gertrude Stein, who's a human, is able to write a poem that fools a majority of human judges into thinking that it was written by a computer. Therefore, according to the logic of the reverse Turing Test, Gertrude Stein is a computer. Feeling confused? I think that's fair enough. So far, we've had humans that write like humans, we have computers that write like computers, we have computers that write like humans, but we also have, perhaps most confusingly, humans that write like computers. So, what do we take from all of this? Do we take that William Blake is somehow more of a human than Gertrude Stein? Or that Gertrude Stein is more of a computer than William Blake? These are questions I've been asking myself for around two years now, and I don't have any answers. But what I do have are a bunch of insights about our relationship with technology. So, my first insight is that, for some reasons, we associate poetry with being human. So that when we ask, "Can a computer write poetry?" We're also asking, "What does it mean to be human and how do we put boundaries around this category? How do we say who or what can be part of this category?" This is an essentially philosophical question, I believe, and it can't be answered with a yes or no test, like the Turing Test. I also believe that Alan Turing understood this, and that when he devised his test back in 1950, he was doing it as a philosophical provocation. So, my second insight is that, when we take the Turing Test for poetry, we're not really testing the capacity of the computers because poetry-generating algorithms, they're pretty simple and have existed, more or less, since the 1950s. What we are doing with the Turing Test for poetry, rather, is collecting opinions about what constitutes humanness. So, what I've figured out, we've seen this when earlier today, we say that William Blake is more of a human than Gertrude Stein. Of course, this doesn't mean that William Blake was actually more human or that Gertrude Stein was more of a computer. It simply means that the category of the human is unstable. This has led me to understand that the human is not a cold, hard fact. Rather, it is something that's constructed with our opinions and something that changes over time. So, my final insight is that the computer, more or less, works like a mirror that reflects any idea of a human that we show it. We show it Emily Dickinson, it gives Emily Dickinson back to us. We show it William Blake, that's what it reflects back to us. We show it Gertrude Stein, what we get back is Gertrude Stein. More than any other bit of technology, the computer is a mirror that reflects any idea of the human we teach it. So, I'm sure a lot of you have been hearing a lot about artificial intelligence recently. And much of the conversation is, can we build it? Can we build an intelligent computer? Can we build a creative computer? What we seem to be asking over and over is can we build a human-like computer? But what we've seen just now is that the human is not a scientific fact, but it's an ever-shifting, concatenating idea and one that changes over time. So that when we begin to grapple with the ideas of artificial intelligence in the future, we shouldn't only be asking ourselves, "Can we build it?" But we should also be asking ourselves, "What idea of the human do we want to have reflected back to us?" This is an essentially philosophical idea, and it's one that can't be answered with software alone, but I think requires a moment of species-wide, existential reflection. Thank you.

Chapter 6

Appendix 1 Key to Exercises

Part I Warm-up

Discuss the following questions in pairs or groups.

1. The prominent authors associated with the Lost Generation literature were Ernest Hemingway,

F. Scott Fitzgerald, and Gertrude Stein, among others. These writers emerged after World War I and were characterized by their disillusionment with traditional values and their exploration of themes such as the loss of innocence, the futility of war, and the search for meaning in a post-war world. Their works often depicted the experiences of the generation that came of age during the war and reflected the sense of aimlessness and disillusionment felt by many in the aftermath of the conflict.

2. Lost Generation literature was characterized by several key themes and characteristics. One prominent theme was the disillusionment and loss of faith in traditional values and institutions, particularly as a result of the devastating effects of World War I. The authors of this movement often depicted a sense of aimlessness and alienation among their characters, who struggled to find meaning and purpose in a post-war world. The literature also explored the destructive nature of war and its impact on the human psyche. Stylistically, the writing of the Lost Generation was characterized by sparse, direct prose and a focus on depicting the inner thoughts and emotions of the characters.

3. The literary scene in the 1920s reflected the social and cultural milieu of the United States through its exploration of themes such as disillusionment, the search for identity, and the clash between traditional values and modernity. Writers of this period, such as F. Scott Fitzgerald and Ernest Hemingway, captured the spirit of the Roaring Twenties in their works. They depicted the excesses and materialism of the era, as well as the disillusionment and emptiness that often accompanied it. The literature of the time also reflected the changing roles of women, the effects of Prohibition, and the impact of war and social upheaval on individuals and society. Overall, the literary works of the 1920s provided a critical commentary on the social and cultural shifts of the time.

4. Gertrude Stein was an American writer and art collector who played a significant role in the development of modernist literature. She is best known for her experimental writing style and her role as a central figure in the Parisian literary and art scene of the early 20th century. Stein's most famous work is *The Autobiography of Alice B. Toklas*, a memoir written in the voice of her life partner. Her writing is characterized by repetitive phrases, wordplay, and a focus on the rhythm and sounds of language. Stein's contributions to literature challenged traditional narrative structures and influenced generations of writers.

Part II The Introduction of the Lost Generation

Watch the video. Write *T* for true or *F* for false for each statement.

1. F   2. T   3. F   4. F   5. T   6. T   7. F   8. F

答案解析：

1. 不是"World War Ⅱ"，是"World War Ⅰ"。
3. 不是"high economic pressure"，而是更小的经济压力。
4. 不是 Hemingway 创造的词，而是他引用 Gertrude Stein。
7. 不是"striving for"，而是"death of the American dream"。
8. 不是"new way of life"，而是"traditional life"。

Part III Gertrude Stein, the Enigma

Watch the video. Answer the following questions.

1. She was referred to as the mother of modernism, and was also a polarizing writer.

2. The writing made her famous, but her writing about ordinary things also caused outrage among readers and critics.

3. She wrote portraits of household items such as stamps, cups, and a red hat.

4. She attempted to replicate abstract painting in literary form. This new style of writing pushed the boundaries of poetry and made innovative contributions to modernism.

5. The work was not appreciated. Although she proclaimed herself as a genius, critics either mocked her or was enraged by her writing.

6. Because in the work she made a compromise, as she wanted to maintain her modernist writing style and theories as well as to make the book accepted by the general populace.

7. Stein made confusion by constructing herself as a character not in a particularly objective or personal way. It subverted the audience's expectations and challenged their desire for Stein's true perspective.

8. It was her desire to make more people understand the modernist art. Through Alice, Stein tried to give the audience permission to have trouble understanding modernism, while urging them to appreciate it.

9. She wanted to tell readers that despite the linearity of proper autobiographies, memory is never linear, and fact and fiction are always blended. There is more than one truth in many things.

10. Her writing encouraged her readers to question assumed perspectives and keep their minds open to the new and unfamiliar.

Part IV Ernest Hemingway — So Ugly, So Beautiful

Watch the video. Answer the following questions for the main ideas.

1. We say Hemingway "ugly" because of his flaws in personality, but he is also "beautiful" for his greatness in writing. The flaws and the greatness combine to make him a character so lively and authentic.

2. Mainly about the troubled time he lived in, for example, the wars and the places he had been to; the novels are also referring to his own pursuits and enthusiasms — to live authentically and be himself.

3. He learned how to use repetition and motion with words from the painters' technique of using "the short, repetitive, concentrated brushstrokes".

4. We can learn about the cold, troubled world of his time and understand the importance of considering what we may become and living according to our values.

Watch the video again. Rearrange the following expressions in the same order as they appear in the speech.

4 – 2 – 11 – 5 – 7 – 3 – 9 – 6 – 8 – 1 – 10

Part V F. Scott Fitzgerald's *The Great Gatsby*

Watch the video. Answer the following questions.

1. He went to Europe for he had been tired of the wildness and extremes around him and wanted to escape from all the extravagance and clamor of his society. He tried to find a new rhythm for life.

2. He thought the writing would be something extraordinarily beautiful but simple at the same time;

on the structure, it would be intricately patterned.

3. The theme was about the American striver (American Dream), about those who wanted to jump higher, leap farther and try harder.

4. The related questions of the theme were about what would the dream do to you, how would it change you, and what would you end up as other than being rich.

5. He admired Gatsby, for Gatsby was not constrained by some social norms or values and was ambitious to pursue what he really wanted. He wanted to be like Gatsby.

6. America offered handsomely opportunities for the young and the ambitious, but there were also impediments, which meant there were limits to which one could go in America.

7. Fitzgerald was very sympathetic to them, but he saw that there was something tragic and something very sad.

8. It symbolized a sense of defeat — the "dying fall" that one could try so desperately but achieve far less than what one wanted. It was also a junk yard of burnt up dreams.

9. They could not truly understand the system that the upper class people (the old money) controlled and made use of.

10. Although Gatsby was rich, he was nevertheless shut out by those people from their circle.

11. She was a working class girl, George's wife, and Tom's mistress. She was a vulgar person, being crazy for Tom.

12. For Tom, she was no more than a mistress to show off to a few friends.

13. The scene is able to illustrate the cruelness and ruthlessness of people like Tom and Daisy — they cost things, yet they would let somebody else pay for them. The scene ought to be ugly in this way.

14. The first kind is the revolutionary fire that belongs to a group; and the second kind is sullen resentment of a peasant that belongs to an individual.

15. Gatsby was all right all along. It was the foul dust on his dreams — those careless and corrupt people like Tom and Daisy — that truly murdered Gatsby.

Appendix 2　Transcripts

Part II　The Introduction of the Lost Generation

The people who came of age during World War I experienced a dark and horrible time in which many of their hopes and dreams had been crushed because of the war. Because of this, they were known as the Lost Generation. Here's the story of the Lost Generation writers.

Once upon a time, there was a city named Paris in France. During the 1920s, lots of Americans moved there to escape institutionalized racism and the associated race riots, xenophobia, censorship, materialism and prohibition; perhaps most importantly they escaped there because they could get a lot more stuff for their money due to a strong American dollar compared to a weaker French franc. Many of these American expatriates or people living outside their home country were writers and artists. They felt like they had more artistic freedom there than in the United States.

Perhaps the most famous representative of this group was a writer named Ernest Hemingway. He wrote a book called *The Sun Also Rises*. Published in 1926, the book is about a group of American expatriates who travel from Paris to watch the running bulls in Pamplona, Spain, among other things. At the beginning of the book, Hemingway quoted his friend and fellow writer Gertrude Stein, saying, the "Lost Generation". Stein herself apparently heard the term from someone else. But regardless, from this point forward, the writers who came of age during World War I widely became known as the "Lost Generation". All of these writers were American while Hemingway, Stein, F. Scott Fitzgerald and T. S. Eliot were among the most famous associated with this group. Other authors and artists that could get lumped in include James Joyce, Sherwood Anderson, John Dos Passos, John Steinbeck, William Faulkner, Aldous Huxley, Isadora Duncan, and Alan Seeger. Even composers like Aaron Copland get associated with the group.

The Lost Generation writers often wrote about exaggerated experiences from their own lives. Generally these experiences revolved around World War I and the years following it. They used common themes in their writings such as pointing out the ridiculously frivolous and materialistic lifestyles of the very rich, the breakdown of traditional gender roles or the death of the American dream. Perhaps no novel better demonstrates all of these themes than the classic novel *The Great Gatsby* written by F. Scott Fitzgerald and published in 1925.

Why were they called as the "Lost Generation"? Perhaps it was the general lack of purpose or ambition caused by having all their hopes and dreams crushed by the war. Having seen pointless death and destruction on a wide scale, many of them have lost faith in the more traditional way of life. Because of this, some became careless with their actions, not setting goals or working toward something great. But they were great. Eventually the term "Lost Generation" referred to all Americans who came of age experiencing the Great War. Basically we're talking about Americans born between 1883-ish and 1900-ish. It's through the art though, we feel like we really get to know who this generation were and what they truly felt while going through such a stressful and anxious time.

Part III Gertrude Stein, the Enigma

Gertrude Stein, referred to by some as the mother of modernism, is perhaps as polarizing as the art she hung on the walls of her home. Born in Allegheny, Pennsylvania to a well-to-do Jewish family, Stein dropped out of her final year at the Johns Hopkins School of Medicine, to join her brother Leo Stein as an American expatriate in Paris. There, Stein met her life partner Alice B. Toklas and hosted a salon that became a nexus for modernist art and literature. Stein's home in Paris was also the center of her most famous book *The Autobiography of Alice B. Toklas*.

While Stein, the connoisseur, was becoming a patron and friend of Pablo Picasso, Paul Cézanne, and Henri Matisse, Stein the writer became a great controversy. The writing that made Gertrude Stein famous, and that caused the most outrage was about ordinary things. In her most lauded work *Tender Buttons*, Stein wrote portraits of household items such as stamps, cups, and a red hat. In *Tender Buttons*, Stein attempted to replicate abstract painting in literary form. Paired with a style influenced by her undergraduate research on automatic writing, she pushed the boundaries of what poetry could be. Today, Stein's *Tender Buttons* is recognized for its monumental and innovative contributions to modernism, but the work was not appreciated during its time. While Stein proclaimed herself a genius insisting that her writing was intuitive and clear, critics either mocked or were enraged by her prose.

In 1933, almost two decades after *Tender Buttons* was published, Stein released *The Autobiography of Alice B. Toklas*. It was different with anything Stein had ever done before: a compromise between Stein's modernist style and her desire to reach the general populace. With Alice as its single narrator, describing her life in Paris with Gertrude Stein, critics described the autobiography as gossipy. Still, the autobiography retained the modernist disregard for conventional perspectives that Stein so embraced.

As Fanny Butcher wrote: "For years everyone, and by everyone I mean everyone who knows about such things, has been trying to get Gertrude Stein to write her autobiography. *The Autobiography of Alice B. Toklas* is Gertrude Stein's novel way of answering that cry without giving up her theories on the new forms of writing."

Stein's writing style wasn't the only thing that perplexed her critics. The public also struggled to understand Stein as a woman, a lesbian, a Jew, and a self-proclaimed masculine genius. In the autobiography, Stein played off of this confusion by constructing herself as a character who has seen through the eyes of a loved one. Instead of letting the readers inside her head by writing a traditional autobiography, she chose to subvert the audiences' expectations and challenge their desire for Stein's true perspective. Stein's name was not even printed on the front cover of the autobiography. Only on the last page did Stein reveal that she had written the book.

As a narrator, Alice B. Toklas was both an outsider and an insider in the modernist world. Stein employed Alice as a translator of the ideology of modernism for a more general audience.

"Picasso and Gertrude Stein stood together talking. I stood back and looked. I cannot say I realized anything, but I felt that there was something painful and beautiful there, and oppressive but imprisoned."

Through Alice, Stein gives the audience permission to have trouble understanding modernism, while urging them to appreciate it anyway.

The autobiography also challenges the audience's expectations of a linear series of events. Alice cycles back again and again to 1907 and her first meeting with Gertrude Stein. She reminds us that despite the linearity of proper autobiographies, memory is never linear, the past is never past, it is always right now. As the structure of the autobiography exemplified modernist theory, so did many details in the narrative. Throughout the book, Stein blended fact and fiction, challenging the assumption that there was one truth. She destabilized the literal, by telling stories where the essence of truth was called into question, and fact was disregarded.

The constructed character Gertrude Stein, the ventriloquist effect through the narrator Alice B. Toklas, the lack of a linear narrative, and the subversion of fact in *The Autobiography of Alice B. Toklas* combined to create a deeply modernist text that confronted a wider audience's assumptions about what an autobiography should look like.

The modernist period was defined in part as a period of political and moral upheaval. In subverting the traditional structure of an autobiography, Stein's writing encourages her readers to question assumed perspectives and keep their minds open to the new and unfamiliar.

Part Ⅳ Ernest Hemingway — So Ugly, So Beautiful

Arrogant, racist, misogynist, narcissist, self-absorbed, self-centered. Who was described in these deeply unflattering terms? Ernest Hemingway. Yes, Ernest Hemingway, the most famous American writer. As an English teacher, every year I think about, "Why do we still teach Hemingway?" I've published three scholarly books on Hemingway, and I've published, most recently, three books on teaching Hemingway, on the topics of war, modernism and gender. And yet every day, I'm asked, "How can you still be teaching Hemingway?"

Who was Hemingway? Born in 1899 in Oak Park, Illinois, he was brought up in an upper-middle-class family with a physician father and an opera-singer mother. He pursued fishing, hunting, journalism, boxing and football. He enlisted in the Italian Ambulance Corps, and in 1918, he was the first American wounded on the Italian Front. He was twice decorated for valor. He wrote about Paris and Spain in *The Sun Also Rises*. He wrote about the Great War in *A Farewell to Arms*. He wrote the first English-language guidebook to the bullfights in *Death in the Afternoon*. He wrote about hunting in *Green Hills of Africa*, and covered the Spanish Civil War and wrote *For Whom the Bell Tolls*. After buying his boat, Pilar, he had four world records in big-game fishing and wrote *The Old Man and the Sea*. He was married four times and had numerous girlfriends. He covered the D-Day invasion, the Battle of the Bulge, and he died by suicide after winning the Nobel Prize for Literature.

Yet Hemingway comes to us as a conflicted figure, somebody who performed masculinity at a time when gender roles were shifting in American culture and women were taking on a more dominant role and men felt the need to strengthen their role. So Hemingway established his reputation in many ways through the manufacturing of different images.

Here we see Hemingway as the wounded soldier. He had 54 pieces of shrapnel in his knee. He looks heroic, but he was blown up while passing out chocolate and cigarettes. Here's Hemingway on safari in Africa. You can now buy kudu horns like that for $20 on eBay. Here's Hemingway pursuing his passion for big-game fishing on the Gulf Stream. The meat from that 486-pound marlin went to waste. He passionately pursued the bullfights in Spain. For many, the bullfights are needless cruelty and not a cultural celebration. He covered the wars—in Spain, in Italy and in France—and afterwards suffered post-traumatic stress disorder. He had many encounters with women and was married four times. He was not a good father. And, of course, there was the drinking. His alcoholism contributed to his manic depression and perhaps to his suicide.

So, Hemingway learned to perform masculinity. He created a manufactured image that told the viewer that he was living life to the fullest; that he was living an authentic life, and you, sitting at home, perhaps, were not. And this image was sold in the media. Hemingway's face appeared on magazines that were aimed towards educated audiences, such as *Time* and *Life*. But more significantly, Hemingway's image was sold to mass audiences in these glossy, slick magazines. For many, he became a representative man, again, at a time when what it meant to be a man was being contested, as women were emerging in the workforce and there were transitions in home and in the workplace.

Thus, with all that are so problematic about Hemingway, why do we still teach his works today? I turn to *A Farewell to Arms*, in many ways, as the best example of why we still teach Hemingway to today's students. It has the literary themes and the style to help students best understand Hemingway's world. For students, to read Hemingway is a sign of something that is cool, cynical, perhaps self-destructive, to for reasons they may not quite be able to articulate. But once they are dropped into the rainy, war-torn landscape of Italy and understand the troubled world of Frederic and Catherine, they recognize that A Farewell to Arms is a great novel. What makes it great? Well, for many of us, it is because Hemingway incorporates the aesthetic principles of Paul Cezanne into his aesthetic code.

In 1924, Hemingway first saw Cezanne's paintings at the salon of Gertrude Stein, in Paris, at a time when he was forming his own aesthetic philosophy, when he was trying to decide what he wanted to do with his own brand of art.

He wrote: "He wanted to write like Cezanne painted. Cezanne started with all the tricks. Then he broke the whole thing down and built the real thing. It was hell to do... He wanted to write about country so that it would be there like Cezanne had done it in painting. You had to do it from inside yourself. There wasn't any trick. Nobody had ever written about country like that. He felt almost holy about it. It was deadly serious. You could do it if you would fight it out. If you'd lived right with your eyes."

Cezanne was a French post-impressionist painter, and in his paintings, he's using short, repetitive, concentrated brushstrokes to break down the plane of the painting. It's a lesson that Hemingway learned from him.

We could turn first to the opening pages of A Farewell to Arms. "In the late summer of that year we lived in a house in a village that looked across the river and the plain to the mountains. In the bed of the river there were pebbles and boulders, dry and white in the sun, and the water was clear and swiftly moving and blue in the channels. Troops went by the house and down the road and the dust they raised powdered the leaves of the trees. The trunks of the trees too were dusty and the leaves fell early that year and we saw the troops marching along the road and the dust rising and leaves, stirred by the breeze, falling and the soldiers marching and afterward the road bare and white except for the leaves."

Notice the repetition of Hemingway's language: he's repeating words like Cezanne are using brushstrokes. We have the word "water" twice, "dust" three times, "leaves" four times, "white" twice. Notice, too, we have things that rise and are raised, fall and are falling. Hemingway is showing the interconnectedness of the natural world: because of the way that the dust rises, the leaves fall early that year—showing us how the war has disrupted the natural cycles; nature is damaged by war.

Notice, too, how Hemingway uses motion. This is part of the trick of Cezanne: to capture life in motion on a canvas. We have the soldiers marching, we have the water flowing, we have the dust rising, and we have the leaves falling. And afterward, everything is bare and white. Hemingway is trying to capture a dominant idea of nature, to show how everything is elementally connected. From Cezanne, Hemingway learned that these short, concentrated brushstrokes would just, in the same way, be employed in his writing. As you look at a Cezanne's canvas, you can see how his brushstrokes give us a house, perhaps a roof, perhaps a tree in the same way that Hemingway's words — dust, leaves, wind— give us that same sense of motion as we get in a Cezanne canvas.

So, as we think about why we still teach Hemingway's fictions, we see, with students, that they embrace Hemingway's realism as their own; they hear it and it echoes. As they navigate the cold world of adults and the treacherous world of teenagers, they find lessons in Hemingway. In the words of a legendary English teacher at Phillips Exeter Academy, Harvard Knowles said: "In giving us stories that root us in our own experiences, Hemingway shows us not only who we are but also forces us to consider what we may become. What greater teacher could we possibly want for our young?"

Bully, racist, narcissist, misogynist, obnoxious and self-centered. Yes, we have to reconcile the tension between an image that is so ugly and an art that is so beautiful, and the role of regressive masculinity in American culture. Yet Hemingway endures, his best writing endures because he teaches us lessons about how to live according to our values and what it means to be human today. Thank you.

Part V F. Scott Fitzgerald's *The Great Gatsby*

27 years old: the most miserable year, since I was 19, full of terrible failures and acute miseries.

September: high hopes for the play, more work on the novel, ballgame...

October: short of money, excitement, parties, on the wagon. The failure and dismal reviews.

December: still on the wagon, fell off Christmas, deterioration, party Goldberg.

January: party with Gloria Swanson, struggling with money, rode all night on...

April: generally bored and feeling bad, decision on 15th to go to Europe.

"We felt that we were escaping extravagance and clamor, and from all the wild extremes among which we had dwelled for five hectic years, from tradesmen who laid for us and the nurse who bullied us. We were going to the old world to find a new rhythm for our lives."

"Dear Max, I may start my novel, and I may not. Its locale will be the Middle West and New York. It will concern less the superlative beauties that I run to usually, and will be centered on a smaller period of time. I wanna write something new, something extraordinary and beautiful and simple, and intricately patterned. After having Zelda draw pictures until her fingers ache, I know Gatsby better than I know my own child. I had him a while and then I lost him. And now I know I have him again."

Fitzgerald chose as one of his great themes, the American striver — the one who won't quit. But with F. Scott Fitzgerald, there is always a shadow that lies over that conception — of all you have to do is jump higher and leap farther and try harder. And what does that do to you inside when you do that? If you spend your life doing that, what will you end up as other than rich?

My economic professor at Huntington College said, read Gatsby. He thought I should become an English teacher, but the message just didn't wash with me that way. Instead, I got out of the book: I wanted to be a bond salesman, I wanted to make the money, I wanted to get to New York, I wanted the glamour, I wanted to have a better life. And I like Gatsby. He was not confined by these constraints that we had in this community, in Montgomery. He was a guy, he was ambitious. He had big parties, he had beautiful women, he had fashionable, powerful friends. I liked that.

Fitzgerald was able to see all of the opportunities that America offered, particularly to the young and to the ambitious. And at the same time, saw the impediments that were also in the way of that kind of glittering gold. So to that extent, there are limits to which we can go in America. And I think Fitzgerald was very sympathetic to those who wanted to go beyond the limits. But he saw that there was something tragic and something very sad, what he called the "dying fall", into those who try so desperately, but they can never quite achieve all that they want. And the valley of ashes in *The Great Gatsby* is a symbol of that whole sense of defeat. It is simply a junk yard between Long Island and Manhattan. It becomes a kind of junk yard of dreams, if you will, of burnt up dreams. George Wilson, the custodian of the valley of ashes, his old sense of dream, his old sense of what he could be in America has been used up and exhausted.

"Well, let's have some gas. I'm sick. I've been sick all day."

"And do I have to help myself?"

And Fitzgerald shows how characters like Tom Buchanan make use of a system that they control in their ruthless way that ultimately is destructive. The system that the young, naive, the auctioneer is not really aware of and doesn't really understand.

"Mr. Buchanan, I was wondering when you would let me have that blue car of yours."

"How do you like this? I bought it last week."

"It's a nice yellow one."

"Like to buy it, would you?"

"A big chance. No, but I could use the other. I need money pretty bad right now. My wife and I want to go west."

"Your wife wants to go?"

Fitzgerald actually has an uncanny ear and eye, for the person who is shut out by these powerful, rich, entitled people — Gatsby himself.

"How much you have that car?"

But who is even more important? I think it's Myrtle, who is Tom Buchanan's mistress. Her husband runs a gas station in Long Island. She is a working-class girl. She's vulgar and she is crazy about Tom. He is the whole world to her. But she is just his mistress that he wants to show off to a few friends. She gets brutally run over.

"She ran into the road. Son of a bitch didn't even stop his car."

"Two cars, one come in, one go I see."

Tom is presumably somewhat upset. But Fitzgerald insisted that he keep a detail describing that her breast was cut off by the on-coming car that struck her down, which, in fact, was driven by Daisy. He just said to his editor that's important, that has to be there. And to me, I thought he is saying its mutilation, what's been done is mutilation of her womanhood, of her heart. It ought to be ugly, it ought to be grotesque. These people cost things. And they don't pay the cost. Somebody else does.

Mr. Wilson was probably Fitzgerald's most memorable portrait of a member of the American proletarians. Fitzgerald says they have two kinds of rebellions, and it can be the fire of a revolutionary or the sullen resentment of a peasant. Wilson is the sullen resentment of a peasant, a man who is beaten down by the world. And at the end, at that extreme moment, picks up a revolver and says, "I'm going to set things right."

"When I came back from the east last autumn, I felt that I wanted the world to be in uniform and at a sort of moral attention for ever; I wanted no more riotous excursions with privileged glimpses into the human heart. Only Gatsby, the man who gives his name to this book, was exempt from my reaction. No — Gatsby turned out all right in the end; it was what preyed on Gatsby, what foul dust floated in the wake of his dreams that temporarily closed out my interest in the abortive sorrows and short-winded elations of men."

Chapter 7

Appendix 1 Key to Exercises

Part I Warm-up

Discuss the following questions in pairs or groups.

1. American literature in the 1930s reflected the social and cultural climate of the era through its focus on the hardships and challenges faced by individuals and communities during the Great Depression. Authors sought to expose the inequalities and injustices of the time, shedding light on the experiences of the working class, farmers, and marginalized groups. The literature of the period also reflected the political and ideological debates of the time, with authors exploring different solutions and critiquing the prevailing systems. Additionally, there was a growing interest in regionalism, with writers like William Faulkner and Zora Neale Hurston capturing the distinct cultures and voices of the American South and African-American communities, respectively.

2. One significant literary movement during the 1930s was the emergence of social realism in American literature. This movement aimed to depict the realities of the Great Depression and the social and economic struggles faced by ordinary people. Authors such as John Steinbeck, with his novel *The Grapes of Wrath*, and Richard Wright, with his novel *Native Son*, portrayed the harsh conditions of poverty, inequality, and racial discrimination. Another notable theme during this period was the exploration of political and social ideologies, with writers like Upton Sinclair addressing socialism and Sinclair Lewis critiquing the rise of fascism in his novel *It Can't Happen Here*.

3. Willa Cather was a renowned American author known for her insightful portrayals of the American frontier and the immigrant experience. Some of her notable works include *My Ántonia*, a novel that explores the lives of immigrants on the Nebraska prairie and their struggles to adapt to a new land. Another significant work is *O Pioneers!*, which depicts the challenges and triumphs of Swedish-American settlers in the Great Plains. Cather's novel *Death Comes for the Archbishop* is also highly regarded for its vivid depiction of the Catholic missionary efforts in the American Southwest.

4. *The Grapes of Wrath* explores several major themes. One central theme is the plight of the working class and the injustices they face. Steinbeck highlights the exploitation of migrant workers and the dehumanizing effects of capitalism. The novel also delves into the concept of family and community, por-traying the strength and unity of the Joad family as they face adversity together. Another significant theme is the connection between humans and the land, as Steinbeck emphasizes the importance of a harmonious relationship with nature. Additionally, the novel explores the idea of social change and the potential for collective action to bring about a more just society.

Part II Sinclair Lewis — The Conscience of His Generation

Watch the video. Answer the following questions.

1. He was called "the conscience of his generation", and his novels horrified both the literary and political establishments.

2. Some people thought he could win the prize because he was making fun of America, and Europe disliked America.

3. Because he was a good storyteller, writing eloquently and being visionary.

4. He wrote about the things happened in American society, about the middle class and all of their flaws.

5. It means Lewis knew what readers preferred, as he knew certainly what was going on in the country, and people loved to read it.

6. It recorded the history of the evangelists and their religious reform at the time; but at the same time, it reflected the character flaws of those reformers, that no man is perfect.

7. Lewis looked at the changes in American culture due to the automobile. He saw far into the future how it was to transform the traditions from the Victorian Era.

8. It was an attack on the provincialism of small-town America, especially small-town Minnesota.

9. It was a boring place to live in, teemed with narrow-minded people, where all culture would merely seem to be reduced to some boring stuff.

10. It was his satire in the novels. He tended to fall out of the canon for he was too limited to his time: the 1920s and 1930s.

Part III Sherwood Anderson's Camden

Watch the video. Answer the following questions for the main ideas.

1. It was a small town among the hills with simple folks. For Anderson, Camden was his hometown, a starting point for manhood.

2. Anderson's Camden embodied his ideal community, where people worked hard honestly with their own hands and the values of human labour were recognized.

3. He had a vital position for other writers such as Hemingway and Faulkner to develop their writing, and for his content, he was deeply respected by some other writers.

4. It meant a small town, the place where we were born and grew up, carried the memory of our childhood and was the starting point for our pursuit of dream and adulthood. No matter how far we had been, it would always stay sharp in our mind.

Watch the video again. Fill in the following blanks.

1) pristine	2) naturalism	3) manhood	4) mechanism
5) embodied	6) community	7) imagined	8) epitaph
9) plowed	10) beauty	11) poetic	12) ultimately
13) harness	14) preserve	15) resents	

Part IV John Steinbeck's *The Grapes of Wrath*

Watch the video. Write *T* for true or *F* for false for each statement.

1. F   2. T   3. F   4. T   5. T   6. F   7. F   8. T

答案解析:

1. 不是"less powerful",而是"no less powerful"。

3. 不是"Central Plains",而是"High Plains";不是银行的帮助,而是因为银行的贷款更多人被迫离开。

6. 不是"at the end",而是"along the way";不是"east of the Mississippi",而是"west"。

7. 不是"to the child",而是"to a dying man";没有代表"pain and anguish"。

Part V Willa Cather's *My Antonia* and *The Professor's House*

Watch the video. Answer the following questions.

1. She wanted her heroine to be like a rare object on the table, which can be examined from all sides, in different perspectives.

2. She means to them the country, the conditions there, and the whole adventure of their childhood.

3. Cather admired her vitality in the face of overwhelming hardship in her life.

4. The conditions were harsh, as survival became the first priority, with no house but a hole in earth to live in and even no materials for construction. The mental damage was huge too, for persons like Pavelka's father who was responsible for bringing the family to such a place.

5. Because in this situation, the will of a person can be either crushed or made. It represents the true and unique life of American pioneers at the time.

6. She faces her hardships with a positive attitude different from her father, working in the fields and cleaning houses in the town all day to support her family.

7. It reveals the meaning of common things in life and the power of life out of darkness. The immigrants went to America, faced the most difficult situation, and yet thrived and sprung out of that as settlers, as the next generation.

8. Cather knew that the world had changed, and it was a century of displacement, pain, suffering, and the imposition of a will on another.

9. She thought the world had broken into two: the former half and the post-1922 years. Cather refused to move on while others stepped on the side of the new; she cherished the great values of the former half.

10. She was old, and she believed youth was the source of power and creativity. She was struggling in the fear of not having any story to tell. She finally decided to write another book.

11. Cather wrote about what happens when the meaning of your life is over long before your life is over.

12. He has built a new house for his family, but he can't bring himself to leave the old one. His study is cluttered with memories and regrets. His daughters care for nothing but fine clothes, and the romance has long gone from his marriage.

13. Tom's climbing up into an undiscovered mesa and discovering an unknown civilization is certainly the metaphor for climbing into one's own life and discovering the civilization of oneself.

14. The fear of loneliness. His work has failed him, his marriage has failed him, and his family's failed him. The World War I killed the best and the brightest, killed the one person who was closest to him. He has nothing to cling to.

15. He learns to make peace with death, he welcomes it. He sees death not as an attack on his consciousness or on his ego. It's not an insult, it's not an assault, it's part of what he comes to accept with an extraordinary wisdom.

Appendix 2　Transcripts

Part II　Sinclair Lewis — The Conscience of His Generation

The rolling plains of Sauk Centre, Minnesota became the launching pad of the most popular American writer of the Jazz Age, Sinclair Lewis. In 1920, America was rocked by the publication of *Main Street*, a satirical novel ridiculing middle-class values and American smugness. He was called "the conscience of his generation", and his novels, which horrified the literary and political establishments, went on to become required reading in English classes for decades.

Sinclair Lewis was the first American to receive the Nobel Prize. Some people feel it was because Europe disliked America, and here was a guy who was making fun of America. "What's the matter, you're wanted for murder? Worse than that. Worse than murder? It's a woman. Well..." He was the most noted Minnesota writer, certainly one of the most noted American writers, the first Nobel Prize winner, and for a while, probably the most popular writer in this country in the early part of the 20th century. He is essentially a storyteller, and a very good storyteller. In the early part of the 20th century, everyone knew who Sinclair Lewis was because he wrote so eloquently about what was going on in American society at the time, rising middle class, American culture, all of the foibles. He was truly, I think, a visionary. ("Oh alright, I always say business is business, that's the American way.")

He had his finger on the pulse of the culture. He knew everything that was going on, mostly to satirize it. But also, people liked reading about what was going on and Lewis certainly knew what was going on in this country. ("When I told my pals I was coming to Jesus, they laughed.")

My favorite book is *Elmer Gantry*, and I just love the book. Maybe it's because of the movie with Burt Lancaster. ("I'm gonna give you all the hell of the Bible, and if you don't like it, you better fix it up with the Lord, because the Lord put it there.") To me, it was the historical reference, the impact of the evangelists of the time like Amy Semple McPherson. ("Who is this uh, this Elmer Gantry?") And the fact that he looked at that movement and found the human side to it, the fact that these religious reformers such as years later, the televangelists had feet of clay. ("In 1917, Mr. Gantry was expelled from a theological seminary in Kansas for seducing the deacon's daughter in the church where he had that day delivered a Christmas sermon.")

Babbitt, the same thing. ("When the city buys a property, they gotta buy from us. Well that doesn't sound exactly honest. I don't see why women can't understand the simplest business deal.") *Babbitt*, which I take as truly a visionary work. Lewis (was) looking at what was happening to American culture because of the automobile. ("Your wife wouldn't grudge me for our friendship; that would be too mean. Women are funny that way.") What effect cars would have, and what effect mass culture would have on this country. I think that in 1922, when *Babbitt* was published, Sinclair Lewis really saw far into the future of the effects of this new invention, and not just the car, but the radio, the phonograph, and everything else that was happening in that age to transform it from what was essentially the Victorian Era, pushing up until World War I.

Certainly the book that all Minnesota school children read for many years was *Main Street*, and it remains as his most famous and well-known book. And that was an attack on the provincialism of small-town America, especially small-town Minnesota. ("Then you think as they do. No Darling, don't get me wrong. See, they're rather a conservative crowd. They're swell people, but just don't ever give 'em a chance to criticize you.") Sauk Centre, his hometown where he grew up, which he called in his writing, Gopher Prairie, the narrow-mindedness of the people, the total boredom of living in a place like that, the way that all culture seemed reduced to the lowest possible common denominator, all those things were certainly present in that book. ("Well I guess it's you they resent." "For what reason?" "Say, plenty of 'em — in the first place you grabbed off the best bachelor in town; the second place you're a stranger, and they were just waitin' for something to crack down on; and did you lead with your chin!")

Sinclair Lewis was, for a while, one of the best-known writers in this country and one of the most popular. His satire especially was what gave him stature. ("Don't you believe in goodness and decency? Holding people together? No. No, I only believe in love.") I think a great deal of what he wrote about was tied to the 1920s and 1930s. ("This thing just about scares me to death. Every time this toaster jumps, I gets me a new gray hair. I never can understand these newfangled gadgets.")

When I had to teach *Main Street*, it was one of the hardest things I ever had to do as a teacher, because the students were almost in open rebellion, because they just did not like the book, because of all of the — getting bogged down in all this material from the 1920s that they didn't understand. Lewis has really tended to fall out of the canon. He is no longer there with Fitzgerald and Hemingway and Faulkner, and my thought of that is simply because he was just too, too limited to the 1920s, a great writer of the 1920s, but still unable to transcend it in important ways.

Part III Sherwood Anderson's Camden

His Camden was a place of mystery—the home of romance, a pristine town tucked in among the hills and cut off from the modern world. Sherwood Anderson was born in Camden, Ohio in 1876 just as summer was fading away. His most famous work *Winesburg, Ohio* tells the story of many people living in a small town. Anderson uses literary naturalism, giving a pessimistic observation of the human condition. When leaving Winesburg, the final character looked out of the car window: the town of Winesburg had disappeared, and his life there had become but a background on which to paint the dreams of his manhood.

Anderson developed relationships with Ernest Hemingway and William Faulkner, becoming a vital mechanism in the development of their writing. Anderson said, "In Faulkner, you feel an inner sympathy with the fact of life itself, but not in Hemingway; in him there was the desire always to kill."

Camden was always alive inside Anderson. His Camden was full of citizens who were honest, hard-working people, who planted their corns by hand and harvested wheats—people that Anderson felt he could understand. Camden embodied ideals the Andersons celebrated and strove for as a writer and as a man. It was full of people who worked with their hands, who recognized human worth—a community, a democracy at work. In his 64 years, he would live in countless places but none could compare with Camden. It was his favorite. And for a very simple reason he did not remember a thing about it.

His family moved away when he was only a year old. Anderson was free to make of it what he would and could retreat there whenever he desired to do so. And in 1934, he and his fourth wife Eleanor set out to visit many towns, including Camden. The ideal community he had imagined as Camden had not come into being. In fact, it might have seemed it never would. But Anderson still heard how strong and decent people were. Although Camden was never the perfect community, it still sits tucked in among the hills with continuing life. And in writing his own epitaph, Anderson says, "Life, not death, is the great adventure." In 1938, Thomas Wolfe wrote, "I think you are one of the most important writers of this century, that you have plowed another deep furrow in American earth, revealing to us another beauty that we knew was there, but no one else had spoken." "I think of you with Whitman and Twain, that is, with men who have seen America with a poet's vision and with a poetic vision of life, which to my mind is the only way ultimately it can be seen." In 1958, Faulkner expressed his view that Anderson had never been given his rightful place in American literature. He said, "In my opinion, he is the father of all my generation."

Anderson's widow Eleanor visited Camden again in 1962. She visited Anderson's birthplace as well as the building where his father owned a harness shop. She spent most of her visit at the local library and was highly impressed with what they had done to preserve the memory of her husband. And later in 1969, his daughter, Marion visited Camden in their library. The visit gave her a good sense of her roots, which she said was a nice feeling.

Sherwood Anderson once wrote, "We are all small-towners." The small-town boy hungers to see the wonders of the world, to be an important figure out there. During all his life in the city, the small town of his boyhood had remained home to him. Every house in the town, the faces of people seen on the street in his boyhood have all remained sharp in his mind. The city man returning to his hometown always has a feeling of sadness. He resents the change in the town, the fact that people of the town have grown older as he has, that strangers have come in. He is shocked, half wishing he hadn't come, and he thinks it would have been better to leave my dream alone.

Part IV John Steinbeck's *The Grapes of Wrath*

There's a reason why *The Grapes of Wrath* is a classic. The story's themes of endurance, sacrifice, and family are no less powerful today than when the book was published in 1939. The well-known tale follows the journey of the Joads, an impoverished family of Oklahoma's sharecroppers pushed off their land by the Depression and drought. They pile into a battered old truck, and head to California in search of a better life. But the Golden State (California) isn't the land of riches they had hoped for. "The book, of course, is a major milestone in American literature, and it is particularly important to our Oklahoma culture. It is in the DNA of the Oklahoma soil." The story is far from fiction. John Steinbeck's novel lays bare the true suffering of Oklahoma families who lost everything but their humanity and faith. The darkest chapter of their lives would become the literary light that is *The Grapes of Wrath*.

The drought hit now 3 quarters of the farmers in the High Plains where the dismal was actually, you know, occurring. They stayed on the farms and saved their places. So most of the dismal farmers actually stayed on their land. But many had no choice but to move. In the Panhandle, Boise City's population dropped 40%, with 1,600 small farmers and their families pulling up stakes. "The banks who have the loans out swoop in and collect or demand payment and of course there's no money to be had.

And they forced folks off the farm. "

"There are tragic things that happen in this play. But finally, it's a play of hope, it's a play of survival, it's a play of love and forgiveness, because the human spirit isn't defeated at the end. "

The central character of the story is the volatile young Tom Joad, an ex-convict, who grows increasingly impatient with the intolerance and exploitation they encounter on their way. " He's not just Tom Joad. He is the vibrant fighting soul of man, wanting to fight for human decency. Like I think, they all have this 'Joad moment' where they say like, 'I will rise up and stand for what I am. ' "

Strong female characters, like Ma Joad, hold the family together through the worst of human tragedy. "There's a kind of a stoicism about Ma. She's all business. She has a couple of lines in the play where she says, 'I don't think about all the things that could happen; I can just deal with what's happening, and what's coming up next. ' "

Along the way west, the Joads stopped at several migrant camps. Cardboard, and corrugated tin shacks that, in reality, were a horrifying fact of life. One of the largest Hoovervilles ran for 2 miles along the banks of the North Canadian River in downtown Oklahoma City. "This was described by one authority at the time as the single worst example of poverty in America, west of the Mississippi. "

"The tragic, Rose of Sharon scene. She's just delivered a stillborn child. She offers her milk-laden breast to a dying man to sustain his life. "

"I think it's a beautiful scene, and I think it's absolutely necessary to the story. There's so much symbolity (symbol) in that last moment: the milk of human kindness, life born out of death. I think it's beautiful. "

The small moments of kindness and grace are so powerful in an atmosphere of death, of suffering, of pain and anguish. You realize what the human touch can mean to someone. " He (Steinbeck) understood the common strivings of people. He understood the lives of ordinary Americans. "

"Steinbeck insisted that the 'Battle Hymn of the Republic' be placed on the inside front cover and back cover. All of the words and music of 'Battle Hymn of the Republic', the Civil War song. And Steinbeck said that this needed to be there, had to be there — this is a deeply American book. "

"There's a great sense of faith. There's a great sense of persistence, that even though the external things challenging them are negative, that these characters don't give up, but they rise to meet each challenge, no matter how dire it is. And I think those are enduring values that all of us cling to as human beings. And I say with a little bit of hometown pride, I think those are particularly strong Oklahoman values. "

"That's what Steinbeck was saying: (it) is that the family has its own strength, and we'll take care of each other. But at times of hardship, we have to pull together as a community to take care of each other. And that's a message that should live forever. "

Part V Willa Cather's *My Antonia* and *The Professor's House*

My Antonia

One evening, in an apartment in New York City, Cather explained the idea for her next novel to a friend. She said: "I want my next heroine to be like this: like a rare object in the middle of a table, which one may examine from all sides. " That rare object would become *My Antonia*, and Willa Cather would tell Antonia's story through a male character's eyes.

More than any other person we remembered, this girl seemed to mean to us the country, the conditions, the whole adventure of our childhood. To speak her name was to call up pictures of people and places to set a quiet drama going in one's brain.

Cather took Antonia straight from life. Her real name was Annie Pavelka, a hired girl who worked for Cather's neighbors in Red Cloud. Cather had always admired Annie's vitality in the face of overwhelming hardship.

"Grandmother didn't know that Willa was writing about her and her family, and she wondered why, why it had to be she. But if she could only understand now the importance of that book and what Willa really meant and what Willa really saw in her — it was her true life, wasn't it?"

In 1880, Annie Pavelka came from Bohemia with her family to homestead on the Nebraska prairie. "And the wagon driver says this is your new home. Oh no and, couldn't you imagine what my great grandfather thought — I'm bringing a family of five children to this hole in the ground. That was their home, their new American home." How did you go about building a house on a Nebraska frontier when there were no trees, you know. How did you do that when you got there the first year? What did you do? How did you survive? And she tells us that story.

In real life as well as in the novel, a heartbreaking story unfolds. It was a brutal winter. Neighbors brought food for the immigrants, or they would have died of hunger. Antonia's father dug a hole near the stove, a place for his daughters to sleep and stay warm. He never once touched the violin that he had brought with him from the old country. "Great grandfather, he just felt so depressed — no one to play for. He said that he was going to go out and shoot some rabbits with the gun that he had brought over from Czechoslovakia, and he didn't go and shoot any rabbits, I guess." He kills himself, commits suicide, can't take it. Some people are crushed by it. It'll either make you or break you. That's a very American theme.

Antonia is different from her father, she survives and even thrives on the frontier. She works in the fields like a man. She moves to town where she cleans houses all day and dances all night. Abandoned by her lover, she gives birth to a daughter. Eventually she marries a farmer, and they raise a family together. In the final chapter of the novel, Jim returns to Nebraska to see his Antonia. She was no longer a lovely girl, but she still had that something which fires the imagination — could still stop one's breath for a moment by a look or gesture that somehow revealed the meaning in common things. And then, in an unforgettable scene Jim meets Antonia's children:

"They all came running up the steps together, big and little, toe heads and gold heads and brown, and flashing little naked legs; a veritable explosion of life out of the dark cave into the sunlight."

That these people coming from another land, emigrating to America, dug themselves into the earth, came at one with the American soil, and then sprung out of that as the settlers, as the next generation.

With *My Antonia*, Cather had created something new out of the old story of the settling of the West. The book was no runaway best seller, but the critics loved it. Journalist H. L. Mencken wrote, "I know of no novel that makes the remote folk of the western prairies more real, and none that makes them seem better worth knowing. And what really counts in the long run is the feeling it leaves you with, the feeling that you have about the book *My Antonia*. Ten years after you've read it, you can still feel that. Why? Because of the transforming magic of art, because Willa Cather told that story and made it immortal."

World War I

She knew when she saw those soldiers returning on the piers in Jersey City from World War I, that life was dreadful. You saw those soldiers gassed and what it did to the skin. I mean, who would want to be part of the world that was emerging from that? Deep down she knew that this was a century of displacement, pain, suffering, and the imposition of a will on another.

In 1922 or thereabouts, Cather wrote, "The world broke into two, and I belong with the former half." Well that was it, the world broke into two, and most people who were writers had broke into two and with a great deal of pain and unhappiness and fear. They stepped on the side of the new; she stepped back into the old. Clearly there was a certain kind of emotional retreat. All right, you know if you say I'm old-fashioned, then I say I belong with the great values of the former half of the pre-1922 years, which in fact the war destroyed — I'm part of that. I was, I am part of a world that was whole. And she doesn't want to move on, because she thinks where the world is going is not a good place.

The Professor's House

Cather had always believed that youth was the source of power and creativity. Now, at age 52, she wondered if she had stories left to tell. She struggled through her fears in the only way she knew — by writing another book.

In *The Professor's House*, Cather wrote — I think as dark a book as has ever been written in America, and what she did — it's really kind of takes your breath away. She wrote about the experience that very few people write about, which is what happens when the meaning of your life is over long before your life is over.

"The moving was over and done. Professor St. Peter was alone in the dismantled house where he had lived ever since his marriage, where he had worked out his career and brought up his two daughters."

Godfrey Saint Peter has written eight historical volumes that brought him fame and money. He has just built a new house for his family, but he can't bring himself to leave the old one. His study is cluttered with memories and regrets. His daughters care for nothing but fine clothes, and the romance has long gone from his marriage. "I tried to make the professor's house stuffy," said Cather. "Then I wanted to open the square window and let in the fresh air that blew off the blue mesa." Outside his window lives everything the professor once knew: adventure, the Southwest, and a young man named Tom Outland, who reminds him of his younger self. In the professor's house, Outland tells his own story.

"Every morning when the sun's rays first hit the mesa top, while the rest of the world was in shadow, I wakened with the feeling that I had found everything... And at night, high above me the canyon walls were dyed flame-colored with the sunset, and the Cliff City lay in a gold haze against its dark cavern."

The story of this cow puncher, this ordinary western man climbing up into an undiscovered mesa and discovering an unknown civilization is certainly the metaphor for climbing into your own life and discovering the civilization of yourself, and that is what Tom Outland leaves the professor — this knowledge. Godfrey St. Peter is all alone now. His work has failed him, his marriage has failed him, his family has failed him, the one person that was closest to him — Tom Outland — dead, killed in the war. World War I killed the best and the brightest. He has nothing to cling to.

"Late in the afternoon, he saw that a storm was coming on. The sky was black and the room was dusky and chilly. He lit the stove and lay down on the couch. The fire made a flickering pattern of light on the wall. He lay watching it, vacantly; without meaning to, he fell asleep."

He had left his window open because the gas stove leaked, but a storm blows the window shut and the flame goes out, filling the room with toxic fumes. His housekeeper finds him close to death.

"He could remember a time when the loneliness of death had terrified him, but now he thought of eternal solitude with gratefulness, as a release from every obligation, from every form of effort. It was the truth."

What St. Peter does is to embrace death. First, he almost does it by dying, and that would be a tremendous mistake on his part; in Cather's mind as well. But at the end of the novel, he makes peace with death, he welcomes it. It's not coming right away, but he is living with the fact that he is going to die, and that's okay, but that means he is going to have to live his life a lot differently now. And he sees death not as an attack on his consciousness or on his ego. It's not an insult, it's not an assault, it's part of what he comes to accept with an extraordinary wisdom. It's like a tree. But he comes out of this, changed, and Cather has written through what it is to give up the self, the ego. Her writing then will be fundamentally changed from that time on.

Chapter 8

Appendix 1   Key to Exercises

Part I   Warm-up

Discuss the following questions in pairs or groups.

1. The Southern Renaissance refers to a literary movement that emerged in the American South during the early 20th century. It was a period of significant artistic and intellectual growth, marked by the rise of prominent Southern writers who explored the complexities of Southern culture and identity. These writers, including William Faulkner, Flannery O'Connor, and Tennessee Williams, used their works to depict the social, racial, and economic issues of the region. The Southern Renaissance in literature often delved into themes such as the legacy of slavery, the decline of the agrarian South, and the struggles of the working class, while showcasing a distinct Southern voice and storytelling style.

2. The Southern Renaissance in literature reflected the social and cultural atmosphere of the American South in the early 20th century by addressing the region's complex history and contemporary issues. The works of Southern Renaissance writers depicted the aftermath of the Civil War and the enduring effects of slavery, exploring themes of racial tension, social inequality, and the clash between tradition and modernity. They also captured the changing dynamics of the South, including the shift from

an agrarian society to an industrialized one. Through their narratives, Southern Renaissance writers offered insights into the struggles, contradictions, and unique character of the South, providing a nuanced portrayal of the region's social and cultural landscape.

3. The concept of "Southern myth" in literature refers to the romanticized and idealized portrayal of the American South in literary works. It encompasses the creation of a distinct Southern identity and the perpetuation of certain cultural, historical, and social narratives. Southern myth often romanticizes the antebellum era, emphasizing notions of chivalry, plantation life, and the "Lost Cause" ideology. It can also involve the portrayal of Southern landscapes, dialects, and traditions as unique and idyllic. However, it is important to note that the concept of Southern myth has been subject to criticism for its tendency to overlook the region's complexities, including issues of race, inequality, and social injustice.

4. William Faulkner's most famous novel is *The Sound and the Fury*. It is a landmark work of modernist literature and is significant for its innovative narrative structure and exploration of complex themes. The novel tells the story of the Compson family, focusing on the decline of the once-prominent Southern family. Faulkner employs multiple narrators, stream-of-consciousness writing, and nonlinear chronology to depict the inner lives of the characters and their struggles with time, memory, and loss. *The Sound and the Fury* is renowned for its experimental style, intricate characterization, and profound exploration of human psychology and the human condition. It solidified Faulkner's reputation as one of the greatest American writers of the 20th century.

Part II　Furious Fiction: Discussing William Faulkner's *Absalom*, *Absalom*

Watch the video. Write *T* for true or *F* for false for each statement.

1. T　　2. F　　3. F　　4. F　　5. F　　6. F　　7. T　　8. T　　9. F　　10. F

答案解析：

2. 只是 possibly。

3. 不是 beach read，而是 very difficult to read。

4. 不是 five narrators，而是 four of them。

5. 因为他认为 the chronology 使他忽略了故事当下的发展。

6. 不是 a Civil War novel，而是 a Gothic novel。

9. 因为这只是 Diane 的感受，而不是真实发生的。

10. 是 20 世纪 Top three American novels。

Part III　Why Should You Read Flannery O'Connor?

Watch the video and choose the right answer for the following questions.

1. B　　2. C　　3. C　　4. B　　5. A　　6. C

Part IV　*To Kill a Mockingbird* and the Southern Gothic Tradition

Watch the video and answer the following questions.

1. The southern Gothic literary tradition.

2. It derives tension from the suppression of dark urges, secrets and past violence.

3. William Faulkner, Flannery O'Connor, Dorothy Allison, Barrie Hannah and Cormac McCarthy.

4. Europe.

5. Gothic novels typically incorporate dark themes, the supernatural and remote settings with severe

weather to explore repressed secrets that continue to influence the present.

6. Because monstrous characters including Bob Ewell and the ghost like Boo Radley populate the novel's rural Alabama setting.

Watch the video again and fill in the blanks.

1) proponents	2) Haunted	3) racism
4) underscores	5) loathed	6) cynical
7) exaggerated	8) mysterious	9) friendly
10) adult	11) perspective	12) dwells
13) hopeful	14) triumph	15) tempered
16) societal	17) prejudiced	18) enlightened

Part V Why Is William Faulkner So Difficult to Read?

Watch the video and answer the following questions.

1. Faulkner used confusion intentionally to explore the mysterious aspects of the human mind and to investigate pressing issues of personal, racial, and regional identity.

2. Many of Faulkner's novels are set in the fictional county of Yoknapatawpha, which is a reimagining of Lafayette County, Mississippi. This setting represents the tensions and contradictions of the American South, including its messy reality, racial divisions, and the legacies of slavery and colonial violence.

3. Faulkner's use of multiple perspectives allows the reader to experience the characters' confusions firsthand and understand their biases and blindspots. It also reflects larger denials of Southern history and allows Faulkner to explore his own anxieties about the South.

4. Faulkner's fiction challenges rigid Jim Crow policies and the region's history of genocide and slavery by inducing ambiguity about racial origins, using evasive language to cover up intolerable history, and exploring the distortions of the past through his characters.

5. Faulkner captivates readers with his verbal acrobatics, convoluted sentences, and outlandish imagery. His writing style can be bewildering but also rewarding, as it invites readers to contemplate the unreliable nature of history and memory.

6. The title *The Sound and the Fury* reflects Faulkner's exploration of confusion and perception. It suggests the chaos and intensity of the characters' experiences and their struggle to make sense of the past and the present.

Appendix 2 Transcripts

Part II Furious Fiction: Discussing William Faulkner's *Absalom, Absalom*

—Hi, I'm Mark Mush and welcome back to Furious Fiction. Here with my co-host Diane Roberts, we're going to talk today about one of the canons of American literature, definitely southern literature, *Absalom, Absalom*, by William Faulkner.

—Absolutely.

—Diane, tell me, you teach this book, tell me, tell me your thoughts, the quick thoughts on this.

—Well, the quick thoughts. Quick thoughts on Faulkner are always tough. Yeah, I'll try. I think this is possibly the greatest American novel of the 20th century. It's my favorite Faulkner novel, and I have said that it's a very difficult book.

—It's yeah, I mean, it's kind of all Faulkner novels that I've read are difficult, and this is maybe at the top of the difficult list. I mean this isn't one that you pick up and go yeah, I kind of knock that out in a weekend.

—Yeah not a beach read, it's not a beach read.

—But I think it is, I mean, somebody had mentioned to me that, you know, you can't kind of read this like you'd read poetry, a little bit at a time, and kind of you've know work your way through it, and kind of you've got to go back and figure out what's going on here. I mean, did you have difficulty figuring out when you first read this?

—Well yeah.

—What is going on?

—Absolutely. The first time I read it, I just thought what a work, because there are five different narrators. Four of them are sometimes misrepresenting, sometimes possibly lying, and definitely not knowing what really happened. These people are trying to reconstruct a story that happened during the Civil War and just before the Civil War, and they don't know all the facts, but sometimes they're just making it up.

—And, I got to ask you, does your book and I didn't notice this until I've almost finished reading this, does your book have a little chronology in the back of it.

—It does.

—And you know, so, and I almost wished I hadn't seen that, because then I'm skipping what exactly is happening here, but you know what I mean is that, good thing, bad thing, what do you...

—Well I, you know, that chronology I don't take too seriously. There's a partner who kind of put it into the best of a publisher.

—Right.

—You don't need it, because, you don't need... You can read it as a detective story. This is about a murder. There is a murder mystery in the middle of it. You can read it at that level to try to figure out, you know, who did what when. You can read it as a family secret story. It's a great Gothic novel, because it happens in the middle of the Civil War, so it's kind of a civil war novel, I mean, but you have your right in terms of Gothic novels, I mean, what gets more Gothic than this?

—Got a haunted house, it's got a curse, it's got a demon, the whole thing. It's actually a really a great read. You know it has doomed young men; it has you know doomed young women; it has doomed a lot of people. And what Faulkner said when he wrote this and one of the fun little things to think about is that it came out in 1936, same year with *Gone with the Wind*. Faulkner said he wanted to write a Civil War novel, without, as he put it, the plug hats and crinoline, and boy, he did, because this is like *The Antigone*.

—Well, it is, and nobody's, you know, there's not a whole lot of gentry here, I mean, this is kind of, you know, some down and out in more ways than one, the folks and family.

—Oh, it just rips the lid off of the genteel fiction of slavery, you know, I mean, this is about the unspoken truth, so who's really related to him.

—And kind of the unhappiness of, you know, a lot of that. Let's say, I'm just a guy on the street. I've always heard of this book. I've never read it. Yeah, why would I, why would you advise me to pick this up and read it? Why should I read *Absalom, Absalom*?

—Because I think it lays bare a truth about America's dependence on slavery, not just the South, and about the kinds of fictions and lies we constructed to make that seem okay, to make it seem okay that these sorts of people over here were, we could abuse them and own them and treat them like they were less than human, because we defined them in a certain way, and these people over here had privileges that the other people didn't have. I think that's one of the wonderful things the book does. The book also does a real number on the secrets families try to keep and how they come back. The rest always returns.

—Now I had, you know, I kind of went into this. I had seen somewhere where this novel was rated by Southern writers as the number one southern novel of all time, so I've kind of figured, well you know, I've never read this. I mean I ought to at least read this and see what's going on, and so I kind of went into the cod liver oil of southern literature. I need to do this because I need to do it. And I didn't come out of it, with they are, why they survive that. You know, I mean, it's good, but it's weird.

—It's rather weird.

—It's difficult, I mean, it's the kind of thing that you guys, maybe I ought to go reread that and make sure I've got what's going on.

—Don't feel bad, because every time I reread it, I am convinced somebody has stuck pages that were never in my book before in my book. And I've read it maybe 15 times, and some of it still seems like, wait, where'd that come from. You know, when you got a novel where two of your main narrators suddenly disappear completely into the past and drag you with them, where we're told they're not in the room anymore, you know, this is what it's about possession. It's about ... Yeah ghosts.

—And pain, the pain, of all of this stuff, and I mean, it's so beautifully done. It is very like much like an epic poem that sort of somehow been blown up and glued back together again. And the sheer beauty of it, I mean, Faulkner, very much a writer of high aesthetic value, let's say, but it is I find it very very compelling, and I think probably as a sudden I find it speaks to me, but it speaks to anybody who's you know got a family, got a history, you know, got an interest.

—And most people do.

—Indeed.

—I mean, so what do you say? Number one southern novel?

—Yeah.

—Number one Faulkner novel?

—Both.

—Okay, that would in the Top Ten American novels.

—Top Three.

—Okay, Top Three. Well, that's pretty strong.

—Yeah right there.

—Yeah I'd have to be there on most of that, Top Three American novels, uh, I don't know, but it is...

—The 20th century.

—Yeah the 20th century, I mean, you know, it's pretty worth reading. I have to say that.

—I'm glad you enjoyed it.

—Well thanks. Mark Mushroom with Diane Roberts were here on Furious Fiction. We're talking today about William Faulkner's *Absalom, Absalom*. Thanks for being with us.

—We'll see you next time.

Part III Why Should You Read Flannery O'Connor?

A garrulous grandmother and a roaming bandit face off on a dirt road. A Bible salesman lures a one-legged philosopher into a barn. A traveling handyman teaches a deaf woman her first word on an old plantation.

From her farm in rural Georgia, surrounded by a flock of pet birds, Flannery O'Connor scribbled tales of outcasts, intruders and misfits staged in the world she knew the best: the American South. She published two novels, but is perhaps best known for her short stories, which explored small-town life with stinging language, offbeat humor, and delightfully unsavory scenarios.

In her spare time, O'Connor drew cartoons, and her writing is also brimming with caricature. In her stories, a mother has a face "as broad and innocent as a cabbage", a man has as much drive as a "floor mop", and one woman's body is shaped like "a funeral urn".

The names of her characters are equally sly. Take the story *The Life You Save May Be Your Own*, where the one-handed drifter Tom Shiftlet wanders into the lives of an old woman named Lucynell Crater and her deaf and mute daughter.

Though Mrs. Crater is self-assured, her isolated home is falling apart. At first, we may be suspicious of Shiftlet's motives when he offers to help around the house, but O'Connor soon reveals the old woman to be just as scheming as her unexpected guest— and rattles the reader's presumptions about who has the upper hand.

For O'Connor, no subject was off limits. Though she was a devout Catholic, she wasn't afraid to explore the possibility of pious thought and impious behavior co-existing in the same person. In her novel *The Violent Bear It Away*, the main character grapples with the choice to become a man of God—but also sets fires and commits murder. The book opens with the reluctant prophet in a particularly compromising position: "Francis Marion Tarwater's uncle had been dead for only half a day when the boy got too drunk to finish digging his grave." This leaves a passerby to "drag the body from the breakfast table where it was still sitting and bury it [...] with enough dirt on top to keep the dogs from digging it up."

Though her own politics are still debated, O'Connor's fiction could also be attuned to the racism of the South. In *Everything that Rises Must Converge*, she depicts a son raging at his mother's bigotry. But the story reveals that he has his own blind spots and suggests that simply recognizing evil doesn't exempt his character from scrutiny.

Even as O'Connor probes the most unsavory aspects of humanity, she leaves the door to redemption open a crack. In *A Good Man is Hard to Find*, she redeems an insufferable grandmother for forgiving a hardened criminal, even as he closes in on her family. Though we might balk at the price the woman pays for this redemption, we're forced to confront the nuance in moments we might otherwise consider purely violent or evil.

O'Connor's mastery of the grotesque and her explorations of the insularity and superstition of the South led her to be classified as a Southern Gothic writer. But her work pushed beyond the purely ridiculous and frightening characteristics associated with the genre to reveal the variety and nuance of human character. She knew some of this variety was uncomfortable, and that her stories could be an acquired taste—but she took pleasure in challenging her readers.

O'Connor died of lupus at the age of 39, after the disease had mostly confined her to her farm in Georgia for 12 years. During those years, she penned much of her most imaginative work. Her ability to flit between revulsion and revelation continues to draw readers to her endlessly surprising fictional worlds. As her character Tom Shiftlet notes, the body is "like a house: it doesn't go anywhere, but the spirit, lady, is like an automobile: always on the move."

Part Ⅳ *To Kill a Mockingbird* and the Southern Gothic Tradition

Harper Lee's 1960 novel *To Kill a Mockingbird* belongs to the southern Gothic literary tradition as the genre that became prominent in the 20th century and furthers the Gothic tradition of exploring the macabre islands lurking beneath the apparently a tranquil surface of reality. As in Gothic novels, the Southern Gothic genre derives tension from the suppression of dark urges secrets and past violence, which threatened to erupt over the course of the novel. These southern Gothic elements are apparent in works by writers including William Faulkner and Flannery O'Connor. The genre was on the wane by the 1960s, but writers have continued to employ its conventions. The works of contemporary writers, including Dorothy Allison, Barrie Hannah and Cormac McCarthy, have attributes of southern Gothic novels. Positioning *To Kill a Mockingbird* within the southern Gothic context helps us understand the novel as part of a dynamic literary tradition and adds depth to its representation of small-town culture and racism.

Emerging in Europe, the Gothic genre saw great success in the 1800s with works including Frankenstein, Jane Eyre and Wuthering Heights, and has remained popular. Gothic novels typically incorporate dark themes, the supernatural and remote settings with severe weather to explore repressed secrets that continue to influence the present. These same Gothic conventions are also found in works of the southern Gothic tradition, but in southern Gothic the narrative is transported from castles or windswept moors to the rural South. The conflict is between the racism and violence of the region's past and present day. Familiar southern Gothic elements exist in *To Kill a Mockingbird*. Monstrous characters including Bob Ewell and the ghost—like Boo Radley populate the novel's rural Alabama setting where, quite unexpectedly, snowfall occurs. Tom Robinson's trial and the attack on Scout and Jem by Bob Ewell represent the struggle between the region's suppressed violent racist history and its more genteel surface image.

To Kill a Mockingbird arrived at the end of southern Gothic's initial flourishing. William Faulkner, the author of novels including *As I Lay Dying* and *The Sound and the Fury*, was one of its earliest and best-known proponents. His stories take place in rural Mississippi and feature characters grappling with the racial and economic anxieties of the post-civil war south. Haunted houses and characters, taboo themes such as incest, and suppressed racism and violence feature prominently in his stories. Faulkner's famous quote "the past is never dead" is not even past, underscores how the characters in his books and in southern Gothic writing in general cannot move beyond the sins of their forefathers. Flannery O'Connor is another writer associated with the genre, even though she loathed the term southern Gothic. She is best known for her short stories, including *A Good Man Is Hard to Find* and *Everything That Rises Must Converge*. O'Connor's works are renowned for their cynical outlook, their exaggerated characters called grotesques, and their complex treatment of race in the segregated south. Shocking acts of violence remind the reader that dark mysterious drives lurk beneath the surface of a small-town life.

While *To Kill a Mockingbird* has many similarities with other southern Gothic works, it also has differences. Its family friendly tone contrasts with the more adult subject matter and language of other southern Gothic works. Since it's told from the perspective of a young girl who doesn't understand many of the adult topics being mentioned, it dwells less on sex, violence and evil than other southern Gothic works. The humor in *To Kill a Mockingbird* is also gentler than other southern Gothic works, whose humor is typically dark and at the expense of the characters. It's also more hopeful. Instead of ending in murder and hopelessness, we see good represented by Boo Radley and the Finch's triumph over Bob Ewell's evil. We still see violence rooted in the past, but it's tempered by hope for reconciling with history and learning from past sins. Some characters are driven by typical repressed torments, but others are motivated by desire to do good and enact societal change. Secrets lose their power to haunt in the light of day, as when Boo finally emerges from his house to be seen. The novel's final words, "Most people are nice when you finally see them", evoke hope for a less prejudiced, more enlightened future.

Part V   Why Is William Faulkner So Difficult to Read?

You're halfway through what's supposedly one of the greatest novels of the 20th century, but nothing quite makes sense. Narrating characters offer clashing versions of the same story and often seem unsure who, what, or when they're talking about. Seemingly minor details trigger intense emotional reactions you don't understand. And the prose is loaded with convoluted sentences and outlandish imagery. Confused? Good—that means you're on the right track.

William Faulkner is considered one of America's most remarkable and perplexing writers. Fortunately, he wasn't just toying with his audience. Faulkner used confusion intentionally, to explore the most mysterious parts of the human mind and investigate pressing issues of personal, racial, and regional identity. The result is a body of work that's shocking, inventive, and often hilarious—but above all, challenging. So what clues should readers look for to navigate his literary labyrinths?

Many of Faulkner's novels are set in the fictional county of Yoknapatawpha—a fantastical reimagining of Lafayette County, Mississippi, where he spent most of his life. Born in 1897, Faulkner grew up steeped in oral storytelling traditions, from folklore and family histories to local legends of Civil War glory. However, these grand myths didn't match the messy reality of the American South, divided by racist Jim Crow laws and plagued by the legacies of slavery and colonial violence. All these tensions come alive inside Yoknapatawpha. Full of horror, humor, and human tragedy, Faulkner's stories feature many memorable characters, like the spurned bride who sleeps beside her would-be husband's corpse, or the duped sharecropper obsessively hunting for imaginary coins. At first glance, these characters seem grotesquely absurd. But under the surface, they all reflect his obsession with how people process the past— what they stubbornly hold on to, unwittingly forget and willingly distort.

Many of Faulkner's fictions are told from multiple perspectives, offering the readers several versions of the story's events. For example, *The Sound and the Fury* combines the narratives of Benjy, Quentin, and Jason Compson, three brothers haunted by memories of their sister Caddy. One brother's narration will occasionally fill the gaps left by another's, but just as often, their accounts contradict each other. To make things more confusing, Benjy's narration is disjointed in time, slipping between past and present without warning. Meanwhile, Quentin's section confuses fact and fantasy as it jumps backward in time from the day of his untimely death. Only the aggressive, money-hungry Jason attempts to embrace the present, but even he is constantly overtaken by past resentments.

Following these threads can be bewildering, but Faulkner wants the audience to share the characters' confusion. This approach allows readers to understand the Compsons' biases and blind spots firsthand. And since his characters' distortions of the past often reflect larger denials of Southern history, it also allows Faulkner to explore his own anxieties about the South. For example, his novel *Light in August* deliberately induces ambiguity about a character's racial origins in ways that undermine rigid Jim Crow policies. And in *Absalom, Absalom!* narrating townsfolk remark that "no one knew how" a local landowner had come into his property, and that his house was built "apparently out of nothing". This kind of evasive language shows how characters are desperate to cover up the region's intolerable history of genocide and slavery.

But even when exploring the heaviest topics, Faulkner spellbinds readers with verbal acrobatics. One particularly bewildering sentence in *Absalom, Absalom!* runs 1,288 words long, and features locals haggling over "violently-colored candy", a "cloudy swirl of chickens", and a hard-drinking planter who's compared to both a worn-out cannon and a showgirl. Even his jokes can breed more confusion, such as when Benjy Compson conflates his sister Caddy with golf caddies.

Reading Faulkner is rarely easy, but it is deeply rewarding. He invites readers to contemplate the unreliable nature of history and memory. And in teaching us to embrace confusion and recognize the limits of our perception, Faulkner can help us listen for hidden meanings in the sound and fury that surround us.

Chapter 9

Appendix 1 Key to Exercises

Part I Warm-up

Discuss the following questions in pairs or groups.

1. The emergence of American realism had a profound impact on the development of American drama. Realist playwrights, such as Eugene O'Neill and Arthur Miller, sought to depict life as it is, exploring social issues and the struggles of ordinary individuals. They moved away from the melodramatic and idealized portrayals of earlier theatrical traditions. American realism brought a sense of authenticity

and gritty realism to the stage, tackling topics like family dynamics, societal pressures, and the American Dream. It paved the way for a more introspective and socially conscious approach to storytelling in American drama.

2. Eugene O'Neill is often referred to as the father of American drama. His plays are characterized by their introspective exploration of complex psychological themes and the human condition. O'Neill's works, such as *Long Day's Journey Into Night* and *The Iceman Cometh*, delve into the depths of human emotions, addressing topics like addiction, family dynamics, and the search for meaning in life. His plays often feature flawed and deeply layered characters who grapple with their inner demons, offering a raw and honest portrayal of the human experience.

3. The Theatre of the Absurd movement had a significant influence on American drama in the mid-20th century. Playwrights like Samuel Beckett and Edward Albee embraced the absurdist philosophy, which rejected traditional logic and explored the existential nature of human existence. Their plays, such as Beckett's *Waiting for Godot* and Albee's *Who's Afraid of Virginia Woolf?*, challenged conventional narrative structures and questioned the meaning and purpose of life. The Theatre of the Absurd movement introduced a new level of experimentation and non-conformity to American drama, encouraging playwrights to push boundaries, challenge norms, and explore the complexities of human existence in unconventional ways.

4. Tennessee Williams's plays often revolve around themes of desire, loneliness, and the search for personal and sexual fulfillment. His works frequently explore the complexities of human relationships, particularly those of dysfunctional families and marginalized individuals. Williams delves into the depths of human emotions, addressing topics such as repression, illusion versus reality, and the destructive power of societal norms. The struggle for identity, the fragility of the human psyche, and the yearning for escape are also recurring themes in his plays. Through his works, Williams offers a poignant and often tragic portrayal of the human condition.

Part II Susan Glaspell's *A Jury of Her Peers*

Watch the video. Answer the following questions.

1. It was difficult and harsh, as the haunting picture at the end of Tocqueville's *Democracy in America*.

2. The weather was terrible; the chores (canning, laundry, boiling water) were draining her life; everything repeated day by day, week by week.

3. He saw the crucial difference of a house with children, and a house without children. And the sacrifice in the house of Minnie Foster is not for the sake of the future.

4. He agreed that the pioneer woman was making a great sacrifice. But in terms of the story, he had realized that it had revealed a stark truth: the sacrifice in the house of Minnie Foster — a place without children — was not for a better future and became meaningless.

5. He mentioned the American way of doing justice outside the law, which was represented by the westerns.

6. It was the American impulse to make things right, and not to rely upon old and established and traditional institutions. This was not unnecessarily sanitary, and could be both good and bad.

7. The law was supposed to make things right and straight, but it did not mean one should surrender all his beliefs of good and bad to the law.

8. Lincoln's opinion is about absolute law-abidingness, which means for no reason one can break laws, be it out of justice or others. It will be crucial for the future and the preservation of self-government.

9. The idea is that there are laws that aren't laws, because they're unjust. It means when we are obeying the laws, we also need to remember that laws are not perfect.

10. Lincoln's idea and Glaspell's are two extremes, with King's being sandwiched in the middle. Lincoln's idea has no tolerance for doing things outside the law, whereas Glaspell's is showing a possibility of doing justice outside the law; King's stands in between, for the law might be imperfect, and going outside the law might also bring chaos.

Part III Clifford Odets's *Waiting for Lefty*

Watch the video. Choose the best answer to each question.

1. C   2. D   3. B   4. C   5. B   6. A   7. B   8. D

Part IV An Interview on Edward Albee

Watch the video. Write *T* for true or *F* for false for each statement.

1. F   2. F   3. F   4. T   5. F   6. T   7. F   8. T   9. F   10. T

答案解析：

1. 不是 *Seascape*，而是 *A Delicate Balance*。
2. 是他原本对于古典音乐的兴趣让他意识到这种相似性。
3. 不是"only"，也不是"not related"。
5. 不是"italicizing"，而是"underlying and capitalization"。
7. 不是"a great playwright"。
9. Albee 认为不能给人带来任何改变的艺术是没有任何价值的。

Part V Eugene O'Neill

Watch the video. Answer the following questions.

1. He always had a lot of ideas in his mind. He could not get rid of them and was deeply troubled.

2. They came in dreams. O'Neill dreamt of all desire under the elms and all wilderness. He dreamt fragments of dozens of other plays.

3. He filled a cultural space that needed to be filled, as America was already rich in novelists but still lacked a great playwright.

4. He knew quite well that American theatre needed him and created a persona for that: he posed for all those gorgeous pictures himself to make himself an expected playwright.

5. Because he always wanted to try something new or different. But most importantly, he focused on life, which is something bigger and more revealing.

6. Being experimental was necessary. For example, he used expressionist technique to the disintegration of his main character (he used savagely stylized dialogue and masks in *Hairy Ape* to present the devastating forces of industrialization to the inner life of workers; he explored the deeply conflicted hopes and fears of a one-time prostitute in *Anna Christie*).

7. He wanted to take us into our interior life by ripping open the life of his characters. He showed people the inner life that was as broad and limitless as the land of America.

8. It mirrored conflicts in O'Neill's own life, past and present.

9. He failed to balance his family life and career. He drank too much and was ill-equipped for the family life, being homesick for homelessness and irresponsibility. The maintenance of his personality brought huge stress to his life, and also formed a gap between him and his family.

10. It is a vehicle to convey the unnamed, undisclosed forces beneath the surface of life.

11. He had been haunted by the loss of religious faith, which he always wanted to look for something to replace. O'Neill's work itself, in a sense, was the mask behind which he hid.

12. It denotes to someone who has all the desires, ambition and feelings to be a great genius writer but just can't make it.

13. O'Neil's obsession with illusive dreams reflected the national question of America as a kind of a hollow dream. It revealed a very tragic and dark vision of what this country is and what this country does to people's dreams.

14. A failing theatre reflected the truth that people constructed their own illusions and dreams to survive the harsh realities in life; but this dream would fall apart one day, like those plays in a theatre, for it cost vigor and energy and one could not hold it forever.

15. The theatre became the perfect medium for those who were heartbroken and disillusioned; the plays were an expression of such an agony.

Part VI Arthur Miller's *Death of a Salesman*

Watch the video. Answer the following questions for the main ideas.

1. For him, the theme of the play was as complicated as life itself and hard to be concluded into one sentence. It could be about the United States, about a man, about an economic situation and about a family.

2. For some, it was a story about the corruption of capitalism. From Willy's perspective, it was a story about love.

3. It revealed that the play was based on Willy's stream of consciousness, with all the scenes being the flashbacks in his mind. The past and the present were merged together.

Watch the video again. Fill in the following blanks.

1) encapsulate	2) boil	3) corruption	4) continent
5) opposite	6) grips	7) architecture	8) recognizing
9) fundamentally	10) dedicate	11) pour	12) triumph
13) insurance	14) gigantic	15) interior	16) marvelous
17) breeze	18) realism	19) verse	20) flashbacks

Appendix 2 Transcripts

Part II Susan Glaspell's *A Jury of Her Peers*

Christopher Demuth: the host
Diana Schaub: the woman on the left

Leon R. Kass: the man in the middle

Amy A. Kass: the woman on the right

In this part, the four speakers are mainly focusing on two issues:

1. The quintessentially American things in the story.

2. The problem of law and justice.

Host: I wondered, uh, as the three editors of this book who selected this story to be included in a section about justice, law-abidingness and public order in America. If you regard this story as saying — we talked about its feminist themes, and we've talked about universal themes, the nature of justice and the practicality of a criminal justice system. Is there anything about the story that is quintessentially American? Does it tell us something about America or the American character? Or is it just (a) story on these other things that happen to be probing into a bit of the author's hometown?

Amy: It really is a kind of window into America. What I have in mind, what came to mind immediately was that very haunting picture at the end of Tocqueville, *Democracy in America*, of the pioneer woman whose life is very difficult and very harsh. She tries to bring to the frontier all of the little things of civilization. But, she is basically drained of her life. One of the things you see very vividly, if you really try to get inside these characters here, is that you get a picture of what it must have been like to be a woman on the frontier; or in the plains, when the weather was terrible, and canning took all summer. And laundry was a big deal. There are (were) no washing machines. You have (had) to get the water, you have (had) to boil the water. It's a whole day, whole week's affair. So it gave me a kind of better understanding. And I would say sympathy with that.

Leon: Could I piggyback on this slightly? I mean I thought you were gonna say, of the pioneer woman in Tocqueville, that she endured all of this because of her children. And what you see in this story is the crucial difference between a house with children, and a house without children. That sacrifice in the house of Minnie Foster is not for the sake of the future.

Amy: So it's really starker.

Leon: It's very stark. It's the frontier without that for which the frontier has been settled. But there's also something else (for) who set this out on the frontier or the Great Plains. It also partakes of a certain American sense of doing justice outside the law. The sheriff is not always in town. The procedures are not always available.

Amy: The Westerns.

Leon: The Westerns. And there's a lot of vigilante justice during this particular time, not unnecessarily sanitary. But, there's something both good and bad about the American impulse to make things right, and not to rely upon old and established and traditional institutions. They step forward, they try to fix things, they try to make things right. And the law is in a way supposed to do this for us. But we don't surrender altogether our sense of our own rectitude or what we think is needed both for better and for worse.

Host: Diana?

Leon: You don't like that.

Diana: Well, this reading is paired with two other readings. One from Lincoln, and Lincoln makes the case for absolute law-abidingness. And that this will be crucial, especially in the future to the preservation of self-government. So you're right that this other element is there from an early point and it's very American. But Lincoln at least regards it as something that needs to be corrected. But, of course, the other reading sandwiches between the Lincoln and the Glaspell is Martin Luther King's, whether from Birmingham Jail, which says there are laws that aren't laws, because they're unjust. So I mean I really do think with the array of these three pieces that students can really see all of the arguments and reach their own conclusions.

Part III   Clifford Odets's *Waiting for Lefty*

Narrator: Responding artistically to the climate of the times, Clifford Odets became the voice of the Group Theatre. His plays mirrored the essence of what the group wanted to be and do. They commented on the social climate of America: the politics, the hopes and fears, and the struggle to survive.

Harold Clurman: There is no doubt in my mind that the Group then had a great effect on Odets. It was the atmosphere of the Group, the intensity of the Group, the fervor of the Group, the optimism of the Group, the belligerence, sometimes — the affectionate belligerence of the Group, and also its desire to get at the truthful expression of human feelings.

Narrator: Looking back, it's no accident that the flowering of the Group Theatre coincided with the Group's discovery of Odets's true gift. Clifford himself said he'd never have become a playwright at all, had not been for the Group. If that's true, he paid them back handsomely. In 1935 alone, four of his plays ran simultaneously in New York. One of them was written in just 3 days and actually made it to the stage 6 weeks before *Awake and Sing*.

Cheryl Crawford: I hadn't seen Clifford for 3 or 4 days. One day he came back stage. I was back there and he had yellow sheets in his hand. I said, "Where have you been? Clifford? I haven't seen you for so long." He said, "Well, I've been writing a play here, one act play, sort of a one-act play." I said, "Let me read it." That was *Waiting for Lefty*.

Ruth Nelson: The play was about the taxi drivers strike, and was a meeting in which they were waiting for lefty. Lefty never appeared. And in the course of this meeting, there were flashbacks to the lives of various cab drivers.

Robert Lewis: It was street language and working-class language, but it was so organized as to have a quality that was a new voice in the theatre.

Waiting for Lefty:

"We'll die for what is right. Put fruit trees where our ashes are."

"Don't wait for lefty, he might never come."

"My god, Joe, the world is supposed to be for all of us."

"I know this."

"Your boss is making suckers out of you boys every minute. Yes, and suckers out of all the wives and the poor innocent kids who grow up with cooked spines and sick bones. Sure, I see it in the papers. How good orange juice is for kids. But damn it, our kids get colds and went on top of the other. They looked like little ghosts. Betty never saw grapefruit. I took it to the store last week and she pointed to a stag of grapefruits: 'What's that?'"

"My god, Joe, the world is supposed to be for all of us."

Ruth Nelson: The first production of *Waiting for Lefty* in New York City at the Civic Repertory Theatre, Eva Le Gallienne's theatre, on 14th street was a night to remember all the days of your life. The audience was so with this play that it was the essence of why the Group Theatre was formed. That night, it all came into flower.

Narrator: A shock of delighted recognition struck the audience like a tidal wave. A kind of joyous fervor seemed to sweep the audience toward the stage. The actors no longer performed. They were being carried along as if by an exultancy of communication, such as I had never witnessed in the theatre before. Audience and actors had become one. Line after line brought applause, whistles, bravos and heartfelt shouts of kinship.

Robert Lewis: Kazan, who's playing a taxi driver. And he was sensational. Sensational. He had because it released him because he had no inhibitions, you see. And he understood the play, he believed in the part, believed in the play, and he loved Clifford and he got out there. At the end of the play, he screamed to the audience "strike".

Margaret Barker: And the whole audience screams "strike". It was true.

Robert Lewis: At the end, pandemonium broke loose that audience went wild.

Ruth Nelson: We stood on the stage with the tears rolling down our faces. And you couldn't believe that this was happening. And I felt all they're going — the balcony is going to come down because of the audience was stomping their feet. They couldn't applaud anymore, so they stumped their feet. And I thought they're going to tear the balcony down.

Shelley Winters: I think I was quite young when I saw *Waiting for Lefty*. I don't know why in Jamaica, there used to be something called the subway circuit. I don't know... But forever after, after I stood up with everybody else and yelled "strike" — the whole audience — I felt that the Union Movement, the CIO-AFL (officially called AFL-CIO), (and it was) were due to the Group Theater. And I still think so.

Narrator: Calls to strike; indictments of a world built on money. "Life shouldn't be printed on dollar bills," goes the famous line from *Awake and Sing*. The spirit of revolt runs through all of Odets's work. And he in the Group were (was) on the cutting edge during the 1930s. Desperate for solutions, many Americans looked to communism, including some members of the Group Theatre.

Phoebe Brand: Almost everybody felt that there was no way out—out of the depression, out of the shooting of the veterans in Washington by Hoover, and out of the horrible Maras (a gang) the country was in at that time, no way out except socialism. The only answer.

Tony Kraber: Anybody who wasn't a bit of a radical in those 1930s should have had his head examined, because the whole country cried out for a solution to the desperate situation that we were in.

Part Ⅳ An Interview on Edward Albee

Ed Wilson: Welcome to the Harold Clurman Seminar on theatre. I'm Ed Wilson and my guest is one of America's foremost playwrights, Edward Albee. Edward, welcome.

Edward Albee: Good to see you.

Ed Wilson: Very nice to have you here. In your play *Seascape*, it's sometimes referred to as a sort of quartet, musical quartet. And in the play *A Delicate Balance*, Tobias has a long speech toward the end that you refer to in the stage directions as an aria. Do you sometimes think of your plays in musical terms that you use? Did you have some analogy between music and playwright?

Edward Albee: I've slowly begun to realize that writing a play is... has a lot in common with writing a piece of music (and) writing a string quartet. The characters are instruments; themes, ideas and musical things are quite related. Even though you don't get the simultaneity of three or four people speaking at the same time, you have the allusion of string quartet writing. The structure of a play, the literal structure of a play and the structure of string quartet can quite often be the same. There's a lot of similarities. They are both performed-out-loud pieces and a playwright notates very much the way a composer does. When a composer wants something loud, he puts triple forte. When a playwright wants something loud, (he) either underlines (or) capitalizes. I began to discover analogies running all the way through, and I think that if I didn't have my enormous absorption with classical music, which I know very well, I probably wouldn't have been aware of these, and I probably wouldn't have been able to write the kind of play that I like to write.

Ed Wilson: I want to change subjects entirely to talk about the content of some of the plays and certain themes that run through your plays, certain ideas that you take up. Several of your plays, a number of your plays are set in a well-to-do setting: perhaps a living room of an upper middle-class family. I'm thinking of all over *A Delicate Balance*. Actually if you want to take *Who's Afraid of Virginia Woolf*, *The Lady from Dubuque*... are all set in this...

Edward Albee: You got to put a play there indoors or outdoors, and I've done a lot of them outdoors, too.

Ed Wilson: Yes. Well, *Seascape* and...

Edward Albee: *The Sandbox* is outdoors, *The Zoo Story* is outdoors, *Seascape* is outdoors, *Listening* is outdoors... A lot of them are outdoors, too. But yes, you're quite right about a number of them are indoors and they are in living rooms. You know what I think that all may come from? Well, probably two places: Chekhov of course; but I think it may also come from a playwright — who I don't think is a very great playwright but whose work influenced me profoundly — that is T. S. Eliot.

Ed Wilson: Oh really?

Edward Albee: Think about *The Family Reunion*.

Ed Wilson: Yes?

Edward Albee: Think about that. Think about *The Cocktail Party*. Places like that probably influenced those decisions that I made a good deal. There is the beating of the great dark wings right outside the window of the cultivated living room.

Ed Wilson: And of course in T. S. Eliot's case, *The Cocktail Party*... I mean the name. It was that whole ambience of it we were talking about.

Edward Albee: So I wouldn't be surprised that if a lot of them came from the...

Ed Wilson: That's fascinating.

Edward Albee: I guess I'm interested in the stripping away of the veneer of the establishment of the people who really really secretly control our society (and) our government and in our culture.

Ed Wilson: You've always been, I think, a bit of a maverick and iconoclast in your... I mean you have your...

Edward Albee: I was, as you may know... Remember, I was adopted into a fairly wealthy family. All of whose values ran totally counter to the values that I seemed to develop very naturally. They were reactionary Republicans; I became a left-wing Democrat. They were filled with prejudices, and therefore I went the opposite way. Obviously, I'm anxious to expose a lot of that and strip some things naked.

Ed Wilson: It seems to me that your plays do make certain demands on the audience. And maybe that's the wrong...

Edward Albee: I've never understood why anybody would want to go to any artistic experience — read a book, see a play, listen to a piece of music, look at a piece of painting — and not come away changed in some way. Not having had an experience that was worth the time and worth the expense. And any play that I go to that leaves me unchanged from the person I was when I went in — that's an absolute waste of time. Life is short, you know. Stay home and turn the mind into cream of wheat on network TV. Why go to the theatre? Serious arts are there to keep us awake and make us think differently about things.

Ed Wilson: How do you feel these audiences respond to the family situations to the personal interactions in your plays?

Edward Albee: I haven't found that my plays are as exotic in Europe as Tennessee Williams's plays are exactly. They don't seem to be as exotic because mine are not as regional I guess.

Ed Wilson: Yes. Like his are Southern.

Edward Albee: My play seemed to translate into the culture of foreign countries fairly well.

Ed Wilson: And the... those relationships, for instance, you have a lot of husband-and-wife situations, a lot of parents-and-children situations. So those translate are accepted.

Edward Albee: No problem. To deal with Czechoslovakia for a moment, when they did *Who's Afraid of Virginia Woolf*, since nobody in Czechoslovakia had ever heard of Virginia Woolf. The only change they made was to change the title to *Who's Afraid of Franz Kafka*.

Part V Eugene O'Neill

First thing you have to understand is that O'Neill is someone who can't get his ideas down on paper fast enough. They're always percolating in his mind, not one idea but dozens of ideas.

He is constantly trying to understand himself. He can't understand that, because a lot of his ideas are unconscious. They come in dreams. O'Neill dreamt all of desires under the elms and all wilderness. He dreamt fragments of dozens of other plays.

Following the success of *Beyond the Horizon*, O'Neill's career would take off with a speed and intensity unparalleled in the annals of American theatre. Over the next 14 years, he would write 18 new plays, see 21 of his works produced on and off Broadway, win two more Pulitzer Prizes, and become the most celebrated and critically acclaimed playwright of his generation.

I mean he was a hugely famous writer. He filled a cultural space that needed to be filled. We had a couple of great novelists, we had Melville, Hawthorne, Henry James, and O'Neill came along at a point when we needed a great playwright and he knew that. I mean it was a created persona as well. I mean he posed for all of those gorgeous pictures of himself and, you know, he was an actor's son and he really knew how to look haunted and, you know, driven.

The fact that he was able to, on his own terms, overturned the very frivolous Broadway that he came into in early 1920s, and that he was able to make producers accept him on his own terms was a remarkable thing for the time, and he never tried to repeat his early success as he always wanted to try something different—often fell on his face, and tried. But each time, he was reaching for something bigger and beyond what he had already done, for something even more important and more revealing—life.

I think that there's a necessity to experiment when you're involved in something as protean as actually literally inventing American theatre. In the *Emperor Jones*, he would use expressionist scenery and the sound of throbbing drums to highlight the disintegration of his main character—a black man haunted by 300 years of American racism in the past. In the *Hairy Ape*, he would use savagely stylized dialogue and masks to evoke the inner life of working men ground to dust by the forces of industrialization. In *Anna Christie*, which would bring him a second Pulitzer, he would explore the deeply conflicted hopes and fears of a one-time prostitute, her father who abandoned her, and the strapping Irish sailor she falls in love with.

Anna Christie:
"And me to listen to that talk from a woman like you and be frightened to close her mouth with a slap! Oh, God help me, I'm a yellow coward for all men to spit at! But I'll not be getting out of this till I've had tomorrow..."

That's where O'Neill wanted to take us: he wanted to take us to that place where the interior life of the characters was ripped open and revealed. And in this limitless America, this land without a horizon, what do we do faced with the desolate boundaries that we feel within us?

To a striking degree, the painful inner turmoil his characters faced mirrored conflicts in his own life, past and present. In 1924, with strains in their marriage already on the rise, he and Agnes moved with 5-year-old Shane to Bermuda, where in 1925 a second child Oona was born, and where the conflict between them intensified. Drinking too much and ill-equipped for the family life he craved, he often felt as he had after the birth of Shane, homesick for homelessness and irresponsibility, he said, and filled with regret that he had gone in for playwriting, mating, and begetting children. Agnes, in turn, increasingly resented the maintenance his personality required, and always more social than him, had little sympathy with his increasingly desperate struggle to give up drinking.

O'Neil stopped cold when he was 40. He had to stop cold because psychiatrists told him that his brain would turn to the white of an egg, and he knew that without writing he would die.

Quitting, however, left him feeling even more strangely unsettled inside, and he compensated by retreating even more deeply into his work. He became increasingly obsessed with masks, and with what they seem to convey of the unnamed, undisclosed forces beneath the surface of life. Conscious at times that his work itself was a kind of mask behind which he was hiding. Haunted more than ever by the loss of his religious faith, he looked increasingly for something to replace it, restlessly searching in play after play for the force behind, he said. Fate, god, our biological past, whatever one calls it, mystery certainly. Ransacking the literature of three millennia, in works of increasing length, complexity and ambition, he would push the boundaries of American theatre to the very limit. Haunted as he drove himself forward by the nagging suspicion that he'd still not created the masterworks of which he was capable.

No one understood better his own limitations than O'Neil. Now the fear of being what Freud called "a pseudo-genius": you know someone who has all the desires to be a writer, and a great genius writer, and all the ambition and all the feelings but just can't make it. That's terrifying. And imagine living with that day by day and not knowing whether you have it or not, and not knowing in spite of all the praise that's been lavished on you. Whether you really are worthy of any of that praise? I'm sure he must have felt that.

"One's outer life passes in a solitude haunted by the masks of others. One's inner life passes in a solitude hounded by the masks of oneself." —Eugene O'Neill

I think that if you look at this obsession that he has with illusions and dreams, and the way that he ties this into the national question of America as a kind of a hollow dream, or a dream that will never be fulfilled: this sort of very, very tragic and dark vision of what this country is, what this country does to people's dreams. The whole obsession with masks in the 20s, I mean, the idea of life as a kind of a failing theatre really, makes it absolutely imperative that he work in the theatre and that he write plays, because the theatre is a perfect metaphor for him for a central question of life, which is the artifice of it: the way that we construct realities to protect ourselves to make it possible for us to survive, and the horrible effort it requires to keep those realities intact and to enlist other people into our own little plays, and how finally one loses the vigor and ruthlessness necessary to keep your dreams. The dominant reality that surrounds you every waking minute, and as those dreams fall apart, you realize that you've lived a lie. And you can't find a better way of expressing that than on the stage because you're of course watching a constantly decomposing dream that cannot remain intact, that has all these holes in it, that the audience is aware of, that frightened and electrified. And I think it makes the theatre the perfect medium for somebody who's as heartbroken about disillusionment, who really finally on some level can't reconcile himself to the fact that there's no salvation, that there's no redemption, that there's no life after death, that everything that made life possible, bearable is really kind of finally a lie.

Part Ⅵ Arthur Miller's *Death of a Salesman*

Host: Arthur Miller is here. It has been over 50 years since his first play, *The Man Who Had All the Luck*, opened on Broadway. With works like *The Crucible* and *A View from the Bridge*, he has become one of the great names in American playwriting. His landmark play, *Death of a Salesman*, is currently celebrating its 50th anniversary with the revival on Broadway. Arthur Miller joins me here for a conversation about life and career. Later we'll be joined by the star of the revival, Brian Dennehy. I am pleased to have, though, one more time at this table and for a conversation. Arthur Miller, welcome back!

Host: *Death of a Salesman* is a play about what?

Arthur Miller: Hmm. Well they asked me that when I was writing it, and I said that it's about a salesman and he dies. It's hard to encapsulate that play. That's about the United States; it's about a man, about an economic situation, about a family; it's about a life. And to try to boil it down to a sentence is beyond me.

Host: Some say it's a play about the corruption of capitalism.

Arthur Miller: Well yeah, accepting and it is. Accepting that when it's played in a place like China, where I directed it.

Host: Is it still playing? And someone said to me it's still playing.

Arthur Miller: God knows, they don't tell me anything.

Host: Not the same production but a variation.

Arthur Miller: Well they have their own good theatres. When it's played there, I ensure that they make a different thing out of it. I was, well in fact — CBS had a crew there where I directed it, and when the opening night came, the crowd came out of the theatre and they found one young guy who could speak English. And they asked him how he liked these at all. "It's wonderful," he said. "It just shows you that Willy Loman is right," he says. "Everybody wants to be number one man." So it depends what continent you're on, as to what it means to you. And in that case it was quite the opposite of what I had originally intended. But...

Host: Some could say Biff Loman is right. It's about coming to grips with the reality of your own life.

Arthur Miller: Well from his point of view, that's what it is. Willy's point of view is quite different. It's a love story basically, between the father and the son. In fact, it just occurred to me a couple of weeks ago, when I was talking to one of the actors, that everyone in this play loves Willy, everybody, but except Willy. And I think basically its appeal probably is that kind of a story. It's about the loss of love and the finding of love again.

Host: One of the great moments in the play is when Willy realizes he is loved.

Arthur Miller: Well that's of course what the architecture of that play is—that both he and Biff, his son, are lost people, and find themselves more or less at the end, by recognizing their love for one another. And that's fundamentally what the story is.

Host: He kills himself because he realizes he is more valuable dead than alive for some other reasons.

Arthur Miller: He wants to give of himself, he wants to dedicate himself, he wants to pour out his love for his son. And in his circumstances, he knows there's no way in this life to do that. And so his great triumph will be his giving his insurance money to his son.

Host: That's the saddest thing about it to me.

Arthur Miller: Well, it happens. Yes, it is sad, but it's just following that tail to its end.

Host: The original title was not "Death of a Salesman".

Arthur Miller: I thought I should call it—I was going to call it "The Inside of His Head", but it was very awkward, and I dropped it soon after I thought of it. But the original set, as I saw it, would be a gigantic, the interior of a skull, and the whole thing would be played in there. But, it didn't take long to see that, that was not really what I should be doing. So, Jo Mielziner, who was one of the great set designers of America, designed this marvelous set for it, and it was by no means the inside of a skull. It was a very wispy house and looked like it could be blown away by a breeze. And (it) was a great triumph that set. But the basic play would be the same anyway, no matter how you did.

Host: You were how old when you wrote this? 31...2?

Arthur Miller: I was 32.

Host: You won a Pulitzer Prize for it.

Arthur Miller: Yeah.

Host: At 33, 32, 33.

Arthur Miller: Yeah.

Host: Changed your life.

Arthur Miller: Well, it didn't. I had written about eight plays before *Death of a Salesman*, and I have been preparing for that play for all those years when I started writing plays in college.

Host: What do you mean (by) "preparing for that play"? I mean everything else is as Churchill said when he became prime minister: "Everything I've done prepared me for this moment."

Arthur Miller: That play, formally speaking, is a kind of invention. The idea was to make everything happen at the same time—that is the past and the present working together, instead of stopping a play and going back. There are no flashbacks in the play, and yet the past is always with us, just as it is in life when you're talking to somebody and you think of something 35 years ago. To make that happen on the stage took a lot of thinking, a lot of feeling, as how to make that happen. And it took a lot of writings over the years, working through straight realism, through poetic theatre, even some verse plays that I was writing, until I came upon that form.

Host: Was it instantly, critically praised?

Arthur Miller: Yes.

Host: It wasn't mixed. It was...

Arthur Miller: No. Almost everybody. Everybody had the same reaction, including the people who read it, except for a few who didn't understand it. They didn't know how it could be done, how the audience could follow the story, because part of it is taking place in the past and then there are, when we were in the past, we're thinking of further back in the past. So there are double, two kinds of past. It's very complicated, but I've made it very simple.

Host: That's the architecture you talked about.

Chapter 10

Appendix 1   Key to Exercises

Part I   Warm-up

Discuss the following questions in pairs or groups.

1. For example, *Black Boy*, *Lolita*, *The Catcher in the Rye*.
2. For example, Richard Wright, John Updike, J. D. Salinger.

3. Many postwar American novels inherit the legacy of realism from the late 19th century and the first half of the 20th century. They focus on the dilemma of everyday life in the postwar American society.

4. The American homeland was not caught up in war and hence the economy survived the devastation of bombs. America became the most dynamic and stable economic body in the postwar world, but the tense conflict between labor and capital was not solved, and so was the alienation of man in capitalism.

5. The postwar novels often feature a sense of loss, disappointment, and an urge to reorient oneself in a society that seemed to be rapidly developing.

Part II The American Novel after 1945

Watch the video. Write *T* for true or *F* for false for each statement.

1. T   2. T   3. T   4. T   5. F   6. T   7. F

答案解析：

5. 不是 *Lolita*，而是 *Franny and Zooey*。

7. 课程安排并不包括这两名作家。

Part III Celebrating J. D. Salinger: Fame, Outsider and *The Catcher in the Rye*

Watch Erica Wagner's interview with J. D. Salinger's son, Matt Salinger. Answer the following questions.

1. Mark David Chapman killed John Lennon, and he said *The Catcher in the Rye* had a great influence on him.

2. 72 million.

3. He thinks it's nonsensical, since there will always be a few lunatics among a huge number of readers.

4. It's about celebrating the works of J. D. Salinger with his readers.

5. You'll be surprised to know how many people out there feel exactly as you do.

Part IV An Evening with Joyce Carol Oates at Cornell University

Watch the video and fill in the blanks.

1) bonus	2) responded	3) reputable	4) reflected
5) letters	6) brutality	7) resilience	8) violence
9) quoted	10) prolific	11) 60	12) 11
13) 42	14) 8	15) 11	16) subjects
17) Gothic	18) majored	19) awards	20) humanities

Part V A Lecture on John Updike

Watch the video and answer the following questions.

1. Lyrical realism.

2. He lived from 1932 to 2009.

3. In eastern Pennsylvanian small towns.

4. Harvard.

5. Philip Roth.
6. The Democrats.
7. He supported the Vietnam War and thought it was necessary.
8. Golf.
9. William Dean Howells.

Appendix 2 Transcripts

Part II The American Novel after 1945

This is "American Novel Since 1945". Welcome. I am Amy Hungerford. Today I am going to do a couple of things. In the first half of class, I'm going to tell you a little bit about the class and introduce some of the questions that we will think about over the term if you stay in this course. In the second half of class, I will introduce you and start telling the first story of the term, and that's about Richard Wright's *Black Boy*, which is our first reading of the term. In between those two parts, I will ask that anyone who is shopping the class and would like to leave at that time, do so then. I would be grateful if you would wait until that point if at all you possibly can. It just makes the whole thing work a little easier and it prevents that drop in the pit of my stomach when I see half of the class leave. So I will indicate when that moment is. Come on. Make yourself comfortable on the floor if you can.

My goal in this course is to allow you or to invite you to read some of the most compelling novels written in the last little over a half century. This includes a whole range of thematic concerns. So when I look down at my list of novels—which I have not brought with me (I trust you can find it on the web; I didn't want to kill trees by making enough of these for all of you) —when I look down at my list of books and I think about what these books are about, I see war. I see war, all the way from the Trojan War, to the Mexican-American War in the 1840s, all the way up to the Vietnam War. I see love, in all kinds of guises: whether they are criminal as in *Lolita*, pedophiliac love; whether they are sort of ideational romantic, John Barth; whether they are campus love, that's *The Human Stain*, Philip Roth; all kinds and forms of sex and love, and then there is politics interweaving with all those things.

There are questions of identity and race. There is a nervous breakdown that actually happens right here in New Haven in one of these novels. That's in *Franny and Zooey*. I see women who give up on housekeeping altogether and let their house go to ruin and become vagrants. I see suicide. I see slavery. All these things you can read about in these novels, but reading these novels is not just about reading about those things. It's also going to be the process of watching an artistic form unfold over a very exciting period of time.

In the second half of the 20th century and up now into the 21st century, writers were thinking very hard about what to do stylistically with all the innovations that come in that powerful period known as modernism. So one of the things we're going to think about together in the course is what happens to all those innovations. Are they abandoned? Are they embellished? Are they stretched? Are they rejected? What happens to those resources that the great modernist writers endowed language with so powerfully earlier in the century? So there are formal questions that we will take up time and again. There are questions that intersect between the form and the content in every single novel that we read.

Now perhaps those of you who like to read fictions, and especially who like to read fictions from this period, will look down at that syllabus and you'll say, "Well, where is?" "Where is Don DeLillo?" "Where is John Updike?" My answer for the question— "Why these writers?" —my answer for the question is the course. It's an answer that unfolds over these 14 weeks of the term. 13? 13. The short answer is that I think these writers best represent all the different threads, all the different forces in the American Novel since 1945. There are lots of other writers we could include, including those two that I named, that would equally illustrate some of the threads that I've got on the syllabus now, but these are the ones for various practical and more substantive reasons that I have chosen.

Part III   Celebrating J. D. Salinger: Fame, Outsider and *The Catcher in the Rye*

Erica Wagner: I think also I wonder, because um, I was asked about this once, you know, some people I think have said, because for instance, Mark David Chapman who killed John Lennon said that *The Catcher in the Rye* had such an influence on him, so that too has, you know, what, what do you say to that kind of stuff?

Matt Salinger: I say nonsense, you know, how many people have read *The Catcher in the Rye*? Perhaps 72-million people, there have been two maniacs that happened to have read it and then went out and killed somebody or did something extreme. What about the other 71 million? The only susceptibility to that is if you write about outsiders, as he did, most artists feel apart from the world in some ways that, they're observers, so many of their characters are observers and that's part of the sensibility and the sensitivity that you have to have as an artist, so you write those characters and people are going to be attracted to them that feel like outsiders and you're gonna get a couple of crazy lunatics in that bunch. What was your answer when you were asked?

Erica Wagner: Pretty much that, I have to say, pretty much that, is that people will always pick up on those exceptions, and yes exactly, how many people have read, so you've been traveling around now and engaging with your father's audiences, you know, we're about to do an event this evening with Penguin and it will be full of people who love your father's works. Now that he's gone, I know what it's like to lose a parent I loved. How is that for you?

Matt Salinger: I was doing this out of a sense of duty because I thought it was the right thing to do, and because I wanted to correct some misapprehensions out there, and to communicate a couple of facts to his readers. I wasn't prepared to enjoy myself. I'm not sure I've enjoyed myself, but I've been moved, and I've been touched by a lot of people have continued to read him. A lot of people have rediscovered him, have gone back to his books at later stages in their lives. I had a fascinating discussion, with somebody recently at one of these talks who had read his work and identified with Holden when he was young, and then identified with Buddy, and then identified with Seymour. It depends where you are in your life and what's happening. But the fact that they're alive in that way, is thrilling and I go back to Mr. Antolini and what he said to Holden. "You'll be surprised to know how many people out there feel exactly as you do." And what a thrill it will be for you to find those people and define clues that they left, how they got themselves out of morass that you're feeling right now. And I think that's what my father did in his four published books and his unpublished material. I think he really was tapped into that, and cared about those people and wanted to help them, and I'm not making him into some saint. I think, he had plenty of faults as he'd be the first to say. But his best self was absolutely including.

Erica Wagner: That's really wonderful. Thank you so much, Matt. It's been really marvelous talking to you. Thank you. It's been fun.

Part Ⅳ An Evening with Joyce Carol Oates at Cornell University

Good evening, and welcome to the last of the summer series. This is a special bonus, and I'm glad to have all of you here. Please silence all of your electronic devices. And I also want to thank Katherine Brewer, the Dean of the College of Agriculture and Life Sciences, for the use of this hall. She's been very generous this year. In the United States, one possible way to find out if you've made it is to check with *The Simpsons*. 11 years ago, Lisa Simpson dreamed she was in prison. And when a guard came around with a book cart, she asked, "Got any Joyce Carol Oates?" The guard replied, "Nope. It's all Danielle Steel." Does anyone know how Lisa responded? Do you remember that? OK, go look it up. But it gets even better. In 2017, in an episode, "Pork and Burns", Joyce actually appears as herself and even voices her own character. But we're at Cornell. And for us, *The Simpsons* doesn't count as a particularly reliable and reputable source of anything. So let's look at a far better one.

In the essay, *Reflecting on Joyce Carol Oates*, Joanne Creighton, an English professor, former president of Mount Holyoke College and the author of two books, and many reviews, and articles about the work of Joyce Carol Oates, reflected, "While Joyce Carol Oates was early called the Dark Lady of American letters, that label is not right. She has a tremendous respect for the dark side of human experience, for the mysterious depth of the conscious, and for the primitive brutality at the core of physical existence. Yet Joyce's vision is not dark. She is, in fact, optimistic about the possibilities of human resilience and transcendence of a distinctly American variety. Despite the violence and duress that her characters typically endure, Joyce respects their tenacious attempt to, as she wrote in the preface to *Marya*, 'forge their own souls by way of the choices they make, large and small, conscious and half conscious'."

Professor Creighton continues, "But she sprints far ahead of those who would attempt to assess her body of work. I agree with Anne Tyler who is quoted in a *Washington Post* article as saying, '100 years from now, people will laugh at us for sort of taking her for granted'." Professor Creighton then finishes, "This we know she is one of the most accomplished and significant American writers of our time." The dictionary definitions of the words productive and prolific surely must have after them these words, as exemplified by Joyce Carol Oates. By my likely incomplete count, she has published at least 60 novels, 11 novellas, 42 collections of short stories, 10 children's and young adult novels, 8 plays, and 6 one-act plays, and 11 collections of poetry. She has also written hundreds of essays and book reviews, in addition to longer non-fiction works on literary subjects ranging from Emily Dickinson's poetry and the fiction of Dostoyevsky and James Joyce, to studies of the Gothic and horror genres, and on such non-literary subjects as the painter George Bellows and boxer Mike Tyson.

How does she do this? I've read—and she'll correct me if I'm wrong—but that she writes daily in longhand from 8:00 am to noon, and then she resumes her writing in the evening. Joyce is a native New Yorker, who attended the same one room school her mother did. While a student at Syracuse

University, where she majored in English and was valedictorian of her class, she won the college short story contest, sponsored by *Mademoiselle* magazine. Some years ago, one of her Syracuse University's professors, Donald A. Dyke, commented that about once a term, "She'd drop a 400-page novel on my desk." He added, "She was the most brilliant student we've ever had here." Joyce earned a Master of Arts in English from the University of Wisconsin, Madison. She has won many, many awards. She still runs, and she is an active hiker and bicyclist. And she is the Roger S. Berlind's professor of the humanities emeritus and professor of creative writing emeritus at Princeton University.

Joyce Carol Oates was last here 9 years and 361 days ago. And it is a genuine pleasure to have her with us again tonight.

Part V A Lecture on John Updike

All right everybody. Welcome back to contemporary American literature. We are continuing our exploration of the realist fiction of the end of the 20th century. And now we have arrived at John Updike, a writer of what I'm calling lyrical realism for reasons I think you'll see. This is unlike dirty realism and magical realism which I applied to Raymond Carver and Louise Erdrich. Those were kind of official terms that were used at the time to describe those writers and other related writers. Lyrical realism is more of a term I'm applying to Updike. It's not like an official term that's been applied to him and I'm borrowing it from an essay that was written in the 2000s by a writer named Zadie Smith, who was contrasting a more experimental fiction with what she called lyrical realism, which she thought was one of the standard types of American fiction writing in the novel and in the short story. And I think that the term lyrical realism, and I'll explain to you what I mean by that shortly, particularly applies to John Updike.

So who is John Updike? He lived from 1932 to 2009. He was born and raised in Shillington, Pennsylvania. So that's on the other side of Pennsylvania from where August Wilson and I are from. So we were in Pittsburgh with fences. That's western Pennsylvania. Shillington is in eastern Pennsylvania near Reading, I think, is the nearest larger city. And he often recurs to this setting in his fiction, this setting of eastern Pennsylvania small town, eastern Pennsylvania with a Protestant Dutch influence. His work is pretty diverse in settings and even some of his later works are more sort of fantastical and some of his works somewhere global. But his most noted realist fiction tends to have that as its setting. He attended Harvard and then he studied in England to be an artist, particularly a cartoonist. Then he comes back to America and he becomes a writer for the *New Yorker* magazine. That's his regular outlet for both his fiction, his short stories and his literary criticism. And he is a very prolific writer, writes many many short stories, many many essays, as a poet, writes innumerable novels. I mean they're not innumerable. One could number them, but I don't actually know how many. Let me think off the top of my head, around 20 novels in a lifetime, 20 or 30 novels. So very prolific and was renowned for his short stories and his literary criticism, etc. And I think one of the ways to think about him, if you think of the authors we've read before in this course, is that he is really I think the heir to John Cheever. Cheever and Updike both have their concerns, this life not lived in the big city but tending to live in suburbs or small towns among the white middle class, the broad middle class from the lower middle class to the upper middle class. Or even Updike often charts his characters sort of moving from the lower middle class to the upper middle class, but that tends to be their concern and with an East Coast setting

231

and a style of lyricism, a very poetic, very richly descriptive, richly evocative writing style, very distant from the minimalism of Raymond Carver or in the generations before Carver, of Ernest Hemingway.

So I think we're starting to see kind of two poles develop in realist writing between a minimalist style and a lyrical style. So what else about Updike? He was married twice. He had four children and in the second half of his life, he lived mostly in Massachusetts, in a relatively small town or at least a small city in Massachusetts. And he is an interesting writer. He is a polarizing writer, a controversial writer for some of the same reasons that Philip Roth was controversial. These were both writers who were contemporaries, both born in the 1930s. We're looking at those 1930s births again, that silent generation that really dominated the second half of the 20th century or the last quarter of the 20th century in American literature. And they were writers who were very interested in chronicling the changes that came about in the 1960s and after with the sexual revolution. And we looked at the kind of emancipatory, the women's movement, the kind of queer movement we see reflected in Adrian Rich's works, but there was a general revolution in sexual mores that wasn't necessarily political in a left-right sense. It just sort of overtook the whole culture in which you have the development of the birth control pill, the liberalization of divorce laws, the full federal legalization of abortion and in general what you have is a relaxation of sexual norms across the society. The idea that you're supposed to get married to someone, you know a man and a woman will get married when they're 22 years old and they'll have children and they'll stay together all their lives. This is no longer really the expectation. You have an elevated divorce rate; you have much more potential for women to control their own reproduction, and in general you have this sexual revolution. And Roth and Updike are both very much male chroniclers of this set of events and they're sort of describing in their works along with some other writers we didn't read, like Saul Bellow for instance. They're describing in their work kind of what it is to experience this development as a man, and so their works are full of adultery. They're full of men with, you know, wives and mistresses, and all sorts of things. And Updike turns his rich descriptive poetic evocative gift often to rather graphic depictions of sexuality because another thing that's happening in this period is a relaxation of literary censorship which I think we've already talked about. That happened kind of, before, in the 1950s and 1960s, and so Updike and Roth and other writers are able to write much more graphically about sexuality in their works which are not simply true of white male writers either. I mean this also applies to James Baldwin and Toni Morrison and Louise Erdrich, all of whom also write rather graphically about sexuality in their works as well. So he has been polarizing in that way. His work was seen as the sort of depiction of male entitlement or the male gaze.

There's also a sense of general kind of conservatism about Updike. He was, I think, politically a lifelong Democrat, but on the very conservative side of Democrat for most of his life. He for instance is notably one of the major writers to have supported the Vietnam War, wrote about why he thought the Vietnam War was necessary. And you know, he's coming to this opinion when that war was largely prosecuted by a Democratic presidential administration, that it was necessary to roll back communism for instance. And in his works, there's a connection here between the style of his works and the politics of his works which is that his gift, his highly poetic style just kind of placidly, complacently seems to describe everything it registers. There's no edge of critique in Updike. That's not true; that goes too far;

but for the sake of a short lecture permit me an exaggeration. There's no critique in Updike. His style sort of pats everything on the head and blesses it as it goes by and literally blesses it. He's a Christian, a very devout sincere Christian who is very concerned about developments within Protestant religion in his writing as well. And in fact, a lot of his fictions take on this kind of frisson from, what does friction mean, this shiver, this tingle up the spine that you get when you read it because of the juxtaposition of the carnality of the sexuality he describes, with also this interest in faith and spirituality. But his particular spiritual view was that everything in the created world was sort of beautiful because God made it all and so everything would be described in this way and that's kind of the utopian way to describe it.

But the negative way to describe it is there's this complacency, this kind of laziness of intellect to his work that he just kind of takes everything in equally and blandly. And so this middle class suburban small town lifestyle that so many other American writers from all different perspectives would want to criticize just isn't there in his work. You know we started this course with that interest in the outsider. There's no sense of outsiderness in Updike's work. He was not an outsider. He became an insider, a consummate insider. And I have him pictured there playing the insider's game of golf. He was very interested in golf; he even wrote a book about golf which I haven't read. So that is John Updike. What do they say in the Norton that I excerpted, "to transcribe middleness with all its grits bumps and anonymities in its fullness of satisfaction and mystery, is it possible or worth doing he asks?" And the editors of the Norton Anthology say that he is arguably the most significant transcriber or creator rather of middleness in American writing since William Dean Howells. William Dean Howells is a 19th century writer who is in many ways the founder of realism as a tradition in American literature. So this lyric poetic description of the middle state of life is what Updike is about.

Chapter 11

Appendix 1 Key to Exercises

Part I Warm-up

Discuss the following questions in pairs or groups.

1. Graffiti, montage, playfulness, deconstruction, fragmentation.

2. Answers may vary. American postmodernism can be associated with a specific period in literature and culture. It emerged primarily in the mid-20th century and gained prominence in the 1960s and 1970s. However, its influence and manifestations can still be seen in contemporary American literature, art, architecture, and other cultural forms.

3. *The Sot-weed Factor*, *Chimera*, and *Gravity's Rainbow*.

4. John Barth, Vladimir Nabokov, and Thomas Pynchon.

Part II An Overview of American Postmodern Literature

Watch the video and answer the following questions.

1. In 1993.

2. The case was when people really saw an explosion of 24-hour news and everybody was getting access to the Internet.

3. From World War II to the mid-1990s.

4. Multiple first-person narrators, unreliable narrators, changes in time.

5. They address social issues related to gender, race and youthful rebellion.

Part III 1001 Nights with John Barth: *The Sot-weed Factor*

Watch the video and answer the following questions.

1. In the 1960s.

2. *Clarissa* and *Pamela*.

3. The epistolary form means that narratives of a novel are facilitated by letters.

4. Henry Fielding.

5. The speaker holds that just like the impenetrable intentions behind Pamela's and Shamela's letters, John Barth's novels are often at play, and that the narratives are unreliable.

6. The protagonist of *The Sot-weed Factor*.

7. Many characters in the novel forge documents to pretend to be someone else.

Part IV An Introduction to Vladimir Nabokov

Watch the video. Write *T* for true or *F* for false for each statement.

1. F   2. T   3. T   4. F   5. T

答案解析：

1. 纳博科夫从小会三种语言，俄语、英语、法语。

4. 纳博科夫一家于1940年移居美国。

Part V A Lecture on Thomas Pynchon

Watch the video again and fill in the blanks.

1) continuation	2) acclaimed	3) esteemed	4) biographical
5) reclusive	6) shunned	7) settlement	8) confluence
9) military	10) intimations	11) obsession	12) defense

Appendix 2 Transcripts

Part II An Overview of American Postmodern Literature

So postmodernism takes these a little bit further and this includes unprecedented prosperity and the 1990s global conflict at the same time. This ranges from after World War II through the 1990s. Some people say 1980; some people say 1990. I would say 1994 to be more specific, but I have my reasons for that. Social protest, the civil rights movement, the women's movement, the gay rights movement, mass culture and consumerism media saturation. This is a little bit before the Internet. The Internet went public in 1993 and then in 1995, this is going to sound strange and if you're still listening to this, but in 1995 we had the O. J. Simpson, 1994 to 1995 was the O. J. Simpson case where we really saw an explosion of 24-hour news at about the same time that everybody was getting access to the Internet. So for me, I would say that postmodernism extends from after World War II until the mid-1990s when the

Internet kind of ushered in a new era but other people can disagree with me. They'd be wrong; I'm just kidding. But the rise of technology, space exploration was during this time; the digital revolution came just at the tail end. I really liked this quote. Quite a bit postmodernism was a reaction to modernism. "Where modernism was about objectivity, postmodernism was about subjectivity; modernism sought a singular truth, postmodernism sought the multiplicity of truths."

To me, this is the key question of postmodernism: what is true and how does your perspective and my perspective, how are they going to differ when looking at the same event. The modernists kind of tried to get rid of traditions, and sorry about that, so postmodernists create traditional works without traditional structure or narrative. For example, multiple first-person narrators, unreliable narrators, changes in time. And really again the idea is subjectivity. Modernists try to look at things objectively without the lens of traditional values and they try to think about things in an objective manner and question what's going on to become more objective. And as the quote says, here the postmodernists are looking at multiplicity and different people's truths and that means sometimes there are no heroes and anti-heroes. There are rarely happy endings; writings are often critical and ironic, so concentrating on surface realities, the absurdity of daily life, questioning of authority, the past morality and again the nature of truth. They address social issues related to gender and race and youthful rebellion. The tone is often detached or unemotional; individuals sometimes seem isolated; movement from small literary circles to diversity and multiculturalism that kind of happens as postmodernism progresses.

And again another reason that I don't feel like we're in this period right now; I think that the idea of diversity with things like changes in publishing and eBooks and things like that; anybody can write and be published doesn't mean that it's going to be good or read by many people. But anybody could be published whereas previously that was really not the case. So post modernism is going to include some of these authors experimental forms, the beat poets pictured here, confessional poets, genre fiction, horror science fiction, fantasy mystery, all of that becomes quite popular during this period. Multicultural literature, more diverse voices. I like the Amy Tan quote: "My work might only be words but behind the words there's a lot of contemplation about human nature." Oops sorry. It should be noted I already said this. So yeah some people would say that our current period is postmodern; other people would say that because of the Internet, the availability of publishing through small presses, print on demand, new media, eBooks, podcasts, blogs, social media, really that began a new movement or a new literary period I think too. It's kind of too soon to tell but I think really that at least since the mid-1990s that writing has changed quite a bit, so we will be looking at books from the realist period, from modernist period, from the postmodern, and then also a book that kind of could be postmodern or could be thought of as contemporary as well.

A few major themes that we're going to talk about. This is not a complete list. The last time I gave this presentation in class, somebody asked me if these were all of them, so I added the words a few. What it means to be American individualism and the self-made man. Those are going to be quite important. We talked about that with transcendentalism but really that's a thought that comes through American literature throughout all time and also questioning those ideals too. Should Americans be so individualistic? Can people be self-made men? If things like genetics or fate or discrimination are working against them? The American dream and who can achieve that and who struggles to achieve it; diversity and difference versus conformity; so things like sexuality, gender, economic differences, regional differences, with regionalism, racial or ethnic or cultural differences and the tension between that and sort of mainstream American culture even differences in thought of people who might seem like they fit into mainstream American culture. Innocence and coming of age, even if that coming of age happens later to someone who is an adult. We're going to look at that in one of our texts, in particular alienation and isolation versus community. A changing moral landscape in each of these periods. The writers are going to question the changes to morality and ask if these changes are really good? Do we want this? Human nature and then truth objectivity and subjectivity. What does it mean to have truth? Is there universal truth? Can we be objective or should we look at things through our own lens and through our own experiences.

So I really look forward to talking with you guys about these things and I hope that in the presentations about the books themselves you can understand. If this was a little bit confusing, once we get into those books, you can understand them a bit more. So that's it. Hope to see you next time. Thanks.

Part III 1001 Nights with John Barth: *The Sot-weed Factor*

Try John Barth's version of *The Sot-weed Factor*, which he published in the 1960s. I would say this is right in the middle of his career, 1968. This is probably his first big selling book. I want to say just a few things. One is that most Barth loves to go back to old books. There are two writers that I always think about when I think about the history of the novel. One is Samuel Richardson, who is really kind of awful and kind of fun at the same time. I have *Clarissa*. I read *Pamela* in college as an undergraduate. I loved it. I've always wanted to reread it and I've been intending to read *Clarissa*, which is possibly one of the longest novels ever written. It's pretty damn big. And to say just a few quick words about Samuel Richardson, I'm cribbing all of this from a wonderful book by Ian Watt called *The Rise of the Novel* which I can't find. It's somewhere on my shelves. I just couldn't find it. There was kind of two or three streams of the novel that started to come out as it is being developed and one was this epistolary stream which was Samuel Richardson, was going to write a book about how young ladies should write letters to show how virtuous they are and what good girls they are, and by doing this, they attract rich men I think basically was the premise. Anyway *Pamela* is about this girl who goes to work for a guy named Mr. B and she is totally virtuous. I think the subtitle is virtually *Virtue Rewarded*.

This is a brilliant and absorbing book. You can't put it down and it's very twisted, very twisted novel. She goes to live with this guy named Mr B, who is this Mr you know. He is supposed to be a nice guy and he is really a lech. And he becomes obsessed with her because she is so beautiful; he wants to sleep with her and he wants to ruin her virtue and he does everything he can to get her into bed. He even locks her into this castle of his and won't let her out. It's a bit like psycho. He runs around; at one point he is wearing like the maid's outfit so he can spy on her. It's a really twisted fun book and ultimately the premise of the book is that, because Pamela is so good and so virtuous, he falls in love with her and he becomes a nice guy and she marries him. It's completely crazy but it presents the notion that this is kind of a realistic vision of the world. It's total but it's somehow going to teach us something about how to be a better person. So this kind of lecturing moralistic type of novel at the same time is filled with these weird twisted notions about people in reply to this. And I can't find this one either, one of my favorite writers we've talked about. I've recommended *Tom Jones* as one of the great long novels to read. Henry Fielding wrote a hilarious book which I can't find on my shelves called *Shamela*, and the premise of *Shamela* is basically anyone who would believe this is an idiot. That's basically the premise of the novel. Pamela is really called Shamela and she is basically writing all her letters to manipulate everybody so that she can get squire a booby to give her all his money, so she is manipulating the whole correspondence. So the idea is that there's a game being played on the reader through the correspondence. That people who believe what's happening in the novel whether it's teaching you virtue or teaching you about history, if you believe you're learning something from the novel, you're an idiot basically. *Tom Jones* is a wonderful book. We're going to take that to the bathtub. I think that's a fair way of describing *The Sot-weed Factor* and almost everything by Barth. If you believe you're going to learn something from a novel, you're an idiot basically; and if you believe any sort of written documentation to some extent, and you don't realize how that person who writes this document is trying to play you, then you're an idiot as well. So it's not just politicians. It's just the whole notion of the novel. The novel is a game and you're just going to play with it.

It's set up as a historical novel. He plays off this poem which is supposed to be about this individual's experiences in the colonies working in a tobacco farm. And he sets up as a historical novel and it's about a kid whose name is Ebony; he is based on Ebenezer Cooke and he starts to set up a whole bunch of really complicated narratives so this is supposed to be a set of twins. There's lots of past histories of where the twins came from and who their father and mother are and who's who, what their relationship is to one another and there's a teacher that shows up named Burlingame. And Henry Burlingame shows up early in the book and you got to keep your eye on Henry Burlingame because he is this sort of shape-shifting character who keeps popping up in the course of the novel. He is always showing up in different guises and giving you a different name for himself and a different explanation of who he is; and in the course of the book, they go to America where the colonies are all a bunch of crooks and pirates all trying to steal land from each other. They're stealing from the king or from the Protestant king or from the Catholics. And the Jesuits are in there and there's all the pirates themselves; there's pirate ships running through it. It is very similar in some ways to a picaresque novel, but it's a little more realistic, a little more like you're kind of in the story. There are lots of complications, lots of broad humor, you know what I mean. Ebenezer is the super serious kid; he takes writing poetry very seriously which means he is the brunt of most of the jokes. He is a fool; he is a fool basically and he believes he is going to write this great poem about merit Maryland which is where he goes to write *The Sot-weed Factor*. There's all sorts of documents that are circulating in this and they're all trying to recover documents to get the history of what's happened to all these people, and who's related to whom, including Henry Burlingame who's got a bunch of different names. And in the course of the book, they're recovering documents. There are lots of forge rings of documents and lots of upending of this. This is very common in all the old great classic comic novels upending of normal relationships. So for example, Ebenezer's valet Bertrand, who's supposed to be serving him, is often going around pretending he is the man; he is

Ebenezer and Ebenezer is his servant. And for various reasons, everybody is trying to kill Ebenezer because they think he is an important person, or he thinks he is an important person. There are a lot of appropriations of identity and appropriations of who wrote the documents, and they're often forging the documents. And often when you meet people, you find out later there are actually other people so it's hard to follow. If you're not really prepared for an immersive type novel, but it's not that hard. The language is written in the 17th century vernacular and dialect, so you have to kind of get into that.

The comedy is very broad in places. There's lots of, you know what I mean. Ebenezer is so super serious; he is a virgin; he wants to be a virgin. He is very much like, you know, Pamela. I write my poetry. And at the very beginning of the novel, he falls in love with a prostitute who wants to sleep with him for five pounds or something, and he says he is so struck by her generosity that she'll sleep with him for five pounds, and he falls in love with her and decides not to sleep with her. And he is basically a 30-year-old virgin and every time he thinks he is going to be really noble, he gets put into some situation where he sees some women and he almost wants to rape her. He is so crazed with sex and then something happens so he never actually does have sex. So his intentions to be Mr. Purity are almost accidentally fulfilled at least in the first half of the novel. Lots of broad comedy you know. The twins at the beginning; I think it's Anna and Ebenezer; they're probably not twins; they're probably not related because it's a very complicated family history, so we're going to go through this book, and the first half of the book is really fun. I've really enjoyed it.

It's not an easy time you know. Right now the whole world is getting crazier literally; we started this series of talks just to find time in the bathtub while the world went ape and it has been going even increasing the ape every single week since we've been doing this. So we still have to find time to read and you really do need to have a good hour a day or you'll get lost to this. You'll get lost and he has got a lot of plates on the sticks running through this. All right, I'm going to leave that, so don't believe everything you read. That's basically what he says and I love both these types of novels I got to say. But I am quite sympathetic towards any writer who basically tells you that, if you take the novel too seriously, you're an idiot. It's for the bathtub; it is for the bathtub.

Part Ⅳ An Introduction to Vladimir Nabokov

All right. Can everybody see and hear everything here? OK. This first quote that I have from the book: "She was Lo, plain Lo in the morning, standing 4 feet 10 in one sock. She was Lola in slacks, she was Dolly at school, she was Delores on the dotted line, but in my arms, she was always Lolita." Her name is one of the themes that we'll talk about a little later.

This is Vladimir Nabokov as a child. He was born in what was then Petrograd, but now St. Petersburg, Russia in April of 1899. He's the eldest of five children; he was raised trilingual, and spoke Russian, English and French fluently. I read that to his patriotic father's disappointment, he could read and write in English before he could in Russian; and after the February 1917 Revolution in Russia forced the abdication of Tsar Nicholas Ⅱ, Nabokov's father became the Secretary for the Russian Provisional Government, which was made up primarily of business owners, capitalists, aristocrats and noblemen; and they generally supported continuing to fight against Germany. Then after the Bolsheviks overthrew the Provisional Government in October of the same year, the Nabokov family fled to Crimea, where they thought they wouldn't have to stay long, they believed that would be temporary. They ultimately had to seek refuge in western Europe, and Nabokov enrolled at Cambridge University. Then in 1920, his family moved to Berlin, where he would join them after he completed his BA at Cambridge. His father was a proud Russian patriot and a classical liberal, who rejected both Fascism and Communism. He was shot and killed in March of 1922 by a Russian monarchist. At the time, he was not the target of the shot, but he was shielding the person who was. After that happened, Nabokov's mother and sister moved to Prague, but Nabokov himself remained in Berlin for 15 years. During his time in Berlin, he wrote his first 9 novels, which were all written in Russian. He also met in 1923 and married in 1925 a Russian Jewish woman named Vera Slonim, and their only child, Dmitri, was born in 1934.

Nabokov's last work of Russian fiction was a 1939 novella called *The Enchanter*, which was written during the relatively short time, just 3 years that he had his family in France. He would later call *The Enchanter* "The first little throb of Lolita". In May 1940, as the German Army advanced, Nabokov, with his wife and son, fled to the United States. They originally settled in Manhattan, and Vladimir, who had studied zoology at Cambridge, volunteered at the American Museum of Natural History as an entomologist. He was a lifelong lover of butterflies in particular, and he was considered an expert lepidopterist.

Nabokov began lecturing at Wellesley College in 1941. He's widely credited with founding the Russian department there; and the Resident Lecturer position was created for him. It gave him the time and income to write and study butterflies. During his time in the United States, he also would teach at Cornell University, where Ruth Bader Ginsburg was among his students; and he also curated a lepidoptery collection at the Harvard Museum of Comparative Zoology. Each summer, Nabokov would make trips to the western United States to collect butterflies; and it was on those trips that he began refining *The Enchanter* into what would become *Lolita*.

Part V A Lecture on Thomas Pynchon

All right everybody. Welcome back to contemporary American literature. This will be a continuation of our discussion of postmodern fiction for this week. The topic of today's lecture is probably the most acclaimed or the most famous of postmodern fiction writers Thomas Pynchon, one of the most acclaimed but also challenging writers in postmodern American literature, comparable in the world of the novel to John Ashbery in the world of poetry I would say. They're both equally esteemed but also not always the easiest writers to engage with. Thomas Pynchon is a difficult writer to do a biographical slide about, because there's not a lot of biography that we know. He is a famously reclusive writer who has shunned all publicity for most of his writing life. There are very few even pictures of him that exist. I think very few recordings of his voice and one of the most notable is his appearance on *The Simpsons* in 2004, in which he appeared with a paper bag over his head but he did do the voice of his own character, so the image of Pynchon on *The Simpsons* and then this early photograph of him as a very young man that I have on the slide are the only images that we have of him.

He was born on 1937 in Long Island to a family whose roots go back to the puritan settlement of New England, and that is a theme throughout his work, the theme of what America is, of its founding, its destiny, its history, is something that's very important to him. He majored in engineering physics at Cornell in the late 1950s, and that's another very important aspect of his life, which is that he is a writer and one of the things that make his writing challenging for literary types like myself is that, he is an expert in and steeped in the sciences, and can write with great fluency and knowledge about science as he does throughout his work. But while he was at Cornell, he attended lectures by the postmodern Russian émigré novelist Vladimir Nabokov who was mentioned in the introduction to the Norton Anthology of American Literature that I had you read at the beginning of the semester. As a major kind of literary figure and major writer and also either a late modernist or a postmodernist novelist, depending on what you do with these terms, and so Pynchon did attend his lectures and then Pynchon went on professionally to work at Boeing in the early 1960s. And I think that one of the things about his work and the politics of his work that is not evident in this early short story is that, he is very worried about the confluence of technology and power so he is working in the aerospace industry in the early 1960s and he is seeing you know some of the ways that military technology is going, some of the ways that surveillance technology is going. There are these eerie intimations even in his early work in the 1960s of the Internet because that's being developed as a military technology. There's also an obsession throughout his work which again is not evident in this short story of the lingering, the lingering presence of Nazism over modern life. Well because he has worked in the aerospace industry, he knows the American space program is being worked on by men who were former Nazis, who were brought out of Germany to do it.

We don't know a lot about his life but we can infer from his not only being steeped in the sciences and the abstract, but in the practical applications of science and the defense industry that the experience is going to shape some of the concerns that we see come back again and again throughout particularly his later work. I mentioned he is a very reclusive writer. He doesn't teach. He refuses media appearances with the exception of his appearance on *The Simpsons*, which will tell you something. He is a very funny writer and his writing has been very influential on popular culture despite the fact that he is a difficult writer. So yes he has influenced some of the later writers we'll read in this course, like Don Delillo, David Foster Wallace and George Saunders.

Chapter 12

Appendix 1 Key to Exercises

Part I Warm-up
Discuss the following questions in pairs or groups.

1. A popular postmodern view holds that truth is relative, as one person's perception of reality doesn't always match another person's perception of reality. In this view, there is no unvarying or permanent truth.

2. Yes, I do. Postmodernist novels are often challenging to read and subsequently analyze, because they tend to use fragmented, or collage-style forms that abandon linear chronology in its writing.

3. No, postmodernism does not necessarily mean anti-modernism. While postmodernism emerged as a reaction to modernism, it is not inherently opposed to all aspects of modernity. Postmodernism critiques and challenges certain assumptions and characteristics of modernism, such as the belief in progress, the grand narratives of history, and the idea of a unified and objective truth. However, postmodernism also incorporates elements of modernism, such as experimentation, self-reflexivity, and a focus on individual subjectivity. Postmodernism can be seen as a continuation or evolution of modernism, engaging with its ideas while also questioning and subverting them. It is a complex and multifaceted movement that resists easy categorization as purely anti-modernist.

4. To start writing a postmodernist novel, I would begin by breaking the rules of traditional storytelling and trying out different ways to tell the story. I would include references to other books and reinterpret them in my own work. Instead of telling the story in a straight line, I would mix it up and jump around in time. I would explore ideas like how different people see things differently, how the truth can change depending on who you ask, and how sometimes language can't express what we really mean. Lastly, I would make the story aware of itself and make readers think about what they're reading.

Part II Unboxed: Lyotard, Postmodernism and the Metanarrative

Watch the video. Write *T* for true or *F* for false for each statement.

1. F   2. T   3. T   4. F   5. F   6. F   7. T   8. F   9. F   10. T

答案解析：

1. 不是 the story of the Renaissance and the Age of Reason, 而是 the story of the European Enlightenment and the Age of Reason。

4. 不是 Christianity, 而是 metanarrative, here referring to the story of the European Enlightenment and the Age of Reason。

5. 不是 encouraged, 而是 be considered an outsider, a dangerous deviant who threatens the safety of the tribe。

6. 不是 lost generation, 而是 beat generation。

8. 不是 dead, 而是 far from dead。

9. 不是 untrue 和 out of date, 而是 unquestioned。

Part III Why should you read Kurt Vonnegut?

Watch the video and answer the following questions.

1. Billy Pilgrim has become "unstuck" in time in such a sense that he can experience events out of chronological order.

2. Through the shapes of stories, Vonnegut tried to make sense of human behavior. To find the shape, he graphed the main character's fortunes from the beginning to the end of a story.

3. Stories that have no clear-cut fortunes, stories without straightforward chronology. For Vonnegut, the tidy, satisfying arcs of many stories are at odds with reality.

4. "To love whoever is around to be loved."

5. Lack of agency. Even though people can see all of time, they can't change the course of events.

6. No, despite the deep concerns about the course of human existence, Vonnegut also advanced the possibility, however slim, that we might end up making something good, or in the speaker's voice,

"a few morsels of hope".

Watch the video again and fill in the blanks.

1) aliens	2) chronological	3) humiliations	4) refuge
5) demolished	6) shapes	7) fortune	8) truest
9) odds	10) ambiguity	11) abandoned	12) moments
13) agency	14) comedy	15) counterparts	16) tenets
17) cosmically	18) associations	19) interspersed	20) slim

Part IV *Catch-22* by Joseph Heller: How to Read It

Watch the video and answer the following questions.

1. Because the phrase "catch-22" has come to be widely used in the Anglophone world to express the very specific kind of frustration that one often feels when faced with the pedantry of authority and the often circular logic of bureaucracy.

2. The word "catch" refers to a frustrating, illogical logic and circular reasoning, as any airmen in the story who makes the case that they ought to be sent home has, in doing so, proven their very "sanity" by being rightly scared of combat. However, having proven themselves "sane", such an airman must therefore stay and continue to fly more perilous missions.

3. According to the speaker, war is weird, war is nonsensical, and war is often downright confusing.

4. *Catch-22* takes a great deal of influence from its author, Joseph Heller's, own experiences as a bombardier in the US Air Force during the final year of World War II.

5. Because World War II had something of a moral clarity to it. It was—and largely still is—viewed as America's "good war" in which a wide range of countries came together to consign fascism to the history books—for a while at least. However, such an image was converted as America found itself engaged in a number of conflicts in the following years.

6. Whilst reading *Catch-22*, apart from World War II, we should also bear in mind two unpopular wars, the Korean War and the American intervention in Vietnam, both fought by doubt-ridden conscripted men.

7. Probably yes, because Heller himself stated that *Catch-22* wasn't really about World War II. It was about American society during the Cold War, during the Korean War, and about the possibility of a Vietnam.

8. Its chapters are, for the most part, named after various characters that exist within this strange world.

9. Yossarian is at the heart of the novel. He is a captain, a bombardier, and is keen to do everything in his power to make it to the end of the war alive.

10. The main plot or central action of *Catch-22* is Yossarian's attempts to either get sent home or, at the very least, avoid flying any further missions

11. The novel has many disconnected anecdotes and the narration often seems to be locked in a kind of stream of consciousness, unable to resist expanding on tiny details of a certain character's backstory. However, it works well in imitating the rambling, mess-hall storytelling that one imagines serves for

entertainment on a military base.

12. According to the speaker, yes. Because he mentions that we could do worse than to describe the novel as a work of absurdism.

13. Because it allows the frustration that Yossarian feels in the world around him to bleed into the very language of the book. Besides, it also echoes the frustrating fixation on often pointless detail which pervades the military bureaucracy in which Yossarian and his comrades find themselves trapped.

14. We can also expect to read about the frustration that one often feels when faced with over reaching and illogical authority.

Appendix 2   Transcripts

Part II   Unboxed: Lyotard, Postmodernism and the Metanarrative

In The Postmodern Condition, Lyotard ("leo-TAR") argues that all cultures, ancient and modern, legitimate themselves through the telling and retelling of narratives, stories that give cultures purpose and meaning.

The story of the European Enlightenment and the Age of Reason separating the West from the rest of humanity remains the metanarrative of today, central to the creation of meaning in our culture, the big story on which countless smaller stories are stacked.

The heroic West, it is said, brings freedom to the world through democracy and reason to the world through science. Lyotard compares this story of "salvation for all" to the similar metanarratives of Christianity.

Without faith and trust in the metanarrative, retelling and rebinding ourselves and others to it, many would have little idea what their lives or our culture mean. Because so many have stacked their own stories and the meaning of their lives on top of the dominant story and meaning, if you question the way of the ancestors and poke the bear spirit, if you doubt that our practices of democracy and science are bringing freedom and wellbeing to everyone, to many you are an outsider, a dangerous deviant who threatens the safety of the tribe.

Unfortunately for the metanarrative, the horrors of World War II and the manufactured genocide at Auschwitz spawned the countercultural attacks of the 1950s, 1960s and 1970s. Counterculturals began asking out loud if the story of Western progress is also a mask for brutality and if the West is much like the rest, ignorant and authoritarian. Jack Kerouac wrote of the "beat generation", the beatnik youth of the 1950s who turned from American conformity, tired and doubtful of consumerism and the Korean War. The Civil Rights Movement of the 1960s called for revolutionary changes to American democracy, which openly excluded many due to race and gender, at the same time protesting the Vietnam War.

Lyotard argues that postmodernism is a playful engagement with many conflicting micronarratives, alternatives that have emerged in the space created by the questioning of the grand metanarrative. While critics argued that postmodernism and the end of the metanarrative is itself a new metanarrative, Lyotard countered that the metanarrative of the progress of the West is far from dead, merely resisted here and there by a variety of countercultures.

For many, the dominance of wealthy nations, the environmental impact of technology on the world's poor and the supremacist nature of the western metanarrative is unquestioned, either out of ignorance or with regret that has no faith in an alternative.

Critics of Lyotard and postmodernism continue to ask whether this is a cure for the condition or merely another symptom. Is postmodernism, like the narrative of modernity, genuine liberation, or is it merely a safety valve to accommodate counterculturals, scholars and gallery goers who are disenchanted but still require entertainment?

Part III Why should you read Kurt Vonnegut?

Billy Pilgrim can't sleep because he knows aliens will arrive to abduct him in one hour. He knows the aliens are coming because he has become "unstuck" in time, causing him to experience events out of chronological order.

Over the course of Kurt Vonnegut's *Slaughterhouse-Five*, he hops back and forth between a childhood trip to the Grand Canyon, his life as a middle-aged optometrist, his captivity in an intergalactic zoo, the humiliations he endured as a war prisoner, and more.

The title of *Slaughterhouse-Five* and much of its source materials came from Vonnegut's own experiences in World War II. As a prisoner of war, he lived in a former slaughterhouse in Dresden, where he took refuge in an underground meat locker while Allied forces bombed the city. When he and the other prisoners finally emerged, they found Dresden utterly demolished. After the war, Vonnegut tried to make sense of human behavior by studying an unusual aspect of anthropology: the shapes of stories, which he insisted were just as interesting as the shapes of pots or spearheads. To find the shapes, he graphed the main character's fortune from the beginning to the end of a story. The zany curves he generated revealed common types of fairy tales and myths that echo through many cultures. But this shape can be the most interesting of all. In a story like this, it's impossible to distinguish the character's good fortune from the bad.

Vonnegut thought this kind of story was the truest to real life, in which we are all the victims of a series of accidents, unable to predict how events will impact us long term. He found the tidy, satisfying arcs of many stories at odds with this reality, and he set out to explore the ambiguity between good and bad fortune in his own work.

When Vonnegut ditched clear-cut fortunes, he also abandoned straightforward chronology. Instead of proceeding tidily from the beginning to the end, in his stories "All moments, past, present and future always have existed, always will exist." Tralfamadorians, the aliens who crop up in many of his books, see all moments at once. They "can see where each star has been and where it is going, so that the heavens are filled with rarefied, luminous spaghetti." Although they can see all of time, they don't try to change the course of events. While the Trafalmadorians may be at peace with their lack of agency, Vonnegut's human characters are still getting used to it.

In *The Sirens of Titan*, when they seek the meaning of life in the vastness of the universe, they find nothing but "empty heroics, low comedy, and pointless death". Then, from their vantage point within a "chrono-synclastic infundibulum", a man and his dog see devastating futures for their earthly counterparts but can't change the course of events.

Though there aren't easy answers available, they eventually conclude that the purpose of life is "to love whoever is around to be loved". In *Cat's Cradle*, Vonnegut's characters turn to a different source of meaning: Bokonism, a religion based on harmless lies that all its adherents recognize as lies. Though they're aware of Bokonism's lies, they live their lives by these tenets anyway, and in so doing develop some genuine hopes.

They join together in groups called Karasses, which consist of people we "find by accident but [...] stick with by choice" — cosmically linked around a shared purpose. These are not to be confused with Granfalloons, groups of people who appoint significance to actually meaningless associations, like where you grew up, political parties, and even entire nations.

Though he held a bleak view of the human condition, Vonnegut believed strongly that "we are all here to help each other get through this thing, whatever it is."

We might get pooped and demoralized, but Vonnegut interspersed his grim assessments with more than a few morsels of hope. His fictional alter ego, Kilgore Trout, supplied this parable: two yeast sat "discussing the possible purposes of life as they ate sugar and suffocated in their own excrement. Because of their limited intelligence, they never came close to guessing that they were making champagne." In spite of his insistence that we're all here to fart around, in spite of his deep concerns about the course of human existence, Vonnegut also advanced the possibility, however slim, that we might end up making something good.

And if that isn't nice, what is?

Part Ⅳ *Catch-22* by Joseph Heller: How to Read It

Hi, my name is Tom. Welcome back to my channel and to another episode of How to Read It, my series in which I aim to provide some accessible introductions to some "classic" bits of literature. This second entry in the series was going to see us take a look at *Pride and Prejudice* but with a new television adaptation of *Catch-22* currently streaming on Hulu and on terrestrial TV (at least here in the UK), I thought there was likely at least one or two people out there who might be thinking about giving the book a go. So, today, we're gonna take a quick overview of the background behind *Catch-22*, its plot and its style to set you off on the right foot in potentially reading it. Before we get going, if you have any questions or thoughts as we go along, then please do feel free to comment those down below in the comments. And, if you're new around here and this seems like your kind of thing, then please do consider sub scribing and, importantly, hitting that notifications bell. With that out of the way however, let's take a look at *Catch-22* and how to read it.

Catch-22 is one of those rare novels which, though being less than 60 years old, has struck such a chord with readers that it's title has passed into common parlance. The phrase "catch-22" has come to be widely used in the Anglophone world to express the very specific kind of frustration that one often feels when faced with the pedantry of authority and the often circular logic of bureaucracy; it's an expression of the exasperation that comes with being at the whim of an overextended higher power which, though seemingly presenting you with choices, damns you if you do and damns you if you don't.

The novel itself follows an ensemble cast of officers in the United States Air Force in the final year of the Second World War. Here, the titular "catch" refers to a contradictory rule which states that, if any airman feels himself to be "insane" and thus in need of being sent home, they need only ask the squadron doctor who is duty-bound to fulfill their requests.

The "catch" being that any airmen who does make the case that they ought to be sent home has, in doing so, proven their very "sanity" by being rightly scared of combat. Having proven themselves "sane", such an airman must therefore stay and continue to fly more perilous missions. This kind of frustrating, illogical logic and circular reasoning finds numerous outlets during *Catch-22*.

General Sherman might once have suggested during the American Civil War that "war is hell" but, viewed through the eyes of Yossarian, *Catch-22*'s protagonist, we might come instead to the conclusion that war is weird, war is nonsensical and war is often downright confusing.

The process of reading the book can, in its attempts to convince us of this fact, often be equally frustrating but hopefully, by the end of this video, you'll be armed with just enough context and framing to embrace it as one of the 20th century's most compelling pieces of literary satire.

Catch-22 takes a great deal of influence from its author, Joseph Heller's, own experiences as a bombardier in the US Air Force during the final year of World War II. Much like the novel's central character, Yossarian, from May to December 1944, Heller found himself stationed in the Mediterranean flying tactical support missions over Italy, where the allied forces were gradually pushing the Axis powers up the Italian peninsula.

Many of the endearing and eccentric characters which populate *Catch-22* were certainly based heavily on Heller's own comrades. Nevertheless, it wasn't until 8 years after the war that Heller began writing the novel, and it wasn't until 1961 that it was finally published. And those intervening years had a significant effect on the overall tone of the book.

See, World War II had something of a moral clarity to it. It was—and largely still is—viewed as America's "good war" in which a wide range of countries came together to consign fascism to the history books—for a while at least.

In the years following, however, America found itself engaged in a number of conflicts which lacked such an image in the popular consciousness. First the Korean War and then American intervention in Vietnam were mired in controversy. As Edward A. Suchman et al. wrote during the former conflict, "the wholehearted support of public opinion which characterized the last war is conspicuous by its absence in the Korean War. Instead of consensus we have partisanship—in place of conviction and faith, we have divided opinion and doubt". Even those who were drafted weren't entirely sure what they were fighting for or whether the cause for which they might lay down their lives was honorable. This context—two unpopular wars fought by doubt-ridden conscripted men—is perhaps even more important to bear in mind while reading *Catch-22* than that of World War.

Indeed, in a 1975 interview with *Playboy*, Heller himself stated that *Catch-22* wasn't really about World War II. It was about American society during the Cold War, during the Korean War, and about the possibility of Vietnamization. We might therefore follow Christina Jarvis in approaching *Catch-22* as a "Vietnamization" of World War II. In place of the moral conviction and organizational lucidity that we tend to see in representations of World War II such as Band of Brothers, say, we see a paranoia, confusion and uncertainty more akin to Forrest Gump's portrayal of Vietnam.

Now, I'm always keen to ensure that these videos avoid any great spoilers but, even so, to try and summarize *Catch-22* by its plot would probably be a bit of a misfire. Of course, things happen within the book but, for the most part, it is not driven by the same kind of narrative progression that we find in most mainstream cultural texts.

The plots of the novel are, instead, highly fragmented, jumping backwards and forwards throughout time and often diverging into lengthy tangents. Its chapters are, for the most part, named after various characters that exist within this strange world and, although the novel does lead to a fairly satisfying conclusion, this is emblematic of Heller's preference for building out a world through disconnected anecdotes and character sketches over telling a "story" in the "beginning—middle—end" sense.

At the heart of the novel is Yossarian. A captain and bombardier, Yossarian is keen to do everything in his power to make it to the end of the war alive. In truth, he and many of his comrades should probably already be on their way home having long since completed. The 25 missions airmen are required to fly on a single tour of duty.

The ruthlessly ambitious Colonel Cathcart, however, is desperate to become a general and is thus keen to impress his superiors. As such, he continually raises the number of missions he expects those under his command to fly. By the beginning of the novel, 25 have become 50 and, by the end, it's a staggering 80.

The central action of *Catch-22*, then, is Yossarian's attempts to either get sent home or, at the very least, avoid flying any further missions. He becomes an expert at feigning a liver condition just serious enough to warrant his being prescribed to bed-rest but not severe enough to warrant any potentially dangerous treatment. Elsewhere, he destroys his own radio headset to ensure that his plane has to return back to base before reaching enemy territory.

Alongside this sits a number of key subplots. Colonel Cathcart's attempts to secure promotion, the squadron mess officer, Milo Minderbinder's, launching of a black market syndicate and Yossarian's comrades' various dalliances with women whilst on leave in mainland Italy all begin as mere anecdotes but grow to be significant elements of the book, containing their own commentary on post-war American society.

It's worth noting, however, that, although much of what makes *Catch-22* notable is its focus on the absurdity rather than horror of war. Terror, loss and violence are not entirely absent. And, as the book progresses we are increasingly given insight into exactly why Yossarian is so fearful of partaking in bombing runs and into the devastating consequences of his superiors' brazen ambition. Seemingly pointless sacrifice lingers at the edges of this novel and the humor of it all increasingly comes to look like a cover for something far more troubling.

When it was first released, the New Yorker criticized *Catch-22* for "not even seem[ing] to have been written; instead [...] giv[ing] the impression of having been shouted onto paper. Although meant as a severe criticism, this actually seems a fair summation of the linguistic style of the novel. I've mentioned above *Catch-22*'s many derivations into disconnected anecdotes and the narration often seems to be locked in a kind of stream of consciousness, unable to resist expanding on tiny details of a certain character's backstory. This can be somewhat discombobulating when reading the novel, yet it works well in imitating the rambling, mess-hall storytelling that one imagines serves for entertainment on a military base. More than this, however, it also echoes the frustrating fixation on often pointless detail which pervades the military bureaucracy in which Yossarian and his comrades find themselves trapped.

I suggested earlier that the world of *Catch-22* often feels absurd and, in terms of genre, we could do worse than to describe the novel as a work of absurdism. Numerous commentators have pointed to the presence of a Kafkaesque element to *Catch-22*. Brian Way, for instance, notes similarities to Kafka's *The Trial* in which the protagonist, Joseph K., finds himself accused of an unspecified crime by a faceless and seemingly unaccountable authority. Certainly, Yossarian's attempts to find meaning for his presence in the Mediterranean and his attempts to navigate the pedantic rules of the military often mirror Joseph K.'s attempts to find a reason for his arrest and secure his own release.

The absurdist influence present in *Catch-22* can often make the novel a frustrating read, particularly as it manifests itself in the novels linguistic form. Conversations between the novel's characters often seem to go round and round in circles indefinitely. Yet I would argue that this frustration is a key element of the novel's success as it allows the frustration that Yossarian feels in the world around him to bleed into the very language of the book.

So, to conclude, *Catch-22* may be a novel about World War II, but it is actually more accurately read as a response to the Korean and Vietnam conflicts which followed it. In many ways it thus likely speaks well to present military interventions which often lack moral certainty or even clear goals. Beyond its astute commentary on war, however, the novel captures more broadly the frustration that one often feels when faced with overreaching and illogical authority. Despite—and often because of—the infusion of this frustration into its very language, it is a warm and often laugh-out-loud funny novel and remains a must-read novel.

Thank you very much for watching this video. I hope you found it interesting particularly if you're planning on reading *Catch-22*. And, if you weren't already, then maybe it has inspired you to do so. Thanks as always to Ash for signing up to the top tier on my Patreon page. If you'd like to support what I do here, creating educational videos here on YouTube, then please do consider popping over to my Patreon page linked down below, and checking that out. Finally, liking this video is always really really helpful, also sharing it with a friend. But, with that all out of the way, thank you very much for watching once again and have a great week!

Chapter 13

Appendix 1　Key to Exercises

Part I　Warm-up
Discuss the following questions in pairs or groups.

1. For example, Saul Bellow, Philip Roth, and Bernard Malamud.
2. For example, *Herzog*, *The Fixer*, *The Assistant*, and *American Pastoral*.
3. Jewish American literature often explores themes such as identity, assimilation, and the tension between tradition and modernity. Authors frequently delve into the complexities of Jewish identity and the

challenges faced by Jewish immigrants and their descendants in adapting to American society while maintaining their cultural heritage. The Holocaust and its impact on Jewish identity and memory are another recurring theme, with authors grappling with the trauma, loss, and attempts to make sense of the Holocaust's legacy. Other common themes include the search for personal and cultural belonging, the role of religion and spirituality, and the exploration of family dynamics and generational conflicts within Jewish American communities.

4. Diaspora refers to the dispersion or scattering of a particular group of people from their original homeland to various locations around the world. In literature, diaspora often serves as a central theme, exploring the experiences, challenges, and sense of identity of individuals or communities living outside their ancestral homeland. Diaspora literature captures the struggles of cultural adaptation, the longing for a lost or distant home, and the negotiation of multiple identities. It provides a platform for marginalized voices, shedding light on the complexities of displacement, exile, and the search for belonging.

Part II The Rise and Fall of Jewish American Literature

Watch the video and fill in the blanks.

1) subtitle   2) institutional   3) legitimate   4) paradigm
5) disciplined   6) articulated   7) prestige   8) interdisciplinarity
9) historicizing   10) nationalist   11) canon   12) venture
13) communal   14) constituting   15) redundancy

Part III Remembering Philip Roth

Watch the video and answer the following questions.

1. 85.
2. More than 25 books.
3. 2 to 3 years.
4. Roth gets a lot of reaction to his works.
5. In 1989.

Part IV Isaac Bashevis Singer, Not a Typical Yiddish Writer

Watch the video. Write *T* for true or *F* for false for each statement.

1. F   2. F   3. F   4. T   5. T   6. T

答案解析：
1. 辛格不太喜欢意第绪世俗世界。
2. 辛格对传统犹太生活抱有尊敬。
3. 辛格是素食主义者。

Part V Zachary Leader on Saul Bellow, with Martin Amis

Watch the video and answer the following questions.

1. In the US, writers usually do not earn much through publishing.
2. In 1964.
3. A biography of Saul Bellow.
4. It was critically acclaimed.
5. A famous club in New York where celebrities frequent.

Appendix 2　Transcripts

Part Ⅱ　The Rise and Fall of Jewish American Literature

　　I'm just wondering if I should give some introductory words but I won't. I'll just start. So part one, my title makes an achingly oblique reference to Irving Howe's famous 1976 cultural history *World of Our Fathers*: *The Journey of the Eastern European Jews to America and the Life They Found and Made*. And for those who don't know the book, the subtitle says it all, though I'm actually not going to spend any time at all talking about the book today. My argument is that Howe's key word "world" reveals the hegemonic legitimation of the Jewish American literary field as part of a larger institutional project to tell the history of the Jews and the innovation of critical practices operating outside the dominion of sort of larger legitimate sphere of ethnohistory system. But first I need to take a few steps back; so I've just finished a new book on the history of the Jewish American literary field. I argue that the field central paradigm, ethnography essentially, has a distinct history and is in fact largely residual now. Ask anyone who cares the dominant event of Jewish American literary history is emergence or breakthrough, right, these are in quotation marks, "the eruption in the 1950s of Jewish American writers like Bernard Malamud, Philip Roth, Saul Bellow, Grace Paley, into the heart of the American cultural scene". More to the point, the fact of breakthrough is the primal scene of the Jewish American literary field. The more or less formalized or academically disciplined study of Jewish American literature grew up around the consolidating self-evidence of the break through narrative, and the field's legibility has from the start been articulated with it. The prevailing accounts of Jewish literature in the US inevitably orbit, even if only implicitly or inconspicuously, or once or twice removed in the gravitational field of this central event. The Jewish American literary study, unlike its brother and sister the US ethnic literary formations, has mostly resisted the urge to explicitly theorize itself, and its practices, the narrative of breakthrough has operated as a deputized proxy for the only real theory, however sporadically or insufficiently acknowledged, of Jewish American literature that has ever been able to carry any currency either professionally in the Academy or publicly among the readers of Jewish American writing, namely immigration. Thus if Jewish American writing before the war can be characterized by a parochial or provincial angst dependably fitting into the US literary historical departments, like immigrant writing or regionalism or urban fiction categories as durable as the dependability with which they are marked by decided second-order prestige, then within two decades of the war's end it had rapidly shed these marginalizing limitations and come to represent American literature at its most central and innovative and ascendant. Accordingly, as Jewish American literary study has tended certainly in some of its recent formations to become more diverse and focused and more sophisticated in scope, it often draws its warrant for these critical investments and it reproduces an image of its own intellectual responsibility in the name of the increasing diversity, sophistication and independence of Jews in America. Jewish American literary study persists in imagining itself as part of the enduring historical reality of breakthrough. Significantly in this narrative of socio-cultural movement from margin to Center, and rearguard to leading-edge, Jewish American literature dependably tracks the career of Jewish America. The breakthrough narrative of Jewish American literature normalizes itself as a straightforward and largely politically innocent reflection or representational lens, as a mode of access that suppresses critical theorization in the name of self-evident history, leveraging its hegemony on the assumption that literary history is itself neither theoretical nor historical.

My new book begins with a critical suspicion about the way in which professional academic formations including both English department-based literary study and Jewish studies-based interdisciplinarity have taken Jewish American literature for granted, and about the way in which Jewish American literary history has itself reflected these predispositions, taking for granted its own literary historical warrant. My critical targets are the disciplinary and intellectual modes in which the Jewish American literary field's Exceptionalist estrangement from the mainstream of humanistic critical self-regard has been carried out. By historicizing the practice of Jewish American literary study and destabilizing the assumption that Jewish American literary history operates entirely under the institutional authority of historical inquiry into the lives and times of Jews in America, I hope to make it easier for humanists to imagine and act on a critically self-aware intellectual practice. I certainly don't pretend that there was no institutionally house study of writing by Jews in America before the 1950s, or that the literary intellectuals of the breakthrough. People not only liked Howe but Leslie Fiedler, Irving Malin, Daniel Walden, Alfred Kazin, Sheldon Grebstein and Allen Guttmann for a few notable examples, invented the idea of thinking about what we now easily call Jewish American writing. To be sure before Wilbur—there was fiction being written by Jews in the United States, there were scholarly works written that is their object, the representation of Jews in English and American literature, and there was of course the persuasive historical tradition of 19th century German Jewish vision, the cultural nationalist logic of a trans historical unity of Jewish expression. But scholarship could not yet take for granted the field unity of a canon of literature organized, defined and indeed interpretable by the Jewish American identity of its authors. This was a post-war development and it has a history that itself cannot be extracted from the gravitational pull of the breakthrough narrative. The innovation of breakthrough was not simply to link inevitably and unimpeachably the Jewish authors and Jewish texts of Jewish American literature, but to reorient thinking about literary texts written by Jews in America around authors as representatives of Jewish American people and experiences. Jewish American literary study would professionalize over the following decades, as scholarly focus shifted from the object of literary representation to its subject, from Jews as a community written about, to Jews as a community writing. More pointedly, the elaboration of breakthrough was often framed in triumphalist terms if colored at times by the tragic, by critics for whom the narrative of emergence was also crucially and fundamentally bound up with a reflexive structure of self-recognition.

As Leslie Fiedler, one of the leading breakthrough intellectuals put it, in a late career reflection on his writing about Jewish American literature, "it was not I realize now a disinterested venture, since I thought of myself at the beginning of my career as part of the movement that had carried such children of immigrant Jews from Eastern Europe from the periphery to the center of American literary culture, making their experience our experience, a part of the communal dream stuff, the myth that makes all Americans one whatever their ethnic origin". And the repetition of first-person pronouns like "our" and "us" in his writings is his marker. The Exceptionalist insiderism that breakthrough inherited from the

Wissenschaft tradition matured in post-war writing and post-war thinking about Jewish American constituting as well a legacy for the consolidation of professional Jewish Studies. The ethnic literary formations we often associate with the emergence of academic multiculturalism and ethnic studies arose from and as institutional arms of active political movements. And they still often identified themselves as part of this struggle in its institutional interdependence with a narrative of breakthrough, however, Jewish American literary study in a sense emerged as part of a perception that a political struggle was in fact over, and as a result to the extent that it continues to constitute itself as a technology for interpreting what Jews do say and write, Jewish American literary study reproduces the grounds of its own redundancy if not in fact its own obsolescence.

Part III Remembering Philip Roth

Host: Finally tonight, we remember the prolific writer and Pulitzer Prize-winning novelist Philip Roth. He died yesterday of congestive heart failure at the age of 85. Roth was the author of more than 25 books, and a giant in American literature. His work evolved through several distinct phases, and often featured Roth's fictional alter egos, including his best-known character, Nathan Zuckerman. The 1969 novel *Portnoy's Complaint* rocketed him to fame for its raunchy, hilarious depiction of a teenage boy's lustful urges and ensuing guilt. Roth would later focus more deeply on Jewish life, mortality, and American history, often setting his novels in Newark, New Jersey, where Roth grew up. During a particularly fruitful period in his 60s, Roth returned to a number of those themes. The accolades and the novels came quickly, including *American Pastoral*, *I Married a Communist*, and *The Plot Against America*. In a moment, William Brangham talks with a colleague and collaborator of Roth's. But, first, how Roth himself saw his work. Jeffrey Brown had the chance to sit down with him for a rare interview back in 2004. Here are some excerpts.

Jeffrey Brown: What is it you want to do when you start a novel? What are you trying to do?

Philip Roth: Get to work. Work.

Jeffrey Brown: Get to work?

Philip Roth: Get to work. Work. Without a novel, I'm empty. I'm empty and not very happy. So, when I get to work on a novel, I begin to do what I'm supposed to do. It's a long process. Usually, it takes between 2 and 3 years to write a novel for me. I don't think about the reader. I think about the book. I think about the—I think about the sentence, I think about the paragraph, I think about the page. I go over it and over it and over it. The book begins to make its demands. The demands are intellectual, they're imaginative, they're aesthetic.

Jeffrey Brown: That's interesting, because you're often described as something of a provocateur, sort of throwing out literary bombshells. I mean, you get a lot of reaction to your work.

Philip Roth: I'm a very bad judge of how people will respond to my work, how the general readers will respond to a book. And I'm always surprised by the responses that a book elicits.

Jeffrey Brown: Many observers have noted this great run of books that you have had over the last, say, 10 years or so. What happened?

Philip Roth: What did I eat for breakfast, you mean? I don't know. Maybe it's a consequence of age. But I did feel energetic, and I do feel ambitious. And I did the work.

Jeffrey Brown: And what was your ambition to do?

Philip Roth: To be able to write this kind of book. To be able to broaden the subject, while, at the same time, keeping it a novel, while, at the same time, having the subject enacted by people.

Jeffrey Brown: And broaden the subject, what is the subject?

Philip Roth: When I came back to live in America in 1989 all the time, I felt enormously energized by being home. But, also, I realized I had in front of me a new subject that was an old subject, which was this country, that it was brand-new to me in a strange way, yet I knew all about it because I had been brought up here. So, being away for 10 or 12 years produced a—I think a burst of running energy.

Part IV Isaac Bashevis Singer, Not a Typical Yiddish Writer

Host: So, can you describe what Bashevis was like as a person?

Marvin Zuckerman: Yes well, first of all let me say his politics. I mean he had two things that were in conflict really. He lived off the Yiddish secular social democratic world because he was supported by the Forward, the newspaper they published. He made a living from that before he became famous; they rescued him really. So he lived off them but he didn't like them. I mean he had no respect or love for that, for you know the secular Yiddish world that I came from and that newspaper represented. On the other hand, he had a great deal of respect for a traditional Jewish life, but he himself wasn't religious or traditional. I mean he, I don't know if he ate, you know, bacon or anything. I think he was a vegetarian. Anyway I forgot, but when he came to visit me for lunch. I had to tell Katy on the phone, "remember he is a vegetarian". And he loved rice and he loved eggs and things like that but he wouldn't eat any meat. Well I probably didn't eat anything that was, you know, blatantly non-Jewish. But he wasn't religious, so you know he was non-religious, but he had this respect for the tradition.

He didn't have any respect for the world that really he came from, that supported him, that he grew up in. Even in Warsaw when he went to the PEN club, the Yiddish PEN club, you know. In Warsaw, the Yiddish sky behind, you know, he grew up in a, it was a secular modern world that gave him a life and a career, but he didn't care about it. So anyhow, you know, even in one of the novels, you remember, in *The Magician of Lublin*, there's a section where the magician goes to rest or something in the, after he has tried to burglarize or something, he goes into the synagogue and he sees some books and he says ah finally a book that tells me what to do, what's right see. So in other words you know, secular literature even the stuff he writes is not really important. I mean it's sort of a traditional view of secular culture that it's irrelevant you know, not important. What's important is what's in the Talmud and in the bible and it's in that novel. If you read it carefully, look for that, you'll see it. And his politics were sort of reactionary. I drove him from Ojai to LA, to my house for lunch, and he asked me. He says you have a good governor here. I said yeah he is not so good, what's the matter? Well he doesn't give enough money for education for example. It was Reagan at the time. And he said well for the police he gives money. He said yeah for the police he gives money. He was sort of conservative in his politics; he was in other words not a typical Yiddish writer.

Part V Zachary Leader on Saul Bellow, with Martin Amis

Martin Amis: Now let's get started on this intriguing, and I agree with Philip Roth, occasionally painful biography. I want Zach to begin in a minute by talking about what success is for a literary

American writer. It's not like it is in Britain. It was Henry James who complained that when Edith Wharton, his friend or acquaintance wrote a new book, or published a new book, she bought a new house. When he wrote a new book, I know he was American, but the same applies, he bought a new wheelbarrow, that was the difference. Zach, can you give us an idea of the magnitude of American success?

Zachary Leader: Well, the success that Bellow had in 1964 with the publication of *Herzog* was on sort of a different level from that of most anyone else one can think of. He was well-known before *Herzog* was published, highly thought of in all the intellectual magazines, and better book's pages, but he wasn't sort of *Time Magazine* successful or celebrated. The book opens with an account of the reception of *Herzog*, and I mentioned to Martin that I might read just a paragraph or two at the very opening to give you a sense of the scope of his success. I'll read just a paragraph or two, not very much.

The book begins: "The launch party for *Herzog* was held on September 22nd, 1964, 2 days after Julian Moynihan pronounced the novel a masterpiece on the front page of *The New York Times Book Review*, and Philip Rahv, the editor of the *Partisan Review* called Bellow the finest stylist at present writing in America in a review in the New York Herald Tribune Book Week. Alfred Kazin was among the guests at the launch, and while waiting for his wife to arrive, he amused himself by picking out, in quotes, the customers for Saul's party from the regulars at 21. The party was held at 21. 'It was so easy', says Kazin. The regulars were better looking, the party goers stamped with the difference of their background and their trade deeply depressing. In they came, Arabel Porter and Katy Carver, all the old loves, would-be lovers, friends and near friends, the hits and misses. All so stale, isn't it? All so bloody familiar? Only Bellow impressed: Saul, our plebeian princeling and imaginative king, standing there, gray, compact, friendly and aloof, receiving his friends whom he had invited to 21."

Chapter 14

Appendix 1 Key to Exercises

Part I Warm-up

Discuss the following questions in pairs or groups.

1. The Harlem Renaissance was an intellectual and cultural revival of African-American music, dance, art, fashion, literature, theater and politics centered in Harlem, Manhattan, New York City, spanning the 1920s and 1930s. At the time, it was known as the "New Negro Movement", named after *The New Negro*, a 1925 anthology edited by Alain Locke. The movement also included the new African-American cultural expressions across the urban areas in the Northeast and Midwest United States affected by a renewed militancy in the general struggle for civil rights for African-Americans that occurred in the wake of civil rights struggles in the then-still-segregated US Armed Forces in World War I and which was further inspired by the NAACP, the Garveyite movement and the Russian Revolution, combined with the Great Migration of African-American workers fleeing the racist conditions of the Jim Crow Deep South,

Harlem being the final destination of the largest number of those who migrated north.

2. Social factors include: 1) the Great Migration; 2) the emergence of an African-American middle class; 3) the development of Harlem into the political and cultural center of black American.

3. Harlem Renaissance redefined how America, and the world, viewed African Americans. The migration of southern Blacks to the north changed the image of the African American from rural, undereducated peasants to one of urban, cosmopolitan sophistication. This new identity led to a greater social consciousness, and African Americans became players on the world stage, expanding intellectual and social contacts internationally. The urban setting of rapidly developing Harlem provided a venue for African Americans of all backgrounds to appreciate the variety of black life and culture. Through this expression, the Harlem Renaissance encouraged the new appreciation of folk roots and culture. For instance, folk materials and spirituals provided a rich source for the artistic and intellectual imagination, which freed blacks from the establishment of past condition. Through sharing in these cultural experiences, a consciousness sprang forth in the form of a united racial identity.

4. African-American literature often explores themes such as racial identity, discrimination, social injustice, and the quest for equality. Authors frequently delve into the complexities of African-American experiences, addressing the historical legacy of slavery, the Civil Rights Movement, and contemporary issues of systemic racism. The exploration of cultural heritage, community, and family dynamics is another common theme, as authors examine the importance of roots, traditions, and the resilience of African-American communities. African-American literature also delves into the complexities of personal identity, including issues of gender, sexuality, and the intersectionality of multiple identities. Overall, these themes contribute to a deeper understanding of the African-American experience and promote dialogue on important social issues.

Part II *Notes of a Native Son*: the World According to James Baldwin

Watch the video. Write *T* for true or *F* for false for each statement.
1. T   2. F   3. F   4. F   5. T   6. F   7. T   8. T   9. F   10. T

答案解析：
2. 只是最畅销的黑人作者之一。
3. 不同意。
4. 是 in France，不是 in Harlem。
6. 没有享有同样的权利。
9. James Baldwin 拒绝了这个标签。

Part III Why should you read Toni Morrison's *Beloved*?

Watch the video and choose the right answer for the following questions.
1. B   2. B   3. C   4. A   5. D   6. D   7. B   8. B

Part IV Can Love and Independence Coexist?

Watch the video and answer the following questions.

1. It inspired an unexpected homecoming for Janie.

2. Zora Neale Hurston wrote the novel and the novel was about a black woman's quest for love and agency in a time that sought to deprive her of both.

3. The whereabouts of her missing husband.
4. Conversation.
5. Both of them were raised in Eatonville, and left Eatonville abruptly.
6. Haiti.
7. By incorporating folkloric elements alongside her own family and romantic history.
8. The third-person narration allows Hurston to unleash her poetic prose on everything, from birdsong, architecture, and fashion to her characters' deepest feelings and motivations.

Watch the second part of the video and fill in the blanks.

1) evident	2) spirituality	3) truest	4) arranged
5) judgmental	6) unknowable	7) threatening	8) complicated
9) navigates	10) infectious	11) restrictive	12) empathetic

Part V Langston Hughes: Leading Voice of the Harlem Renaissance

Watch the video and fill in the blanks.

1) leading	2) prominent	3) dignity	4) visible
5) forefront	6) lonely	7) celebrates	8) everyday
9) weaving	10) vitality	11) collaborate	12) prolific
13) anthologies	14) aspiring	15) connected	16) legacies
17) tribute	18) average		

Appendix 2 Transcripts

Part II *Notes of a Native Son*: The World According to James Baldwin

Over the course of the 1960s, the FBI amassed almost 2,000 documents in an investigation into one of America's most celebrated minds. The subject of this inquiry was a writer named James Baldwin. At the time, the FBI investigated many artists and thinkers, but most of their files were a fraction the size of Baldwin's. During the years when the FBI hounded him, he became one of the best-selling black authors in the world. So what made James Baldwin loom so large in the imaginations of both the public and the authorities?

Born in Harlem in 1924, he was the oldest of 9 children. At age 14, he began to work as a preacher. By delivering sermons, he developed his voice as a writer, but also grew conflicted about the Church's stance on racial inequality and homosexuality.

After high school, he began writing novels and essays while taking a series of odd jobs. But the issues that had driven him away from the Church were still inescapable in his daily life. Constantly confronted with racism and homophobia, he was angry and disillusioned, and yearned for a less restricted life. So in 1948, at the age of 24, he moved to Paris on a writing fellowship.

From France, he published his first novel, *Go Tell it on the Mountain*, in 1953. Set in Harlem, the book explores the Church as a source of both repression and hope. It was popular with both black and white readers. As he earned acclaim for his fiction, Baldwin gathered his thoughts on race, class, culture and exile in his 1955 extended essay, *Notes of a Native Son*.

Meanwhile, the Civil Rights Movement was gaining momentum in America. Black Americans were making incremental gains at registering to vote and voting, but were still denied basic dignities in schools, on buses, in the work force, and in the armed services. Though he lived primarily in France for the rest of his life, Baldwin was deeply invested in the movement, and keenly aware of his country's unfulfilled promise. He had seen family, friends, and neighbors spiral into addiction, incarceration and suicide. He believed their fates originated from the constraints of a segregated society. In 1963, he published *The Fire Next Time*, an arresting portrait of racial strife in which he held white America accountable, but he also went further, arguing that racism hurt white people too. In his view, everyone was inextricably enmeshed in the same social fabric. He had long believed that: "People are trapped in history and history is trapped in them."

Baldwin's role in the Civil Rights Movement went beyond observing and reporting. He also traveled through the American South, attending rallies, giving lectures of his own. He debated both white politicians and black activists, including Malcolm X, and served as a liaison between black activists and intellectuals and white establishment leaders like Robert Kennedy. Because of Baldwin's unique ability to articulate the causes of social turbulence in a way that white audiences were willing to hear, Kennedy and others tended to see him as an ambassador for black Americans—a label Baldwin rejected. And at the same time, his facility with words led the FBI to view him as a threat. Even within the Civil Rights movement, Baldwin could sometimes feel like an outsider for his choice to live abroad, as well as his sexuality, which he explored openly in his writing at a time when homophobia ran rampant.

Throughout his life, Baldwin considered it his role to bear witness. Unlike many of his peers, he lived to see some of the victories of the Civil Rights Movement, but the continuing racial inequalities in the United States weighed heavily on him. Though he may have felt trapped in his moment in history, his words have made generations of people feel known, while guiding them toward a more nuanced understanding of the society's most complex issues.

Part III Why should you read Toni Morrison's *Beloved*?

A mirror that shatters without warning. A trail of cracker crumbs strewn across the floor. Two tiny handprints that appear on a cake. Everyone at 124 Bluestone Road knows their house is haunted, but there's no mystery about the spirit tormenting them.

This ghost is the product of an unspeakable trauma, the legacy of a barbaric history that hangs over much more than this lone homestead.

So begins *Beloved*, Toni Morrison's Pulitzer Prize-winning novel about the suffering wrought by slavery and the wounds that persist in its wake. Published in 1987, *Beloved* tells the story of Sethe, a woman who escaped enslavement.

When the novel opens, Sethe has been living free for over a decade. Her family has largely dissolved. Sethe's mother-in-law died years earlier, and her two sons ran away from fear of the specter. Sethe's daughter Denver remains in the house, but the pair live a half-life. Shunned by the wider community, the two have only each other and the ghost for company. Sethe is consumed by thoughts of the spirit, whom she believes to be her eldest daughter. When a visitor from Sethe's old life returns and threatens the ghost away, it seems like the start of a new beginning for her family. But what comes in the ghost's place may be even harder to bare.

As with much of Morrison's work, *Beloved* investigates the roles of trauma and love in African-American history. Morrison writes about black identities in a variety of contexts, but her characters are united by their desire to find love and be loved, even when it's painful.

Some of her novels explore when love challenges social conventions, like the forbidden affection that grows between the townsfolk of "Paradise" and their fugitive neighbors. Other works examine how we can be blind to the love we already possess. In *Sula*, one character realizes that it's not her marriage, but rather, one of her friendships that embodies the great love of her life. Perhaps Morrison's most famous exploration of the difficulty of love takes place in *Beloved*. Here, the author considers how the human spirit is diminished when you know the things and people you love the most will be taken away. Morrison shows that slavery is destructive to love in all forms, poisoning both enslaved people and their enslavers.

Beloved examines the dehumanizing effects of the slave trade in numerous ways. Some are straightforward, such as referring to enslaved people as animals with monetary value. But others are more subtle. Sethe and Paul D., the visitors from her old plantation, are described as trying to "live an unlivable life". Their coping mechanisms are different. Sethe remains mired in her past, while Paul D. dissociates himself completely. But in both cases, it's clear each character has been irreparably scarred.

Morrison also blends perspectives and timelines, to convey how the trauma of slavery ripples across various characters and time periods. As she delves into the psyche of townspeople, enslavers, and previously enslaved people, she exposes conflicting viewpoints on reality. This tension shows the limitations of our own perspectives, and the ways in which some characters are actively avoiding the reality of their actions. But in other instances, the characters' shifting memories align perfectly, capturing the collective trauma that haunts the story.

Though *Beloved* touches on dark subjects, the book is also filled with beautiful proses, highlighting its characters' capacity for love and vulnerability. In a stream-of-consciousness sequence written from Sethe's perspective, Morrison unspools memories of subjugation alongside moments of tenderness, like a baby reaching for her mother's earrings, spring colors, and freshly painted stairs. Sethe's mother-in-law had them painted white. She recalls, "so you could see your way to the top... where lamplight didn't reach."

Throughout the book, Morrison asks us to consider hope in the dark, and to question what freedom really means. She urges readers to ponder the power we have over each other, and to use that power wisely. In this way, *Beloved* remains as a testimony to the destructiveness of hate, the redeeming power of love, and the responsibility we bear to heed the voices of the past.

Toni Morrison once said, "If there is a book you want to read, but it hasn't been written yet, then you must write it." Unimpressed with *The Samphire* she wrote as a kid, writer Actevial Bartler did just that. Explore her stunningly inventive works with this video.

Part Ⅳ Can Love and Independence Coexist?

Baritone thunder. Snarling winds. Consuming downpours. Okeechobee, the disastrous hurricane of 1928, tore through the North Atlantic basin, laying waste to entire communities.

In Eatonville, Florida, the storm forced many to flee. But for Janie Crawford, it inspired an unexpected homecoming. Janie's return begins *Their Eyes Were Watching God*, Zora Neale Hurston's acclaimed novel about a black woman's quest for love and agency in a time that sought to deprive her of both.

When Janie arrives back in Eatonville, her arrival is shrouded in mystery. Her neighbors and friends are quick to gossip about her reappearance, her finances, and most importantly, the whereabouts of her missing husband. But only Janie's friend Pheoby gets to hear the whole story. Over the course of a conversation that spans most of the novel, Hurston untangles Janie's life story, from her complicated childhood and her life in Eatonville to her scandalous departure and the shocking events that followed.

The specifics of Janie's story are often larger than life, but many of the book's details reflect the incredible experiences of its author. Zora Neale Hurston was raised in Eatonville, one of the first planned and incorporated all-Black communities in America. Like Janie, she also left Eatonville abruptly, traveling first to Jacksonville and DC, before eventually moving further north. In New York City, Hurston studied anthropology and became a renowned author in the Harlem Renaissance, a cultural, literary and artistic movement that's still considered a golden era of Black artistry and creativity. Here, her work garnered enough support to fund research trips through the South, where she collected stories and folktales from Black Americans.

By 1937, her fieldwork had taken her all the way to Haiti, where she wrote most of *Their Eyes Were Watching God*. Hurston drew on all these experiences for the novel, incorporating folkloric elements alongside her own family and romantic history to bring readers into the intimate spaces of Black southern life. She uses regional phrases and sayings to capture the dialect of her Floridian characters. And the novel's omniscient third-person narration allows Hurston to unleash her poetic prose on everything, from birdsong, architecture, and fashion to her characters' deepest feelings and motivations.

Perhaps more than any specific details, Hurston's experiences of being a black woman in America at this time are more evident in the novel's themes. Over the course of one long evening, Janie and Pheoby discussed the nature of family, marriage, spirituality and more. But their conversation always comes back to Janie's truest desire: to live honestly and be truly loved in return. As a teenager, Janie resents an arranged marriage, despite the safety it offers her and the wishes of her loving grandmother. When her family becomes well-respected in Eatonville, she struggles with the judgmental eyes of strangers and a husband who wants her to be something she is not.

Throughout her life, Janie frequently feels she is at the whim of natural and spiritual forces that can shift the course of her existence without warning. And when she finally does find true love, these unknowable powers continue to act on her, threatening to destroy the life she has so painstakingly built.

The story takes place during a time where women had little to no agency, and Janie's life is full of complicated characters who demand different kinds of love and submission. But despite of the loneliness of her situation, Janie navigates these trials with defiance and curiosity. Her questions and commentary push back in subtle, clever ways. And as the reader follows Janie's journey from childhood to middle age, her confidence becomes infectious.

Just like Hurston, Janie defies the restrictive expectations for a woman in her time. Early in the novel, Hurston writes that "there are years that ask questions and years that answer", suggesting that life can only truly be understood by living it. But through her empathetic storytelling, Hurston invites us into Janie's life, her life, and the lives of so many other women.

Part V Langston Hughes: Leading Voice of the Harlem Renaissance

—Langston Hughes was a great author because he spoke to, for and about black people in America.

(Poet, novelist and playwright, Langston Hughes was the leading voice of the Harlem Renaissance.)

—America was changing during the time that Langston Hughes was so popular. Black Consciousness was becoming more and more public, more prominent. I think that Langston Hughes was important because he was one of the early figures to show the dignity and the beauty of ordinary black life.

—He was one of the most visible of the younger black poets, a new generation that described themselves as the New Negro. They covered new topics, took on new poetic forms and sought a wider audience, and Langston Hughes was at the forefront of that.

(James Mercer Langston Hughes was born in Joplin Missouri on February 1st, 1902.)

—He wrote a lot about being lonely when he was young, and I think that was a tremendous part of the result of moving around so much.

(After graduating high school, Hughes published his first and most famous poem *The Negro Speaks of Rivers*.)

—It is the first poem that celebrates Africa and dignifies the image of Africa in American literature.

—*The Negro Speaks of Rivers* was published in a popular black journal, and so he was really rather widely read from the beginning. His poetry and his prose actually had access to everyday people.

(While studying at Columbia University, Hughes discovered the Harlem art scene, spending hours in jazz and blues clubs, weaving the rhythms of music into his work.)

—Jazz and blues were great influences on Langston Hughes. He sought to capture the energy and vitality of the music in his poetry.

—He was very familiar with the Harlem nightlife. He knew the musicians and later in this life he would even collaborate with some of the key figures at that time such as Duke Ellington.

(Hughes was a prolific writer and one of the first African-American authors who could support himself through his writing.)

—Langston Hughes wrote plays. He edited anthologies of poets of African descent across the Diaspora. He wrote short stories. One of his most famous series of short stories center around Jessie Be Simple. These are tales told by a resident of Harlem to an aspiring writer who is a stand-in for Langston Hughes.

—He was one of the more widely published of the young poets of the period. He was also among the better connected. He really worked hard to promote the careers of other young writers in Harlem and also throughout the rest of his life. That's also one of his big legacies.

(Langston Hughes died of cancer on May 22nd 1967. His Harlem residence was given landmark status, a fitting tribute for a legendary writer.)

—His influence, his ambition as a creative writer, his success and accessibility. He wrote for the average person. He was not writing for college classrooms. He was not writing for the elite. All of those things, I think, require that we recognize and acknowledge him as a great American literary voice of the 20th century.

Chapter 15

Appendix 1 Key to Exercises

Part I Warm-up
Discuss the following questions in pairs or groups.

1. For example, Amy Tan, author of *The Joy Luck Club* and other novels exploring Chinese American experiences; Jhumpa Lahiri, known for her Pulitzer Prize-winning collection of short stories, *Interpreter of Maladies*, and the novel *The Namesake*; Celeste Ng, author of *Everything I Never Told You* and *Little Fires Everywhere*, which examine the dynamics of Asian American families.

2. Well, for me, it's Amy Tan. I would recommend you to read her debut novel *The Joy Luck Club*, as it not only depicts the Chinese American and immigrant experiences, but also uncovers a deeper truth, that is, the need to be seen and understood by the ones you love.

3. Yes, I believe that literature is a good medium, or can be a bridge to help people in the West to know Asia better. Reading classics by Asian American authors is a great way for them to appreciate Asian languages and culture.

4. Asian American literature contribute to the broader field of American literature by offering diverse perspectives and narratives that challenge and enrich the national literary canon...

Part II Celeste Ng and Maxine Hong Kingston answer your questions about *The Woman Warrior*

Watch the video. Write *T* for true or *F* for false for each statement.
1. F   2. T   3. T   4. F   5. T   6. T   7. F   8. F   9. F   10. T

答案解析：
1. 不是 Little Fires Everywhere，而是 The Woman Warrior。
4. 不是 Little Fires Everywhere，而是 Everything I Never Told You。
7. 不是 had been to，而是 had not been to。
8. 不是 voice of America，而是 Asian-American voices。
9. 不是 their particular ethnicity，而是 things other than just their particular ethnicity。

Part III Philosophies of Self: East-West Distinctions

Watch the video and answer the following questions.

1. In the United States, generally we have a mode of self where the self is kind of like an avocado, right. We have a "pit" inside of us. The pit is ourselves, our essence, our identity. We like that self and we want it to be unique.

2. In Asia, people frequently have a "flexi-self". It is a self that is oriented more to duty than to rights

for instance. And very importantly, it does not have a cultural mandate to be different and to be unique.

3. The difference is not, "How different are we from each other?" The difference is, "How much significance do we attach to that difference?" In other words, do we think it's very important to differentiate ourselves from others?

4. Because everyone is always making choices. Every little choice that you make—even in private, because it defines of who you are—is a little loaded. They feel like they just choose.

5. Westerners feel that we are actually less free than they are. So they think that we are the ones who are kind of in this prison where, you know, like I say, every moment we must define ourselves.

6. In the West, people want to feel that it's an extension of our great love and the nature of our being to be able to take care of the elderly, and it should be an expression of their inner nature. In the East, people just go and take care of the elderly parent because that's their duty, and for them this is really liberating.

Watch the video again and fill in the blanks.

1) pit   2) essence   3) unique   4) reflect
5) duty   6) mandate   7) alike   8) significance
9) peculiar   10) endlessly   11) choice   12) anxious
13) individualistic 14) loaded 15) overlay   16) define
17) freely   18) extension   19) interdependent 20) liberating

Part IV Why Should You Read *The Joy Luck Club* by Amy Tan

Watch the video and choose the best answer for the following questions.

1. B   2. A   3. D   4. C   5. B

Watch the video again and answer the following questions.

1. The mahjong table gathering serves as a starting point for interconnected vignettes, allowing the characters to share their stories and explore themes of heritage, identity, and the generation gap.

2. The book is divided into four parts, mirroring the four rounds of mahjong, with each part consisting of four chapters, reflecting the hands in the game. This structure imitates the format of the Chinese game and organizes the narratives within the novel.

3. Jing-Mei struggles to fill her mother's place in *The Joy Luck Club* because she feels inadequate and ignorant compared to her mother and the other members. She worries that she doesn't possess the same wisdom, knowledge, and understanding of her mother's experiences and the cultural heritage they represent.

4. The mothers in the novel feel divided from their daughters due to the cultural and generational gaps between them, as well as the daughters' struggle to understand and reconcile their mothers' experiences, expectations, and heritage with their own identities and lives as American-born individuals.

5. The daughters in the novel feel divided from their mothers due to the cultural and generational gaps between them, as well as the daughters' struggle to reconcile their own identities and aspirations with their mothers' expectations and the weight of their mothers' past experiences and unfulfilled hopes.

Appendix 2 Transcripts

Part II Celeste Ng and Maxine Hong Kingston answer your questions about *The Woman Warrior*

Judy Woodruff: A memoir of stories of ancestors in China and the lives of Asian-American immigrants.

Jeffrey Brown has our August book club selection.

It's part of Canvas, our ongoing series on art and culture.

Jeffrey Brown: We tried something different for August. We asked one of today's leading writers to choose a book she loves to return to when time slows down in the summer.

Celeste Ng is the author of the bestselling novel *Little Fires Everywhere*, which is now being adapted as a new streaming video series.

Her choice for our book club was *The Woman Warrior*, which *The New York Times* recently named as one of the best memoirs of the last 50 years.

And to our delight, its author, Maxine Hong Kingston, is here as well.

So, this is a special pleasure to have both of you.

Celeste, thank you for doing this for us.

Celeste Ng: Thank you so much for having us.

Jeffrey Brown: Tell me why you picked this book.

Celeste Ng: This is just a book that has been so important to me and so influential to me personally, that, as soon as you asked, it is what came to mind.

It spoke to me when I was younger, as a Chinese American girl, speaking about some of the experiences of Chinese American women. And every time I have come back to it, it sort of gives me something new.

Now that I am a parent, I am looking at it from the parent's side and thinking a lot about what parents don't tell their children.

Jeffrey Brown: So, Maxine, written in the mid-1970s, right?

What were you — how you can encapsulate? What were you trying to do?

Maxine Hong Kingston: Well, the first sentence in *The Woman Warrior*, it says, "Don't tell anyone, my mother said, what I am about to tell you."

Jeffrey Brown: Mm—hmm.

Maxine Hong Kingston: And...

Jeffrey Brown: So, we have secrets right away.

Maxine Hong Kingston: Yes, and taboos, the adventures, the lives of people who had to keep their lives secret.

Being born a writer, I had to tell, I had to blab these stories out.

Jeffrey Brown: And you did it in a very creative way that jolted people then and to this day, because this is a mix of sort of fact, mythology, all kind — fact and fiction, in a sense, in a memoir.

Maxine Hong Kingston: Yes, I had to do it this way, because — well, one reason is that we were illegal aliens and always felt the threat that we were going to be deported.

And — but I had to tell the stories, especially the stories of crossing borders against the law. And so I made up a new way of storytelling, so that you can't tell whether I'm writing fiction or nonfiction.

Jeffrey Brown: And, Celeste, you were starting to say how this had sort of felt connected to your own life in some ways.

Celeste Ng: Yes. I'm an American-born Chinese, but there are so many things about my parents' lives in Hong Kong, where they came from, and in Mainland, where my dad was born, that were just so opaque to me when I was growing up. I would get sort of maybe the end moral of the story, but I didn't get all the details along the way.

And that was one of the things that *The Woman Warrior* sort of made clear to me, that these stories filter down to us, and along the way, we lose track of what really happened versus sort of what the message that the story is supposed to be telling you.

It's a reading experience sort of unlike any that I had ever had.

Maxine Hong Kingston: So when you don't know the story or they don't tell you what else happens, that is when the fiction writer in you writes it.

When I was — *The Woman Warrior* starting with, don't tell anybody what I am about to tell you, that is much like the title of your first book, which is *Everything I Never Told You*.

So you had that impetus too. I am just going to tell everything.

Celeste Ng: And I think it's the writer's impulse too that, when there is a secret, there is a power there. There is something there that is dangerous.

And one of the ways to sort of deal with that danger is to shine a light on it and tell it, and imagine your way in, and fill in all those details that have been sort of left out.

Maxine Hong Kingston: Yes.

Jeffrey Brown: One of the things I love about having you both here is that we can talk about the power of influence. Right?

Maxine Hong Kingston: Yes.

Celeste Ng: Yes.

Maxine Hong Kingston: Yes.

Jeffrey Brown: Where it comes from, what you read, what sticks with you.

Maxine Hong Kingston: And the power of the imagination too.

I had not been to China, where all these stories came from or where my family came from. And so I would imagine it just from the bits of information. And I would imagine what that village was like, and what that well was like, where my aunt killed herself and the baby.

And so I would imagine it. And then, decades later, I went to those places. And so I could test the power of the imagination against reality. And, you know, it was there. What I imagined was actually there.

And then I think, wow, it's the power of the writer to actually make something appear.

Jeffrey Brown: What about — you know, Celeste, I know you have worked hard to mentor, to bring up new voices as well.

We're seeing sort of connections here, right, especially voices in America, Asian-American voices. Where are we today?

Celeste Ng: I think we're making progress.

I think there have been more and more stories getting told, not just Chinese-American stories, but stories from lots of different kinds of Asian-American styles, Asian, East Asian. And we're seeing more books too, by writers with Asian heritage that aren't — quote, unquote — "about being Asian", which I think is a wonderful thing, that there is space now, I think, for those writers to talk about things other than just their particular ethnicity.

Jeffrey Brown: Yes.

I mean, also notable, of course, in reading your book is the themes that have stayed with us, right, very much here with us.

Maxine Hong Kingston: I feel that we have created an Asian-American, Pacific Islander literature.

And we didn't have this as part of American literature just 40 years ago. And I have seen it grow from just a few books to now there's so many of us.

Celeste Ng: Well, I think your book was a very big part of that.

I mean, I read your book first when I was a teenager because my mother had it on the shelf. But when I got to college, it was on my syllabus, and it was often the only book by an Asian-American writer of any kind.

And it was wonderful to have it there, but I'm seeing now that it is now being taught alongside other books. And I think that is part of your influence. You paved the way for a lot of other writers.

Jeffrey Brown: All right, this is great.

For now, I want to say thank you, Maxine Hong Kingston, *The Woman Warrior*.

Maxine Hong Kingston: Oh, you're very welcome.

Jeffrey Brown: And Celeste Ng, *Little Fires Everywhere*.

Thank you for...

Celeste Ng: Thank you so much for having us on.

Jeffrey Brown: And we are going to continue our conversation online, including getting our authors to recommend some of their favorite books and other passions.

And you can find that later on our website and on our book club Facebook page.

But, before we go, our pick for September. It's one of the most talked about debut novels in recent years, *Conversations with Friends* by the young Irish writer Sally Rooney. She will be with us right here next month.

Judy Woodruff: And love that conversation with those two women writers.

Part III Philosophies of Self: East-West Distinctions

In the United States, generally we have a mode of self where the self is kind of like an avocado, right. We have a "pit" inside of us. The pit is ourselves, our essence, our identity. It is the thing to which we must above all be true. And, of course, very importantly, we see that pit as unique. So that everything we do we want to show, to reflect that pit. We like that self and we want it to be unique.

In Asia, people frequently have a "flexi-self". So it's a different kind of self. It is a self that is oriented more to duty than to rights for instance. And very importantly, it does not have a cultural mandate to be different and to be unique. People in the East are not all alike. So if you look at my family, believe me, every single person is very, very different. That is true, of course, throughout Asia.

The difference is not, "How different are we from each other?" The difference is, "How much significance do we attach to that difference?" In other words, do we think it's very important to differentiate ourselves from others? So if you're asking, "Are they individuals?" Of course they're individuals. You know, are they different? Of course they're different. But of course for them it's like, "Well of course I'm different. Why would I make a big deal about that?" And they think it is very peculiar that in the West that we feel that we must differentiate ourselves from others endlessly.

So one of the ways that we do that of course is through choice, you know. Choice in the West is very, very important. Everyone is always making choices. And honestly a lot of those choices make us a little anxious. If you do a study where you are just sitting in an empty room and you're making a choice and you come from a more individualistic culture, you actually show signs of a little anxiety, you know. Every little choice that you make—even in private, because it's defining of who you are—is a little loaded. They feel like they just choose. In other words, when they make those choices, it doesn't have this overlay.

And that's one of the reasons they feel that actually we are less free than they are. So they think that we are the ones who are kind of in this prison where, you know, like I say every moment we must define ourselves. Well isn't that awful? And of course the way that we live, we feel that we want to be freely electing to live the way that we live, right?

And so, even when we're doing things like taking care of the elderly, for example, we want to feel that it's an extension of our great love and the nature of our being to be able to take care of the elderly. The other day I was having dinner with somebody and they said, "You know, I just don't feel that, and it's just very, very hard." So somebody from a more flexi-self or interdependent culture would say, "It's just your duty." And so for them it's like, you know, they help their elderly parent, they just go take care of the elderly parent because that's their duty. For them this is really liberating. You just go do it and you don't expect there to be, you know, an expression of yourself. It's just what people do. From their point of view, we have made things very, very hard for ourselves to demand that everything should be an expression of our inner nature.

Part Ⅳ　Why Should You Read *The Joy Luck Club* by Amy Tan

In her Auntie An-mei's home, Jing-Mei reluctantly takes her seat at the eastern corner of the mahjong table. At the north, south, and west corners are her aunties, long-time members of the Joy Luck Club. This group of immigrant families comes together weekly to trade gossip, feast on wonton and sweet char siu, and play mahjong. However, the club's founder, Jing-Mei's mother Suyuan, has recently passed away. At first, Jing-Mei struggles to fill her place at the table. But when her aunties reveal a deeply buried secret about Suyuan's life, Jing-Mei realizes she still has a lot to learn about her mother, and herself.

In Amy Tan's 1989 debut novel, *The Joy Luck Club*, this gathering at the mahjong table is the point of departure for a series of interconnected vignettes. The book itself is loosely structured to imitate the format of the Chinese game. Just as mahjong is played over four rounds with at least four hands each, the book is divided into four parts, each consisting of four chapters.

Alternately set in China or America, each chapter narrates a single story from one of the four matriarchs of the Joy Luck Club or their American-born daughters. These stories take the reader through war zones and villages of rural China, and into modern marriages and tense gatherings around the dinner table.

They touch upon themes of survival and loss, love and the lack of it, ambitions and their unsatisfied reality. In one, Auntie Lin plots an escape from the hostile family of her promised husband, ultimately leading to her arrival in America. In another, the Hsu family's all-American day at the beach turns dire when Rose is overwhelmed by the responsibility her mother assigns to her. The resulting tragedy traumatizes the family for years to come.

These tales illustrate the common divides that can form between generations and cultures, especially in immigrant families. The mothers have all experienced great hardships during their lives in China, and they've worked tirelessly to give their children better opportunities in America. But their daughters feel weighed down by their parents' unfulfilled hopes and high expectations.

Jing-Mei feels this pressure as she plays mahjong with her mother's friends. She worries, "In me, they see their own daughters, just as ignorant, just as unmindful of all the truths and hopes they have brought to America."

Time and again, the mothers strive to remind their daughters of their history and heritage. Meanwhile, their daughters struggle to reconcile their mothers' perception of them with who they really are. "Does my daughter know me?" some of the stories ask. "Why doesn't my mother understand?" others respond.

In her interrogation of these questions, Tan speaks to anxieties that plague many immigrants, who often feel both alienated from their homeland and disconnected from their adopted country. But by weaving the tales of these four mothers and daughters together, Tan makes it clear that Jing-Mei and her peers find strength to tackle their present-day problems through the values their mothers passed on to them.

When *The Joy Luck Club* was first published, Tan expected minimal success. But against her predictions, the book was a massive critical and commercial achievement. Today, these characters still captivate readers worldwide. Not only for the way they speak to Chinese-American and immigrant experiences, but also for uncovering a deeper truth: the need to be seen and understood by the ones you love.

Chapter 16

Appendix 1 Key to Exercises

Part I Warm-up

Discuss the following questions in pairs or groups.

1. Here are a few Native American writers and their representative works. Louise Erdrich: A prolific writer, Erdrich has written numerous novels, including *Love Medicine*, *The Round House*, and *The Plague of Doves*. Her works often revolve around the experiences of Native American characters, blending elements of history, spirituality, and contemporary life. Leslie Marmon Silko: Silko's novel *Ceremony* is a widely acclaimed work that weaves together Native American mythology, history, and personal narratives to explore themes of healing, identity, and the effects of colonization. N. Scott Momaday: Momaday's novel *House Made of Dawn* won the Pulitzer Prize for Fiction in 1969. His writing combines poetic language and vivid imagery to depict the experiences of Native Americans in both traditional and contemporary contexts.

2. The oral tradition is significant in Native American literature as it serves as a means of passing down cultural knowledge, history, and values from one generation to another. It preserves the authenticity and richness of Native American storytelling and fosters a sense of community and interconnectedness.

3. Native American literature often portrays the relationship between humans and the natural world as one of interconnectedness and harmony. Nature is seen as a living entity with its own spirit, and humans are depicted as an integral part of this web of life, emphasizing respect, balance, and reciprocity.

4. Contemporary Native American literature has evolved by incorporating personal experiences and addressing current social and political issues faced by Native communities. While traditional forms of Native American literature heavily relied on oral narratives, contemporary literature embraces various written mediums, including novels, poetry, and plays, to convey the diverse experiences and realities of Native peoples.

Part II Samson Occom: The Father of Native American Literature

Watch the video and choose the best answer for the following questions.

1. B   2. B   3. A   4. D   5. A   6. C   7. B   8. D

Part III New Erdrich Novel Deals with Crime and Jurisdiction

Watch the video and answer the following questions.

1. *The Round House*.

2. The story is set on a Native American reservation in North Dakota.

3. She explores clashes of culture and law between tribal and state jurisdictions in investigating a crime.

4. The jurisdictional problem revolves around the question of who has authority over crimes committed on Native American reservations.

5. It is a recommendation aimed at addressing the issue of violence against Native women and restoring some sovereignty and jurisdiction over non-Native people in such cases.

6. The main character is a 13-year-old boy named Joe.

7. She was interested in writing in Joe's voice, and it took over as she delved into the story.

8. The Round House is a sacred place on many reservations, often associated with ceremonies and the resilience of Native American culture.

Part Ⅳ Leslie Marmon Silko: How to Connect to Nature, Even in the City

Watch the video. Write T for true or F for false for each statement.

1. T 2. F 3. F 4. T 5. F 6. T 7. F 8. T

答案解析：

2. 风景有改变。

3. 是贪婪造成的。

5. 不是 fear and avoidance, 而是 a deep connection and friendship。

7. 文章描绘了 Tucson 为一个隔离的城市，某些社区被边缘化。

Watch the video again and select one word for each blank from a list of choices given in a word bank following the passage.

1) concern   2) greed   3) laments   4) urban
5) segregated   6) habitats   7) awareness   8) preserving
9) underscores   10) destructive

Appendix 2 Transcripts

Part Ⅱ Samson Occom: The Father of Native American Literature

Samson Occom, born in 1723 in New London, Connecticut, and died on July 14th, 1792, in Stonebridge, New York, was a reverend of the Mohegan nation and a Presbyterian cleric known as the father of Native American literature. He fought for the protection of the edges of American lands but became aware of the limitations a Native American had in the quota of white world. He originally converted to Christianity after his mother Nana's widow, Sarah Occom, who was one of the first Mohegan converts during the Great Awakening.

The Great Awakening was the first of several awakenings that America had. It was a revitalization of religion and faith, and not only in America, but also occurred in England, Scotland, and Germany. It rose to counter the Age of Enlightenment, and the earliest manifestations of the awakening appeared in Pennsylvania and New Jersey. Preachers such as Jonathan Edwards, famous for sermons such as *Sinners in the Hands of an Angry God*, used vivid imagery to discuss the horror and corruption of human nature.

In his earlier years, he enrolled in a school belonging to a lessor Wheelock in Lebanon, Connecticut. He had already begun teaching himself English and took to the tasks of learning Greek, Hebrew, and Latin. His progress as a student encouraged Wheelock to open the Indian Charter School, which was a charity school for educating Native American missionaries. He spent 4 years at the school but due to failing health and poor eyesight, he was unable to go to college. So, he began teaching near his home and then transferred to Long Island, where he taught Native Americans and ministered to them. He sang and invented card games to help teach his students. Later on, he assumed the duties of the Presbyterian minister who had retired.

While teaching, he met and married his wife, Mary Fowler, in 1759. They had 10 children. Also, in 1759, he became ordained by the Long Island Presbytery, and in 1765, he traveled to England with Reverend Nathaniel Whitaker, hoping to raise money for the school Wheelock opened. While in England, he preached on over 300 different occasions and raised over 11,000 pounds. Upon returning 2 years later, Occom saw that Wheelock hadn't cared for his family as he promised to, and then Wheelock took the funds that Occom had raised to move the school to New Hampshire and chose to exclude Native Americans. He only taught white settlers and renamed the school Dartmouth after a wealthy donor.

"I am very jealous that instead of your seminary becoming Alma Mater, she will be to Alba Mater to suckle the 24 she has already adorned up to much like the Popeish Virgin Mary way Lux treatment of outcome is actually a great irony that happens during the Great Awakening." During this time, Native American converts were highly prized, but once the Native Americans were converted, they were treated like second-class citizens. Occom himself was made one-fifth of the salary of a white missionary.

Becoming concerned with the marginal rights for Native Americans, this led to his opposition to slavery. He published a sermon condemning slavery, and this caught the attention of poet Phyllis Wheatley. She wrote to him, saying, "In every human breast, God has implanted a principle which we all call love of freedom. It is impatient of oppression and pants for deliverance."

He kept a journal from December 6th, 1743, to March 6th, 1790, in which he documented his daily activities, and this diary has become an extremely important historical document. His most famous work would be the sermon that he gave on September 2nd, 1772. As he preached about the hanging of Moses Paul, the sermon was turned into a book and became the first known book published in English by a Native American, and it was a best-seller.

At the beginning of his decline from fame, rumors began to spread that he was a heavy drinker and not even Mohegan, both of which were started by those who despised him for defending the Native American land claims. Throughout the 1770s and 1780s, he lost support from his denomination and began preaching to Native American tribes in New England. After the American Revolution, he led a coalition of seven Native American tribes to form Brother Town in New York. He founded a Presbyterian Church in Brother Town in 1792 but died shortly after. Brother Town was relocated to Wisconsin during the War of 1812 because Congress wanted all Native American tribes to move east.

The Brother Town Indian Nation still exists today but remains locked in a battle for recognition by the federal government. Though not regularly studied in today's society, Samson Occom had a major impact when he was alive. Not only did he fight for Native American rights, but he wrote sermons to help convert Native Americans to Christianity. He wrote the first book that was published by a Native American in English, and that is why he is known as the father of Native American literature.

Part Ⅲ   New Erdrich Novel Deals with Crime and Jurisdiction

JEFFREY BROWN: And finally tonight, a woman is attacked and the life of her 13-year-old son,

Joe, is altered forever, along with his family. That's the dramatic outline of the new novel *The Round House* by Louise Erdrich, which has been nominated for a National Book Award. The story is set on a Native American reservation in North Dakota, and it explores clashes of culture and law between tribal and state jurisdictions in investigating a crime. I talked with Louise Erdrich recently and asked her first how she came to write the book.

LOUISE ERDRICH, author of *The Round House*: I was really haunted for years by the background, the political background of this book. But I didn't want to write a political diatribe of any sort. So I waited and waited to have some characters come to me and speak to me about this situation.

JEFFREY BROWN: So, if it started with this issue, then let's explain the issue, because—and it's not giving away much of the novel to say there is this jurisdictional problem, right, of law, who is a Native, who has jurisdiction over crimes. But what is it that you wanted to explore? Explain the problem.

LOUISE ERDRICH: Well, there is a legacy of violence against Native women that has gotten worse and worse over time. And, historically, the underpinnings lie in the complex nature of the land tenure on Native reservations. Each piece of land has a different jurisdictional authority. A lot of this— there are attempts to solve this. One of the most recent was sponsored by Senator Patrick Leahy of the Senate Judicial Committee, and their recommendation was termed *The Violence Against Women Reauthorization Act* in 2012. So there have been attempts, but there is a kind of fear of restoring some pieces of sovereignty to Native tribes. And the statistics are that one in three Native women are raped. About 67% of those rapes fall under federal jurisdiction and are not prosecuted. Something like 88% are believed to be committed by non-Natives. And the tribes have no jurisdiction over non-Natives. So part of the fix is to restore some sovereignty, some jurisdiction over non-Native people only in these situations.

JEFFREY BROWN: So, this it started with this issue, a political issue.

LOUISE ERDRICH: It started with the background, but I didn't know who was going to talk to me. And I was digging little trees out of the foundation of my own parents' house. And as I drove away and left, this voice started to talk to me. And I knew once I had written those words into this, that when I got to those words, "Where is your mother?" I knew that this was the book. I knew I had the book.

JEFFREY BROWN: So you saw this decidedly nonfiction huge problem?

LOUISE ERDRICH: It's a big tangle, isn't it?

JEFFREY BROWN: Yes.

LOUISE ERDRICH: The way I'm explaining it, it's like you—you start unraveling, and it's everywhere.

JEFFREY BROWN: Yes. But you had to find a way in as a novelist.

LOUISE ERDRICH: I had to find a way to go straight in, and Joe gave me the in with the innocence and heart. Well, he's not all that innocent. He's a 13-year-old kid, but he is so protective of his mother and so ambivalent as a 13-year-old about both his mother and his father. So he is growing up in a tremendously short time over the course of a summer.

JEFFREY BROWN: Yes. I know in other of your works, you like to have multiple voices sort of explaining the story. This one really is focused on this young 13-year-old Joe. Was that hard to get that voice right? And why did you decide to just focus it on one voice?

LOUISE ERDRICH: I didn't really decide. It just happened to me. I was so interested in writing in his voice that it really took over. I feel now that I see that book sitting at your elbow that I sort of want it back. I want to be writing in that voice again. (LAUGHTER)

JEFFREY BROWN: You want the book back.

LOUISE ERDRICH: I want the book back and I want Joe back. He was mine. Now he's out there. But I loved writing… (LAUGHTER)

JEFFREY BROWN: Does that always happen? I mean, you can't have him, right? This is ours, right? (LAUGHTER)

LOUISE ERDRICH: You've got him, but…

JEFFREY BROWN: Is that normal for you to feel after you've finished a book?

LOUISE ERDRICH: Somewhat, but in this case, it's very special because Joe just took me through this entire book. As you said, his voice is the major voice in the book.

JEFFREY BROWN: Now, this sense of place, you know, I talk to a lot of writers, and some have it and really feel it, and others, you know, they could be writing about any place. But, with you, it's often a specific place and it's often a culture that is otherwise not much written about in our culture. Is that important to you? Is that part of what you are doing? Or is that just where you are from and what you know?

LOUISE ERDRICH: It's who I am. I grew up in Wahpeton, N.D., and I didn't leave until I was 18, and I have kept going back. My parents still live in Wahpeton. My family works in the Indian health service in the school system. And North Dakota, really—the Red River Valley specifically and the Turtle Mountain Chippewa Reservation, are really where I'm from, so—and what I know. So that's all I'm doing.

JEFFREY BROWN: Is there a sense—I mean, even the name, "The Round House", it is a sacred place on the reservation.

LOUISE ERDRICH: Yes. Exactly.

JEFFREY BROWN: And I'm wondering, in writing about this culture, is there a fear of losing some of those traditions, losing that culture?

LOUISE ERDRICH: Well, I think this is at the heart of the book. *The Round House* is a sacred place on many reservations. There is a kiva, or there is a sweat lodge, round places. The tepee is round. You know, this is the circle that depicts the turn of the Earth itself. And to have this violated does speak to the violation of the culture. But what I think happens and what I think the book talks about is also the resilience of the culture.

JEFFREY BROWN: And the book can help preserve it, I suppose, or at least let the rest of the culture know about it.

LOUISE ERDRICH: I'm hoping this particular issue gets—is—becomes more widely understood. It's very complicated.

JEFFREY BROWN: All right the new book is *The Round House*.

LOUISE ERDRICH: Thanks so much.

LOUISE ERDRICH: Pleasure.

Part IV Leslie Marmon Silko: How to Connect to Nature, Even in the City

What inspired you to write *The Turquoise Ledge*?

Well, I decided that the time had come to do something with the notes I've been keeping over the years, those little notes. And then, too, I was really struck by the way the world has changed so fast, and I thought that if I didn't write about the way things were when I was a girl, that no one would ever know that there had been or that there was this different way of being. And I thought about the old folks and how they were and how they lived, and I realized that if I didn't put something, write something down about it, that it would just be, you know, it would just go away or be forgotten. And I wanted the younger generations to know that there were different ways of living and being in the world, other than what we see around us today.

How have the landscapes that you know changed over the past few decades, and what's driving those changes?

What's driving those changes is greed, and the landscapes have changed in shocking ways, heartbreaking ways. And the way I was raised, in a way, a lot of the people in the Southwest were raised, was that we related to the land as extensions of ourselves. In the years since I've moved to Tucson, it's shocking the way they just crush the 200-year-old saguaro cactuses, the way all kinds of beautiful living things are just crushed. These foothill palomero days, they get the beautiful yellow blossoms in the spring, it takes hundreds of years to grow, and these people come, and they have no understanding, they're just driven by greed to build these badly built houses, which they then sell to people with bad mortgages, and well, we know how that all turns out now.

How can those of us who live in urban environments or perhaps in environments where we just don't appreciate nature, to see it with better eyes?

Well, I think it would be a process, it's not an instant thing, and I think that you can find connection anywhere. I think that if you open your heart and open yourself to these other beings and realize their consciousness isn't so different from ours, that even in the city, maybe with pigeons, this sort of life of firming, you know, this connection that we can make with other living beings, it really just takes an openness and openness of the heart, and then a little bit of solitude can help, a little bit of time alone to take a walk alone so that we aren't talking to somebody.

Can you tell me about your relationship to the land and particularly to animals? I know that's a big part of *The Turquoise Ledge*.

Yeah, well, in *The Turquoise Ledge*, I wanted to describe the kind of friendship and even affection that I receive from the wild animals. Tucson is a lonely place to be if you're a newcomer. There's a lot of transient population that comes through. By transient, I don't mean transient Reds, but people come, they teach at the University of Arizona for a while, and then they don't feel comfortable there, and they move on. And there's just a few of the wealthy founding families, and they're very insular. They don't, you know, allow people in. Tucson is a very segregated city. There's a whole town called South Tucson, and that's where the Spanish-speaking people live, that's where they're sort of pushed. It's an unfriendly town. And so when I settled up in the hills, the most friendly beings were the rattlesnakes, the pack rats, and, you know, just the wild things, the bees and the hummingbirds. With just a little bit of showing that I was, I didn't mean harm, it was really wonderful. The animals and birds and things were ready to be, ready to be friends of mine. And so those are my longest friends in the 30, more than 32 years I've been there. So when I wrote the book, I wanted to pay notice to them and, in a way, help protect their lives because they're the ones who get crushed under the bulldozers. And so I wanted other people to understand that these creatures want to be connected with us and that they, in a sense, are part of us and that they can really give us sustenance and hope when nothing else in the human world can.